GU00806289

The Use and Abuse
of Sovietology

The Use and Abuse of Sovietology

LEOPOLD LABEDZ

With a preface by Zbigniew Brzezinski
Edited by Melvin J. Lasky

Transaction Publishers
New Brunswick (U.S.A.) and Oxford (U.K.)

MOST of the essays which I have anthologized here were published either in *Survey* or in *Encounter*. The essay on E. H. Carr appeared in the *Times Literary Supplement*; the pieces on Solzhenitsyn and on Sinyavsky and Daniel appeared as introductions to books published by Penguin and Collins, to all of whom we are grateful for copyright permission. Special thanks due to Rebecca Penrose for her quick-witted editorial diligence.

M.J.L.

Copyright (c)1989 by Transaction Publishers, New Brunswick, New Jersey 08903.

All rights reserved under International and Pan-American Copyright Conventions. No part of this book may be reproduced or transmitted in any form or by any means, electronic or mechanical, including photocopy, recording, or any storage and retrieval system, without prior permission in writing from the publisher. All inquiries should be addressed to Transaction Publishers, Rutgers - The State University, New Brunswick, New Jersey 08903.

Library of Congress Catalog Number: 88-20083
ISBN: 0-88738-252-5
Printed in the United States of America

Library of Congress Cataloging-in-Publication Data

Labedz, Leopold.
    The use and abuse of Sovietology / Leopold Labedz: with an introduction by Zbigniew Brzezinski.
    p. cm.
    ISBN 0-88738-252-5
    1. Soviet Union--Intellectual life--1917-   2. Dissenters--Soviet Union.   3. Sovietologists. 4. Totalitarianism. I. Title.
DK287.L33 1988
947.084--dc19   88-20083 CIP

Contents

Preface   *Zbigniew Brzezinski*   1

I Great Dissidents

1. Solzhenitsyn's Nobel Prize   3
2. On Trial: The Case of Sinyavsky & Daniel   12

II False Prophets

3. Isaac Deutscher: Historian, Prophet, Biographer   33
4. E. H. Carr: Overtaken by History   94
5. Chomsky Revisited   112
6. Alexander Werth   126

III Portraits & Profiles

7. Kolakowski: On Marxism and Beyond   135
8. Will George Orwell Survive 1984?   155
9. Appreciating Milosz   205
10. Raymond Aron's "Vindication"   217
11. The Two Minds of George Kennan   223

IV Lessons of History

12. Holocaust: Myths & Horrors   240
13. The Student Revolt of the 1960s   264
14. *Détente*: An Evaluation   291
15. The Question of European Unity   319
16. On Literature & Revolution   332

Preface

Zbigniew Brzezinski

THIS IS a work by a fighter, a thinker, and an idealist. Leo Labedz is a fighter who minces no words in his contempt for the apologists of totalitarianism. He never rests in his efforts to enlarge the scope of human freedom, and many have felt the sharp edge of his polemical scalpel. He is a thinker, with a penetrating mind and encyclopaedic knowledge. He is an idealist who believes in sacrificing for the just cause to which he has dedicated his life. And he is my friend. . . .

This last personal consideration notwithstanding, I feel confident in asserting that the work of Leo Labedz, which has spanned the four decades from the days of Stalin to the rise of Gorbachov, stands far above the general literature of the Kremlinologists. The sampling of his writings contained in this volume represents an excellent model for those scholars who intend to study the phenomenon of Soviet Communism and a preceptive analysis for those statesmen who need to understand the Soviet Union.

Leo Labedz never suffered from any of the illusions which periodically have blinded Western scholars to the truth of the repressiveness and aggressiveness of the Soviet Union. This was a result in part of what he once described to a friend as his personal lesson in "comparative totalitarianism". He was 19 years old in 1939, having returned from studies in Paris and living again in his native Poland. With the wartime partition of Poland between Hitler's Germany and Stalin's Russia, many families had to face the stark choice of deciding whether to flee East or West, into Nazi- or Soviet-occupied territory. One of his aunts, recalling memories of the First World War and the Kaiser, chose to move westward toward "civilized Germany". Others chose to run eastward toward the "progressive anti-fascist homeland of socialism". Leo understood the two myths, and the mortal dangers of both *Gulag* and *Kazett*. He believed that going west would mean certain death and that going east, while perilous, would at least offer a chance to survive. As it turned out, between Siberia and Holocaust, he saw his entire family suffer great casualties, leaving him with an acute sense of how both German National-Socialism and Soviet Communism were manifestations of the same tragic phenomenon of totalitarianism.

Leo did not allow these wrenching personal experiences to cloud his academic judgement. Instead, these events have informed his writings with a sharper understanding of reality. He is a scholar in the best sense of the term, with an ability to work in many languages and with a wide knowledge of history, political science, sociology, and other social sciences. He is obsessed with acquiring as much information as possible, leaving no pages unturned in the pursuit of a footnote citation. He can address with ease all the arguments about the validity of Litvinov's diary, the importance of missing verses in the Soviet edition of Pushkin's *Commander*, or other minutiae in the study of the Soviet Union, all the while distinguishing between what is traditionally Russian and innovatively Soviet.

At the same time, Labedz is not an ivory-tower academic but an activist-scholar. While his house is crammed full of books and documents—with innumerable large black plastic bags full of thousands of cuttings and stacks of back issues of *Pravda*, *L'Humanité*, the *Daily Worker*, and other Communist publications—he did not isolate himself from events. An argumentative man, he sought to convince whoever crossed his formidable path, from German diplomats, to Italian socialists, to French *gauchistes*, and even to English Communists and American Trotskyites (present and past), of the rightness of his point of view. He participated in the revolutionary developments in Poland in 1979–81 from the London centre of the *KOR* and Solidarity. He organized petitions for political prisoners in the Soviet Union. He argued with J. Robert Oppenheimer on nuclear issues and exchanged views with Chinese generals at Peking briefings. He spoke out publicly on Soviet policy in Paris from the time of the Moscow "show trials" and in Washington through the era of *Détente*.

In his writings, Labedz demonstrates a tenacious independence of mind. Even if he were the only proponent of a particular point of view, he would not be swayed from his convictions by the climate of general opinion. If he did not convince everyone, he did influence international public debate through his polemical strength.

His greatest legacy will be the continuing publication of *Survey*, the journal that Walter Laqueur founded which Labedz edited with him for several years and later published alone. It is respected by scholars all over the world and has served for decades as an indispensable forum for the ideas of Western authorities on the Soviet Union, communism, and East–West relations. His own works on the future of Soviet society, the evolution of Marxist thought, (and especially Revisionism), the history of Russian literature, the prospects for international Communism, and the Soviet dissident movement all stand as testaments to the breadth of his mind.

This collection, which draws many of its essays from the pages of *Survey*, demonstrates the way in which Leo Labedz effectively fused practical knowledge with historical knowledge, with each reinforced by and benefiting from the other. Like another naturalized British citizen a hundred years earlier, writing and thinking in London, he knew that while scholars had in the past understood the world the point was now to change it.

Washington DC
June 1987

1. Solzhenitsyn's Nobel Prize

ON purely literary grounds there is nothing extraordinary about the award of the 1970 Nobel Prize for Literature to Alexander Solzhenitsyn. He is widely recognized in his own country as its greatest living writer, although his works are banned there, and he is highly praised by critics and readers all over the world. His books, *One Day in the Life of Ivan Denisovich*, *The First Circle*, and *Cancer Ward*, have become best-sellers in all the countries where they were published. On the face of it there should be nothing surprising in the fact that honour has been given where honour was due. In conferring the world's highest literary award on the Russian author, the Swedish Academy was not taking a political decision. If anything, *not* to have awarded the prize to Solzhenitsyn would have been a political decision arising from other than literary considerations. This can be clearly seen from the account given to an Italian correspondent (Pietro Sormani) by a member of the Swedish Academy (the communist writer, Arthur Lundquist):[1]

> "The decision was difficult and not unanimous. The eighteen Academicians, who during the summer had examined the works of the candidates, were divided to the last between Solzhenitsyn and the Australian writer, Patrick White, the latter being a compromise choice favoured by many who wanted to avoid precisely those 'political machinations' of which they were accused by the Soviets. They even put out feelers in Moscow through Ambassador Jarring in an attempt to discover what the reactions of the Kremlin would be to the possible choice of Solzhenitsyn. . . . In the end, however, the decision to award the prize to Solzhenitsyn prevailed.

---

[1] *Corriere della Sera* (25 October 1970). Arthur Lundquist is a Lenin Prize winner and a friend of Sholokhov. He is one of the committee of six which presents to the Swedish Academy the candidatures for the Nobel Prize for Literature.

When Sholokhov received the award in 1965, Lundquist's praise for the Academy's decision was quoted with approval in the Soviet press which expressed great pleasure at the award and referred warmly to Dr Karl Ragnar Gierow (the same Swedish Academy spokesman who was later to notify Solzhenitsyn of his award). Gone was the abusive condemnation (made at the time of the Pasternak affair) of the Swedish Academy as "a tool of the imperialists". In the grand climax Sholokhov received a telegram of congratulation on the award, signed jointly by the Central Committee of the Communist Party of the Soviet Union and the Soviet Government (*Pravda*, 28 October 1965).

On 21 October 1970 Dr Karl Ragnar Gierow informed the press conference in Stockholm that he had sent a letter to the chief editor of *Literaturnaya Gazeta*, Alexander Chakovsky. He said that the decision was taken to make the letter known to the world when *Literaturnaya Gazeta* had not had the courtesy to publish his letter or to correct in any way at all the misapprehensions and errors of fact about the administration of the Nobel prizes which it had published a week earlier.

'We were of course aware of the political consequences of this kind of choice', Lundquist went on; but he vigorously rejected the charges which Moscow directed against the Swedish Academy. It was not true, as the Soviet press had asserted, that the Academy had yielded to outside pressures or that it had lent itself to the manoeuvres of 'White' émigrés in France and Germany. . . ."

As the Pasternak affair had already demonstrated, the definition of what is political is quite different in the Soviet Union from what it is elsewhere. In the Soviet Union, a refusal to submit to political dictates of the Party on aesthetic or ethical grounds is in itself termed "political". In the West the definition is less comprehensive; fortunately it does not yet completely cover the ethical and aesthetic. *as it now does in 2016*

Yet, given that this important point has been grasped, the fact remains that the decision of the Swedish Academy is one of the most remarkable it has ever taken, and it was based not only on literary criteria. The Academy was clearly aware of this when it stressed in its citation not just Solzhenitsyn's purely literary achievement, but "the ethical force with which he has pursued the indispensable traditions of Russian literature".

Solzhenitsyn's writings, well known in the West, provide ample evidence for this citation. But its full significance can be gauged only against the background of his life, of his fate as an individual and a writer (a fate shared by millions of Soviet citizens and hundreds of Soviet writers), and of his own ethical fortitude in adversity, a fortitude amounting to heroism. Presenting a documentary record of the Solzhenitsyn case may help the reader to understand this background.[2]

ALEXANDER ISAYEVICH SOLZHENITSYN was born on 11 December 1918 in Kislovodsk (a spa in the Caucasus well liked by Lermontov). His father died in an accident before his birth. When the boy was six years old, his mother moved to Rostov-on-Don to earn a meagre living as a typist. Life was even harder for a young widow with a small son than for the population in general during the 1920s and '30s, the years which included the post-Revolution and post-collectivization famines.

Alexander was extremely good at school and later, while studying mathematics and physics at Rostov University, he won a Stalin scholarship for postgraduate studies. The gods are ironical: the future author of *One Day* and of *The First Circle* used it to follow his literary bent (of which he was conscious before he was ten), and enrolled at the Moscow Institute of Philosophy, Literature and History for a correspondence course which he completed in 1941. In the previous year he married a fellow-student, Natalya

---

[2] See *Solzhenitsyn: a Documentary Record* (ed. Leopold Labedz) which was first published in 1970 by Penguin, revised edition 1974, and to which this article constitutes the introduction.

Reshetovskaya, and took a job as a teacher of mathematics in a Rostov secondary school. When he sent his first attempts to the journal *Znamya* they were rejected—another ironical incident, for the man who rejected them was none other than Konstantin Fedin, who nearly 30 years later was to prevent the publication of *Cancer Ward* in *Novy Mir*.

After the outbreak of the Soviet–German War Solzhenitsyn joined the army (on 18 October 1941) and served as an artillery officer all the way from Kursk to Königsberg (now Kaliningrad). He was twice decorated and in 1945 was promoted to a captaincy. What followed was the first step on his road to Calvary: he was arrested for criticizing Stalin in his letters to a friend. In July 1945, while in the notorious Lubyanka prison in Moscow, he was sentenced by the special board of the *NKVD*, the secret police, to eight years hard labour in a prison camp. The verdict was pronounced in his absence, a standard procedure during the years of Stalin's rule of terror.

He served his sentence partly in a special prison in Moscow, where he was sent because of his training as a physicist, and partly in the Karlag concentration camp in Dzezkazgan in the province of Karaganda where a vast network of such camps had been built. The earlier experience provided the canvas for *The First Circle*, the later for *One Day* and for the play *The Tenderfoot and the Tramp*.

On his release from the camp in 1953, Solzhenitsyn was again sentenced, this time to "perpetual exile". He was to serve it near Dzambul in southern Kazakhstan. During his stay there he was striken by a cancer of the stomach and was sent to Tashkent for a course of radiology. The treatment was successful. It was this experience which sets the scene of his third novel, *Cancer Ward*.

Solzhenitsyn was released from exile in 1956 and "rehabilitated" a year later. He had spent eleven years in prisons, in camps and in exile, among millions of other prisoners, facing the questions of life and death in what was a microcosm of Soviet life at the time: Stalin's *univers concentrationnaire*. Now he settled in Ryazan, a hundred miles south-east of Moscow, and took a post as mathematics teacher in the local school. He was rejoined by his wife, who, while he was in exile in Kazakhstan, had given him up for dead and married again. He was soon to achieve world-wide fame and his genius was to be universally acclaimed, but his *via dolorosa* was not at an end. He had a debt to pay to the ghosts of his fellow prisoners. He began to write *One Day in the Life of Ivan Denisovich*.

THE PERIOD after the 20th Congress of the Soviet Communist Party was one of considerable political and intellectual ferment in the Soviet Union. Having denounced Stalin in his "secret speech", Khrushchev constantly oscillated between thaw and freeze, between the policy of relaxation and the policy of repression. The sorcerer's apprentice of Soviet politics assumed the mantle of a moderate reformer who condemned Stalin's methods of rule, but who was determined to preserve as the basis of his power the machine built by his predecessor. While scolding the more liberal intelligentsia (among whom the writers were naturally the most articulate), Khrushchev was also facing the sullen resentment of the *apparatchiki* who felt their position being undermined by his demolition of the Stalin myth and his other "hare-brained schemes".

It was at the climax of Khrushchev's until then successful struggle with his more die-hard opponents in the Party, and because it could be used against them, that Solzhenitsyn made his explosive literary debut with the publication of *One Day* in November 1962.[3] It was not long, however, before the die-hards' counter-offensive began, and Solzhenitsyn drew the first fire from his critics. They still hailed his talent and had to go carefully in their attack because he was launched by Tvardovsky with Khrushchev's personal *nihil obstat*, but that only meant that the attack had to be veiled. The formula used was that he had failed "to rise to a philosophical perception"[4] of the Stalin era (i.e. that the Party was building socialism despite Stalin's "mistakes"). While Solzhenitsyn provided the simple truth about it, his critics demanded a more dialectical approach: "Without a vision of historical truth, there can be no full truth, no matter what the talent".[5]

The counter-offensive fizzled out in the spring of 1963 when an interview with Tvardovsky (containing warm praise of Solzhenitsyn) appeared in *Pravda* (12 May). But towards the end of the year the battle flared up again. So long as Khrushchev stayed in power, Tvardovsky was able to publish several short stories by Solzhenitsyn in *Novy Mir*. After Khrushchev's fall in 1964, only one more tale by Solzhenitsyn appeared in print. The struggle between his friends and enemies became more intense in 1965, with the former on the defensive and steadily losing ground.

At the meeting of the prose section of the Moscow writers' organization he was still supported by the majority of those present, who passed a resolution calling for the publication of *Cancer Ward*. But by then the battle for the publication of *The First Circle* in *Novy Mir* had already been lost, and at the end of 1967 Konstantin Fedin torpedoed the appearance of *Cancer Ward*—already set up in print for *Novy Mir*. By that time hundreds of *samizdat* ("publish-it-yourself") editions of Solzhenitsyn's novels were circulating in typewritten form in the Soviet Union, and even without the help of the *KGB*—which was, as it were, forthcoming—they were bound to reach the

---

[3] The introduction (by Max Hayward and the present writer) to its first American edition, published in January 1963 in New York, began with the words:

"[This book] is beyond doubt the most startling work ever to have been published in the Soviet Union. Apart from being a literary masterpiece, it is a revolutionary document that will affect the climate of life inside the Soviet Union."

[4] Lydia Fomenko, "Great Expectations", *Literaturnaya Rossiya* (11 January 1963).

[5] Vadim Kozhevnikov in *Literaturnaya Gazeta* (2 March 1963).

West and find publication there in spite of Solzhenitsyn's protests and pleas to the Writers' Union to have them published in Russia first. During 1966 and 1967 Solzhenitsyn was subjected to increased pressure: he became the target for a growing slander campaign and his manuscripts and archives were seized by the KGB.

DURING ALL THIS TIME he fought a vigorous defensive battle and found many supporters and admirers. His open letter to the 4th Writers' Congress (May 1967) is the most eloquent plea for the freedom of literature that has ever appeared in the Soviet Union. His hard experience and his knowledge of the law were important assets in his conduct of the battle, but he increasingly was facing opponents who were not just hard-liners, but were ready to use the weapon of political provocation and so to swell the KGB file on him, a file which could be used against him at the appropriate time by his enemies. By obscure channels, his manuscripts began to reach the West. It became clear that a "case" against Solzhenitsyn was being prepared and that he might eventually face trial, as Sinyavsky and Daniel had done. The two meetings of the Writers' Union which were held to discuss his "case" before his expulsion already treated him like a pariah and put him in the dock. He was duly expelled from the Union, an action which he contemptuously castigated in another magnificent open letter.

His detractors accused him of being a "tool of the imperialists" and a "slanderer of the Soviet Union" (*Literaturnaya Gazeta*, 26 November 1969). He was called a "liar" by the Russian Federation section of the Writers' Union which invited him to leave the country and live in the West. Sholokhov called him a "pest" (*Literaturnaya Gazeta*, 3 December 1969).

The *samizdat* publications conducted a vigorous defence of Solzhenitsyn, but the Soviet "democratic opposition" was itself coming increasingly under fire, its members being arrested and sent to "mental prisons", corrective labour camps or to exile in the remoter parts of the country.

WHEN, in 1970, the Soviet authorities were preparing the final act in the Solzhenitsyn drama, the Swedish Academy announced its award of the Nobel Prize for Literature to Solzhenitsyn. Bitterly stung, the Soviet propaganda machine quickly announced the "literary and political bankruptcy" of Solzhenitsyn and condemned the Nobel Prize Committee for its nefarious decision. It was no longer ready to concede to Solzhenitsyn even a literary talent.[6] Now he had become a "run-of-the-mill writer" (*Soviet Weekly*, 17 October 1970). With his friend and protector Tvardovsky on his

---

[6] Earlier even his opponents granted him at least that. Fedin said at the meeting of the Secretariat of the Writers' Union (on 22 September 1967): "None of us denies his talent." And Alexi Surkov said that Solzhenitsyn was dangerous "because he has got talent".

death bed, Solzhenitsyn was facing the greatest honour and another great ordeal in his life.

During the Pasternak affair and, again, when the Nobel Prize was awarded to Solzhenitsyn, the Soviet press denounced the Swedish Academy as "conservative and reactionary", pointing out that in 1901 the first Nobel Prize for Literature had gone to the now forgotten French poet, Sully Prudhomme, and not to the great Leo Tolstoy (*Literaturnaya Gazeta*, 21 October 1970). The Academy has indeed made many errors of judgement during the 70 years in which the Prize has been given, but this particular argument was not used in the Soviet press when it was Sholokhov who received the award.

If there are certain historical continuities in the treatment of even the greatest Russian writers by the authorities, they only underline how much worse that treatment is now. Tolstoy was denounced by the Holy Synod, an episode which forms the basis of his novel *Resurrection* (it is also recalled in *Cancer Ward*). But the Holy Synod would hardly have dared to press Tolstoy to renounce the Nobel Prize, if he had received the award, or to attack the Swedish Academy for making it. True, when Tolstoy died without returning to the Church, the Holy Synod forbade the local priest to say a mass for his soul—and instructed the local police to exact obedience from the population to its decree forbidding the chanting of religious songs for Tolstoy and laying wreaths on his grave. Later, authorized by the governor of Ryazan, the police relented and permitted the placing of wreaths. Today the Ryazan authorities are less liberal, as the expulsion of Solzhenitsyn from the Ryazan writers' organization testifies.

Of the four Nobel Prizes awarded to Russian writers, three are not acknowledged by the Soviet authorities. Pasternak was forced to renounce it; Solzhenitsyn was denounced for receiving it; and although Ivan Bunin, who received it in 1933 as an émigré, has been posthumously rehabilitated, an article in *Pravda* (22 October 1970) commemorating the one hundredth anniversary of his birth did not mention that he was a Nobel Prizewinner. Would any other country in the world feel "ennobled" if it had to disclaim the highest honour for their finest writers? What would—say—the French think if they had to repudiate André Gide, François Mauriac and Albert Camus, three of their Nobel Prize laureates?

But perhaps in the historical perspective all this is not so important, provided of course that what one has in mind is the literary prizes and not the persecution of the writers. As we all know, literary prizes, including the Nobel Prize, do not in the long run make any difference to the stature of the writer. What matters is the quality of the writing, and here time is the most ruthless judge. It is by such criteria that Solzhenitsyn will be judged by posterity, and although literary predictions are notoriously risky, one can venture the opinion that the combination of his literary gifts and his nobility of spirit will make him "an immortal". In the Soviet context his historical as well as literary significance cannot be exaggerated. He is the first great Russian writer to emerge after the Revolution whose humanity can be compared to that of Tolstoy, his awareness of suffering to that of Dostoyevsky, his lack of sentimentality to that of Chekhov.

His style may seem old-fashioned in the light of literary developments elsewhere, but not in the context of the historical development of the Russian language and literature, or indeed in the general course of European culture. And who can tell what effect it will have on his readability a hundred years hence? In any case there is no doubt that Solzhenitsyn is the best example of those writers whom the late Konstantin Paustovsky described as the only ones whose works will endure (*Novy Mir*, No. 11, 1967):

> "They see the truth and they write the truth. Therefore their books survive. They live and they will go on living and there is no need to worry about the fate of their books. In that lies the strength of true works of art; having served their own time, they retain their irresistibility and their power of conviction even when that time moves into the past. And not only as a document, but also as a passionate human response to what is happening in the world."

Konstantin Paustovsky was (as I know from a personal conversation) an admirer of Solzhenitsyn.

L IKE OTHER major novelists, Solzhenitsyn makes his own experience the centre of his literary work and the point of departure for its symbolic significance. The concentration camp and the cancer ward are for him places in which to reflect not just on the problems presented by "extreme situations", but on the wider questions of Soviet reality and of our epoch, of good and evil, in short *la condition humaine*. Like other great novelists he is uncompromising in his attitude to truth and he restores to Russian literature the moral universalism which had been lost during the Stalin era. His writing is philosophical in the traditional sense; with its complexity and sense of tragedy, it is the antithesis of the shallow optimism and vulgar sociologism which, under the sign of "socialist realism", has for so many years dominated Soviet prose writing.

One of the characters in *The First Circle* reflects that "for a country to have a great writer is like having another government". Solzhenitsyn is such a writer. He ended his beautiful story, *Matryona's Home*, with these moving lines:

> "We all lived beside her and did not understand that she was that just person without whom, according to the proverb, the village could not endure.

Nor the city.
Nor all our land."

Solzhenitsyn is himself such a person.

In regard both to the man and the writer, the Nobel award to Solzhenitsyn and the words of its citation are singularly appropriate in stressing "the ethical force with which he has pursued the indispensable traditions of Russian literature".

(*1970*)

S INCE the above was first published, Solzhenitsyn's name has constantly been in public view. He continued in his struggle for civic and artistic integrity between the publication of the first volume of his literary epic on war and revolution, *August 1914*, and his banishment from the Soviet Union. He was subjected to new pressures and chicaneries, but his growing world fame at first protected him from more drastic measures.

It was not an easy situation: as he made clear in interviews with Western journalists it was nerve-racking and precarious. He had to exert himself to the utmost to continue his literary work and his struggle. It was not only civic courage which was required to face political adversity; it also necessitated an iron self-discipline and a methodical devotion to work. Sheer guts would not have been enough to enable him to continue his artistic endeavours in such strained circumstances.

The authorities were making life difficult for him in all sorts of ways. His application for a Moscow residence permit had been rejected, even after he had been granted a divorce from his first wife, Natalya Reshetovskaya, and was finally able to marry in May 1973 his long-time companion, Natalya Svetlova, the mother of his two children. As his Swiss lawyer, Dr Fritz Heeb, said (*The Times*, 18 January 1973), with reference to the article in the *New York Times* (8 January 1973) by an official of the Soviet *Novosti* agency, Semyon Vladimirov, who painted a picture of Solzhenitsyn living a life of "luxury and leisure", he was subject to a continuous "campaign of defamation" which culminated in surreptitious threats to his life and in open official threats (after the Yakir–Krasin trial) that he might be criminally charged. But Solzhenitsyn was undeterred.

When the long drawn out "Case No. 24" conducted by the *KGB* finally led to the suppression of the Moscow *samizdat* publication, *Chronicle of*

Current Events, there were only two dissidents who, because of their world-wide fame, could effectively pursue the struggle: Solzhenitsyn and Sakharov. Both of them have risen to the occasion magnificently: in ringing tones, they denounced the arrests, psychiatric "treatment" and other forms of repression which have taken such a toll among their friends in the Soviet Union. They let the world know in a way which no one else could match about the other side of *détente* and in doing so they disregarded completely any personal risks involved in such a frontal challenge to the Soviet authorities.

The manuscript of *The Gulag Archipelago* had by then been seized by the KGB. Solzhenitsyn decided that "the time has come" to publish it, whatever the personal consequences for him might be. He saw in this the hand of God. "As Macbeth was told: Birnam Wood will walk."

The rest of the drama followed inexorably. After yet another campaign against him, Solzhenitsyn was arrested and expelled from the country on 13 February 1974. The spectacle of a Nobel Prize winner being dumped abroad was, like so many other elements in the Solzhenitsyn affair, unprecedented.

What was not unprecedented was the fact that the practice of producing "un-persons" continued. The name of the greatest contemporary writer did not appear in the seventh volume of the Soviet *Literary Encyclopaedia* published in 1973. Officially, Alexander Solzhenitsyn had already ceased to exist as a writer before he was expelled from the Writers' Union and long before he was banished from the Soviet Union itself. After his banishment the authorities ordered that all his works which were published in the Soviet Union and still remained in public libraries (like his short stories in old copies of *Novy Mir*) should be removed.

There were many attempts under Stalin to erase certain writers from the memory of the people, but, as the subsequent period has shown, such attempts mostly failed. Is it any more likely that the author of *One Day in the Life of Ivan Denisovich* will be permanently eradicated from Russian literature and Soviet history?

(1974)

2. Sinyavsky & Daniel

> **Phædo**: *Haven't you even heard how this trial went?*
> **Echecrates**: *Yes, someone told me about it . . .*
> **Plato**, THE DEFENCE OF SOCRATES

THE CASE OF Sinyavsky and Daniel will no doubt be given its place in the history of famous trials.[1]

Its significance can be better seen today than when it was the centre of attention of the world press. The hearings, held in Moscow between 10 and 14 February, 1966, were not open to the public or to foreign observers, and only fragments of the evidence and of the drama in the courtroom reached the outside world. This book gives a detailed account of the proceedings and allows a fuller assessment to be made.

The record shows that the trial of Sinyavsky and Daniel was so conducted as to invite comparison with other cases of malevolent prosecution of freedom of thought and expression—the trial of Socrates, the condemnation of Giordano Bruno, the theological arraignment of Galileo, Voltaire's "*l'affaire* Calas", the Tennessee "monkey trial", to mention a few such *causes célèbres* which have acquired universal significance.

The record also shows that sympathy with the two writers was expressed in almost every country, including their own—difficult as it was to manifest it there. But when they took up and maintained their moral stance at the trial, it was in almost complete unawareness of this fact (they had been kept in isolation since their arrest), and in the knowledge that by their attitude they risked the likelihood of a heavier sentence.

It is true that they did not face the risk of death sentence for their literary activities, as did Socrates for his activities as a philospher: but in other respects their ordeal was more servere. Socrates had a genuine chance of influencing the five-hundred-strong jury of Athenian citizens—had 30 of them voted the other way, he would have been acquitted. If there was a miscarriage of justice in his case, the trial was at least an open contest conducted in accordance with the current rule of law. The travesty of law at the Moscow trial is perhaps best illustrated by Judge Smirnov who, at one point, indignantly rebuked Sinyavsky for referring in *The Trial Begins* to the use of "bugging" devices by the secret police:

> "That's the sort of thing covered by Article 70—slander. Doesn't this malign our people, our society, our system?"

---

[1] This essay constitutes the introduction to *On Trial: The Case of Sinyavsky (Tertz) and Daniel (Arzhak). Documents Edited by Leopold Labedz and Max Hayward* (Collins and Harvill, London, 1967).

Yet the learned judge had no qualms in allowing as evidence the tape-recorded conversation of Sinyavsky, secured by means of precisely such a device installed in his flat!

In one respect the two trials were similar. In each the prejudiced attitude of the court prevented its taking into account the explanation given by the accused of the character of their work, literary in the one case, philosophic in the other; in each, the case of the defendants fell on deaf ears.

On hearing the verdict, Socrates—according to Plato—said:

> "It is not my lack of arguments that caused me to be condemned but . . . the fact that I refused to address you in the way which would have given you most pleasure."

Twenty-four centuries later, Sinyavsky echoes the complaint:

> "The arguments of the prosecution give one the feeling of being up against a blank wall, on which one batters one's head in vain, and through which one cannot penetrate in order to get to some kind of truth."

Daniel made the same point:

> "I was not told, 'You are lying, this is not true'—my words were simply ignored as though I had never said them . . . This refusal to listen to what we were saying, this deafness to all our explanations, was characteristic of the whole of this trial."

But it is in the specific framework of Russian and Soviet history that the case of Sinyavsky and Daniel seems most important.

SINCE THE 19TH CENTURY, political trials have played a special rôle in Russian life. Revolutionaries used them as a tribune to inspire the young and the intelligentsia. Their behaviour in the courtroom was the test of strength of their devotion to their ideals. Stalin knew this tradition well and applied the Potemkin technique to his courtrooms. His use of "show trials", with their ritual recantations and self-accusations by the defendants, not only helped to demonstrate his absolute power, but greatly reinforced the mechanism of ideological conditioning and psychological *Gleichschaltung* of the population. Henceforth the most fantastic official propositions were to be unquestioningly accepted, even if they violated the most elementary sense of reality. Those who knew that "the Emperor has no clothes" had better not only keep quiet, but repress the knowledge into their subconscious. In literature the officially inspired fantasy was implemented by means of the doctrine of "socialist realism", another didactic mechanism combining orthodoxy with surrealistic naturalism.

To break its shackles is not as simple for the Soviet writer as for the innocent child from Andersen's tale to say that "the Emperor has no clothes". Externally, he has to face the same obstacles and to bear the same unpleasant consequences for telling the truth as all those in history who were saying things challenging the established orthodoxies. As Voltaire wrote to Diderot (on 26 June 1758): "It is a real pity that we cannot tell the truth in anything touching metaphysics and even history . . . We are compelled to lie, and then we are still persecuted for not having lied enough." But internally, the problem is more complex today, because of the deep psychological consequences of totalitarian thought-control and of cultural isolation on the "captive minds".

Facing the moral blackmail of being branded as disloyal to their people and their country, it is psychologically easier for them to approach the problem indirectly. It is also natural that Soviet writers interested in truth should in the first place be concerned with the ways to get rid of compulsory perception and obligatory didacticism. Sinyavsky defined his artistic "credo" as the question of "how to be truthful with the aid of the absurd and the fantastic". For him the right to an *autonomous* fantasy is a precondition for the elimination of the distorted uniformity of reaction imposed by the Emperor on the courtiers and the population, by the established system on "Soviet man" and the Soviet writer.

SINCE STALIN'S DEATH, and more particularly since Khrushchev's "secret speech", the mechanism of this compulsory surrealistic consensus has begun to break down. By refusing to plead guilty, by behaving like normal men and not like conditioned robots, by expressing authentic thoughts and emotions instead of synthetic formulae, by speaking the truth as they saw it and not the conventional lies expected of them, Sinyavsky and Daniel exposed in effect the artificial character of this "consensus". Their conduct in court broke the magic spell of the Moscow Trials. They have shown that—despite years of indoctrination and psychological conditioning—critical intelligence, independence of mind and the courage to speak it continue to survive. Their fate has a bearing not only on the struggle between the Russian literary "liberals" and "diehards", but on the whole internal evolution of the Soviet Union.

★   ★   ★

"The man of letters is without recourse. He resembles the flying fish—if he raises himself a little, the birds devour him; if he dives, the fish eat him up."
Voltaire

THE LAST SCENE in *The Trial Begins* takes place in a prison camp where the narrator and his fellow prisoners, having failed in their "essential duty of co-operating in the effort to bring the Glorious Future nearer", are digging ditches. The trial of Andrey Sinyavsky and Yuli Daniel had a similar epilogue.

One cannot help being fascinated by the strange, dramatic prescience of the author. Here was a Pirandellesque double involvement in both life and literature, and also perhaps, as in Greek tragedy, an element of impending destiny. Sinyavsky's and Daniel's trial in 1966 confirmed Tertz's ironical foresight.

Some 10 years earlier, the narrator of the epilogue to *The Trial Begins* had written:

"The contents of my story, finished except for the epilogue, had become known to some highly placed officials. As could be expected, the cause of my downfall was the dragnet, which had been fixed in the big sewage pipe under our house.

The rough drafts I had conscientiously flushed down the drain every morning went straight to Interrogator Skromnykh's desk. The important personage whose instructions I had carried out, though not perhaps to the letter, was by then dead, and his personality was indeed undergoing a widespread public reappraisal. Nevertheless I was accused of slander, pornography and giving away state secrets.

I had no defence. The evidence was there. Besides, Globov, who was called as a witness, produced documents which proved my guilt conclusively and in full. In the course of the interrogation, it was established that everything I had written was pure invention, the product of a morbid and ill-intentioned mind."

It would be difficult to give a truer summary of what happened in the trial. "The evidence was there" in the form of Tertz's and Arzhak's books; the *Glavlit* report proved the two writers' guilt "conclusively and in full". Sinyavsky and Daniel were accused of "slander"; if not of pornography, then of obsession with sordid sexual situations; and if not of "giving away state secrets", then of entering the service of the foreign enemies of the state. "It was established that everything they had written was pure invention, the product of morbid and ill-intentioned minds."

THE TRIAL GAVE RISE to anxiety throughout the world. The press was flooded with articles, letters, protests, and appeals from individuals and organisations to the Soviet authorities, urging them to reconsider their actions. By contrast with the Pasternak affair in 1957, no voice was raised in the West to defend their attitude. Even usually friendly and sympathetic observers were shocked. The protest from the Left was no less vocal than from the Right. The socialist *Tribune*'s editorial called on the Soviet Government to "stop this stupid trial"; *The New Statesman* wrote that, by staging it, Soviet justice had put itself on trial.

The international community of writers showed particular concern over Sinyavsky's and Daniel's fate, and the Secretaries-General of International PEN and of COMES (David Carver and Giancarlo Vigorelli) applied for permission—which was refused—to attend the trial. The movement of protest spread far beyond purely literary circles.

In the event, attendance at the trial was restricted to a carefully selected public. The Soviet press insisted throughout, that "the trial was public and reported by the press" (*Pravda*, 22 February 1966) and that the defendants had been granted their full rights. But it succeeded only in making the travesty of justice plainer. As the *New York Herald Tribune* (14 February 1966) put it, "These rights included the right to be laughed at by a hand-picked audience of 70 persons, the right to be told that they are not telling the truth in their answers to questions, the right to have only the prosecution side of the case reported in some detail to those who cannot claim access to the 'open' trial because they have no passes . . . ." "Because of lack of space" in the small courtroom to which the hearing was transferred at the last moment, foreign journalists and observers were refused entry. So were the friends of the accused, who had gathered outside the court and, according to *The Guardian* (11 February 1966), told the police: "Of course it's an open trial—here we are, out in the open!"

Le Monde (12 February 1966) rightly claimed that Soviet press comments "were totally lacking in objectivity". The hypocrisy of some of them could have been envied by Tartuffe. Feofanov, who subsequently covered the trial for *Izvestia*, wrote before it started (30 January 1966):

> "The law must stand above passions and emotions. If those who serve the law infringe this very first commandment, we shall all suffer. For any retreat from the law means the direct road to arbitrary rule. Let the law function, free from (outside) influence."

This, in the paper which had launched the slanderous campaign against Sinyavsky and Daniel while their case was *sub judice* and they were being held *incommunicado* in prison, a campaign which was to continue throughout and after the trial! The title of Feofanov's report of the first day of the trial was THE LAW RULES HERE; that of *Tass* in *Pravda*, THE FACE OF THE SLANDERERS!

On the second day of the trial, Feofanov assured his readers that:

"The court cannot be quite sure [of its verdict] until everything has been explained which aggravates or mitigates the guilt of the accused."

Thus the presumption of innocence was replaced by the presumption of guilt; the question before the court was only that of degree.

The defendants' plea of "Not Guilty" aroused the indigation of the press. *Tass* reported:

"Sinyavsky and Daniel are trying to escape responsibility for their crime, although their hostile attitude has been confirmed not only by their anti-Soviet works but by the evidence of experts and witnesses . . . ."

and *Radio Moscow* added: "What impudence! they try to deny the evidence, but they were put with their backs to the wall by the Prosecution."

Similar "indignation" was aroused by the defendants' "attempt to reduce the essence of their actions, punishable by law, to purely literary matters". Feofanov complained that "the same familiar, grating words were heard from both defendants about the artist's right to self-expression . . . literary conventions, hyperbole, and so on", adding that "the court tore away their window-dressing and laid bare their hostile essence" (*Izvestia*, 16 February 1966). He added: "One can hardly imagine a greater moral fall."

Shortly after the verdict, a Government spokesman promised the official publication of a "detailed account" of the trial to supplement the picture given by the press. It has not appeared.

ONLY THE TRANSCRIPT of the proceedings and the protests of liberal Soviet intellectuals (reproduced in our book, but unpublished in the Soviet Union) give the arguments of the defence and details of what went on during the preliminary investigation, as well as in the courtroom.

Thus, from the letters of the wives of the accused we learn that witnesses were intimidated, while the transcript reveals the drama in the courtroom with its "electrically charged atmosphere" and the "wall of misunderstanding or unwillingness to understand" which Sinyavsky felt it "impossible to breach to get at any kind of truth". The transcript highlights the astonishing disregard for legal precision shown by lawyers. Asked if he had sent his manuscript abroad "illegally", Sinyavsky answered, "No, unofficially." No one contradicted him, for the good reason that to send manuscripts abroad is not illegal. Yet, undeterred by this, the Prosecutor in his final speech again referred to the prisoners having sent their manuscripts out "illegally". It also highlights the ignorance, or disregard, of literary principles shown by the court, and its exclusive interest in quotations which, taken out of context, could be interpreted as "anti-Soviet"—although, as Sinyavsky's Counsel pointed out, the law required proof, not merely of anti-Soviet attitudes (whatever that may mean) but of deliberate intent to undermine the state.

It was left to the protesting members of the Soviet intelligentsia to draw attention to violations of the elementary legal safeguards, formally guaranteed by the Soviet Constitution, which the press and the court failed to observe. Thus Meniker for the defence pointed out that the press campaign before the trial was a violation of Article 16 of the Criminal Code, according to which the judges and public assessors must reach their final verdict in conditions which preclude their being "influenced from outside". Rodnyanskaya (in her protest) commented on this "blatant disrespect for the court and its important task, a disrespect bordering on the nihilist view that judicial procedure is nothing but an empty formality".

But the protests went much further: they questioned the legality of the very basis of the trial and brought out its wider moral and intellectual as well as legal implications.

Lydia Chukovskaya asserted that "Sinyavsky's and Daniel's committal to trial was in itself illegal"; and five members of the Institute of Linguistics declared:

> "Never before in the history of the Soviet State has a writer been arrested and *publicly* tried for anti-Soviet, anti-State activities[2] which consisted (merely) in his writings . . . whether published at home or abroad. Furthermore, (this is unprecedented) in the history of Tzarist Russia. . . ."

This aspect of the case strongly impressed the liberal intelligentsia. In spite of the insistence of the Prosecution and the press that the accused were not being tried "as writers" but "as criminals", it was clear that their "crime" was their literary work, the only *corpus delicti* produced at the trial. The arguments of the Prosecution showed that they were "guilty" of writing in a particular way, different from "socialist realism". Sinyavsky and Daniel had to defend themselves against the accusation that there were no "positive heroes" in their works and that they had used unsuitable metaphors. (One can imagine a Western writer's reaction to the idea of a court of law reproving him for such

---

[2] When, seven months after the trial, changes in the criminal code were made, aimed at the suppression of various forms of criticism, they evoked a letter of protest by 21 prominent scholars and artists—including Shostakovich, Tamm, Nekrasov, Engelgardt, Sakharov, and Romm—who argued that "the passing of such laws at the present time seems to us a quite unjustified action likely to result in judicial abuses, breaches of the law, and an atmosphere of suspicion and denunciation".

Later on, there was also a youth demonstration in Moscow (on 22 January 1967) demanding the abolition, as contrary to the Constitution, of the legislation of 16 September 1966 and of Article 70 of the criminal code (under which Sinyavsky and Daniel, and, subsequently, several young writers and poets, among them Natalie Laskova, Alexander Ginzburg, Yuri Galanskov, Valentin Khromov, were arrested and sentenced).

lapses: for it must be remembered that this was no literary or even ideological debate—these were judicial proceedings.)

THE BELIEF THAT it was for this that they were condemned was implicit in the letter from the 63 Moscow writers who offered to stand surety for them. Pointing out that the Prosecution had failed to prove subversive intent, they stressed that

> "The condemnation of writers for writing satirical works is an extremely dangerous precedent. Neither learning nor art can exist if paradoxical ideas may not be expressed, nor hyperbolic images used."

Both in Tzarist and Soviet Russia writers have been persecuted only too often; many were sentenced to *katorga*, prison, forced labour camps; and some were shot. But none before had been tried in a regular court of justice specifically for their writings. They were dealt with (as the sinister Russian phrase has it) "on the administrative level", or tried for some alleged crime other than their literary works.

Catherine the Great sent Radishchev to Siberia for writing his *Journey from St Petersburg to Moscow*—by the imperial order of an autocrat. Dostoyevsky was sentenced to hard labour—as a terrorist. Gumilyov was shot in 1921—as a participant in an anti-revolutionary plot. Under Stalin, Pilnyak, Mandelshtam, Babel, and thousands of other intellectuals and writers were sent to prison or to Siberian labour camps, where many of them died. But (except for the Jewish writers, who were tried *in camera* and executed as 'cosmopolitans' in 1952) none was put on trial: they were sentenced summarily by special boards of the *NKVD*—an arbitrary practice, officially condemned by Stalin's successors.

After Stalin, Olga Ivinskaya was sentened by a court to eight years in camp for a currency offence—not for her loyalty to Boris Pasternak. Joseph Brodsky was sent to the Arctic as a "social parasite"—not as a poet.

If hypocrisy is the tribute vice pays to virtue, these trumped-up charges were a hypocritical tribute paid by Soviet courts to Russian literature.

Until the Sinyavsky–Daniel affair, it was only in the eyes of ideologists, not of the judiciary, that a work of art as such could be a crime. For ideological functionaries such as Zhdanov or Ilyichev, art and propaganda were one and the same, serving either the Children of Light (i.e. the Soviet state) or the Children of Darkness (i.e. the Enemy). Whatever the artist's "subjective" intention, it was therefore asserted that the only true yardstick by which literary work must be judged is its value to one side or the other. But although the whole of Soviet life was permeated by this eschatological outlook, it was not formally embodied in the legal code; and it was not applied to literature by the judiciary. Stalin, who believed in political prophylactics, used the Moscow Trials as morality plays *pour décourager les autres*. But writers *qua* writers were not prosecuted in court even under him.

After his death, the liberal intellectuals hoped that the growth of "legality" would increasingly afford artists and writers a measure of protection, precisely because they believed that legally they could not be prosecuted in their professional capacity.

T HE TRIAL OF Sinyavsky and Daniel was a blow to this hope. It showed that the problem of security from persecution transcended that of legality, important though it be for the writers and the Soviet public in general to see legality upheld. It brought home the fact that some literary works could be regarded as crimes; and that, in any case, new legislation could be introduced to make them punishable as such.

This is what actually happened during and after the trial of Sinyavsky and Daniel. They were charged under Article 70 of the *RSFSR Criminal Code*, which deals with "propaganda conducted for the purpose of undermining the state" and which, for the first time, was applied to fiction and *belles lettres*. To make the suppression of literary and other forms of non-conformism still easier in future, the Soviet legislature introduced (on 16 September 1966) the appropriate amendments to Articles 142 and 190 of the *RSFSR Criminal Code*.

Now it was no longer a case of arbitrary decisions overriding the rule of law, but of the law itself being so framed that it could be used against writers and literature. If it is true that, under Stalin, Sinyavsky and Daniel would almost certainly have been shot out of hand, and that at their trial they no longer faced the death sentence, it is also true that the trial not only violated existing legality, but foreshadowed measures designed to make sure that legal prosecution of literature would, in future, offer no judicial problems.

BUT, UNDOUBTEDLY, the deepest significance of the Sinyavsky–Daniel trial for Soviet intellectuals lies in the fact that the behaviour of the defendants raised, for the first time, the issue of the intellectuals' right to independent thought. In their protests, they were explicitly concerned with freedom of thought and conscience, with the artist's right to creative freedom, without which literature cannot fulfil its proper function. Golomshtok wrote:

"... [Tertz's writing can be described as] the work of a mature writer with sharp insights into the contradictions which disturb and torment modern man—and not only in a socialist society. The problems he raises—the alienation of the individual from society, the contrast between man's technical progress and his spiritual emptiness, the relationship of means to ends, etc.—are those which stand at the heart of modern culture. They make up the inner sense of the work of Kafka and Joyce, Faulkner and Hemingway, Böll and Steinbeck, Babel and

Pasternak. . . . These problems are imposed on modern man by the enormous complexity of twentieth-century life. . . . To deny that these problems confront our own society as well as others is not only to contradict the basic teaching of Marxism but also to fly in the face of common sense and of the facts of our everyday experience. Nobody who claims to be a modern writer can afford to close his eyes to them. . . ."

The writer cannot be required merely to preach the official catechism, he has the duty to navigate the uncharted sea of the problems of his age. He must not confuse patriotism with blind conformism. Two protesters (Yu. J. Levin and A. Yakobson) quoted the celebrated words of Chaadayev:

"I have never learned to love my country with my eyes shut, with bowed head, and sealed lips. I consider that no one can be useful to his country unless he sees it clearly. I think that the time for blind infatuation is past. I suppose that we have come after others in order to avoid their mistakes, illusions and superstitions. . . ."

The Sinyavsky–Daniel case has, for the first time in Soviet history, provided the occasion for Soviet intellectuals to declare that they no longer wish to live "with eyes shut, head bowed and lips sealed". Because they wish to exercise their own critical intelligence in dealing with various contemporary problems, the trial has dramatically highlighted the limitations imposed on them in this respect. In the circumstances, the issue is as much that of "truth" as of "freedom". Commenting on what it called "the old problem of truth in the arts", *Novy Mir*, the journal to which both Sinyavsky and Daniel were contributors, declared (November 1965):

". . . [To those who say that] not all truth is needed, we reply: No, our art needs the whole truth."[3]

This, as the trial showed, is the crux of the matter. There is, firstly, the truth about the past, without which it is impossible to face the truth about the present. Asked why he had sent his manuscripts abroad instead of submitting them to Soviet publishers, Daniel referred to the taboos surrounding the Stalin period:

---

[3] Since then, *Novy Mir*, which has been under fire so many times before, has been subjected to renewed pressures. On 27 January 1967, *Pravda* attacked it for "stubbornness in defence of erroneous positions". On 19 February 1967, *Izvestia* castigated it for preaching "passive humanism". Its joint deputy-editor (A. G. Dementiev) and its lay-out editor (B. G. Zaks) were removed. Its editor, Tvardovsky, who earlier in March still stood his ground, saying that he would accept criticism only if it was based "on the lofty notions of a literature of Soviet society worthy of the great traditions of Russian realism bequeathed by the classics", was forced to retreat. At a special meeting of the Writers' Union devoted to the "shortcomings" of *Novy Mir*, he made a statement (published on 29 March 1967, in *Pravda*, *Izvestia*, and *Literary Gazette*) in which he promised "to study critical comments attentively" and to "take them into account in the future work of the magazine".

"Our literature and press are silent about the things on which I write. But literature is entitled to deal with any period and with any questions. I feel that there should be no forbidden subjects in the life of society."

In his final plea, he elaborated on this point:

"The Public Accuser, the writer Vasiliev, said that he was accusing us, both in the name of the living and in the name of those who fell in the war. . . . Their memory is sacred to me. But why, when he quoted from Sinyavsky's article the words 'so that not one drop of blood should be shed, we killed and killed and killed', why . . . did Vasiliev not remind us of certain other names, or are they unknown to him? I mean the names of Babel, Mandelshtam, Bruno Jasienski, Ivan Katayev, Tretyakov, Kvitko, Markish, and many others. Perhaps Vasiliev has never read their works or heard their names? But perhaps the specialist in literature, Kedrina, knows the names of Levidov and Nusinov? Or even if they are so phenomenally ignorant in matters of literature, perhaps the name Meyerhold rings a bell with them? Or, if they are in general unversed in matters of art, perhaps they have heard the names of Postyshev, Tukhachevsky, Blücher, Kossyor, Gamarnik, Yakir? Evidently these people must have died in their beds from a cold in the head, if we are to believe the assertion that we did not kill. Well, what is the truth of the matter—did we kill or didn't we? Did all this happen or didn't it? . . ."

These questions, needless to say, remained unanswered.

Sinyavsky and Daniel stressed that what they had criticised in their works was mainly the past, though they were also concerned with its effect on the present and the possibility of its revival. Clearly, had the authorities decided to make a clean sweep of the "survivals of the cult of personality", they would have welcomed the support of the two writers. But the state failed to pass this test. It was easier to establish, as Tertz said in *The Trial Begins*, that "everything they had written was pure invention". In the words of Daniel, " 'slander' was the easiest reply to everything said by the defendants".

THERE WAS ALSO THE QUESTION of the truth about the present. The way it was handled by the Prosecution was strikingly illustrated by the references to Sinyavsky's and Daniel's "anti-semitism". Sinyavsky remarked with bitter irony: "Since it is difficult to make Daniel out to be an anti-semite, the fascist Daniel, hand-in-hand with the anti-semite Sinyavsky, tramples on everything that is sacred. . . ." Later on, Daniel pointed out that the lunacy of the accusation went even further:

"Sinyavsky need not think that only he has been declared to be an anti-semite. I, Yuli Markevich Daniel, a Jew, am also an anti-semite. All this by virtue of the fact that one of my characters, an old waiter, says something about the Jews, and so the entry goes down in my dossier: 'Nikolai Arzhak (Daniel) is a consummate and convinced anti-semite.' Do you think that this was written by some inexperienced consultant? No, this report was written by Academician Yudin."

There is a double and prophetic irony in this context about the words of the prosecutor, Globov, in *The Trial Begins*:

"No Rabinoviches shall undermine the basis of our society. We shall not allow our enemies to destroy us, it is we who will destroy them."

IF THE ISSUES WERE "truth" and "freedom", so—on a different but almost as significant a level—was humour.

Daniel's vain attempts at the trial to explain his motives in writing *This is Moscow Speaking*, and the satirical, not exhortatory, significance of the idea of "Public Murder Day" on which its plot is based, were to receive an ironical postscript after he had spent more than a year in a "strict regime" labour camp. In his final plea he had complained that the *Glavlit* "expert evidence" on his story read literally: "The author thinks it possible that a 'Homosexuals' Day' could be held in our country." Little did he imagine that soon, when the amended Criminal Code made it possible to sentence Soviet citizens to three years' imprisonment for telling "anti-Soviet" jokes, a solemn discussion would take place in the Soviet press of the suggested plan to introduce an official "Laughter Day". In the circumstances, the idea of such a "Day of Public Murder of Jokes" is not without its melancholy humour. At the trial, the authorities instinctively showed their fear of any sayings which, by their tone, could conflict with established sacrosanct formulae; they showed their fear of humour.

Tertz had said in his essay, *On Socialist Realism*, that humour was out-of-place in the Soviet era (as in that of Catherine the Great)— Mayakovsky had started by making fun of things, but soon learned his lesson. This truth could not have been made plainer than it was at the trial. So thick was the atmosphere of solemnity that the writers themselves were precluded from claiming their right to make gratuitous jokes.

Humour (though never mentioned) was itself on trial. It was the gratuitousness of art that, above all, was, by implication, denied. This was particularly unfortunate for Sinyavsky, whose sense of the grotesque is the very quality which makes him see the whole of life in a fresh light, and with a vividness so different from what he called "its passport likeness". If ever there was an occasion to demonstrate the fact that Soviet artists were required to be the earnest, respectful servants of established second-hand "truths", this was it.

Regrettable as we may find this—since for us gratuitousness is so essential a characteristic of art, as it is of play—we are no doubt sufficiently accustomed to the Soviet view of the writer as the mouth-piece of state policy, not to be surprised. But we may feel an extra sympathy with the writer in the dock, forced to defend not merely his right to professions of principle, but his right to the lightest of his gifts—his openness to the grace of laughter.

One and the same attitude towards humour can make it obligatory (as on "Laughter Day") or illegal (as when it is expressed in "Radio Erevan" jokes). It would seem that the Soviet state is so dependent upon the Byzantine verbal reverence of its subjects—on a frozen, outward ritual of piety—that it feels itself truly "undermined" and "weakened" by spontaneous laughter, and is thus forced to bring it under the operation of the Criminal Code.

THE TRIAL LED TO a new form of reaction on the part of many of the most distinguished members of the Soviet intelligentsia.

Less than 10 years ago, at a meeting of Moscow writers in October 1958, even such admirable poets as Martynov and Slutsky joined in the witch hunt against Pasternak and the cry for his expulsion from Russia.[4] This shameful servility has now been replaced, not just by dignified silence, but by an unprecedented wave of protests.

It seems that many among even the more liberal Soviet intellectuals, when they learned of Sinyavsky's and Daniel's activity as Tertz and Arzhak, were at first shocked by their "duplicity" in publishing abroad and under pseudonyms. They may have been unaware that this was not illegal. Moreover, it is certain that, had Sinyavsky published his first "Tertz" book under his own name, he would have found it impossible to publish any other. Should he have resigned himself to this? Those who might think so, because they hold that a law, however unjust, must be obeyed (though it is easier to believe this in countries where laws can be changed under pressure from public opinion), should realise that there was no call for this heroic Socratic attitude in his case. Not only were the two authors within their legal rights in using pseudonyms and publishing abroad—it was not even illegal for them to by-pass the Soviet censorship, since officially no such censorship exists. All that Sinyavsky and Daniel did was to risk prison by defying—not the

---

[4] A stenographic report of the meeting appeared in *Survey*, No 60, 1966, pp. 134–63, under the title, "Judgement on Pasternak". The flavour of the "debate" can perhaps be conveyed by a quotation from the statement by Boris Polevoy.

"Pasternak is, in my view, a literary Vlasov, a man who, whilst living with us and eating our Soviet bread, earning his living in our Soviet publishing houses, and enjoying all the benefits of a Soviet citizen, betrayed us, deserted to the enemy camp, and is now fighting on their side. A Soviet court had General Vlasov shot (voice from the audience—'hanged'), and the whole people approved of it because, as we rightly said, it was good riddance to bad rubbish. I think that a Cold-War traitor should also be given a fitting and extremely heavy punishment: 'Get out of our country, Mister Pasternak. We do not want to breathe the same air as you.' (Applause) . . ."

law—but the conventions which, they knew, the police and the courts could enforce with or without support from the law.

To the charge of "double dealing", Sinyavsky answered simply and truthfully that, had he been able to write "from an idealist point of view" for Soviet publications, he would have done so; and that he did "everything possible to express his real thoughts" in the writings published under his own name in the Soviet Union. A comparison of the work he published at home and abroad confirms that this is so. For the reasons why the defendants had published their work abroad, the Judge and the Prosecution might have consulted Herzen (*Selected Philosophical Works*, published in 1956—in Moscow—where on page 561 they would have found the explanation)—

> "Was there ever a country with a censorship and an arbitrary government where secret presses and the underground distribution of manuscripts did not exist once an intellectual movement and the desire for liberty existed? That is just as natural a state of affairs as the publication of manuscripts abroad . . . ."

That many, even liberal-minded, Soviet intellectuals should at first have reacted in a way implying a certain reluctance to face the issues raised by the Sinyavsky–Daniel case, is not surprising, given their conditioning. It was only later that sympathy with the two writers and their brave and honourable stand began to crystallise among the Soviet intelligentsia. Only gradually did some of its members appreciate the real issues at stake. What is astonishing is that so many of them, who either changed their mind or had no need to do so, spoke out fearlessly before and after the trial.

The policy of alternate "thaw" and "freeze"—even if it has meant two steps forward and one-and-a-half back, and even though it has discouraged so many hopes—has not remained without effect. There is a fresh wind of courage. It is difficult for people in the West to realise the significance of open protest, not only by individuals but by groups, in a country where for so long "group" has been synonymous with "conspiracy" and a "demonstration" was either "pro-government" or a "crime".

DURING THE TRIAL, Sinyavsky taught the Judge a lesson in literary criticism by proving effectively that authors cannot be identified with the characters in their books. In the prologue to *The Makepeace Experiment*, the narrator says:

> "If I'm caught, I'll deny everything. If I have to stand my trial, hands and feet bound, face to face with a terrible judge, I'll recant."

Judge Smirnov asked Sinyavsky (perhaps hopefully):

> "Here is what you write about the fears of Proferansov [one of the characters in the novel]: 'If I'm called to account by dread judges. . . .'

These thoughts of Samson Samsonovich, do they reflect your own fears and anxieties?"

Sinyavsky drily replied:

"This is not said by Samson Samsonovich but by Savely Kuzmich [a descendant of the other Proferansov], and these are not my thoughts."

Later on, the same Judge Smirnov (in a conversation with Professor Harold Berman of the Harvard University Law School, in August 1966) called Sinyavsky a "scoundrel".

Had Sinyavsky "recanted", he would presumably have received a lighter sentence. But nothing else was likely to help him. For it was not only his double identity as Sinyavsky-Tertz but his identity *tout court*, to which he owed the hostility of the Soviet *bien-pensants*.

In his report in *Izvestia* (13 January 1966), Feofanov asked the rhetorical, but relevant, question, which he put in the usual eschatological perspective:

"How could it happen . . . that two relatively young men, living amongst us, educated in Soviet schools and universities, have suddenly become accomplices of our worst enemies?"

This he attributed, in the usual stereotyped way, to the "extreme lack of ideological discipline and moral responsibility of the accused". The explanation is of course irrelevant: it only begs the question. Avoiding the "objective" causes of Sinyavsky's and Daniel's reaction to the historical reality surrounding them, it replaces such causes by "subjective" demonology.

Sinyavsky himself drew attention to this most sensitive point in his final plea, when he said ironically:

"One cannot help asking oneself: where did these monsters come from, out of what bog, out of what underground did they emerge? Apparently a Soviet court (I know this from books) in coming to its decision, usually concerns itself with the origin of the crime, with its cause. In the present case this is of no interest to the Prosecution. All the same, where did we come from, Daniel and I? We must have been dropped by parachute from America and immediately begun to work havoc—scoundrels that we are. . . . Has the Prosecution really not pondered the question of our origin? How could a fascist arise in our midst? Surely, if you come to think of it, this is a far more terrible matter than that of a couple of books, however anti-Soviet they may be in content. The Prosecution has not even raised this question. . . ."

Not only the "cult of personality", but also present reactions against it, have to be reduced, in this 'Marxist' perspective, to peculiar, individual aberrations. Yet the official position seems to be that Stalinist crimes were peccadilloes compared with the sins committed by those who are concerned with the truth about them. There must be demons either inside or outside; real personal motivations remain unfathomable within the psychological framework of the official mythology.

In an article, "Socialist Realism and its Detractors" (published in *Foreign Literature* in January 1962), Boris Ryurikov reproached Western reviewers of Tertz's essay, *On Socialist Realism*, with failing to appreciate that Tertz was a White émigré who masqueraded as a Soviet writer living in Russia:

> "The identity of the anonymous author of the article, published in *Esprit*, is of little interest to us. No one has any intention of trying to expose his incognito. If he feels like wearing a mask, let him. But whoever he is, he does his work crudely. The spirit, the style, the form and the 'erudite' arguments advanced, show that the article was concocted in the same school of intellectual snobs (probably connected with White Guard émigré circles) who are trying to keep alive the traditions of *Vekhi* and of the Religious-Philosophical Society which proclaimed a crusade against materialism. By repeating what reactionary publicists said in the most shameful period of Russian social thought, the author indicts himself.
>
> Several magazines in Britain, the U.S.A. and West Germany promptly re-reprinted the anonymous article, even commenting that it was the authentic evidence of an eye-witness. Surely, they ought to have suspected the fraud—it is such a clumsy one—but they were blinded by their hatred of Communism, and hatred, as everyone knows, is a poor counsellor. . . ."

The ludicrous idea of Tertz as a White émigré living in Paris could no longer be maintained in court; but apart from this, there was no difference in the style of the accusations. What a contrast with the philosophical serenity of Sinyavsky reflecting in *Unguarded Thoughts*:

> "Man becomes a truly sincere and valuable being once he loses his official attributes—his profession, name, age . . . ."

Both under his own name and under his *nom de plume* Sinyavsky remained true to himself. For him (as for the Soviet critic Pomerantsev who was the first to raise this cry after Stalin's death) genuine literature is impossible without sincerity. "Socialist realism" is not merely another literary style, but a basic obstacle to literary creativity: it prevents the sincere expression of the writer's own emotions and thoughts.

In the "socialist realist" scheme, tragedy has to be "optimistic", and drama is reduced to stilted pathos. For Sinyavsky, facing the facts of Soviet history and its tragic dramas, fantasy and the grotesque are ways of escaping from the falsification and trivialisation of emotions, and from the reduction of individual thoughts to the shallow level of official didacticism. He has the same reverence for suffering, life, and death, as other writers who have reached the understanding of tragedy—Pasternak, Akhmatova, Solzhenitsyn.

There is no sign in Sinyavsky of hypocrisy or "double-dealing", two characteristics shown by his detractors; and his attitude throughout has been very different from that of Sholokhov, for instance, who re-wrote his novels to suit changes in the Party line, and who, after eulogising Stalin, was later on the best of terms with Khrushchev.

Sinyavsky, after Khrushchev's speech, expressed the horror felt by his generation for Stalin's crimes, but he placed the guilt where it belonged and did not hesitate to show his compassion for Stalin's daughter Svetlana.[5]

THE CONTRAST BETWEEN the style of thinking and the respective *finesse de sentiments* of the accused and the accusers is also the contrast between the best and worst representatives of contemporary Russian literature. The behaviour of the two Nobel-Prize-winners, Pasternak and Sholokhov, is a direct illustration of this contrast.

The attitude of Sinyavsky to Pasternak on the one hand, and that of Sholokhov to Pasternak and to Sinyavsky on the other, are symbolic of two mentalities, of two traditions in Russian literary life. In her magnificent *"J'accuse"*—her open letter to Sholokhov—Lydia Chukovskaya made the point bluntly:

> "In the whole history of Russian culture I know of no other case of a writer publicly expressing regret, as you have done [at the 23rd Party Congress]—not at the harshness of a sentence but at its leniency. . . . You said in your speech that you are ashamed for those who tried to get [Sinyavsky and Daniel] pardoned by offering to stand surety for them, but, quite frankly, I am ashamed not for them or for myself, but for you.[6] In making that plea, they were following the fine tradition of Soviet and pre-Soviet Russian literature, whereas you, by your speech, have cut yourself off from this tradition."

By a paradoxical coincidence, at the very time when Sinyavsky—a follower of Pasternak and the leading Soviet exponent of his poetry—was

---

[5] At a press conference after her arrival in the United States, Svetlana Stalin said of the trial of Sinyavsky and Daniel that it "produced a horrible impression on all the intellectuals in Russia and on me also, and I can say that I lost the hopes which I had had before that we are going to become liberal somehow. . . ." (*Time*, 5 May 1967).

[6] An "Open Letter to Sholokhov" written at the same time in the West, by Alberto Moravia, uses almost the same words: "When you declare that the defenders of Sinyavsky and Daniel should be ashamed of themselves, we must tell you that you should be ashamed of yourself. . . ." (*Espresso*, 10 April 1966).

arrested, Sholokhov (who called Pasternak "a poet for old maids") was awarded a Nobel prize for literature. *Le Monde* promptly suggested that Sholokhov, now that he had joined "the community of great writers", should intervene with the Soviet authorities on behalf of Sinyavsky: by so doing he would show, not only aesthetically but also morally, that he deserved the internationl honour bestowed upon him. On the eve of the prize-giving ceremony, Mr Mark Bonham Carter, representing Sinyavsky's English publisher, went to Stockholm to urge Sholokhov to do so; but his efforts to reach him were in vain—which was not surprising, as Sholokhov's press conference at the time, as well as his subsequent regrets at the "mildness" of Sinyavsky's sentence, have shown only too plainly. It was, therefore, no more than poetic justice that Sholokhov in turn should be branded as "a traitor" by the Peking *People's Daily* (15 May 1966) for accepting the Nobel Prize.

IT IS CHARACTERISTIC that among the world reactions to the harshness of the sentences passed on Sinyavsky and Daniel—reactions which united *L'Humanité* and *Le Figaro*, *L'Unita* and *La Stampa*, *The Daily Worker* and *The Daily Telegraph*—the only support for the Soviet authorities came from what, in the present state of Sino-Soviet relations, can only be considered a tainted source. The Chinese approved of the verdict, and the pro-Chinese Belgian journal, *La Voix du Peuple* (25 February 1966) warmly commended what it called "a real political trial". It added, however, that this would not be much help to the "revisionists" Brezhnev and Kosygin, who "hide behind the verdict on Sinyavsky and Daniel as if it were a smokescreen for the continuation of their dirty acts of treason. . . ."

The Soviet authorities appear to have paid little attention to so ambiguous a compliment, just as previously they had failed to respond to the world-wide appeals against the staging of the literary trial and the condemnation of the two writers. Later, fresh efforts were made to influence their attitude, and new appeals for clemency came from prominent intellectuals, civil rights associations, and writers' organizations.

A major initiative to that effect was undertaken by International PEN and COMES (European Community of Writers), whose Secretaries-General went to Moscow for talks with the officials of the Soviet Writers' Union and the Soviet authorities. They failed to reach the latter; and their efforts were stone-walled, although the Soviet Government must have been well aware of the effect of its unbending attitude upon intellectuals the world over.

Meanwhile, it became known that Sinyavsky and Daniel were serving their sentence in two "strict regime" camps in the Autonomous Republic of Mordovia. The conditions were poor, the two "literary prisoners" were overworked and undernourished. Daniel was suffering from an old war wound, and Sinyavsky's more delicate health was deteriorating.

The camps to which they were sent—No. 11 and No. 7a respectively—form part of the Dubrovlag complex in the Potma region, about 300 miles from Moscow, on the middle Volga (*The Daily Telegraph*, 14 March 1967). The camps are controlled by the Chief Administration of Places of Detention (*GUMZ*, formerly known as *GULAG*), itself a branch of the Ministry for the Maintenance of Public Order (*MOOP*, formerly *MVD*). In the two camps in which Sinyavsky and Daniel are being "punished", prisoners must perform hard physical work which is sometimes dangerous to their health, they are forbidden to spend more than 5 roubles a month in the camp store, and allowed only one visit a year from their wives. (The attitude of their wives recalls that of the wives of the Decembrists, of whom Lermontov wrote so movingly, a heroic tradition enshrined in the folk-lore of the Russian intelligentsia. The wonderful letters from Mrs Sinyavskaya and Mrs Daniel show that their loyalty, fortitude and steadfastness of character are no less impressive than those of the Decembrists' women.)

Although the situation in the camps is not quite as grim as under Stalin, it remains very harsh indeed. Each camp contains about a thousand prisoners, mainly political, or members of religious sects such as Baptists and Jehovah's Witnesses.

In March 1967 the Presidential Bureau of COMES met in Rome and issued a statement agreeing to resume the "dialogue" with the Russians "in the hope that this demonstration of good will would not remain without echo", i.e. that "the fate of Sinyavsky and Daniel may be settled in a manner comparatively satisfactory to world opinion in the not too distant future" (*The Times*, 1 April 1967, letter from John Lehmann, British Vice-President of COMES). This hope was based on Soviet hints to that effect, and on rumours in Moscow that Sinyavsky and Daniel might benefit from the amnesty to be proclaimed on the occasion of the fiftieth anniversary of the October Revolution.

In the meantime the two prisoners continue to suffer detention in forced labour camps for having committed the sin of expressing their own authentic emotions and thoughts in a state where the rulers are still unwilling to allow their subjects to think or feel for themselves.[7]

A MORE STRIKING JUXTAPOSITION than any comment on the Sinyavsky–Daniel case and on the two writers' situation today, is provided by two prophetic scenes in *The Trial Begins*. The first takes place soon after the arrest of Seryozha, a young and somewhat naïve character in

[7] Andrey Sinyavsky was released from the labour camp in Potma in 1971. The following year he emigrated to Paris where he continues to write, to run, with his wife, a publishing house for émigré writers, and to edit the literary journal *Sintaksis*. Yuli Daniel was released at the same time as Sinyavsky. He has since been living in Moscow, his health ailing as a result of his time in the camp. He has been translating poetry from Georgian and English into Russian. His new poems will be published in *Novy Mir* later this year.

the novel, who is harking back to the lost idealism of the early revolutionary movement.

". . . 'Well, young man', the Interrogator said at last. 'Now we have been into your views in detail. One thing I would like to get straight—how did you manage to get in touch with foreign agents?' . . . 'What kind of an idiotic joke is that?' Seryozha paled. 'Please remember, I have not so far been condemned, I am only on trial.'
    The Interrogator looked amused and drew back the window curtain. . . .
    'That's where they are, the people who are on trial. See how many of them?'
    The Interrogator pointed at the crowds milling below. Then he stroked Seryozha's shorn head and explained gently:
    'You're different now, my boy. You're not on trial, you are condemned.'. . ."

If, in Voltaire's time, the writer was "without recourse", like "the flying fish", what can be said of the condition into which Sinyavsky and Daniel were born? They were helpless vis-à-vis the authorities—they could not "dive"; nor were they able to "raise themselves" to influence public opinion. Two centuries after Voltaire, they were facing a state considerably more all-embracing in its demands on the conscience of the writer and incomparably more exacting in its ideological claims. Like Seryozha, they were not on trial, they were condemned long before the verdict.
    The second scene is described on the last page of The Trial Begins, when the narrator and another charcter in the novel, Rabinovich, now both in a forced labour camp, are discussing the future of the human race in the light of their experience. Rabinovich refers to the transformation of means into ends in history, and exclaims:

"And now there is no God, only dialectics. Forge a new dagger for the new Purpose at once!"

At this point, the narrator concludes the epilogue:

"I was just about to object when the soldier who guarded us from the danger of escaping, woke up on his hillock and shouted:
    'You there, in the ditch! You've been wagging your tongues long enough. Get on with your work.'
    We took up our spades as one man."

If they were together in the same camp, this conversation might well have taken place—not between two characters in a novel—but between Sinyavsky and Daniel. They too are "still digging". But this could not, and cannot, be the end of the epilogue, for a reason which Sinyavsky-Tertz gives in the same novel, in which he so amazingly anticipated his later fate.

"The Court is in session, it is in session throughout the world. And not only Rabinovich, unmasked by the City Prosecutor, but all of us, however many we may be, are being daily, nightly, tried and questioned. This is called history."

(1967)

3. Isaac Deutscher

(I) Historian & Prophet

"The prophets prophesy falsely, and the priests bear rule by their means; and my people love to have it so; and what will ye do in the end thereof? . . ."
—Jeremiah, v. 31.

"ISAAC DEUTSCHER, the most eminent, accurate, and informative of all commentators on Soviet affairs. . . ." Thus the London *Tribune* (20 October 1961) in what is by no means an exceptional tribute to one who has been widely hailed as an analyst of Soviet affairs and highly complimented as a historian. John Dewey said that "he has freed himself from the method of praise and blame and leaves the reader with understanding"; Bertrand Russell commended his "historic impartiality". The scope of the influence of Deutscher's ideas is astonishing. In the last two decades he has found a sympathetic hearing from markedly different political audiences ranging from left socialists to conservative Blimps. His articles have appeared in the *Manchester Guardian* and *The Times*, in *Corriere della Sera* and the *Washington Post*. He was published by the liberal *Observer* and the staunchly conservative *Sunday Times*, by the left-wing *l'Express* and the bourgeois *France-Soir*. The Catholic *Esprit* and Sartre's *Les Temps Modernes*, the anti-communist *Reporter* and the anti-anti-communist *New Statesman* had him as a regular contributor. The pillars of the British Establishment listened to him in 1956 explaining the historical ambivalence of the unprogressive Hungarian (counter-) revolution, and comrades Leduc and Pajetta, leaders of the French and Italian Communist Parties, heard him pontificating in 1961 on the necessary conditions for the unification of the Socialist and Communist parties, which he favoured. Neutralist statesmen from the underdeveloped countries, representing in Marxist terms the "national bourgeoisie", repeated his arguments in and out of season, and so did the Trotskyist revolutionaries from *La Quatrième Internationale*, endorsing the Maoist line against the "national bourgeoisie".

Deutscher may, like other Marxist historians, be a prophet looking backwards, but he certainly has not been a prophet without honour. What are the reasons for his popularity? Were his prognostications right, as he constantly asserts? How accurate is he as a historian? Has he in fact, as a reviewer in the *Economist* declared, brought "to the study of contemporary history a calm temper"? Deutscher has always said that he is politically engaged. At the opening meeting of the "New Left Club" in London he ended his speech with the call: "Forward to the Red Sixties". The dialectical (and political) feat of being at the same time *engagé* and *au-dessus de la mêlée* may look like an impossibility to ordinary mortals, but has not Deutscher claimed to follow the Olympian tradition of Goethe?[1] Or are all these proclamations no more than the thinly veiled rationalizations of a passionate ideologue, reflecting the far from calm temper of a frustrated politician?

To answer these questions is not enough for an understanding of the phenomenon of "Deutscherism"; for this a wider examination is necessary, an analysis of the reasons why so many were inclined in the '50s to accept as gospel truth the ambivalences of their prophet. But it may be helpful to look at the roots of his beliefs, to scan his writings again, to check them against the facts, to examine more closely his method of handling the evidence, and to discover the relation between Deutscher's historical vision and his running commentaries on current political events. Only in this way can we fairly assess his claim to be in the tradition of Goethe, Shelley, and Jefferson, which he invokes together with Marx's own patronage.

Personal Background

ISAAC DEUTSCHER was born in 1907 in an orthodox Jewish family in Poland. His grandfather and father were owners of a printing firm publishing Jewish religious literature; his uncle was a member of the Polish Upper House before the war, representing the Jewish clerical party, *Agudah*. As a boy Deutscher attended a rabbinical school and until he was in his late teens he wore the traditional Chassidic attire. He rebelled, however, against both school and home, left his *Yeshiva*, and put on ordinary clothes. Before that, he had started writing poetry in Polish and his translations of Hebrew poetry into Polish were read at the gatherings of the literary *avant-garde* at Cracow University where a Chassidic youngster writing poetry in Polish was something of an attraction. His poems were published in the Cracow Polish-language Jewish journal, *Nowy Dziennik*. Some had a Zionist character, but soon Deutscher became a socialist and hoped to be able to work for the socialist Cracow daily, *Naprzod*; but he gave up the idea and moved to Warsaw, where he became a communist and at the age of 19 joined the illegal Communist Party.

This was not an unusual evolution. Many other members of the Jewish intelligentsia looked to communism for a solution of the "Jewish question" in a country where anti-semitism was endemic, where discrimination barred the way to a career, and poverty and obscurantism were rampant.

There were many paradoxes which the ironic Clio kept in store for the young talmudist-turned-dialectician. As things turned out, there was indeed a "final solution" of the Jewish question in Poland: it came through the Nazi annihilation of over three million Jews; and after the War, the Communist

---

[1] Cf. *Heretics and Renegades* (London, 1955), p. 21.

ruling minority, top-heavy with the Jewish remnant (often concealing its ethnic origin), only helped to continue the traditional popular anti-semitism in a country from which the Jews had practically disappeared. Anti-semitism was without doubt the most important factor turning many Jews towards communism, but—to crown the irony—those among them who survived witnessed the persecution of the "rootless cosmopolitans", when (in Tertz's phrase) "anti-semitism was implemented in the name of internationalism".

This was, however, in the future. Before Hitler took care of the "Jewish problem" in Poland (and elsewhere), Stalin had in 1937 dissolved what the communist Jewish idealists regarded as the instrument of its real "solution", the Polish Communist Party, and annihilated its leadership. By that time Deutscher had been long out of the Party. He was expelled in 1932 for writing a series of articles criticising the party line in Germany (where the Communists were busy attacking the "Social-fascists" of the SPD). Before his expulsion, Deutscher was secretary of the editorial board of the Yiddish communist literary monthly, Literarische Tribune, published legally (his articles there appeared under the pen-name "Krakowski").[2] After leaving the Party, Deutscher collaborated with a small Trotskyist group which published some anti-Stalinist pamphlets. In 1934 the members of the group joined either the Bund (Jewish Workers Party) or the PPS (Polish Socialist Party). Deutscher joined the latter. While in the Communist Party he was writing both in Yiddish and in Polish (in the legal communist monthly, Miesiecznik Literacki). He now started working in a modest capacity on the Jewish daily in Polish, Nasz Przeglad, published in Warsaw. This was a "bourgeois" pro-Zionist paper, and Deutscher stayed with it until 1939 when he left for England. There, after the outbreak of War, he joined the Polish army under General Sikorski. He was released from military duties in 1942 and was subsequently employed in the Polish Ministry of Information of the government-in-exile. Although he had published some articles in England earlier, it is from this time that his journalistic career in Great Britain begins, with regular contributions to the Economist and the Observer. Considering his linguistic handicaps, his technical achievement as a journalist was remarkable.

The Heretic & the Revolution

AN ASSESSMENT OF Deutscher's views is impossible without taking into account his youthful traumas. His attachment to some illusions of his youth and his ambiguities are rooted in the earlier, little-known part of his biography. His pro-Soviet sympathies, his Trotskyist hagiography, his work for "bourgeois" newspapers while remaining on the side of History

---

[2] Ksiega Wspomnien, 1919–1939 (Warsaw, 1960), p. 240.

and the Proletariat—all these characteristic elements are already present in the earlier experience.

It is not enough, however, to indicate the genesis of Deutscher's views to invalidate them. Such a method is a favoured trick of those Marxists who assert that truth is socially determined, and of those psychologists who think it sufficient to locate the motives behind the beliefs to dismiss them. For others it is still necessary to examine their relation to facts and to professed values.

With this proviso it is legitimate to try to discover the social and psychological sources of his bias, which despite his "Olympian" affidavits is more marked in his writings than in the work of many other students of Soviet affairs who do not attribute to themselves such lofty intellectual parentage. And, if one wants to find out where Deutscher's pattern of thinking originates, there is no more indicative essay than "The Ex-Communist Conscience" (which appeared in the *Reporter* in April 1950, and which was then reproduced in 1955 as the opening chapter in *Heretics and Renegades*).

In this essay Deutscher formulated his ideological *credo*. In it he opposes Communist Heretics to Communist Renegades. He implies that he himself belongs to the former category, but does not define it directly and leaves the reader to infer what it is and what it is not from his criticisms of the renegades:

> "Nearly every ex-communist broke with his party in the name of communism. Nearly everyone set out to defend the ideal of socialism from the abuses of a bureaucracy subservient to Moscow. Nearly everyone began by throwing out the dirty water of the Russian revolution to protect the baby bathing in it. Sooner or later these intentions are forgotten or abandoned. Having broken with a party bureaucracy in the name of communism, the heretic goes on to break with communism itself. He no longer defends socialism from unscrupulous abuse; he now defends mankind from the fallacy of socialism. He no longer throws out the dirty water of the Russian revolution to protect the baby; he discovers that the baby is a monster which must be strangled. The heretic becomes a renegade."

Not so the "Heretic". He will remain true to his ideals, even though this may involve some semantic confusion (such as indiscriminate mixing of the terms socialism and communism), and the straining of metaphors and historical parallels. He will refrain from breaking with communism, notwithstanding the Leningrad affair, the hanging of Kostov and Rajk, the Crimean case, the Slansky trial, and the Doctors' plot.

For the "Heretic", "the world is split between Stalinism and an anti-Stalinist alliance in much the same way as it was split between Napoleonic France and the Holy Alliance". He considers therefore that "the only dignified attitude the intellectual ex-Communist can take is to rise *au-dessus de la mêlée*. He cannot join the Stalinist camp or the anti-Stalinist Holy Alliance without doing violence to his better self," but he does not renounce the cause of the prevention of cruelty to bathing children and continues to defend it in the most influential press organs of the wicked Holy Alliance. Somewhat inconsistently, he justifies this attitude by recalling "some great 'intellectuals' who, in a similar situation in the past, refused to identify themselves with any established Cause". He, the "Heretic", unlike the Communist "Renegade", follows in the footsteps of Goethe, and Shelley: like these three "outsiders to the great conflict of their time", he prefers not to commit himself. Unfortunately, "most ex-communist intellectuals are inclined to follow the tradition of Wordsworth and Coleridge rather than that of Goethe and Shelley", and that implies that they are ready for anything: "our ex-communist, for the best of reasons, does the most vicious things. He advances bravely in the front rank of every witch hunt. His blind hatred of his former ideal is leaven to contemporary conservatism. Not infrequently he denounces even the mildest brand of the 'welfare state' as 'legislative Bolshevism'."

This description of the ex-communist Conservative die-hard hardly applies to the six writers—Koestler, Silone, André Gide, Louis Fischer, Richard Wright, and Stephen Spender—whose book, *The God that Failed*, Deutscher was ostensibly reviewing in his essay. None of them became a reactionary socially and all of them remained liberal politically. But it is true that some ex-Communists have a tendency to reaction-formation or to manic denial. Georg Simmel in his classical analysis of the phenomenon of apostasy described it with far greater perception than Deutscher; according to surveys on the subject, the majority of ex-Communists tend to settle on the social-democratic and not on the conservative positions.[3] There is of course a variety of psychological reactions among former communists. To the present writer, who belongs to a later generation, and was not (like Deutscher) involved in the political struggles of the 1930s, it seems that Deutscher's ambivalence derives from what may be called an inverted "apostasy-complex". For this reason he remains fixated in his adolescent stage in the 1920s and tends to romanticize his early beliefs, the "heroic period of the revolution". Nor is the "Heretic" free from failings with which he charges others, such as, for instance, "the ex-communist's characteristic incapacity for detachment". It would not be easy to disentangle what is projection and what displacement in Deutscher's description of a "Renegade":

[3] Cf. G. A. Almond, *The Appeals of Communism* (Princeton University Press, 1954). The same applies to the young Polish revisionists whom Deutscher scolded in 1957 and implored not to become "renegades".

"He is haunted by a vague sense that he has betrayed either his former ideals or the ideals of bourgeois society; like Koestler, he may even have an ambivalent notion that he has betrayed both. He then tries to suppress his sense of guilt and uncertainty, or to camouflage it by a show of extraordinary certitude and frantic aggressiveness. He insists that the world should recognise his uneasy conscience as the clearest conscience of all."

This can hardly be excelled as a description of Deutscher himself.

1942–1947: Predictions & Comments

DEUTSCHER began to display "historical impartiality" in his writings even before Stalin began to lay, at Teheran, Yalta, and Potsdam, the foundations of his post-War empire.

In an article which appeared seven months after Hitler's attack on Russia in the Polish weekly, *Wiadomosci Polskie*, published in London,[4] Deutscher, writing under the pen-name Ignacy Niemczycki (a Polish rendering of his name), was already putting forward the main ideas and prognostications which he was to repeat during the next 20 years, whatever the current historical evidence at his disposal. For him subsequent events are not relevant evidence to confirm or modify his opinions. These are an expression of faith of the "true believer" and therefore not to be measured by the normal yardstick by which political expectations can be accepted or rejected as realistic or not; that is, by testing the predictions against what has actually happened; not at some time in the future, but at the time when the predictions are politically relevant, when they affect political attitudes and behaviour. Deutscher goes on repeating his optimistic prognostications and claims credit for them whenever things are improving in the Soviet Union, but conveniently forgets all the *specific* predictions he made which were disproved by events. Whenever possible, he follows in the footsteps of the Delphic oracle and makes his predictions vague, conditional, and qualified enough to leave himself a way out whatever happens. But this type of insurance is not always available, nor is his other favourite line of retreat, the claim that he forecasts long-term developments only. The blurb for *Heretics and Renegades* states that the "author's forecasts have a way of coming true with astonishing accuracy, as even the sceptics have found". In his foreword to *Russia after Stalin*, Deutscher wrote: "I willingly admit that I had not expected that my prognostications would begin to come true so soon" (p. 5). Here is what he wrote in his 1942 article mentioned above:

"Since the 22nd of June 1941 the Russian revolution is sealing with the

---

[4] 22 February 1942. Ironically enough, the weekly was closed two years later by the British Government for its anti-Soviet attitude.

blood of the Russian workers and peasants its indissoluble link with the European workers' movement . . . Underlying Soviet expansion there were none of the typical factors which determine the behaviour of any genuine imperialism. There was no search for markets, for sources of raw materials, or for profitable investment opportunities. Soviet annexations were not necessitated by the socio-economic structure of the country, but were only moves in the defensive politico-strategic game . . . Before the eyes of the Soviet people the war is dispelling the myth of totalitarian infallibility, and it must push the Soviet regime towards deep internal transformations, towards the freedom of the working masses. The democratisation of the Soviet regime will not only be a powerful stimulus for the development of socialism in the whole world; it will ultimately establish the indissoluble link between the workers' movement in all countries and the fighting peoples of the USSR."

Well, this particular prediction did not come true; the sceptics were justified. The Soviet "working masses"—and many of them shared some of Deutscher's illusions during the war—were disappointed; they were not pushed "towards freedom". The non-imperialist Stalin, lacking any Marxist motives for expansion, established his control over a hundred million East Europeans, and these changes were promptly accepted by Deutscher as "the irreversible post-War revolutions in Eastern Europe". This might have been expected. In the same article he had stated that "revolution brought on the point of bayonets, and realised by barbaric means, is *still* a revolution", and is that not enough to justify it in the "progressive" mind? In his articles in the *Economist* and the *Observer*, published between 1942 and 1947, Deutscher repeated his thesis of 1942, predicting Soviet democratization. It was of course quite wrong, but was well received at the time; for the public in the West was war-weary and looked forward to a post-War world of stability and peace.

After the War, as "Peregrine" in the *Observer*, Deutscher continued to enlighten the British public about developments in the Soviet bloc. Thus, Stalin's switch from the "patriotic" line during the War to the more "leftist" line consonant with the post-War expansion was presented as a revival of internationalism:

"The most striking feature in Russian life during the first months of peace has been the ebb of the nationalist mood [11 November 1945]."

This on the very eve of the "Russia First" discoveries campaign. At that time, too, the spectre of the Soviet Marshal appeared, which later on regularly made its entrance to frighten the Western public and to show that an accommodating attitude of non-resistance was really best, as the alternative was too frightful to contemplate. The reshuffle of the Soviet government, which included Voroshilov and Budenny, but not Zhukov, Rokossovsky, Konev, or Tolbukhin, brought the following comment:

> "The formation of the new government looks like a victory of the peace party over the group that might be regarded as a potential war party [31 March 1946]."

This not so long before the Berlin Blockade and the Korean War. Nor did the satellites under the progressive bayonets fare too badly. In his despatches from Germany, Deutscher discovered much to praise in Ulbricht's future Reich:

> "Here in the Russian zone, German culture has unexpected life and liberty . . . One could not help reflecting that the much overworked phrase 'Soviet cultural revolution' had not been an empty sound after all . . . The Russian Military Government, whatever its failings and faults, does give a sense of purpose and direction to many Germans. This is perhaps the most important fact which impresses itself upon the mind of the visitor to the Russian zone [3 March 1946]."

In Poland Deutscher did not notice the accumulating grievances which 10 years later were to bring about the October revolt. But he resented the remark of the American Ambassador in Warsaw, who was alleged to have warned the Poles that American credits would not be forthcoming if nationalization of industries continued:

> "This is an act of intervention as unceremonious as any to which the Russians have yet committed themselves [13 January 1946]."

This was when the Russians were establishing full political control of the country and continuing its economic exploitation. Deutscher was pooh-poohing the steps then being taken by the Communists towards a more thorough Stalinist *Gleichschaltung* of Eastern Europe. He did not like the expression "Iron Curtain", but (2 June 1946) found that it "has been lifted over most of Europe". On the other hand the policy of the "national front", with the drive by the Communist parties to swallow the Socialist parties as a preliminary to their own total domination, was warmly recommended:

> "The objective which Communists professed to pursue—the creation of a united Socialist Party—is a legitimate and sound objective [7 April 1946]."

His other dispatches during this period were in the same strain.

1948–1953: Conscience & Perception

WHEN THE Curtain finally fell over Eastern Europe and Stalin- ism entered its terroristic heyday between 1948 and 1953, Deutscher found it difficult to detect signs of the predicted democratization. He withdrew to a defensive position, disapproving of the persecutions but also of those who voiced their outrage without realizing the dialectic of terror and progress. He deprecated Stalinist malevolence, but even more the aggrieved outcries on behalf of its victims by the "cold warriors" and the "anti-communist crusaders". His was "the clearest conscience of all"; in contrast to others he possessed a historical perspective on the crimes at the time when they were being committed. This gave him the proper sense of proportion to assess their significance with equanimity until the time when "history will cleanse and reshape Stalin's work".

It is interesting to compare the tenor of Deutscher's writings on Stalin's misdeeds at different periods. Before the War he denounced them, using the word "crimes" (as Trotsky did then and Thorez is doing now). After the War he still condemned them, of course, but avoided using the word itself. After Stalin's death his references to the previous period are still muffled in circumlocutions, in which the moral condemnation is indirect, such as the repeated description of the last of the Stalin crimes as "the scandal with the Kremlin doctors". "Through this incident", said Deutscher in *Russia after Stalin*, "Stalinism reduced itself to ghastly absurdity. It committed moral suicide even before the physical death of its author" (p. 112).

It is difficult to see why it is this "incident" which is such a scandal that it amounts to the "moral suicide" of Stalinism, and not a myriad other crimes committed earlier. But the choice of words becomes clear in the light of his earlier writings on the end of the Stalin era. For instance, at the time now referred to by Soviet Jews as the "black years"—when all Jewish cultural activities were completely liquidated, many Jewish writers annihilated, and the persecution of "rootless cosmopolitans" was preparing the ground for a more radical solution for which the "doctors' plot" was to be the prelude—Deutscher denied the existence of governmental action specifically directed against Soviet Jews (hence his subsequent alarm about "the scandal"). On 7 December 1951 the London *Jewish Chronicle* reported a symposium on "Can Jewish Community Life Continue under Communism?", held under the auspices of the World Jewish Congress, in which Deutscher took part:

> "Mr Deutscher said he did not believe that one could accuse the Soviet Government of any special anti-Jewish attitude. It seemed to him that the Jew remained in Russia equal to every other citizen in regard to the law. He added that he dissociated himself from the assumption which seemed to be implied in the question. . . ."

In general, Deutscher leaned over backwards to give the mildest picture of the last years of Stalin and the most charitable interpretation to his post-War actions. The heresy hunts "amounted to little more than shadow-boxing",[5] and anyway at the 19th CPSU congress "the young Stalinist guard witnessed a partial self-repudiation of Stalinism".[6] Who would recognize this era— when the country was blanketed by terror, and fear seeped into every nook and cranny of Soviet life, when the Byzantine adulation of the tyrant reached its zenith as he was preparing another blood-bath—from Deutscher's description?

> "As a rule the 'deviationists' were not imprisoned or deported. They were required to confess the error of their ways and were punished by some mild form of demotion. Sometimes the government honoured them with the highest awards only a short time after they had been singled out for attack. Even the confessions of error were different in kind from those to which Russia had become accustomed earlier on. Having uttered the conventional words of recantation, the 'deviationists' often defended themselves and their views in a veiled yet transparent manner."[7]

Mein Liebchen, was willst du noch mehr?—as Heine would have said. But there is more of the same in Deutscher's perception of the period in which, according to him, "the terror seemed to have spent much of its impetus" (this at the time of the Leningrad and Crimean cases, etc.). Here is his verdict on it in an essay (based on a series in *The Reporter* (New York) in the summer and autumn of 1951, subsequently updated in his book):[8]

> "Up to the time of the scandal with the Kremlin doctors, that is up to 1953, there was no unearthing of sinister conspiracies in Moscow, no hectic search for traitors and enemies of the people, no witches' Sabbath comparable to that of 1936–8. During the whole closing phase of the Stalin era only one member of the Politbureau, N. Voznesensky, the head of the State Planning Commission, was purged. He disappeared suddenly and noiselessly, without being called upon to prostrate himself and confess his crimes in public. Other party members charged with heresy or deviation suffered mild demotion but escaped the extreme form of punishment."[9]

Deutscher, who at the time and later indignantly rejected accusations of

---

[5] *Russia after Stalin*, p. 108.   [6] *The Reporter*, 23 December 1952.
[7] *Russia after Stalin*, p. 107.   [8] *Heretics and Renegades*, p. 128.
[9] At the time Bulganin told Khrushchev: "I'm just on my way to see Comrade Stalin. We shall talk like friends. But where I shall be going when I leave him—home or gaol—I don't know." The Soviet student quoting this remark added "That was how everybody felt at that time." (*Survey*, No. 26, p. 56.)

writing apologies for Stalin,[10] has been overtaken by events, not least by official Soviet statements on the Stalin era. But he never admitted having been wrong. His own summary was that "far from refuting my prognostications, events have confirmed them" (Esprit, March 1954).

1953–1962: Expectations & Realities

AFTER March 1953, Deutscher's forecasts suddenly acquired a new look. The disappearance of the Deity obviously presaged changes. The question was what forms the changes would take, how they would affect the Soviet political system, what the outcome of the struggle for the succession would be. Here Deutscher's optimism was bound to be less misplaced than in the previous periods, for some improvement for the population as a result of the conjunction of the political crisis, economic growth, and social changes was certain. About many of the changes he was quite correct; but his political prognostications were again off the mark, because of his simplified notions about the relationship between economic and political change.

Deutscher began to commit his expectations to print one day after Stalin's death when, in an article in The Manchester Guardian, he asserted that the post-Stalin crisis could "be solved only in one of two ways: through a democratic regeneration of the Revolution or through counter-revolution". This restricted view of the alternatives was soon replaced by another dichotomy: development towards democracy or military dictatorship, which he expounded in detail in his Russia after Stalin. He explained that "a military dictatorship would signify neither a counter-revolution, in the Marxist sense, nor the restoration of Stalinism". But he thought that "the prospect of a military dictatorship, while not altogether unreal, is improbable", therefore he envisaged "a gradual democratic evolution". He repeated the assertion that "the alternative is still between a democratic evolution of communism and some sort of military dictatorship" more than once;[11] and while prudently stressing the long-term character of this alternative, he tended to stretch the facts of the post-Stalin struggle for power to fit the Procrustean bed of his dichotomy.

Thus, although he had already been obsessively overplaying the analogy with the French Revolution and had declared that "the Russian counterparts to the Jacobin, Thermidorian, and Bonapartist phases of the revolution had in a curious way overlapped and merged in Stalinism",[12] he now discovered that "between January and March 1953 a Russian Bonaparte cast his shadow ahead".[13] The shadow has been reappearing ever since, without becoming

[10] Cf. Partisan Review, Fall 1956, p. 515, and Preface to the Vintage Edition of Stalin, (N.Y., 1960), p. viii.
[11] Heretics and Renegades, p. 188 & p. 209.
[12] Heretics and Renegades, p. 54. This was written in 1950 in the introduction to the French edition of Stalin.
[13] Russia after Stalin, p. 167.

long enough to bridge the gap between prediction and fulfilment. After the elimination of Beria in July 1953, Deutscher discovered a gap "between the galvanised Stalinist method of government and the un-Stalinist mechanics of power. Across this gap a potential Bonaparte once again cast his shadow".[14] Malenkov resigned on 8 February 1955 because "the marshals joined hands with the leaders of the Gosplan in an otherwise somewhat unnatural alliance against the Prime Minister and his supporters".[15] The Soviet marshals had been on the upgrade in the West, and Zhukov was already being cast for Bonaparte by the press fed on Deutscher-type commentaries. On the June 1957 showdown he wrote in *The Times* (10 July 1957) that "for some time past Marshal Zhukov had already acted as virtual umpire *vis-à-vis* the opposed factions; and he now threw his decisive weight behind Khrushchev". Therefore Zhukov's inclusion in the Presidium meant that "from the moment of his appearance there he seems as if cast for the arbiter's role".

It must have been a great disappointment when shortly afterwards Zhukov was expelled from the Presidium without so much as causing a ripple on the surface; the Army did not raise a finger to defend its best candidate for the role of Bonaparte. Evidently, the relation between the Party and the Army was not what the prophet believed it to be.

But there were some saving graces: Deutscher was after all more committed in his predictions to the "democratic" part of his alternative. As always, he underlined any element in the situation which could be interpreted as a stepping-stone towards democracy.

From the beginning he derided those who stressed the inevitable rivalries among the post-Stalin leaders. In *Russia after Stalin* he did not even mention the struggle for power among Stalin's heirs as a likely development. But after Beria's fall he immediately wrote a *Postscript* to the American edition (reproduced in *Heretics and Renegades*) in which he tried to cover his traces by an attack on George Kennan for his alleged belief that there were no "genuine divisions within the Soviet ruling group".

Deutscher could not have been more mistaken. First of all he said that Malenkov "merged the Ministry of State Security with that of Internal Affairs and placed Beria at the head of the united department". Beria gained

---

[14] *Heretics and Renegades*, p. 189. Characterizing Bulganin, Deutscher wrote in the *Manchester Guardian* (9 February 1955): "The new Premier is in the Army but not of it. But behind his back stand the real leaders of the officer corps, Marshals Vassilevsky, Govorov, Zhukov and others, the real candidates for the still vacant post of a Soviet Bonaparte."

[15] *Manchester Guardian*, 12 February 1955. Deutscher immediately detected the personal and social divisions behind the fall of Malenkov: "From the beginning Bulganin and Kaganovich were apparently the chief opponents of this powerful pro-consumer programme . . . Bulganin and Kaganovich found powerful allies in the Army and in the Gosplan. The Malenkov–Mikoyan view, on the other hand, found widespread but less influential support in academic and journalistic circles, among the intelligentsia, among the heads of the light industries, and in party cadres concerned closely with the nation's morale."

the reputation of being "one of the more moderate and educated men in Stalin's entourage" (*Russia after Stalin*, pp. 129–130). "In the last period of his activity Beria represented the curious paradox of a semi-liberal police chief in a totalitarian state" (*Heretics and Renegades*, p. 177). It was, therefore, a great shock when the "liberal" Malenkov proclaimed that the "liberal" Beria was an enemy of the people and an imperialist agent. Both of them, Deutscher had suggested (*Russia after Stalin*, p. 120 and *Heretics and Renegades*, p. 184) had been *dvurushniki* (double-faced) under Stalin, concealing their liberal leanings. The fall of Beria represented "half a victory" for "the die-hards of Stalinism" (p. 187). "The same old hands of the political police, resentfully straining to recover their sacred right to extort 'confessions' from their victims, and the Great Russian chauvinists, joined hands to wreak vengeance on him" (p. 177).[16]

But *nil desperandum*. This setback to the "liberal Malenkov" did not mean the end of "collective leadership". Deutscher explained that the Russian Communist Party favours "the substitution of collective leadership for the party régime controlled by a single leader. Collective leadership or government by committee implies free debate at first within that committee and later also in the lower grades of the Party. . . ."[17] It is only natural that, in view of this, Deutscher tended at the time to diminish Khrushchev's role. At the time of the 20th Congress, he referred again to "the change from autocracy to collective leadership" and declared that Khrushchev (previously depicted as the leader of the Stalinist wing) clashed at the Congress with Mikoyan. They "represented two different and in part conflicting attitudes. Mr Khrushchev appears to take a middle line between the die-hards of Stalinism and the anti-Stalinists".[18]

After the fall of Malenkov, Deutscher suggested that it was Bulganin who was the chief opponent of his consumptionist policy.[19] Shortly before Khrushchev's June 1957 victory, he still stressed the existence of the institution of "collective leadership" and pointed out that "the essence of collective leadership is dispersal, diffusion, and therefore limitation of power".[20] After the June 1957 *coup* he wrote that "Khrushchev's ascendency may well be short-lived",[21] but reluctantly admitted in *The Great Contest*

---

[16] A simpler version, based on Khrushchev's indiscretions, indicates that Beria was shot or strangled by his Presidium colleagues, who, fearing his power, with the help of some military commanders sprang a trap on him.

[17] *Manchester Guardian*, 4 November 1954. In *Russia after Stalin* Deutscher declared: "Historically, the Communist party has lost its own freedom because it denied it to others. When at last it regains freedom it cannot but return it to others" (p. 147). But he mentioned only social organizations, not other parties.

[18] *The Times*, 28 February 1956. He reverts to this assertion again: "Khrushchev's prestige and influence are on the decline. His conciliatory attitude certainly did not stand up to the test of events" (*France-Observateur*, 8 November 1956).

[19] *Manchester Guardian*, 10 February 1955.

[20] *Universities and Left Review*, Vol. 1, No. 1, p. 4.   [21] *The Times*, 11 July 1957.

(London, 1960, p. 12) that although Khrushchev had not become the autocrat that Stalin was, "he appears to have done away with collective leadership as Stalin did". Since then Deutscher has refrained from talking about "collective leadership".

Libertarian Hopes & Anti-Libertarian Commitment

ALL THIS TIME struggles for greater freedom were indeed taking place in the Communist countries, and it was not difficult to recognize the protagonists and to identify those who were for freedom and those who were against it. Many such issues and events could be used to test the libertarian spirit of the observer. What was Deutscher's attitude towards them? Was he on the side of the oppressed or the oppressors? His pronouncements provide a guide to his commitment to what he designates as "a fully fledged Soviet democracy" of the future. To take a few instances:

Shortly after the Polish "Spring in October", the Warsaw weekly, *Swiat*, reproduced Deutscher's essay, "The Ex-Communist's Conscience". A few months later a young communist writer, A. Braun, expressed some misgivings:

"Deutscher recommends abstention from activity as the only attitude worthy of an intellectual. Unfortunately this is an impossible attitude for an intellectual living . . . in such a society as ours. One has to remember that in our country people were destroyed and liquidated not for any activity but for that very attitude." (*Nowa Kultura*, 3 March 1957).

Deutscher sent a letter to the editor of *Nowa Kultura* (7 April 1957) in which he warned the young Communist "revisionists" that they might be wrong in their attitude "to the Russian revolution because they are too near to it". That was precisely their chief complaint; but Deutscher, who was farther away and more alert to "historical perspectives" reminded them that "the distinction between a 'heretic' and a 'renegade' is relevant not only in the West, but also in the East—in Poland". He was applauded by the official *Polityka*, but the "revisionists" were unimpressed. One of them, K. T. Toeplitz, gave a pointed summary of the issue.

"Measuring our problems by the abstract norms of the traditional 'socialist struggle', Deutscher (at present living in England) has entirely misplaced his support and his sympathies. This misunderstanding reminds me of a well-known anecdote about a young Jew who was studying Marxism. Troubled with doubts about the doctrine, he went to a Rabbi and asked: 'Tell me, Rabbi, is it possible to build socialism in just one country?' 'Certainly', said the Rabbi, after pondering a while. 'You can build socialism in one country, but you have to live in another.'. . ." (*Nowa Kultura*, 21 April 1957).

Deutscher was undeterred. At the time of the Party counter-offensive against the press in Poland, when the "springboard of October", the celebrated magazine *Po Prostu*, and other periodicals were being suppressed, he gave an interview to the weekly *Swiat* in which he approved of "limitations on democratic freedoms at certain periods" provided that such practices were not presented "as a virtue, still less an eternal virtue". Thus when it came to a concrete political issue, he found himself as usual on the side of the censors, a singularly uncomfortable position for one who dreams that the goddess of freedom may yet be tempted into the Communist camp.

The same attitude was consistently displayed on other issues when freedom was at stake. He would always adorn it, of course, by a "realistic" argument, but so did all the acolytes of all the autocrats in history. In this matter what is important is not a rationalization but a political attitude. And in the case of Deutscher the political attitude is unmistakable. The Hungarian revolution provided another test.

Deutscher rationalized the renewed restrictions imposed by the Party in Poland by discovering the "proletarian movement from below which kept the Polish Thermidorian forces at bay in October".[22] But in Hungary the issues were clear-cut and it was difficult to embrace the goddess of freedom while condoning her rape. That is, however, precisely what he managed to do.

In the first place he proclaimed that here was "a Thermidor which in appearance is also, or even primarily, a war of national liberation", that "Hungary in effect rejected Russian bayonets together with the revolution which was originally brought to that country on those bayonets". Although it was "the ardent work of the whole insurgent people" it was a counter-revolution nonetheless, a counter-revolution in which "Nagy and his faction played the role which Trotsky at one time assumed Bukharin and Rykov would play in Russia". Therefore his plain verdict was that "in October-November [1956] the people of Hungary in a heroic frenzy tried unwittingly to put the clock back".

It was not, however, his last word on the subject. In a lecture before a Canadian audience (1959), the unwitting counter-revolution of the whole people—crushed by Soviet intervention—became simply and euphemistically "a civil war".[23] Thus ended Deutscher's romance with the goddess of freedom in Hungary. There are other instances indicating his libertarian spirit.

He was indignant with Orwell for his untimely literary exposure of Stalinism, when the crimes were being committed, and later with Pasternak for his post-Stalin testimony to the epoch in *Doctor Zhivago*. Even the letter of

---

[22] *Universities and Left Review*, Vol. I, No. 1, p. 10. In fact it was the proletariat which had to be restrained "from above" from fear of Soviet intervention in October 1956.

[23] *The Great Contest*, pp. 12, 16, 48.

rejection by the editors of *Novy Mir* was not so disparaging as Deutscher's review of *Doctor Zhivago*. Obviously, these two authors touched Deutscher on the raw, and it is not difficult to see why.

Orwell's complete intellectual integrity and the metapolitical serenity of Pasternak were in striking contrast to his own equivocations. Orwell, he said, "lacks the richness and subtlety of thought and the philosophical detachment of the great satirists". His political reasoning struck Deutscher as "a Freudian sublimation of persecution mania".[24] Pasternak "speaks the language of the dead and not of the living". His was "the voice from the grave" (even though he was still living at the time). In Deutscher's interpretation, *Doctor Zhivago* is a "political novel", or even just a "political history", and Zhivago only "a sterile egotist, a humanitarian moralist". Not so the prophet himself, who in his philosophical detachment roundly asserted (in December 1958, i.e. when Pasternak compared himself in a poem to "a hunted beast") that "the individual freedom and welfare of Pasternak have never been interfered with until now" and reproached him for putting up only "passive resistance" in Stalin's time: "In his poems he escapes from the tyranny, he does not defy it". And that is why he survived when the majority of poets and writers of his generation either committed suicide, were deported or arrested and annihilated. Stalin himself "watched over his security and welfare" because he knew "that he had little to fear from his poetry".[25]

Here, then, was a man who took a solitary stand against a totalitarian state impugned by an author who more than once had served as apologist for Stalin's tyranny. There is not much evidence here of the Goethean *Höflichkeit des Herzens*.

Deutscher's Facts & Figures

IN ALL HIS pronouncements, Deutscher emphasises the scientific character of his Marxism. "Stalinism", according to him, was "the Marxism of the illiterate"; his own is the genuine product. How rigorously does he apply it to the analysis of Soviet developments?

Not only is his handling of facts and figures often less than precise; sometimes he is amazingly ignorant of the matters he writes about with such expert self-assurance. Here, for instance, is Deutscher's verdict on the development of Soviet planning theory under Stalin:[26]

---

[24] *Heretics and Renegades*, pp. 36, 48. This remark shows: (*1*) A singular insensitiveness to the subject of persecution in the biographer of the hunted and murdered Trotsky; (*2*) An ignorance of Freud for whom sublimation applied only to primary instincts, and was in any case positive. In Freud's scheme, persecution mania (an obsolete concept) cannot be sublimated.

[25] "Boris Pasternak et le calendrier de la Revolution", *Les Temps Modernes*, January 1959, pp. 1061, 1064, 1070, 1081.

[26] *Heretics and Renegades*, p. 117.

"The theory of planning was one of those very few fields in which the general intellectual depression of the Stalin era did not prevent the achievement of definite progress. The planners had at their disposal an amazingly effective 'secret weapon': the famous theorems of 'simple and expanding reproduction' which Karl Marx had developed in the second volume of *Das Kapital*. Those theorems, modelled on Quesnay's *Tableaux Economiques*, describe the composition and circulation of a nation's productive resources under capitalism. Adapted by Soviet planners to a publicly owned economy and further developed, they helped to produce results which future historians may well describe as the most momentous feat in social technology achieved in this generation. . . ."

It is difficult to decide what to admire most in this passage: the audacity of its author or his ignorance. Everything here is wrong. The theory of economic planning under Stalin shared the fate of other social sciences; the "thaw" in economics began only after Stalin's death; the "secret weapon" has very little to do with actual Soviet planning, and in particular Quesnay's *Tableaux Economiques* have no practical application in the activities of Gosplan. Deutscher was evidently led astray by the ideological embellishments of Soviet economic writings because, if anything, *Das Kapital* prevented a further development of Soviet planning theory. In point of fact, the whole post-Stalin discussion on planning centred on this obstacle, and its further development depends very much on the acceptance of un-Marxist importations from Western economic theory and on mathematical economics, as well as of the native revisionist theories of Novozhilov and Kantorovich. The Marxist theory of value was, and still is, a stumbling block to progress; and if the techniques of input–output analysis and of linear programming are being adapted to Soviet planning it is in spite and not because of *Das Kapital*.[27]

Notwithstanding the fact that "the most momentous feat in social technology" had already been developed under Stalin, Deutscher later discovered "some revival of theoretical discussion" in Soviet economics. He went on to give his Canadian academic audience some gratuitous advice (*The Great Contest*, p. 32).

"A great deal of this discussion must, I am afraid, remain unintelligible to Western students trained in the economics of Marshall or even Keynes, because it is conducted in terms of Marxist theory. Here is one more reason, a severely practical one, why Western universities should at last begin to encourage serious and first-hand study of Marx's work.

---

[27] On this see A. Zauberman, "Revisionism in Soviet Economics", in *Revisionism*, edited by L. Labedz (London, 1962); and R. W. Campbell, "Marx, Kantorovich, and Novozhilov", in *Slavic Review*, October 1961.

You cannot understand the present Russian economic debates and planning practices without knowing *Das Kapital*. . . ."

Deutscher seems quite unaware of the vast amount of research being done in Western universities on Soviet economics, and of the fact that the Association of Economists studying this subject in America alone numbers hundreds of scholars.

The same type of ideological prejudice vitiates his appreciation of Soviet agricultural realities. His references to the subject are consistently misleading because of his ideological commitment to the Collective Farm system. In his first dispatch from Germany to the *Observer* (29 July 1945) Deutscher reported that some of the German soldiers on the Eastern front had been "very favourably impressed by the collective farms in which, they said, they saw efficiency as well as social justice". In 1953 he endorsed Stalin's rejection of the proposed transfer of the Machine Tractor Stations to the *kolkhozes* by saying that this "might indeed mark the beginning of a powerful development of modern capitalism in Russian farming", and that "Stalin is undoubtedly right" in believing that "the result would be an enormous strengthening of the anti-socialist elements in the Soviet economy".[28]

But a few years later, when the MTS were transferred, he endorsed Khrushchev's "new deal" for the farmers which, he said, was undertaken "in the belief that state-owned industry, with its greatly expanded resources and power, has nothing to fear from an increase in the economic strength of farming".[29] These ideological gyrations, although not always following the current Soviet line, are related to it. His approach is uncritical, not only to Soviet facts, but also to Soviet figures. He quotes unreservedly the official Soviet statistics whenever it suits his argument, although he knows quite well that they have to be approached with caution.

Speaking about the 19th congress (in Stalin's time) in an address to Chatham House, Deutscher referred to the choice between guns and butter in the context of the time: "I think that in this respect Russia's situation compares favourably with that of Western Europe".[30] And in his 1959 Canadian lectures, with the same sanguine credulity, he is confident that 10 years later Soviet standards of living "are certain to have risen above Western European standards" (*The Great Contest*, p. 65). Is it surprising that a Soviet

---

[28] *Soviet Studies*, April 1953.
[29] *The Great Contest*, pp. 15 and 16. In *Russia after Stalin* Deutscher gave a mildly critical, but relatively favourable picture of Stalin's agricultural legacy (pp. 65–66). Nowadays, even the Communist *l'Unita* (31 January 1962) declares that Stalin left "a grave stagnation in agriculture, which in many sectors could not progress beyond the pre-War levels". And "Khrushchev himself has told *The Times* that when Stalin died agriculture was in a state of stagnation" (*The Times*, 2 March 1962).
[30] *International Affairs* (London), April 1953, p. 153.

writer, referring to this prediction, quotes with approval "the English economist, Deutscher"?[31]

As a legal expert, Deutscher reported the Soviet debate before the adoption of the new legal code, stating that "under the old code, of Vyshinsky's ill-famed inspiration, the legal trial, especially in political cases, was based on the presumption of the defendant's guilt". The new code, on the contrary contains "neither the presumption of guilt nor the presumption of innocence".[32]

This is casuistic nonsense. The 1958 Soviet debate did indeed centre on the issue of the "presumption of innocence" which the more liberal Soviet lawyers wanted to embody in the new code; but the old code did not actually contain "the presumption of guilt". It rejected the "presumption of innocence", but that is not the same. In his book, *Teoria sudebnykh dokazatelstv v sovetskom prave* (Moscow, 1946), Vyshinsky even argued the superiority of Soviet law because, he said, it embodied the principle of the presumption of innocence, and put the burden of proof on the prosecution (pp. 190–198).

On other matters of some historical interest, and not without a certain sociological and doctrinal significance, Deutscher again gets his facts mixed up. Reviewing Trotsky's *The Revolution Betrayed* (in the *New Statesman*, 24 August 1957), he informs his readers that James Burnham "based his *Managerial Revolution* on a few fragments of Trotsky's theory". In fact, Burnham did precisely the reverse. After a long dispute in which Trotsky rejected the ideas first expounded by Bruno Rizzi in *La bureaucratisation du monde*, Burnham left the Trotskyist movement and elaborated these ideas in *The Managerial Revolution*. It was precisely on this question that Trotsky conducted his last political struggle, as his last writings (in the collection *In Defence of Marxism*, New York, 1942) show. Burnham's position, as can be seen from this volume, was diametrically opposite to Trotsky's.

It would be too tedious to enumerate more of Deutscher's errors; they are not conscious mis-statements, but rather subconscious misrepresentations. They have a definite pattern, reflecting a bias so strong that, evidently without realizing he is doing so, he often manipulates reality to suit his argument. When it comes to damning Orwell, he notes "some points of resemblance in the life stories" between him and Zamyatin, and the biography of the Russian gets distorted:[33]

"In 1917 Zamyatin viewed the new revolution with cold and disillusioned eyes, convinced that nothing good would come out of it. After a brief imprisonment he was allowed by the Bolshevik

---

[31] A. Startsev, in *Mirovaya Ekonomika i Mezhdunarodnye Otnosheniya*, No. 2, 1961, p. 31.
[32] *The Great Contest*, p. 37.   [33] *Heretics and Renegades*, p. 37.

Government to go abroad; and it was as an émigré in Paris that he wrote
We in the early 1920s. . . ."

Everything here is wrong. Zamyatin was not only not against the revolution,
but "greeted it with enthusiasm and spent endless hours in lecture halls and
conference rooms on its behalf".[34] He became disillusioned only later. He
wrote *We* in Russia and not in Paris; it was only published abroad. He was not
in Paris in the early 1920s—he went there in 1931 after a campaign of
vituperation against him in the Soviet press. He wrote a dignified and ironical
letter to Stalin, asking for permission to leave, which was granted. But he
was not imprisoned, nor as an émigré did he seem "at times half-reconciled
with the Soviet régime when it was already producing its Benefactor in the
person of Stalin", as Deutscher asserts.[35]

But it is in his commentary on current political developments that
Deutscher's approach to facts leaves most to be desired. He does not present
his speculations about Soviet political developments as hypotheses but as
established historical facts. His stylistic devices include such practices as
reporting conversations between Soviet leaders in inverted commas, as if
Deutscher himself had heard them, and describing their attitudes and actions
in a way which suggests that, if he was not present, he was at least
eavesdropping. So, for instance, his description of the angry exchanges
between Malenkov and Khrushchev in the *New Statesman*, and of the
conversation between Mao Tse-tung and Ferhat Abbas (whose own version
of it in *Afrique Action* was very dissimilar from the one given by Deutscher in
The Reporter, 10 November 1960). One of the descriptions reads as follows:
Khruschev, pointing to Molotov and Kaganovich exclaimed: "Your hands
are stained with the blood of our party leaders and of innumerable innocent
Bolsheviks!" "So are yours!" Molotov and Kaganovich shouted back at him.
"Yes, so are mine", Khrushchev replied, "I admit this. But during the purges
I was merely carrying out your orders. I was not then a member of the
Politbureau and bear no responsibility for its decisions. You were. . . ."
(the *New Statesman*, 24 January 1959), and there are many other instances of
such inside knowledge.

He "knows" that the future leader of the "anti-Party group", Molotov,
was "semi-retired" at the time of the 20th Congress (*The Times*, 29 February
1956), and is "still influential" now (*Observer*, 28 January 1962). He "knows"
in 1953 that Malenkov's "peace party" began "to explore the lines of retreat
from Germany" (*Russia after Stalin*, p. 153) and that the "Malenkov-Beria
bloc" was "really prepared to abandon the government of Pieck and
Ulbricht" (*Heretics and Renegades*, p. 175)[36]—just as he "knows" now that

---

[34] Eugene Zamyatin, *We* (New York, 1959), p. vi.   [35] *Heretics and Renegades*, p. 42.

[36] He repeated this assurance a year later: "Moscow was almost openly preparing to abandon
the government of Pieck and Ulbricht in the first few months after Stalin's death" (*Manchester
Guardian*, 3 August 1954).

"Khrushchev will abandon East Germany", and is already contemplating a withdrawal "to be carried out, if necessary, unilaterally and regardless of the consequences to East German Communism", because it is "a millstone round his neck" (Observer, 28 January 1962). The point about all these speculations is not that they are or might be mistaken—Deutscher, like everyone else, can sometimes guess right—but that highly conjectural suppositions are presented as actual events, when in reality they are nothing but his own (usually wrong) inferences, deductions, and constructions. He is, of course, not supposed to apply the same degree of rigour in his political commentaries as in his historical writings; but even so such practices in his essays, often reprinted in book form, fall well below accepted standards. Nor is his reputation for critical acumen enhanced by extensive quotations (in Russia after Stalin) from fake memoirs such as My Uncle Joe (Joseph Stalin) by Budu Svanidze, a book fabricated by the notorious Paris factory of "Sovietological" forgeries.

Between Khrushchev & Mao

THE STATE OF suspended animation which characterizes Deutscher's approach to Communist affairs makes him as reliable a commentator on the Chinese as on the Soviet scene. Soviet developments are constantly related to the French Revolution and its aftermath, with a limited number of operative bogeys (Thermidor and Bonapartism). The Chinese developments in turn are always being compared to the Soviet ones (NEP and Stalinism). Deutscher once said that "In drawing any analogy, it is . . . important to know where the analogy ends. I hope that I shall not offend badly against this rule".[37]

He is, however, a serious offender against his own golden rule. After Mao's "Contradictions among the People" speech Deutscher rushed into another of his historical metaphors. In the New Statesman (29 June 1957) he proclaimed that "it represents a most radical repudiation of Stalinism", that "it contributes solidly to the winding up of the Stalinist orthodoxy and method of government", that "in effect, Mao proclaims China's NEP".

A striking prediction indeed, but, as so often before, hopelessly wrong. Exactly three weeks earlier, on 8 June 1957, the People's Daily had initiated the attack on the "Rightists" and made it clear that the "liberal" interlude was over.

Another of Deutscher's emphatic hopes was disposed of only post hoc. Mao, he wrote, "leaves us with no doubt that he envisages no such 'second revolution' [as Stalin's of 1929–32] for China", and that he now preaches the "inevitability of gradualness". The 1958 "Great Leap Forward" and the Commune movement provided their own postscript to these assurances. In

---

[37] Heretics and Renegades, p. 53.

his enthusiasm for the progressive Mao, whose "repudiation of Stalinism" was "certainly more thoroughgoing than was Khrushchev's 'secret speech' ". Deutscher asserted that he "argues exactly as Trotsky did nearly 35 years ago". But this supreme compliment was to undergo some dialectical twists.

By 1961 Deutscher came to the conclusion that "the international communist movement remains divided into three wings: left, right, and centre. These wings [represented by Mao, Khrushchev, and Tito] are in some respects the indirect descendants of the three rival communist schools of thought of the 1920s—Trotskyist, Stalinist, and Bukharinist". Deutscher never was a follower of Bukharin, and anyway Tito did not provide enough of a wave of the future to attract adherents to his not-so-big battalions. Of the two remaining "indirect descendants", Mao offered radicalism, fundamentalism, revolutionary drive, in short the "pristine Marxism" of Deutscher's Trotskyist dreams. Khrushchev was "anti-dogmatic", "de-Stalinising" Russia, and for "peaceful coexistence". The one was nearer "the heroic period of the revolution", ready to use "barbaric means to drive barbarism" out of China, and presumably as much entitled to elevate "the *sacro egoismo* of his revolution to a supreme principle", as was Stalin. But the other, too, was the chosen instrument of "historical necessity" which would establish pure "Leninist democracy" in Russia, ushering in "a new phase in the development of Marxism as free from dogmatism as the pristine Marxism was—or even freer—but immensely enriched by new experience and able to comprehend and interpret it".

The revivalist spirit pointed to the "dogmatist" Mao with his "proletarian internationalism". The "democratic" professions indicated the "liberal" Khrushchev, even though *embourgeoisement* rather than proletarian revival might be the outcome. A cruel dilemma for the ex-Trotskyite biographer of Stalin. Was he to choose the "great revolutionary despot", Mao—or "the last *muzhik* Prime Minister" of Russia?

The manifesto of the 81 Communist parties issued in Moscow in November 1960 still induced a hopeful prediction that Mao and Khrushchev

> "and their supporters must go on arguing and patching up their differences as best as they can. They are, so to speak, condemned to do this in mutual tolerance, which does not come easy to either of them. This relative tolerance is quite new to contemporary Communism, which has been formed in the monolithic mould of Stalinism. . . . "[38]

But soon Deutscher found it more and more difficult to make a virtue of necessity, as the "mutual tolerance" between the two instruments of "historical necessity" was becoming both less mutual and less tolerant.

---

[38] *The Reporter*, 5 January 1961, p. 30.

He did not gloss over the differences, but chose an odd way of dealing with them, presenting in the *Sunday Times* (2 July 1961) as a sensational discovery a "secret circular" said to have been sent by Khrushchev to several Communist parties in which Mao was charged with "disloyalty" and "incitement to world war". In fact the article only reproduced, in slightly altered form, the contents of a statement of uncertain origin which had appeared a month earlier in a dissident French communist paper, *La Voie Communiste* (which, oddly enough, contained in the same issue an article by Deutscher). These facts were given in articles published in the *Guardian* (19, 20, 24 July 1961) and *Est et Ouest* (1961, Nos. 262, 263). In replying (in the *Sunday Times*, 23 July, and the *Guardian*, 26 July), Deutscher assured his readers that he had not used the document from *La Voie Communiste* (aware of its existence though he was); his own document was different, and had been obtained from a source he was unable to disclose; and he reiterated his belief in its authenticity. It was one of the less convincing examples of his dialectical skill.

The Dialectic of Political Ambiguity

A T THE FUNERAL OF Natalie Trotsky, several of the speakers referred to this tragic figure of a revolutionary Niobe, who lost her husband and sons through the vengeful terror of "the great revolutionary despot". Deutscher was one of them.

Describing the occasion in *France-Observateur* (1 February 1962), Maria Craipeau reported the following conversation:

> "*Nous sommes fidèles, n'est-ce pas? m'a dit quelqu'un.*"
> "*Fidèles a quoi? Dis-moi, a quoi sommes-nous fidèles?*"
> *Il me regarda, étonné.*
> "*A notre jeunesse, non? A nous mêmes? Je ne sais pas, moi.*"

Indeed, faithful to what?

All great men have their epigones and some of the epigones are not always faithful. In Deutscher's case this involved not so much the "permanent revolution" as permanent ambiguity. Moral indignation, that inevitable companion of political idealism, is curiously inhibited in his writings; and this is strangely out of key in an author who can be so lyrical about his ultimate ideals. His formal disapproval of Stalinist iniquities is always coupled with an apologetic note, either in the form of retrospective determinism or of a prophecy that economic determinism will ensure a happy ending "in the long run" (when, as Keynes said, we will all be dead). What is more, this moral ambivalence is matched by political equivocation. This equivocation is present whether it is a question of past or present, of Stalin and Trotsky, of Khrushchev and Mao, of the "non-Jewish Jew" and the state of Israel, or of the "objectively progressive" East and the "formally democratic" West. When the Italian communist leader, Pajetta, pointed out that the persons who were prematurely telling the truth about Stalinism "have not been very helpful to the Revolution", Deutscher reverted to his old theme:

> "I can agree with you on this point. Some years ago I wrote an essay about heretics and renegades directed against those ex-Communists who exploited the truth about Stalinism, or rather part of the truth about Stalinism, to help reaction. . . ."

More than that:

> "We should indeed not forget that European Social-democracy has a big responsibility for the birth of Stalinism, because by isolating and combating the Russian revolution it contributed to its degeneration."[39]

In short, the Socialists first helped Stalinism to emerge, and then the ex-Communists helped reaction by telling the truth about it.

Deutscher was no less liberal in his advice to Soviet Jews. Referring to their grievances, he said he believed that few would wish to emigrate, should the occasion offer, "because the Soviet Union is evolving in the direction of a genuine Socialist democracy", and even now we are witnessing the beginnings of a resurgence of communist internationalism which "must provide a source of hope to Jews of all political convictions" (*Jewish Chronicle*, 14 November 1958).

The "friend of Israel" is no less generous in his friendly advice to the West, but here his loyalties are even less divided. Although Deutscher is not too clear-cut about it, there can really be little doubt on which side his sympathies are in what he himself terms the "great contest". As communism is bound to win, because it is both desirable and historically inevitable (this is never made quite explicit), it is not surprising that his policy recommendations tend to weaken the West and strengthen the Soviet Union, and that they usually coincide with the policies currently advocated in Moscow. What is rather more bizarre than the picture of Deutscher offering solemn advice to the "capitalist side" on how to handle the situation "intelligently", is the sight of people devoted to the survival of the West looking for guidance to a man whose sympathies and political philosophy indicate that it should go under.

For two decades now, Deutscher has been defending the Soviet moves on the international scene which shifted the balance of power in favour of the Soviet bloc; and if his advice had been taken it would have shifted even further to the West's disadvantage. At the time of Yalta he argued that Stalin was not an imperialist because the Soviet Union had no economic motives for expansion. Later on he could not maintain that the subjugation of 100 million

---

[39] *Espresso* (Milan), 14 and 21 November 1961.

East Europeans happened in a "fit of absent-mindedness", so he found that it was an expression of Stalin's policy of self-containment (*Russia after Stalin*, pp. 78–9). After Stalin's death he still believed that while the practice of imperialism had secured surplus profits to capitalists, "an exactly opposite development is taking place within the Soviet bloc" (*Partisan Review*, No. 4. 1956, p. 514). But now he dispels doubts about the sincerity of the Soviet commitment to the *status quo* in a different way:[40]

> "Can the Soviet government be trusted to refrain from aggression? Will it not, circumstances permitting, seek to dominate Western Germany? Is the urge for conquest not inherent in communism and Soviet power politics? Such questions, based on the experience of imperialist conquest, were still partly relevant to Stalin's policy; but they bear, in my view, little or no relation to the new phase of Soviet diplomacy and to its power-political background. . . ."

Shortly after the *Sputnik* propaganda started pouring from every medium of communication, and not long before Khrushchev's Berlin nuclear-rocket-rattling, Deutscher declared that

> "It is to the credit of Khrushchev's government that, on the whole, it has not tried to exploit the sputniks and luniks to foster a mood of arrogance and aggressiveness, a mood which, unfortunately, was not absent from the West during the years of the American monopoly in atomic power."

Advising the West to accept disarmament without controls, the historical materialist, who preached in and out of season that economic growth must bring political freedom in the Soviet Union, now discovered that in the great contest "ultimately the challenge is a spiritual one".[41]

AFTER A CAREFUL ANALYSIS OF Deutscher's sayings and writings, precious little remains of critical independence and historical impartiality. This explains the suspicion that all his protestations of liberalism and objectivity, justified by occasional reservations and reluctant strictures, are nothing but a mask necessitated by "bourgeois" journalism and academic convention. Deutscher appears to be, at bottom, unable to shed his dogmatic style of thinking and cannot understand free thought unbound by a body of scriptures. A heretic is after all only a rebel against a particular interpretation of dogma, not against orthodoxy as such. His vision of Soviet affairs is essentially simplistic. Despite the difference in political sophistication, it does not deviate all that much from that of the "Red Dean", Hewlett Johnson. Deutscher's sense of reality is of course too strong to permit him to project his

---

[40] *The Great Contest*, pp. 51–2. Cf. also the *Manchester Guardian*, 5, 7, 9 April and 29 December 1954.
[41] *The Great Contest*, pp. 41–2, 62, 78.

vision on to the present, as Hewlett Johson does, so he projects it on to the future. But although in his case there is no complete substitution of reality by a vision, his prophecies tend to overlap with his diagnoses.

His analysis of Soviet developments is, thus, essentially a continuation of the tradition which in the 1920s and 1930s made so many innocents believe every word of Stalinist propaganda. He is far from being a simpleton à la Hewlett Johnson, but he remains a *simplificateur*. As an analyst he permits his opinions to interfere with his perception of reality too much to provide a picture that is not a caricature. It is not just a question of a "normal" amount of bias which is probably unavoidable, but of an addiction to myth-making which prevents a sober analysis of Soviet affairs.

Forty-five years after the revolution it is high time to look at it as a fact of life, and not as an elixir of life. In the approach to Soviet affairs the double dangers of chiliastic faith and political paranoia are always present. There is a certain symmetry between the tendency of a revolutionary prophet to whitewash Soviet reality because of his simple faith, and the attitude of an anti-Communist die-hard who can never recognize any changes in it, because he looks at it only through the spectacles of the "conspiracy theory of history". The one sees liberalism and democracy where they do not exist; the other may refuse to recognize the reality of the Sino-Soviet conflict because of his "demonological" preconceptions. Deutscher often tries to present his *lettres de crédence* of objective moderation by pointing out his opposition to die-hard Stalinists and die-hard anti-communists; but truth is not a matter of equidistance from misconceptions.

Objectivity and a realistic attitude to facts cannot be based on a prophetic approach, but only on sober critical analysis. The picture that emerges is of a man who takes himself much too seriously as an analyst, who is careless about evidence, always ready to shift the argument to prove his oracular prescience, reluctant to admit an error, more concerned with the recovery of faith than with the discovery of truth.

Granting his undoubted talents as a *littérateur*, his vivid style and historical imagination, a careful reader finds that as a political analyst he fails just too often, and we can only hope that in the long-run *some* of his prophecies come true (in the short-run they are politically self-defeating). As a *homo politicus* he is less than candid: As a prophet he was, and still is, in demand because he constantly provides a political anodyne in a dangerous world. His own private unpuzzled vision of the communist wave of the future coincides with a universal longing for peace which induces many people to look at Soviet affairs through rose-coloured spectacles, thus assuaging their anxieties. He satisfies the hankering after the chiliastic myth and enhances the allurement of peace at any price by providing a simplified *rationale* for wishful thinking. These attitudes, as we know, are quite widespread; *mundus vult decipi* is still a relevant maxim.

(1962)

(II) Deutscher's "Stalin"*

> *"The Moscow Trials, which so shocked the world, signify the death agony of Stalinism. A political régime constrained to use such methods is doomed. Depending upon external and internal circumstances, this agony may endure for a longer or shorter period of time. But no power in the world can any longer save Stalin and his system."*
> **Leon Trotsky,** THE STALIN SCHOOL OF FALSIFICATION *(1937)*

> *"The coming epoch may bring with it a breathtaking reversal of the process by which the Soviet democracy of the early days of revolution was transformed into an autocracy. . . . However half-hearted the intentions of the Malenkov government may have been and whatever its ultimate fate, it already has the historic distinction that it has taken the first steps which should lead towards democratic regeneration."*
> **Isaac Deutscher,** RUSSIA AFTER STALIN *(1953)*

> *"When Stalin's body was evicted from the Mausoleum on the Red Square . . . a prominent editor of a great bourgeois paper remarked wistfully: 'Now we may have to raise monuments to Stalin. Without Stalin the Soviet Union may indeed become so much more attractive to our working classes that we shall face dangers infinitely more real and threatening than those we had to face during his reign of terror' . . ."*
> **Tamara Deutscher,** DÉTENTE & SOCIALIST DEMOCRACY *(1975)*

THE 25th anniversary of Stalin's death has been dutifully marked in the "bourgeois" press and dutifully ignored in the Communist press. There were no surprises on either side. In the West the picture of Stalin has been subjected to a steady process of realistic exposure during this quarter of a century: from Khrushchev's "secret speech" to Solzhenitsyn's *Gulag Archipelago*. Various other influences contributed to this process: reminiscences by Milovan Djilas and Svetlana Stalin; books on Stalin's terror like those by Robert Conquest; Western studies of Soviet history, such as the biographies of Stalin by Adam Ulam or Ronald Hingley; writings by Soviet survivors of the Stalin epoch like Nadezhda Mandelshtam or dissidents like

---

* Readers of Leo Labedz's remarkable first article on Isaac Deutscher waited for years in vain for its sequel. But it never appeared. The author now explains why, and offers his original text with a new introduction as a contribution to the anniversary of Stalin's death (1953–78). – *Ed.*

Andrei Sinyavsky. Five years before the fateful date, Orwell's fear in *1984* that humanity may be deprived of its memory through the manipulation of history is not really likely to materialize.

In the East the picture of Stalin has been subject to historiographical reappraisal of quite a different kind. Its outcome may have been the official silence on the anniversary, but none the less Stalin received sympathetic treatment in recently published memoirs by the Minister of Foreign Trade, Nikolai Patolichev; and the mention of Stalin's name by the Minister of Defence, Marshal Dmitri Ustinov, at the Army Day meeting in the Kremlin Palace of Congresses, brought a burst of applause from the 6,000 officers present.

None of the type of writings first mentioned has, of course, ever been published in the Soviet Union. The Soviet leaders may not be able to implement completely Orwell's dictum that "He who controls the past, controls the future"; but they know that if they do not try, they will lose not only the future but the present as well.

SOVIET HISTORIOGRAPHY remains the Eighth Wonder of the World. Bending the historical evidence did not begin with Stalin, though the surrealistic falsification of historical facts certainly reached "yawning heights" under him. But the "memory hole" technique certainly did not end with him and his treatment in Soviet history books under his successors is a vivid illustration of this. Under Stalin, as the late Bertram D. Wolfe put it:

> "Party historiography was in a steadily deepening crisis. Histories succeeded one another at a faster and faster rate, as if they were being consumed by a more and more irritable gigantic chain-smoker who lit the first page of each new work with the last page of the old. . . . The heroes of one work became the dubious weaklings of the next and the villains and traitors of the third; persons of one work became unpersons in the next . . . ."[1]

It was only the publication in 1938 of the celebrated "Bible of Stalin's era", *The Short Course on the History of the CPSU*, which stopped this particular "chain-smoking" for the next 15 years.

The first new Party history under Khrushchev (published in 1959) was only a pale shadow of his "secret speech". Stalin was of course dethroned, he had made "mistakes" and "violated Leninist norms of Party life", but apart from his mistaken idea about the sharpening of the class struggle during the "construction of socialism", there was no indication of his wrong doings. Even the murder of Kirov was given the (slightly attenuated) old Stalinist twist. Only in its second edition (published in 1962, a year after the 22nd

---

[1] Bertram D. Wolfe, *An Ideology in Power* (1969), p. 296.

"de-Stalinisation" Congress) was there a sharply different treatment of Stalin. It has not only dropped the wild panegyrics about him contained in the *Short Course*, but admits mass repressions under him during which "leading Party and Government officials and military men" had perished. It did not, of course, explain the nature of these repressions or provide a true picture of the scope of Stalin's Great Terror. But if the Moscow Trials remained taboo, Kirov's murder no longer was.

> "The assassination of Kirov had a most adverse effect on the life of the Party and the state. It was committed under the cult of personality. Stalin used it as a pretext for reprisals against persons unacceptable to him. Many arrests took place as a result. It was the beginning of wholsesale repressions and flagrant violations of socialist legality."[2]

The announced investigation of the crime has never been concluded; but it was revealed later in *Pravda* (7 February 1964) that Kirov was a candidate of a group of Party leaders who planned to replace Stalin, thus suggesting a motive.

The same edition of the Party history rewrote (falsely) Stalin's role during the War and (less falsely) put the blame on him for the "excesses" of the forcible collectivisation.

UNDER BREZHNEV the process of denigration of Stalin has been reversed. The book by Alexander Nekrich (now at Harvard) revealing Stalin's responsibility for Soviet unpreparedness for the Nazi attack on 22 June 1941 was condemned and withdrawn. The attacks on the de-Stalinisers, the Sinyavsky-Daniel trial, the fulsome homage in *Pravda* (26 February 1966) to his henchman Zhdanov—all these worrying pointers induced several Soviet notables to make an appeal to Brezhnev against rehabilitating Stalin. But although there was no complete rehabilitation, his image was being restored; the "de-Stalinising" historians were attacked, references to repressions, arrests and deaths resulting from them disappeared from print, even phrases like "the Personality Cult" and "the Era of Errors and Distortions" have become unacceptable in spite of their euphemistic timidity.

In 1969 Stalin was described in *Kommunist* (No. 3) as "a prominent figure of the CPSU and the Soviet State" and "a fighter for the working class". An article in *Pravda* (21 December 1969) commemorating the 90th anniversary of his birth played down his defence blunders and moved in earnest towards

---

[2] *Istoriya Kommunisticheskoi Partii Sovetskogo Soyuza* (Moscow, 1962), p. 486. On Soviet Party historiography under Khrushchev see: John Keep, *Contemporary History in the Soviet Mirror*, London, 1962; on historiography under Brezhnev see: Kenneth A. Kerst, "CPSU History Re-Revised", *Problems of Communism*, May-June 1977.

restoring his name as a great War Leader. The three Brezhnev editions of the Party history (1969, 1971, 1976) made an increasingly radical break with the Khrushchevian 1962 version, and rewrote it quite thoroughly. Criticisms of Stalin were either left out or became paltry; the references to the collectivisation and the purges were discreetly reformulated (in the last two editions the Red Army purge in the 1930s is no longer mentioned); credit is given to Stalin for his role in the War and he is praised as a "theoretician and great organiser".[3]

The Kirov episode has been gradually brought back to a slightly retouched *Short Course* variant. Instead of the Khrushchev innuendo implicating Stalin in the crime, it is now said to have reminded the Party and the Soviet people "once again of the need to increase revolutionary vigilance" (which is the old Stalinist watchword). And the 1976 edition has dropped altogether even the emasculated reference to "violations of socialist legality" after Kirov's assassination which was still being printed in the 1969 and 1971 editions.

In short, the picture of Stalin has been refurbished quite fundamentally under Brezhnev. While Khrushchev has become an "unperson", a "balanced" biography in the Soviet calendar for 1979 marks the 100th anniversary of Stalin's birth on 21 December.

It is against this background that one should read the accompanying essay. I wrote it at the end of 1962 at the height of Khrushchevian de-Stalinization, shortly after the publication of Solzhenitsyn's *One Day in the Life of Ivan Denisovich* and of the second edition of Isaac Deutscher's biography of Stalin. I was fresh under the impact of *One Day . . .* and it was just at a time when I had persuaded an American publisher to produce an English translation of Solzhenitsyn's novel (for which Max Hayward and I provided an introduction). It was then that I wrote this essay on Deutscher. But it was never printed. I may perhaps be permitted to explain the circumstances.

My essay—reproduced below—is the second part of a study which I published in April 1962 in *Survey* (No. 41). It criticized quite sharply Deutscher's writings, mainly his journalism. At the end of it there was an announcement that there would be a continuation of the study which would deal with his historical works.

After the appearance of the first essay I received a letter from Mr Deutscher's solicitor threatening me with a libel suit and demanding an apology. I consulted several lawyers. After grilling me on the subject they advised me that there was "no case to answer". Accordingly I refused to budge. Mr Deutscher, after a sharp exchange of correspondence, did not implement his threat and did not issue the threatened libel writ.

---

[3] The late Marshal Vasilevsky explained in *Voenno-Istoricheskii Zhurnal* (No. 2, 1978) that "historical interests of our socialist motherland justify Stalin's policy to avoid providing Germany with the pretext of unleashing war. His fault was that he did not draw the line beyond which such a policy became not just unnecessary, but dangerous."

But when I had written the second part my lawyers advised me not to publish it. The publication of the second article might suggest "a deliberate campaign to destroy Deutscher's reputation". I could not understand this reasoning, in view of the fact that the first article already contained the advance announcement about the forthcoming publication of the second. But legal technicalities are beyond the comprehension of a mere layman; and it was impractical to try to straighten out the issue by a transatlantic correspondence. I was then a Senior Fellow at Columbia University in New York, and I had other things to do. So I postponed publication.

WHEN I EVENTUALLY RETURNED to London I was again busy with other matters. I harboured the idea of publishing it, but then Isaac Deutscher suddenly died (in Rome on 19 August 1967, at the age of 60) and I saw no point in engaging in posthumous polemics. I therefore put the article aside, and did not think about it until some 11 years later, when in a conversation the Editor of *Encounter* suggested to me the idea of publishing it at long last on the occasion of the 25th anniversary of Stalin's death. I put together the pages of the original text with some difficulty, and it is reproduced here without updating (which I have tried to provide in this introduction) and with no changes whatsoever.

ALTHOUGH THE STALIN ERA and the Soviet epoch in general are by now no longer "a mystery wrapped in enigma" for the Western public, the ability and readiness to draw lessons from them are far from impressive. "Progressive" stereotypes and myths about the Soviet Union are no longer what they used to be; yet Western understanding of the Soviet phenomenon is not all that much better. This applies in particular to the question of the Soviet attitude to truth and facts.

Recently Boris N. Ponomarev headed (for the second time) the delegation of Soviet "parliamentarians" visiting the USA (he also had talks not long ago with the British Prime Minister, James Callaghan). In April 1978 he attended the Socialist International conference on disarmament in Helsinki. He lectured there on the "peaceful policy" of the Soviet Union.[4] He is the Party ideological spokesman on such matters as dissidents and Euro-Communism. Like the head of the *KGB*, Andropov, Ponomarev is concerned with disinformation (but, unlike Andropov, he is only a Candidate Member of the Politburo). He is the head of the International Department of the Central Committee of the CPSU and as such officially in charge of Soviet relations

---

[4] Cf. *Kommunist*, No. 7, May 1978, pp. 38–50. At the December 1962 meeting of Soviet historians Ponomarev used a quotation from Lenin to say that Party mindedness requires historical analysis to be based on "a foundation of precise and indisputable facts".

In a *samizdat* historical review, *Pamyat* (reproduced by Chronicle Press, New York, 1978),

→

with the foreign Communist parties. He is the embodiment of official Soviet double-think and double-talk. Whether his Western parliamentary or socialist "colleagues", who consider him an *interlocuteur valable* at *détente* parleys, realize all this or not, they are likely to be blissfully unaware of another title to glory of Mr Ponomarev. He is the Grand Vizier of Soviet historical falsification, a Talleyrand of Soviet historiography. He epitomizes the Soviet customary perversion of truth and window-dressing in matters of the past as in matters of the present, and the two are inextricably linked.

He began his career by helping Vilgelm G. Knorin in writing a Party history in the 1920s. When, in the words of Bertram Wolfe, "histories, and a little later historians, were disappearing without trace", Knorin's work suffered the usual fate and he himself was shot afterwards as "a *Gestapo* agent". But that is not what happened to Boris Ponomarev. He flourished under Stalin (whom he probably helped, with Professor Yudin, in the preparation of the *Short Course*). He flourished under Khrushchev for whom he prepared the two versions of the "de-Stalinised" Party history. And he flourishes under Brezhnev for whom he revised it radically by producing the three new editions in which Stalin is partially rehabilitated. He is, in fact, the chief editor of all five divergent editions of the post-Stalin Party history! This is something even beyond George Orwell's imagination.

But should one really complain that too few learn from the past? One must remember that the intellectual *cognoscenti* "upstairs" influence the rank-and-file "downstairs". In May–June 1976, the *New Left Review*, on whose editors Isaac Deutscher was so seminal an influence, introduced a new editorial section, "Memories for the Future". It explained that

> "the Left—despite the importance it habitually attaches to the experience of this past [i.e. of the 1920s and '30s]—. . . has too often neglected this precious and dwindling inheritance of memory. At best, it has concentrated exclusively upon the great names—and erratically in that. Of course, the account given by major participants, in memoirs or interviews, can be invaluable. But the testimony of less central figures is often equally illuminating—and may at times even be more reliable."

To make up for it, the *New Left Review* published extracts from David Wilson's autobiography *Living in My Time*. The memoir of this "ordinary

---

L. Nadvoitsky demonstrates how the book published in 1974 by the Institute of Marxism–Leninism, *Lenin: A Collection of Photographs and Movie Stills*, which allegedly includes "all" the photographic material on the subject "in existence", with the exception of 53 photographs—uses the old "memory hole" technique; eliminating the "unpersons" and systematically "masking out" from the photographs and unrehabilitated "enemies of the people" (Trotsky, Bukharin, Zinoviev, Kamenev, et al.).

Some of these doctored photographs were reproduced in the article by Christopher Hitchens, "Mutilating Russia's photographic history", *New Statesman*, 1 September 1978.

Labour man" is indeed illuminating, but perhaps not in the way intended by the *New Left Review*. In it, Wilson describes his encounter with Prince Dmitri Svatopelk-Mirsky, who had fought with the Whites against the Soviets, became a refugee and taught Russian Language and Literature at London University. Their encounter was a turning point for Mr Wilson (who eventually joined the Communist Party), and he eloquently expresses his gratitude to Prince Mirsky:

> "He had come to accept the rightness of the revolution for the Russian people and wished to help the Soviets in any way he could.
> On Sunday morning we had a long walk and, for me, an interesting discussion. He asked me how I saw the political situation, and in course of this I told him of the dread I had of the power of the press to mould the minds of people and to create opinion. He said 'Oh yes, of course, Bourgeois opinion' and seemed puzzled at my fears. It was quite extraordinary that at that moment it was as though the scales dropped from my eyes. Until that very moment I had always thought that the capitalist press could create working-class opinion, and the thought had obsessed and frightened me. And here was this Russian aristocrat for whom it was simply an observed fact that the English bourgeois press could instil bourgeois opinion into the British proletariat; but of course they could not create proletarian opinion. It seemed quite simple to him. Since then I have read with profit everything that I have been able to get by Mirsky in English. He eventually went back to Russia, and what became of him I do not know, but I owe him a step in my mental development."

The subsequent fate of Prince Mirsky is, of course, well known. He did not enjoy for long the truthful proletarian features of the Soviet press.[5] He was arrested during the Great Purge and with countless others—an aristocrat among the people—perished in the Gulag Archipelago of Stalin's forced labour camps. So much for the *New Left Review*'s history lessons for those who want to use memories for the future!

IN HIS AUTOBIOGRAPHICAL *Chronicles of Wasted Time* (1973), Malcolm Muggeridge recollected Prince Mirsky in Moscow:

> "Mirsky never discussed with me how he felt about having returned to the USSR as a Soviet citizen. It was obviously an act of great

---

[5] Shortly after the *New Left Review* printed Mr Wilson's piece of autobiographical wisdom, the *Journalist*, the organ of the National Union of Journalists published (in August 1976) an article by Alice Barstow, "The Soviet Press—A Weapon of Democracy". It elicited a vigorous protest in its correspondence columns.

imprudence, and it was clear that he disliked living in Moscow, and having to associate with other Soviet penmen. In London his position had been quite comfortable; as a crossed-out prince he had an assured social position both in upper-class and intelligentsia circles, besides being welcome at working-class gatherings. Even—perhaps particularly—the Communists were glad to have a prince with them on the plinth in Trafalgar Square when they assembled there. In Moscow he was completely at the mercy of the authorities. I don't, of course, know whether he ever meditated trying to escape, but once, when we happened to be looking at a map together, his finger moved to Batum, on the Turkish frontier, and stayed there. I never heard for certain what happened to him, but know that he was arrested and taken off, either to be executed or to die in a labour camp. The ostensible cause of his fall from favour was, it seems, an article he had written on the occasion of the centenary of Pushkin's death in 1937. Following what he supposed to be the Party Line, he wrote of Pushkin as a court lackey and toady. Alas for him, the Line had changed, and Pushkin had been reinstated as a national hero. So, it turned out, Mirsky was liquidated for denigrating Pushkin—a delectable example of Fearful Symmetry, whose cruel whimsicality may have appealed to his own savage temperament. When I heard how his fall had come about, I recalled Luciani's [*Le Temps* correspondent] remark about him that Mirsky had pulled off the unusual feat of managing to be a parasite under three régimes—as a prince under Tsarism, as a professor under Capitalism, and as an *homme-de-lettres* under Communism; of his three essays in parasitism, it was the last that had proved the most hazardous and exacting. . . ."

ONE OF MY OWN personal reminiscences throws an even sharper light on the relation between the Communist historical and mental development.

In 1940 I became friendly with the Soviet film-maker Alexei Kapler. He wrote scripts for some films in a series of movies which presented the history of the Revolution and of the Civil War according to the historiography of Stalin's *Short Course*. Among them were such films as *Lenin in October, Man with Arms, Lenin in 1918, The Unforgettable 1919*, etc. Stalin discussed Kapler's scripts with him personally. Kapler was perfectly aware that the *Short Course* was a concoction of lies, historical fabrications, and surrealistic distortions; but, needless to say, he did what Stalin "suggested" to him. In our own conversations he was quite cynical about it. His was not a case of "double-think"; he was conscious of the falsification of history involved in his work. But when I met him some 25 years later in London he was in some respects a changed man. He retained his pleasant qualities and warm personality. But what had happened to his cynicism, or scepticism, or critical awareness?

His personal history might have accounted for his rather unusual evolution. He had received prizes and privileges from Stalin for his work, but he was sent in 1943 to the Vorkuta concentration camp—because of his romance with Stalin's daughter, Svetlana. He spent more than 11 years in the Gulag Archipelago and was "rehabilitated" after Stalin's death. When I saw him again, in 1965,[6] he stressed his political loyalism, and he implored me "not to write slanders about the Soviet Union".

Some 12 years later, during a visit to Shanghai, I noticed that a local Chinese cinema was showing a Soviet film. A member of the Shanghai Revolutionary Committee who was accompanying me explained that it was the 60th anniversary of the "October Revolution" and China had decided to commemorate it by showing in all the cinemas 10 Soviet feature films on early Soviet history. They included *Lenin in October, Man With Arms, Lenin in 1918, The Unforgettable 1919*, etc. This, he explained to me, was being done because these films were banned in the Soviet Union. So it was urgent to prevent the falsification of history by Soviet "revisionists" who refused to show the true picture of the Soviet past. He obviously believed it. I felt that the ghosts of Kafka and Pirandello in a surrealistic embrace had been hovering over the scene.

WE LIVE IN AN AGE of polycentric surrealism. When Paul Neuberg, the producer of the 1978 British TV series "Stalin—the Red Tsar", was searching for copies of *Lenin in October, Lenin in 1918*, and *The Unforgettable 1919*, he discovered to his surprise that all the copies of these faked "documentary" films had actually been re-faked, and the new versions could therefore not provide relevant material. As *The Guardian* (12 August) reported:

"He found versions in Paris, Brussels and Stockholm, as well as in London. But all versions had been censored in the 1960s to remove references to Stalin. Mr Neuberg claims that there are now no original prints with any public archive or distributor in the West. He had been obliged to go to private sources for a complete print.

He was first alerted to the censoring last summer in a British film archive while viewing *Lenin in 1918*. He knew the original version featured Stalin prominently.

'The chief purpose of this film was to portray Stalin in the role of Lenin's right-hand man in the period of revolution and the Civil War.

---

[6] Svetlana, with whom I was in touch at the time, excluded (when she came to the West somewhat earlier) a number of references to Kapler from her book. But Kapler did not know of this act of reticence on her part until the book was published later. His own behaviour was personally decent. For instance, as eye-witnesses testify, he went out of his way to help his fellow prisoners in the Vorkuta prison camp (cf. Antoni Ekart, *Vanished Without Trace*, London, 1954).

You can imagine our amazement when, by the end of reel three, it was clear he had been entirely cut.'

Lenin in October contained a scene of actors portraying Lenin and Stalin walking through a crowded hall and on to a platform. The Stalin character had been excised from the scenes—but since the actor could not be removed from the platform without losing a vital scene, the film had been re-processed to put the figure of a sailor between the camera and the platform, blocking out the actor playing Stalin.

According to Mr Neuberg, the censoring was easy enough to execute, as none of the Western archives or distributors held master prints or negatives of the films, only prints. When the prints began to deteriorate, the Russians offered new versions."

In 1954, after the fall of Beria, the subscribers to the Large Soviet Encyclopaedia received from its publishers an instruction recommending that they should replace, "using scissors and glue", an entry on Beria by an entry on the Behring Straits, conveniently provided on a newly-printed page. Even though, as in the case of Beria, the purpose of the film-erasures was falsification, the new rearrangement of reality actually happened to involve a removal of an historical fraud and not just a creation of an "unperson".

B UT WHAT CAN ONE MAKE of a prominent English historian whose mind is still so much in the grip of the mythical stereotypes formed in Stalin's time that they condition his perception even today? For A. J. P. Taylor, the bogey of a "Riga correspondent" sending his anti-Soviet false dispatches about the situation in Russia to the "bourgeois press" is still luridly alive. In the New Statesman (12 February 1978), Professor Taylor wrote the following about some BBC TV programmes on China:

"I remark from the BBC series that correspondents in Hong Kong are as qualified to judge China as those in Riga were qualified to judge Russia in the inter-war years."

Yet again, Muggeridge's memoirs are apt:

". . . at that time the paper [The Times] had no correspondent in Moscow and relied on the reports of a man named Urch in Riga. Anyone who had the curiosity to look up Urch's dispatches would find that they maintained a high level of accuracy and reliability; certainly by comparison with [Walter] Duranty's, so prominently displayed in the columns of the New York Times. Again one marvels at the almost mystical importance attached to the location of a newsgatherer as distinct from the truthfulness of the news sent. . . . if the New York

Times went on all those years giving great prominence to Duranty's messages, building him and them up when they were so evidently nonsensically untrue, to the point that he came to be accepted as the great Russian expert in America, and played a major part in shaping President Roosevelt's policies *vis-à-vis* the USSR—this was not, we may be sure, because the [NY] *Times* was deceived. Rather, because it wanted to be so deceived, and Duranty provided the requisite deception material. Since his time, there have been a whole succession of others fulfilling the same role—in Cuba, in Vietnam, in Latin America."

Evidently neither Khrushchev's "secret speech" nor Solzhenitsyn's *Gulag Archipelago* made any difference to A. J. P. Taylor's mind-set. Evidently, if you were a "correspondent in Riga" you told lies—even if history subsequently proved that honourable journalists had been reporting facts and truths.

Professor Adam Ulam once wrote:[7]

"We who study Soviet affairs have—why try to conceal it—a skeleton in our filing cabinets. To describe this skeleton let me invoke a fictitious case of two fictitious characters, *X* and *Y*. In his attempt to learn as much as possible about the Soviet Union, *X*, between roughly 1930 and 1950, read nothing but the works of reputable, non-communist authors. He grounded himself on the writings of the Webbs and Sir John Maynard. Turning to the American academicians, he followed the studies of the Soviet government, law, and various aspects of Soviet society which might have come from the pen of a professor at Chicago, Harvard, Columbia or Williams. This serious intellectual fare would be supplemented by the reading of the most objective non-academic experts on Russia, and finally of those few journalists who had no axe to grind, especially the ones who had spent a long time in the Soviet Union.

His friend *Y* had an equal ambition to learn, but his taste ran to the non-scholarly and melodramatic. Indifferent to objectivity, he would seek the key to Soviet politics in the writings of the avowed enemies of the régime, like the ex-Mensheviks; he would delight in the fictional account *à la* Koestler or Victor Serge. Sinking lower, *Y* would pursue trashy or sensational stories of the 'I was a Prisoner of the Red Terror' variety. He would infuriate *X* by insisting that there were aspects of Soviet politics which are more easily understood by studying the struggle between Al Capone and Dan Torrio than the one between Lenin and Martov, or the dispute about 'socialism in one country'.

[7] *Survey*, No. 50, January 1964.

Which of our fictitious characters would have been in a better position
to understand the nature of Soviet politics under Stalin?"

Alas, true characters are stranger than fictitious ones. A. J. P. Taylor still has
not learned who was telling the truth—for even now he implies that the
reports of the "Riga correspondents" about Stalin's murderous reign were
just anti-Soviet slander.[8]

T HE 25TH ANNIVERSARY of Stalin's death provided a focus on the
   problems involved in all the esoteric points of historical interpretation.
Our Western public still does not fully realize that the vicissitudes of
communist historiography are concerned with vital Party concerns, its
current policies and legitimacy, and that ultimately they bear upon its
ideological identity and its attitude to reality itself. That is why a critique of
the interpretation of the significance of the Stalin era and the highlighting of
the events in it which have proved to be particularly sensitive for communist
historiography are important.

My essay on Isaac Deutscher is, I hope, not just an exercise in pedantry. It
retains, I believe, contemporary relevance, particularly as Deutscher's book
still exercises a considerable influence on the readers who may not have
"heightened consciousness"—this applies especially to the New Left
generation. Many of its "true believers" reacted to Deutscher in the same
way as David Wilson did when "the scales dropped" from his eyes on
encountering Prince Mirsky and his writings. Like Deutscher himself, they
are "critically" sympathetic to both Trotsky and Stalin. They do not realize
how trapped they are in a no man's land between Soviet historiography and
Deutscher's hagiography.

In his *The Prophet Outcast* (which is the subject of my final study),
Deutscher quotes approvingly Trotsky's prediction that the monuments
which Stalin had built himself

> "will be pulled down or taken into museums and placed there in
> chambers of totalitarian horrors. And the victorious working class will
> revise all the trials, public and secret, and will erect monuments to the
> unfortunate victims of Stalinist villainy and infamy on the squares of a
> liberated Soviet Russia."

---

[8] A. J. P. Taylor approvingly reviewed in the *New Statesman* (13 January 1978) the book
Shattered Peace (Andre Deutsch, 1978) by the young American historian, Daniel Yergin, for
whom what he calls "the Riga axioms" (i.e. the "counter-revolutionary" image of the Soviet
Union) are the basis of his indictment of the post-war American foreign policy. Thus the old
stereotype is perpetrated by the new generation of "progressives".
  Ironically, A. J. P. Taylor's *idée fixe* does not save him from abuse by other Old Believers in the
myth about the "Riga correspondents". Reviewing Taylor's *Introduction* to the Penguin edition
of John Reed's *Ten Days That Shook the World*, Andrew Rothstein dismissed it in the Communist
Morning Star (11 April 1977) as "14 pages of misinformation".

This is, to be sure, strong language. Deutscher himself did not use it in his biography of Stalin (only after his death did he introduce "the Borgia perspective"). But *no* monuments were erected to Stalin's victims during the 25 years since the demise of the old tyrant. Its anniversary coincided with the 40th anniversary of the Bukharin trial (which took place between 2 and 13 March 1938 and which was completely disregarded not only in the Soviet but, with one or two exceptions, such as the Italian liberal daily *Il Giornale* and the communist *l'Unità*, also in the Western press).[9] In the Soviet Union Nikolai Bukharin has not been rehabilitated. Nor of course has Leon Trotsky. Instead of monuments to his glory, the victim of Stalin's assassin[10] in Mexico has been given a treatment which reaches even more absurd lengths than Stalin's own *Short Course*.

IN THE SECOND VOLUME of his novel, *The Eternal Appeal* (1978) the Soviet author Anatoli Ivanov now claims that it was Trotsky who instigated the Great Purge in the 1930s. Together with his *Gestapo* masters, he manipulated the honest Chekists who were murdering innocent communists and other Soviet citizens. It was Trotsky who prepared the demonic plan: "We will physically annihilate people who are most loyal to Soviet ideology . . . in all walks of life."

According to Ivanov, Trotskyism presented a terrible threat, of which the Great Purge was evidently only a foretaste. The Soviet Union was only saved from its menace by the indomitable Stalin.

The novel was published in the mass-circulation *Roman-Gazeta* (No. 2, 1978) as well as in book form (first printing: 1,600,000 copies).

But if the rehabilitation of Deutscher's hero, Trotsky, has not occurred in the East, the first biographer of his anti-hero, Stalin, has been "rehabilitated" in the West. Boris Souvarine's classical book on Stalin has been re-issued in France 40 years after its original appearance and received praise in the French "progressive" journals which ignored him disdainfully for close to half a century. Now suddenly it appears that he was right all along. He is hailed as a pioneer of "the whole demythification process" (as Sam White put it in the *Evening Standard*).

---

[9] The case of Bukharin has been raised by the Communist Party historian, Paolo Spriano who wrote in *l'Unità* (16 June 1978) that there was "a sacrosanct necessity" to rehabilitate the victims of the Moscow trials, after the son of Bukharin, Yuri, wrote a letter to Berlinguer appealing to him to intervene on behalf of his father's honour (it was originally published in *La Republica* on 22 June 1978, and in English in *The New York Times* on 7 July 1978 and in *Tribune* on 14 July 1978). The Italian Communist senator Umberto Terracini addressed the Italian, French, Spanish and English Communist Parties with a plea that they should declare the Mosow 1938 trial of Bukharin as a case of "simple assassination", and called for the rehabilitation of Bukharin. The appeal was also made by several other West European Communists and Left figures.

[10] After his release from the Mexican prison, Ramon Mercader received a high decoration in the Soviet Union. It was recently reported that he died in Cuba, but *Der Spiegel* claimed that he is "still alive and living in Moscow".

For Deutscher in his historical dialectics Stalin and Trotsky were, somehow, *both* right. In fact he himself was profoundly wrong about both antagonists. It was Souvarine who was right in his perspective on Stalin. But Deutscher dismissed Souvarine in a contemptuous reference, writing that Trotsky:

> "preserved in his prose—as one preserves insects in amber—the names of quite a few scribblers who would otherwise be forgotten . . . ."

Am I, in publishing the second part of my old essay, preserving the name of a "scribbler" who is being forgotten? Or should I have left my own pages "in amber"? Let the reader decide.

> *"One must be careful to avoid stirring up feelings when talking of the Revolution; no one was in a position to resist it. The blame lies neither with those who perished, nor with those who survived. It was not within the power of the individual to change the elemental forces and to prevent the course of events which were born from the situation and the circumstances."*
> **Napoleon** (*1808*)

> *"The real adepts put on the mask of impartiality."*
> **Julien Benda,** on historians, in THE TREASON OF THE INTELLECTUALS (*1928*)

TEN YEARS AFTER Stalin's death his role in history is being rewritten in the Soviet Union. Not only has his body been removed from the mausoleum, his pictures withdrawn, his monuments destroyed, and his name erased from enterprises and places; the new edition of the Party history[11] has shifted from a regretful to a generally hostile attitude towards him. In the circumstances, Deutscher's political biography of Stalin[12] looks like the only remaining and the most persuasive historical justification for the actions of his hero.

It is therefore somewhat ironical that while the "heirs of Stalin" are taken to task in *Pravda*, his Western biographer seems to repeat after Horace:

> *"Exegi monumentum aere perennius (I have erected a monument more durable than bronze)."*

In the recent new edition of his book,[13] Deutscher declares that he was always confident that his interpretation of Stalin and Stalinism would stand the

---

[11] *Istoriya Kommunisticheskoi Partii Sovetskovo Soyuza* (Izdanie Vtoroe, Moscow, 1962).

[12] I. Deutscher, *Stalin, A Political Biography* (Oxford University Press, 1949).

[13] I. Deutscher, *Stalin, A Political Biography* (Vintage Russian Library, 1960). All quotations unless otherwise indicated are from this edition.

test of time, and that although "a great deal of fresh documentation has become available" since the first edition, "on the whole I *do* stand by the interpretation of Stalin and Stalinism given here."

As a prophet Deutscher claimed: "Far from refuting my prognostications, events have confirmed them."[14] As a historian he echoes the sentiment: "This new documentation, however, far from contradicting the story as I have told it, amply confirms it." Thus, whether about the future or about the past, Deutscher "is always right" and the subsequent evidence only seals the verdict. A historian is less exposed than a prophet because he does not have to anticipate the facts, but only to reconstruct and select them. In his interpretation, however, he can fit them into a predetermined pattern in which the past is as inevitable as the future. In such a scheme evidence, old or new, is of limited relevance only and serves as an illustration for a *roman à thèse*.

For this he does not need any new illustrations, particularly such as could introduce a jarring note into the old text. The facts for which the late dictator is now being condemned are not exactly new to him. He did not have to wait for the Smolensk archives, and certainly not for the new Soviet Stalinography, to learn about them. At the time of his writing there was in the West an abundant literature on the subject. Since then it has grown still further and is now coming to the surface in the Soviet Union itself; but Deutscher shows little inclination to elaborate upon this aspect of Stalin's reign.

A reader of *Stalin* would look there in vain for more than a cursory reference to such an historic Stalinist institution as the forced labour camps. In Deutscher's "historical perspective" the fate of the millions rotting in them deserved no more than a few sentences in a 600-page book. Now that a Soviet author has published a story in *Novy Mir* (1962) describing it in detail, the contrast with the attitude of our free historian is particularly telling. And Deutscher's treatment of the subject is not only extraordinarily brief, but also hazy and misleading.

He does not refer to the development of the Stalinist *univers concentrationnaire* during the two decades preceding the publication of his book. He reduces it there to two instances only: forced labour "imposed on peasants who had resorted to violence in resisting collectivisation", and the deportations in the spring of 1935, after the assassination of Kirov, of "tens of thousands of suspect Bolsheviks, *Komsomoltsy*, and their families" from Leningrad and other cities who "filled prisons and concentration camps". A reader unfamiliar with the subject would hardly suspect that it was not only the peasants "who had resorted to violence" who were deported to the North, that apart from them and the "suspect Bolsheviks, *Komsomoltsy*, and

[14] Cf. *Survey* (No. 41, April 1962), p. 129.

their families" there were millions (not thousands) of the inmates of the forced labour camps who did not belong to these categories. However, although both time and magnitude of the grim *NKVD* empire are blurred, "objectivity" is carefully preserved:

> "Soviet penitentiary reforms of earlier years, inspired by humanitarian motives, viewed the imprisonment of criminals as a means to their re-education, not punishment. . . . Amid the famine and misery of the early thirties the provisions for their protection were completely disregarded, 're-education' degenerated into slave labour, terribly wasteful of human life, a vast black spot on the picture of the second revolution."

This is all Deutscher has to say about Stalin's prison camps. He contrasts the "humanitarian" penal practice under Dzerzhinsky and Menzhinsky with its "degeneration" under Yagoda, and attributes it to the famine of the early '30s, without mentioning that this famine was caused by Stalin's own forcible collectivization. And although later the conditions of the camp inmates had not improved, even though the famine had passed, and the camps became an important part of the Stalinist system there is nothing more on the subject in Deutscher's book.

He completely glosses over subsequent mass deportations, which included entire nationalities, and which were swelling the prison camps long after the "second revolution". For those deriving their information about Stalin's deeds from this biographer, some of the post-Stalin rehabilitations must be rather unexpected, as so many of his victims were not even mentioned by Deutscher. It would also be impossible to realize from this source the inhumanity of the camps when Beria (Deutscher's future "liberal") was in charge, described so vividly, though with restraint, in Solzhenitsyn's *One Day in the Life of Ivan Denisovich*.

IRONICALLY ENOUGH, its author began his prison sentence before Deutscher's story ends. It was in 1949, while Solzhenitsyn was involuntarily "collecting material" in the camp for his novel, that the biography of his jailer who "undertook to drive barbarism out of Russia by barbarous means" appeared. Its easy formulations and fluent phrases appealed not only to the prejudiced and the unwary, but also to many people of good will who mistook its special pleading for objectivity. It has also evoked, as Deutscher notes, a "passionate resentment and hostility". This he deplores. But it is more clear than ever before that his book not only undermined resistance to Stalinism, but through its main thesis was in effect, even if not in intention, reassuring Stalin that, being an agent of history, he was on the whole doing only the historically inevitable in using forced labour in the process of industrializing Russia. And, being a chosen instrument of history, he did not have too many scruples about the means used. Djilas testifies in his *Conversations with Stalin* (1952) that cruelties "did not worry him one bit, for he was convinced that he was executing the judgment of history".

In this last respect, in fact, Stalin shared his biographer's view, and although he needed no reassurance, it must have been pleasant to have his actions presented as the verdict of history by an "objective historian" who also believed that *die Weltgeschichte ist das Weltgericht.* He had a job to do, given to him by history itself, and, unlike his biographer, he could not afford to be squeamish about it.

If it was too early for the tribunal of history, whose "judgment" was still uncertain, the roles were already indicated. The despot was "progressive" and the historian not only disinclined to be a "hanging judge", but in effect quite ready to overlook a good deal of the existing evidence in his assessment of the case. However, the victim had not yet been admitted to the witness stand, and, as could have easily been predicted, he was less interested than Deutscher in the "historical perspective", shaped as it was by the disembodied abstractions of a teleological theory, rather than by the real fate of flesh-and-blood humanity. Solzhenitsyn, the witness, was concerned with Ivan Denisovich, who had suffered in the camps. Deutscher, the historian, had his perspective in common with Yosif Vissarionovich, who had created them.

Blame & History

LEO TOLSTOY noticed that with the passage of time everything in the past begins to seem inevitable. This "deterministic effect" clashes with the realization of choices—political, social, existentialist—with which we are faced in our actions before they are taken. The paradox is heightened when a deterministic theory of history is linked with a call to action. In so far as the theory is influencing its field of perception, it becomes a self-fulfilling or a self-destroying prophecy.

But it is still confronted with historical facts which do not correspond to its expectations. Faced with this, Marxist historians who have to interpret them can even declare such facts irrelevant to the basic propositions of Marxism. Deutscher, for instance, says:[15]

> "I cannot see the importance for the validity, or otherwise, of the materialist dialectic and of historical materialism of the fact that the development of the class struggle in the West has not confirmed some of the optimistic expectations of Marx, Engels, or Lenin."

---

[15] *Nuovi Argomenti* (No. 57/58, 1962) p. 64.

But a much more important role in Deutscher's method of argumentation is played by the "deterministic effect" in the perception of history. Falling back upon it he introduces his "historical perspective", which he uses as a mask for political evaluation. He created it synthetically when Stalin was still alive, and when (as he himself puts it in the new edition of his book) "we had none". At that time the outcome of the political battles being fought was still in the balance, events were decided on a day-to-day basis, and evaluated by contemporary actors; but Deutscher already knew that "Stalin belongs to the breed of the great revolutionary despots, to which Cromwell, Robespierre, and Napoleon belonged".

This was rather flattering to Stalin, as none of these historical figures, whatever their misdeeds, engaged in systematic genocide. Cromwell had his Ireland, Robespierre his Madame Guillotine, and Napoleon his Duc d'Enghien, but none of them was associated with crimes of an order and magnitude comparable to Stalin's. None of them resembles the man who was responsible for the Grand Guignol of the Moscow Trials, the horrors of the *Yezhovshchina*, the mass deportations, starvation, the death of the anonymous millions who perished in all these Vorkutas and Kolymas, the death sentences on children, the execution of prisoners of war in Katyn, and the innumerable other crimes committed on his account. To use Deutscher's language, to give "full value" to his work, "history" has quite a lot more to "cleanse" after Stalin than it had after Cromwell and Napoleon.

But whatever theoretical construction one puts on it, barbarism is barbarism, and history is not a detergent. The "full value" of Stalin's work is not much appreciated nowadays. Deutscher washes whiter than Clio allows. His anthropomorphic language only obscures the realization that "history" cannot "cleanse" anything. Stalin's victims are in their graves, millions of them unknown, and they cannot be raised from the dead. And a moral restitution involves not a historical apologia, but an unequivocal condemnation.

BOTH THE Khrushchevian and Deutscherian interpretations of Soviet history admit Stalin's merits. Deutscher, of course, demands a full rehabilitation of the communist opposition, and Khrushchev has not done this. But, on the other hand, since the 22nd Congress, Soviet pronouncements on Stalin are already more damning than Deutscher's own.

In Soviet historiography "progress" is attributed to the Party and Stalin is said to have "seriously hampered it".[16] Deutscher "dialectically" related his "retrograde" and his "progressive" features and is acclaimed for his "objectivity" in the "bourgeois press".

---

[16] *Istoriya Kommunisticheskoi Partii Sovetskovo Soyuza* (Izdanie Vtoroye) p. 505.

But the difference between the two versions of history is not just one of focus, it is also one of the degree of blame put on Stalin. Deutscher is more inclined to put the blame on "History". It is therefore not surprising that, having prematurely identified his own perspective with the "historical perspective", and his own political verdict with the "verdict of history", he should declare in the introduction to the new edition of *Stalin* that "the historical perspective in which we can now view Stalin is perhaps still too short".

It is indeed not entirely unrealistic to imagine that, when the anti-Stalin campaign no longer serves a politically advantageous purpose, when the cries of the victims have lost their immediacy, and the next generation of Party bureaucrats is no longer personally involved in Stalin's crimes, the time may come for his rehabilitation for a measured assessment of his contribution to the might of the Soviet state. Should such a situation ever arise, Deutscher's biography of Stalin, with its "bourgeois objectivism", will be on hand and could easily be used for such a revaluation. The Tolstoyan "deterministic effect" will by then really come into its own; the passage of time may blunt indignation and make the crimes appear inevitable or statesmanlike. No generation is really very much concerned with the horrors of the past; and although they are registered in the memory of humanity, they are not comparable with the horrors of the present. We all look at St Bartholomew's Day and the Smyrna atrocities with a much greater degree of detachment than did their contemporaries.

But if Deutscher's book may serve for Stalin's rehabilitation in the future, just as it served as an adroit apologia in the past, its philosophy of history may not be entirely adequate for that future purpose. Because, if it should ever happen, it will be more influenced by Russian patriotic attitudes, which are alien to the "internationalist" Deutscher, than by the abstractions of revolutionary theory applied by a member of that almost extinct species, the cosmopolitan Jewish intelligentsia. With the advent of communist polycentrism, the historical parallels are more likely to be, again, figures from the Russian past, Ivans and Peters, rather than Deutscher's Cromwells and Robespierres.

It is a melancholy thought, however, that, whether the omelette is national or international, the broken eggs will not necessarily loom large. There may be something in Deutscher's "historical perspective": Genghis Khan is, after all, a national hero of modern Mongolia.

Of Poets & Peasants

THE SELECTION AND PRESENTATION of historical facts should, in Deutscher's frequently used phrase, be made *sine ira et studio*; but this lofty prescription is not followed in his historical writings.

A historian need not be impartial to be objective, but to qualify as such he must fulfil certain demands. He must use all sources and not disregard those which do not happen to fit his preconceived ideas. He must keep his bias within reasonable limits, and in selecting his material be ready to learn from it and not only to use it for the benefit of his scheme. Intuitive understanding is necessary, but it is not a sufficient condition; omissions must not be blatant, and imaginative creation should not replace evidence. In short, there is a distinction between the work of a historian and the work of a historical novelist, between a study and a piece of fiction, however well written.

IF IT IS NECESSARY to restate such platitudes, it is because Deutscher's historical works often fall short of such minimum requirements. To begin with, his sources on the Russian revolution are heavily one-sided. In line with his political sympathies, he relies almost entirely on Bolshevik accounts or on Trotsky's version. One has only to glance at the bibliography of the sources to which he refers in *Stalin* to see that, with very few exceptions, the non-communist sources, Russian and foreign, are conspicuously absent, and that even Stalin's own masterpiece of historical falsification, the celebrated *Short Course* of Party history, now securely buried, is still listed among the "sources", although it is clear, now as before, that not a single line in this "definitive version" of Stalinist history can be used as a historical reference, but itself has to be checked against genuine sources.

Deutscher is, of course, entitled to his general ideological bias. Even now the history of the French Revolution is still subject to formidable partisan re-interpretations. Ever since Napoleon gave his instructions on how it should be approached (and his angle not unnaturally coincided with Deutscher's own), French historians have continued their battle of re-interpretation, from Michelet through Aulard to Lefevre. But no respectable historian discussing the French Revolution can look at it through a strange combination of Babouvist and Napoleonic spectacles, and then maintain that this restricted view entitles him to claim objectivity. And yet this would be a counterpart to Deutscher's approach to the Russian Revolution and its aftermath. He does not refer to all to the non–Bolshevik material on it (such, for instance, as has been used by Haimson, Treadgold, Keep, or Schapiro). He disregards completely writings by Mensheviks (except Dan), Social Revolutionaries, and Kadets. He has not consulted or pays no attention to various non-Bolshevik documents, ranging from papers by Axelrod to Tsarist police records, which are deposited in various libraries all over the world (such as the Institute of Social History in Amsterdam, Bibliothèque Nationale in Paris, Columbia University Butler Library in New York, Hoover Library at Stanford and the Library of Congress in Washington). He establishes his credentials by making a sanctimonious reference to Western writers and memoirists on the Second World War: "I hope that in using their evidence I have made sufficient allowance for inevitable bias." However, such primary data as the German Foreign Office documents, published in the book of Zeman and Hahlweg, are not worthy of mention in the new edition of *Stalin*.

In his enthusiasm, Deutscher even implies in one place that the victory of the February Revolution (which, he says, "came from the people itself"), should be attributed to the Bolsheviks. He begins an imaginary conversation between Stalin and the last Tsar with the words "Surely you were defeated not by the war itself, but by the Bolshevik party". A more accurate impression of the subject can be found in C. P. Melgunov, *Martovskie Dni 1917 goda*. Among secondary sources, Deutscher does not even mention the two volumes by W. H. Chamberlin, *The Russian Revolution*, published in 1935. There are only two footnotes to Souvarine's pioneering work on Stalin, although clearly Deutscher must be indebted to it.

But perhaps the greatest defect of Deutscher as historian is his talent as *littérateur*. There is everything to be said for a historical study which is well written. But if this happens only rarely, it is because the literary mind is not well adapted to the utilization of fact in historical setting, the criteria of literary creation being quite different from the criteria of historical studies. The historical truth and the "artistic truth" do not necessarily coincide. The first obligation of a historian is accuracy. Not dramatic effect, not wistful improvisation, not tidiness in constructing a story, and not a passionate expression of hope, despair, or even of inner understanding—but the cool and sceptical discovery of evidence. Unless he distinguishes between fact and supposition, not after deliberation but as a mental habit, his literary flair will betray him; and the line between history and fiction will be blurred.

THIS IS precisely the case with Deutscher. He started as a poet, and he has a tendency to dramatize history, to present it in a series of effective juxtapositions—historical metaphors—to give it literary colour; and all these gifts, which could be splendid in a good historian, are dangerous in one who uses them as substitutes for sober evaluation. His revolutionary romanticism leads him to project himself on to the "scene" of history with which he identifies himself. There the revolutionary *manqué* can strike all the attitudes for which real history offered him no chance. He can identify himself with the actors without genuinely appraising their roles and without really caring much about the wider drama which, as in Marx, involves the masses in the audience, and not, as in Carlyle, just the stage. He can supplement his early fixations with *la révolution intrahisable* by an eternal love of hypostasis and histrionics. In short, writing history can be a compensation rather than a vocation.

This, perhaps, is a lesser evil. We have had in our time enough unaccomplished painters · and schoolteachers, seminarists and poet/ philosophers projecting their frustration in the opposite direction. It is Deutscher's seductive style which to some extent accounts for the success of his books. The style carries with it the emotional exaggerations, the flights of imagination, and the metaphorical confusion which makes them more often than not historical fiction, which, indeed, is stranger than truth.

IT IS IMPOSSIBLE to analyse in detail all the inaccuracies in the Stalin biography, just as it is impossible to analyse in detail the connection between Deutscher's style and his historical method. Such textual analysis would require several pages for every one written by Deutscher. But a combination of his literary assets and historiographical liabilities can be illustrated by a fairly representative example. Here, for instance, is how he describes Stalin's "second revolution".

> "The whole experiment seemed to be a piece of prodigious insanity, in which all rules of logic and principles of economics were turned upside down. It was as if a whole nation had suddenly abandoned and destroyed its houses and huts, which, though obsolete and decaying, existed in reality, and moved, lock, stock, and barrel, into some illusory buildings, for which not more than a hint of scaffolding had in reality been prepared; as if that nation had only after this crazy migration set out to make the bricks for the walls of its new dwellings and then found that even the straw for the bricks was lacking; and as if then that whole nation, hungry, dirty, shivering with cold and riddled with disease, had begun a feverish search for the straw, the bricks, the stones, the builders and the masons, so that, by assembling these, they could at last start building homes incomparably more spacious and healthy than were the hastily abandoned slum dwellings of the past. Imagine that the nation numbered 160 million people; and that it was lured, prodded, whipped, and shepherded into that surrealistic enterprise by an ordinary, prosaic, fairly sober man, whose mind had suddenly become possessed by a half-real and half-somnambulistic vision, a man who established himself in the role of super-judge and super-architect, in the role of a modern super-Pharaoh. Such, roughly, was now the strange scene of Russian life, full of torment and hope, full of pathos of the grotesque; and such was Stalin's place in it; only that the things that he drove the people to build were not useless pyramids. In his own mind he saw himself not as a modern Pharaoh, but as a new Moses leading a chosen nation in the desert."

What *can* one do with this type of history writing? Count the number of *omissio veri*? Or of *suggestio falsi*? Point out that Deutscher *knows* what was happening in Stalin's mind, "suddenly possessed by a half-real and half-somnambulistic vision"? that he attributes to the *whole nation* motives and initiatives which were not there? that he confuses Don Quixote and Sancho Panza? How *can* such a style be related to historical facts?

And would not such an anti-histrionic demonstration seem ungenerous, just as Deutscher's own high-handed generalizations about what ultimately are individual sufferings seem morally insensitive, if historically imaginative? We are all strong enough to stand up to other people's sufferings, particularly if our historical heroics can be done at a distance. To fortify ourselves we only have to repeat after Pope, "Whatever is, is right"; or after Hegel, "Whatever is real, is rational"; or after Marx, "History never puts on its agenda the tasks which cannot be accomplished".

Yet in no case are flights of imagination a substitute for evidence in the biographies of historical personalities. Deutscher's work reflects his Immaculate Conception of the Revolution, which underlies everything he writes ("I do not see how the revelations about Stalin's crimes can convert anybody, except persons vacillating under the shock, to believe in private property or in the Immaculate Conception", *Nuovi Argomenti*, No. 57/58, 1962). As for any true believer, it is all a matter of faith and conversion, one way or another.

IN THIS LIGHT it is possible to understand the special meaning he attaches to such expressions as historical objectivity and writing *sine ira et studio*. His scientific model is Lenin, that "critical student in the laboratory of thought", who pursued research "with an open and disinterested mind" (*Stalin*, p. 118). It is not surprising that with such an idea of scientific disinterestedness Deutscher wrote his book the way he did. In his mind Leninist *partiinost* coexists with "bourgeois objectivity", and his own partisanship with the claim to be *au dessus de la mêlée*. In the new introduction to *Stalin* he writes:

> "Although, or rather because, I had written my book as an outsider to the cold war and refused to echo the battle cries and shibboleths of the two camps, my book implicitly made a hash of this notion; and so inevitably it became involved in the cold war and became the crusader's target. *Habent sua fata libelli*."

Deutscher is mistaken in thinking that his *Stalin* is an objective or impartial work because it was criticized both by the *Daily Worker* and by Dr Franz Borkenau. For the conflict with Borkenau was fundamental, whereas the dispute with the *Daily Worker*, however bitter, was a kind of family quarrel within the common Leninist heritage. What Leninist, after all, has not been attacked at one time or another by the *Daily Worker*, especially in Stalin's days? If Mr Deutscher's book aroused so much passionate resentment and hostility (as he notes in his 1960 introduction) this had to do not so much with what he said. After all there were far more emphatic apologies for Stalin published at the time; but none tried to pass as an objective study by a detached scholar. What antagonizes so many foreign observers of Russia is not only Soviet reality but also the persistent attempts to embellish that reality, to declare it the best of all possible worlds. In a similar way, Deutscher's *Stalin* minus the pretence of objectivity would almost certainly have created much less resentment.

Between Doubts & Certainties

THE BIOGRAPHY OF STALIN was published at the height of the "cult of Stalin's personality" in the Soviet Union. The summit of historical sycophancy had been reached. *Pravda* was carrying lengthy panegyrics for months on end to celebrate his seventieth birthday. Tito was already excommunicated and Moscow Trials were being exported to the countries of Eastern Europe. Internally, Zhdanovism reigned supreme and the *NKVD* was taking care of the rest.

Faced with this situation, a free historian chose to elevate its creator to a certain sinister dignity and sombre grandeur. That was his right: historians do not just collect information, they have also to use their powers of interpretation and imagination. But it is not only a matter of taste and bias. Admitting the necessity of interpretation, and hence of the inevitable bias of the historian, there remains a certain minimum of rigour without which history would indeed only be "a tale told by an idiot".

Some facts can be established and there is no room for argument about them. There is a difference between bias and inaccuracy, and this is particularly important in the context of Soviet historiography. Confronted with a falsification of history on an unprecedented scale, the suppression of facts and the creation of myths on a conveyor belt by state-historians, it is not just an elementary duty of the historian to be pedantic about the facts, he has to re-establish the truth.

IN THIS RESPECT TOO Deutscher's work falls short. Not only because of his tendency to mythologize through his interpretative flights of imagination, but also because he is often wrong about "primary facts". These lapses are not conscious distortions, but arise from his ideological obsessions. He was caught between his own cult of history and the contemporary "cult of personality", and the result was that many facts acquired a slant which helped to shape the Stalinist myth from the outside while it was being synthetically elaborated from within.

This was pointed out at the time, in a long memorandum to which Deutscher refers in the introduction to the new edition of *Stalin*, by David and Boris Shub, who accused him of a "multitude of inaccuracies". Deutscher says that the supporting quotations were "torn out of context or crudely distorted" but does not dispute the actual charges. He dismisses them high-handedly as an "underhand attack" and a "comic incident", which could have had some effect only in "the political climate of the time".

But no amount of obfuscation and one-upmanship will change the fact that the inaccuracies in *Stalin* are no more acceptable in the post-Stalin climate of opinion than at the time when Deutscher's subject was committing his own "errors and distortions". Deutscher's cloak of objectivity conceals not only a definite political tendency but serious scholarly deficiencies as well, which often makes his presentation of facts misleading. His historical technique often corresponds to his journalistic technique. As a counterpart to his eavesdropping at the meetings of the Presidium we have *historia arcana* whose only basis is Deutscher's imagination. In neither role does he indicate that his statements are guesses, and what may or may not be considered excusable in a journalist dealing with the current scene is certainly not pardonable in the writing of history. Two instances can be quoted: Deutscher's treatment of the Kirov and the Tukhachevsky affairs.

THE KIROV MURDER, which unleashed the wave of terror and served as a prelude to the Great Purge, is described with the confidence of one who has full knowledge of the circumstances of the case:

> "The quasi-Liberal spell was suddenly interrupted when on 1 December 1934 a young oppositional communist Nikolayev, assassinated Sergei Kirov in Leningrad. Stalin rushed to Leningrad and personally interrogated the terrorist in the course of many hours. He established that the assassin had belonged to a small group of young communists embittered by the oppressive atmosphere in the country. . . . He probably also found out that it was Kirov's liberalism that enabled the terrorists to gain access to his offices in the Smolny Institute. . . . He drew the conclusion that the time for quasi-Liberal concession was over."

The source for this version is given: it is Stalin's own *Short History of the CPSU*, which in fact does not contain all the details given above. Some of them are invented independently by Deutscher, who in fact knew no more than anybody else what had actually happened. Among other signs of the "quasi-Liberal spell" Deutscher mentions the renaming of the *GPU*, now the *NKVD*, and the nomination of Vyshinsky as Attorney-General. As to the circumstances of the murder, he simply repeats the official Stalinist case, without so much as hinting that there might be some doubt about its authenticity, and without indicating that his own presentation of it is pure guesswork. He must have heard of other versions, some of which attributed Kirov's murder to Stalin. There was the thesis of his murdered hero in *Bulletin Oppozitsii*, where Trotsky put forward some of the speculations which much later were reinforced by Khrushchev's admission in his "secret speech" that "the circumstances of Kirov's murder hide many things which are inexplicable and mysterious and demand a most serious investigation. . . ." But on this occasion Deutscher preferred to suppress the voice of his murdered hero and give the version of his murderous anti-hero who was still alive. A grand historical synthesis requires a dramatic treatment, in which the certainty of details, and qualifications as to their reliability are unnecessary academic paraphernalia. Trotsky's and Nikolaevsky's speculations were known when *Stalin* was first published (both *Bulletin Oppozitsii* and *Sotsialisticheski Vestnik*, where they appeared, are in Deutscher's bibliography); Khrushchev's remarks on the subject were made long before the appearance of the second edition. They are passed over in silence.

At the 22nd Congress Khrushchev made even more explicit allusion to Stalin's responsibility; and the new edition of the Party history reiterates that "the circumstances of the case are still being clarified". Thus we have a somewhat ironical situation: while Soviet readers are no longer compelled to read Stalin's own presentation of the case, the Western readers of Deutscher's new paperback edition are still today learning the "established historical facts" about the Kirov affair in their unadulterated Stalinist version!

O N THE TUKHACHEVSKY AFFAIR Deutscher admits that "the exact circumstances of Tukhachevsky's plot and of its collapse are not known", but he has no doubt about its existence:

"The real conspiracy was begun by the leaders of the army, Tukhachevsky and his associates. . . . All non-Stalinist versions concur in the following: the generals did indeed plan a *coup d'état* . . . Tukhachevsky was the moving spirit of the conspiracy."

All non-Stalinist versions referred to turn out to be three references in a footnote, of which two are highly unreliable and the third, Krivitsky's *I Was Stalin's Agent*, has no page reference, which is not surprising as Krivitsky not only does *not* "concur", but directly contradicts Deutscher's version. General Krivitsky in fact describes how "Stalin's scheme to 'frame' Tukhachevsky and the other generals had been set in motion at least six months before the alleged discovery of a Red Army conspiracy" (p. 234).

The use of a reference which proves exactly the contrary is not scholarly custom. But Deutscher goes further. He does not disclose that Tukhachevsky's name was mentioned 11 times in an exchange between Vyshinsky and Radek at Radek's trial on 24 January 1937. This was a sure sign that Stalin had begun to draw his net round the Soviet Marshal, just as those implicated in the earlier Moscow trials were the next on the list of victims for the subsequent trials. Neither does he mention Krivitsky's allegation that the "evidence" against Tukhachevsky was fed to the *Gestapo* through the *OGPU* agents in the Tsarist émigré organization and then fed back to Russia through Czechoslovakia. This is a version partly confirmed by Hoettl, Schellenberg, and Churchill's memoirs; and referred to by Khrushchev at the 22nd Congress (although he doubtless had more direct sources); and by Gomulka at the IX Plenum of the Polish Communist party. Tukhachevsky has now been declared "a loyal son of the motherland" and a victim of "unjustified repression" (*Red Star*, 24 March 1962).

Khrushchev's historiography cannot, of course, be taken at face value any more than Stalin's; but it is clear that even now the case remains highly conjectural, and was even more so when *Stalin* first appeared. Deutscher committed the double offence of presenting a pro-Stalinist version as the anti-Stalinist version, and of treating it as an established fact:

> "The men who tried to put an end to Stalin's rule, Tukhachevsky and his associates, acted behind the back of the people, as a small, strictly secret group of conspirators. Therein lay their fatal weakness. . . ."

Knowledge & Knowing

THE Kirov and Tukhachevsky affairs are examples of Deutscher writing as if he knows when he does not. But he also has the opposite tendency of being more cautious than the available evidence permits and when the benefit of his doubt is all *ad usum Stalini*. Such, for example, is the case of the Katyn massacre on which Deutscher writes that:

> "there were reasons to suspect that the Germans themselves, who were then putting millions of people to death, might have been guilty of the deed."

This statement sounds reasonable enough to a reader who may not know that at the time it was written there was *already* a formidable body of evidence in Polish (and thus available to Deutscher) which indicated clearly that this particular crime should not be attributed to Hitler but to Stalin.

Other examples of Deutscher's misleading technique are legion. Thus,

Stalin's distrust of the old intelligentsia is explained in terms which match his own accusations:

> "Old technicians and administrators viewed his projects with cool scepticism and even open hostility. Some sided with one or the other opposition. A few persisted in an attitude of defeatism which led them to obstruct or even to sabotage the economic plans."

This innuendo could easily be used to justify the trial of the Mensheviks (which Trotsky condemned in his exile); of the Industrial Party; or even of the Moscow Trials which Deutscher so eloquently denounced.

His writing technique also includes what might be called a "double treatment", i.e. a presentation of an unfavourable item followed by a softening of it by a philosophical ratiocination, some form of qualification, or a plain misstatement of fact. Stalin's Great Purge is summarized thus:

> "It is not necessary to assume that he acted from sheer cruelty or lust of power. He may be given the dubious credit of the sincere conviction that he did serve the interest of the revolution and that he alone interpreted those interests aright."

Indeed, it is difficult to see how it could have been otherwise; both for himself and for Deutscher, Stalin was an instrument of history itself. He embodied the Marxist historical necessity in his ruthlessness, and in his alleged bursts of "liberalism". When in 1939 the Great Purge had come to an end, "the statutes of the party were amended in a quasi-Liberal spirit". It was just then that Beria was appointed (replacing Yezhov), and Beria was to become in Deutscher's phrase "a liberal chief of police" after Stalin's death.

Stalin's callous role *vis-à-vis* the Warsaw anti-Nazi uprising of 1944 can hardly be discerned in Deutscher's biography. His description of this historical episode is wrapped up in all kinds of circumlocutions and allowances, including the statement that the uprising was "unexpected". As a matter of historical fact the Soviet-sponsored radio in Polish appealed for weeks on end to the inhabitants of Warsaw to rise in revolt.

Magical Metaphors

B UT THE MOST DECEPTIVE ELEMENTS in Deutscher's writing technique are the historical metaphors. He is ready to produce them, like rabbits out of a magician's hat, on any occasion. They usually centre around the French Revolution, but sometimes they stray to other periods. They are as suggestive as they are misleading.

Not only Cromwell, Robespierre, and Napoleon, but also Tsar

Alexander, the Iron Chancellor Bismarck, and even Pope Alexander Borgia—all serve to explain the inevitability of Stalin. And so does Marx:

> "In spite of its 'blood and dirt', the English industrial revolution—Marx did not dispute this—marked a tremendous progress in the history of mankind. It opened a new and not unhopeful epoch of civilisation. Stalin's industrial revolution can claim the same merit."

Soviet industrialization has many common features with other processes of industrialization, but it also differs from them in important respects. Some of its economic features may be comparable; but its political, cultural, technological and demographic background is *sui generis*. However, a sweeping historical metaphor takes care of all these peculiarities. A glance at the Time-table of History—obviously privately revealed to Deutscher—is supposed to dispel any doubts about the progressive character of the Stalinist method of industrialization:

> "It is argued against it that it has perpetrated cruelties excusable in earlier centuries but unforgivable in this. This is a valid argument, but only within limits. Russia has been belated in her historical development."

Deutscher does not care to explain what these "limits" are, but in another of his historical comparisons he stresses that Stalin was not quite unique.

> "As an inspirer of revolution from above, Stalin does not stand alone in modern European history. He takes his place by the side of Napoleon and Bismarck, from whom in other respects he differs so much."

But the "differences" are not emphasized, and the analogy is extended to foreign policy.

> "It is mainly in Napoleon's impact upon the lands neighbouring France that the analogy is found for the impact of Stalinism upon Eastern and Central Europe."

Is there really an "analogy" between—say—Scharnhorst and the recently rehabilitated Traicho Kostov or between Andreas Hofer and the unrehabilitated Nikola Petkov? (At least, neither Scharnhorst nor Hofer ever needed rehabilitation. . . .)

Napoleon–Stalin liberating Poland from the Tsar Alexander imperceptibly changes into Alexander–Stalin who subjugated it:

> "The complaints of British and American negotiators about Stalin's capriciousness may still be best expressed in Byron's words about Alexander:

Now half dissolving to a liberal thaw
But hardened back whene'er the morning's raw. . .

How nobly gave he back to Poles their Diet
Then told pugnacious Poland to be quiet.

It is curious how the analogy can be extended from major issues down to details."

These details do not include the suppression of the democratic parties in Eastern Europe. Deutscher admits that when during the War the Polish issue was negotiated by Stalin, his granting of "testimonials of good democratic conduct was extremely grotesque". But this is immediately followed by a remark that "it would be wrong to describe Stalin's action as mere trickery, strong as was the element of trickery in it", because (apart from other reasons) "he undoubtedly believed that what he did served a profoundly democratic purpose. . . ."

However, "only after the War was the Bolshevik in Stalin to reassert himself so strongly as to efface Alexander's likeness. . . ." By then his "eyes were fixed primarily on revolutions in Warsaw, Bucharest, Belgrade, and Prague". The revolutions were not there, but can't they always be exported "on bayonets" for progressive purposes? In the Baltic countries, Stalin "had no intention of tampering with their social system" and it was only his sense of danger after the collapse of France which "impelled him to stage revolutions in the three small countries". And after the War—

"The gradual integration into the system of planned economy of several small and medium-sized countries, most of which had been industrially more developed than Russia before the thirties, promised to quicken the tempo of Russia's as well as of their own reconstruction. The first condition of that integration was that communism should be in power in the countries concerned. In treading this path Stalin tacitly admitted that the productive forces of the Soviet Union revolted, to use Trotsky's favourite expression, against its national boundaries."

With this Marxist argument for Soviet imperialism, it is not quite clear whether it was Napoleon or Alexander in Stalin who propelled him in all these actions. But internally, once the War was over—

"Stalin's effort to restore moral supremacy of the party was coupled with his endeavour to re-establish the party outlook as against the nationalist mood of the preceding years."

This was not easy, particularly as Stalin was soon to launch the "Russia First" campaign in which it was stressed that "Popov" invented almost everything, from radio to penicillin. Deutscher notes that at that time "millions of former forced labourers returned home from a long sojourn in Germany", but does not mention that after their return they were deported to the Soviet forced labour camps (like the Buchenwald inmate, Senka Klevshin, in Solzhenitsyn's novel). He stresses instead—

> "the abolition of capital punishment, the quasi-Liberal modification of the criminal code, the emphasis on *habeas corpus* and on the rule of law, and a number of post-war reforms."

The reason for this was apparently that Stalin–Alexander remembered Stalin–Napoleon. He knew that the Red Army soldiers saw foreign countries during the War and this generated in them "a yearning for freedom and a curiosity which the government was ill-equipped to satisfy". Stalin decided to have these "quasi-Liberal" reforms because he was aware of

> "the sequel to the ferment which arose in the army of Alexander I from its contact with Europe. Barely a few years after the victory over Napoleon the Tsar's officers' corps was riddled with secret societies, formed by men whom the observations of life abroad had induced to fight for reform at home. After Alexander's death those secret societies prepared and staged the Decembrist rising of 1825, the forerunner of a long series of revolutionary convulsions."

Having been subjected by Deutscher to so many retrospective reincarnations, the reader is not surprised that the Bolshevik in Stalin reasserted himself not only against Alexander but also against Napoleon; and he dismissed Zhukov.

ALL THESE HISTORICAL METAPHORS were used when Stalin was alive. After his death they were supplemented by another one, shifting the parallel from Alexander I, the head of the Russian Orthodox church, to Alexander VI, the head of the Roman Catholic church. In a debate organized by the Italian journal *Espresso* (17 December 1961), Deutscher declared:

> "To speak about the influence of Stalinism on Russia and upon international communism is much more complicated than to speak for example about the influence of the Borgias' period on international Catholicism and upon Italy. There is, however, a certain vague similarity between the two historical situations, in so far as we, the Marxists, never believed that it would be possible to have in our movement a 'period of Borgias'. And yet we did have it. If one wants

"Unimpeachable Sources"

L ET ME ADD (in 1978) a few remarks on the preface to the 1967 subsequent edition of *Stalin*, in which Deutscher wrote:

"It is possible . . . that my account of the Tukhachevsky affair may need some revision; but if so, Khrushchev and his successors have not provided the elements necessary for such a revision, despite the fact that they have rehabilitated Tukhachevsky and cleared him of the charge that he plotted against Stalin in Germany's interest, as Hitler's agent. In my account of the affair I emphatically refuted that accusation; but I related a version drawn from unimpeachably anti-Stalinist sources (quoted in a footnote on p. 380), according to which Tukhachevsky planned a *coup* against Stalin, in order to save the army and the country from the insane terror of the purges. This version may be mistaken; but Khrushchev and his successors have not revealed a single document or a single fact that would throw light on the affair and allow us to dismiss altogether the anti-Stalinist accounts which insisted on the reality of the plot."

This self-exculpation shows the typical traits of Deutscher's self-righteousness: unwillingness to admit error, retrospective verbal apologetics, artful fact-twisting.

The footnote on p. 380 contains references which are anything but "unimpeachable" or are even all "unimpeachably anti-Stalinist". As noted above, Krivitsky's account is precisely opposite to what Deutscher claims it is. Krivitsky wrote that Stalin "plotted the extermination of the High Command of the Red Army . . . long before [he] 'suddenly' discovered a Red Army plot against his power", that he "used fake 'evidence' imported from Germany and manufactured by the Nazi Gestapo in his frame-up of the most loyal generals of the Red Army . . . ."

Of the other two sources quoted, one, E. Wollenberg, *The Red Army*

(1938) can hardly be treated seriously as evidence. The author maintained (pp. 239–247) that "according to reliable sources of information there was actually a plan for a 'palace revolution' and the overthrow of Stalin's dictatorship by forcible means". The plot was headed by Gamarnik and Tukhachevsky. The plan (fixed for the middle of May 1937) was that the Red Army units were to break the resistance of the *GPU* troops commanded by Marshal (*sic*) Yagoda, occupy the Kremlin, and restore "the Soviet democracy". But the conspirators were arrested in the early weeks of May and "promptly shot". Thus not only were they prevented from seizing power, but also from carrying out "the foreign political programme of the Tukhachevsky–Gamarnik group" which consisted of "the activization of the Soviet foreign policy in dealing with Japanese imperialism and German and Italian fascism and promoting the Socialist World Revolution". Wollenberg did not disclose his "reliable sources of information" and his allegations are unsupported by any proof.

Deutscher's third source, an article by M. Bobrov, published in *Sotsialisticheskii Vestnik* in 1947 has even less claim to credibility. *Sotsialisticheskii Vestnik* published in September, October and November 1947 three articles by M. Bobrov. The last of them was accompanied by an editorial note stating that "much in the views and conclusions expressed in them is wrong or not demonstrated, as we will try to explain in our reply to the author". In the subsequent, December 1947 issue, the editor of *Sotsialisticheskii Vestnik*, R. Abramovich, wrote that Bobrov "uses the word 'plot' in a specifically *GPU* sense", that "one does not know where he got his information", and that "it is difficult to know how much truth there is in all this". So much for Deutscher's "anti-Stalinist" accounts of the Tukhachevsky affair! But there is even more to it. In 1962, the other editor of *Sotsialisticheskii Vestnik*, Solomon Schwartz, explained to me that the editors regretted the publication of these articles because they discovered that they were written (under a pseudonym) by a shady character whom they suspected of being a Soviet *agent-provocateur*.

Such are the "unimpeachable" sources which are the basis of Deutscher's version of the Tukhachevsky affair, a version which after all was left unchanged in the last, 1967, edition of *Stalin*.

to push the analogy still further, we can find a precedent also for
Khrushchev, considering that after the death of Alexander VI there was a
phase devoted to the 'liquidation of the crimes of the Borgias'. . . ."

The Italian Communist party leader, Giancarlo Pajetta, was evidently not
over-impressed by this reasoning, and he replied somewhat ironically:

> "The parallel between Stalin and Borgia does not seem to me too well
> founded, even if the analogy may have some brilliant aspects. From the
> point of view of the Marxist analysis it is devoid of all significance. The
> Church before Alexander VI was certainly not dominated by followers
> of apostolic communism, nor afterwards did we have popes who
> wanted to restore the primitive christianity of the evangelical epoch."

The moral seems to be that neither the Cult of History nor the Cult of
Personality offers the right views about history or personality.

I T WAS NOT NECESSARY to have a "historical perspective" to assess
Deutscher's *Stalin*. Shortly after its publication many reviewers pointed
out its methods and its political bias. Others, however, like the anonymous
reviewer in the *Times Literary Supplement* (10 June 1949), proclaimed that
"until the coming of a new generation allows a new perspective to be
attained, the present biography will not easily be superseded".

   That new generation is evidently not yet with us, not even in the Soviet
Union; still, Deutscher's book badly needs to be superseded, and now more
than ever. Fourteen years have passed since its publication and today its
perspective looks more twisted than before, its mistakes more glaring, its
misconceptions more obvious; its whole tendency seems anachronistic. It
was only with the progress of "de-Stalinisation" that Deutscher finally
thought of mentioning the "Borgia perspective". He had used the words
"quasi-Liberal" or "semi-Liberal" with monotonous frequency to describe
attitudes or acts of Stalin and Beria. If he stresses today the "critical" elements
of his analysis, that only shows his dexterity. He is a historian whom his own
Deity, History, has proved wrong on so many points, but he goes on
confirming his own rectitude:

> "I prepared *The Great Contest* [1961] for its first publication in the Winter
> of 1959–60. Subsequent events seem to me to have confirmed in all
> essentials my analyses and forecasts, even though these were concerned
> with the long-term prospects of Soviet policy rather than with
> immediate developments."

There is one apt remark in *Stalin*:

"The semi-intelligentsia from whom socialism recruited some of its middle cadres enjoyed Marxism as a mental labour-saving device, easy to handle and fabulously effective."

Deutscher contrasts with it a more refined form of "pristine" Marxism, but it still seems relevant to his own intellectual processes. In Deutscher's scheme the shining knights of the Leninist epoch were slain by the Dark Knight who performed a "progressive" work which will usher in an epoch when the pure faith in its "pristine" form will be restored and implemented. Many, though not all, deficiencies of Deutscher's political biography of Stalin derive from this infantile fixation.

It is a melancholy comment on our period, full as it is of gullibility, ignorance, and the corruption of standards, that a book of this sort, with its political fantasies and scholarly shortcomings, could have been praised by famous men and even acclaimed by some as a "classic".

(1978)

4. E. H. Carr:

An Historian Overtaken by History

WHEN Edward Hallett Carr began the writing of his *History of Soviet Russia*, he was three years older than Edward Gibbon had been when the last volume of *The Decline and Fall of the Roman Empire* appeared. Carr took 33 years to conclude his work, 10 years longer than Gibbon. Unlike Gibbon, however, Carr did not later publish his Memoirs (although, according to Tamara Deutscher, he did leave "an unpublished autobiographical memoir"). Instead he published a book on the Comintern, a kind of coda to his *History* (although it is not formally incorporated in it). *The Twilight of Comintern, 1930–35* appeared shortly after Carr's death at the age of 90 (in 1982).

Of course it would have been more interesting to have had his memoirs as the terminal point of Carr's grand enterprise. Nonetheless, the publication of his last book provides an occasion to look back at his *magnum opus* in the context of his other writings. Is it indeed, as so many enthusiasts have said, a work deserving of classic status, such as Gibbon's *Decline and Fall* instantly achieved?

"Superb", "luminous", "masterly" were some of the adjectives used by early reviewers. One admirer, Chimen Abramsky, later suggested (in his introduction to the *Festschrift* in honour of Carr published in 1974) that he "will always be remembered for the monumental history of Soviet Russia".

It is indeed monumental and impressive in many respects, but one must be sceptical about its status as a classic. In my view it is a deeply flawed work; and the fact that an immense amount of labour and research went into it cannot alter the fundamental objections to Carr's approach to the subject. His perspective is rooted in a philosophy of history which all too often manifests a lack of understanding of contemporary developments, and leads to inconsistencies in the interpretation of the events and issues of our time. Underlying all this is a certain continuity of attitudes which permeate the entire body of his work, colour his writings, and even override his political persuasions. They frequently clash with some of his professed values and result in certain important shifts of emphasis in his arguments and formulations (with no retrospective admissions of misjudgment).

1. The Shadow of Gibbon

GIBBON'S political attitudes also underwent change: he was in turn a Jacobite, a Tory, and a Whig. But Gibbon, unlike Carr who focused on the actions of rulers, was in his great work concerned with liberty, and not just with power. He argued that when Romans lost their freedoms, Roman civilization went into decline. Carr's preoccupation with power is such that all his protestations to the contrary notwithstanding, he loses sight of the question of the outcome of the whole exercise of establishing "really existing socialism".

What of the taste and texture of the Soviet omelette in the making of which so many unlamented eggs had to be broken? The reality of the outcome disappears behind an abstract formula which often combines "progressive" stereotypes with the lexicon of Soviet terminology. This point is illustrated by three sentences which furnish the summing-up of Carr's conclusions on Soviet history from *1917: Before and After* (1968).

> "What happened in Russia in October 1917 could still be plausibly called a proletarian revolution, though not in the full Marxist sense" (p. 32).

> "Leninism is Marxism of the epoch no longer of objective and inexorable economic laws, but of the conscious ordering of economic and social processes for desired ends" (p. 10).

> "In the space of fifty years a primitive and backward people has been enabled to build up for itself a new kind of life and a new civilization" (p. 170).

This latter judgment echoed that of Sidney and Beatrice Webb. Unlike theirs, however, it was based not on a naive fantasy, but on solid research (and knowledge of at least another three decades of Soviet history, over half of which was in the worst period of Stalin's ruthless dictatorship).

Gibbon deplored "the triumph of barbarism and religion". Carr hardly concerns himself with barbarities in his *History*. It was only long after the impact of Khrushchev and Solzhenitsyn had been felt that he began to condemn the barbarities, and then only in incidental remarks which were few and far between. ("An historian is not a hanging judge. . . .") One could hardly infer from reading Carr's *History*—particularly the early volumes— that (as he put it in 1967 in his essay on "The Russian Revolution: its Place in History") "after Lenin's death, sinister developments occurred, the seeds of which had undoubtedly been sown in Lenin's lifetime . . . ." But he hastened to add that although

> "it would be wrong to minimize or condone the sufferings and the horrors inflicted on large sections of the Russian people . . . it would be idle to deny that the sum of human well-being and human opportunity in Russia today is immeasurably greater than it was fifty years ago".

The old historical conundrum of means-becoming-ends-in-themselves is shifted by Carr from the plane of action to the realm of analysis, and the results are extolled. History is thus transmogrified into his *History* through the identification of the historian's perspective with that of the ruler. It was a tendency to which Carr was always particularly prone.

But he also extolled freedom. "No history, no freedom; and conversely, no freedom, no history" (*The New Society*, 1951). His interpretation of freedom can be inferred from the following:

> "If Soviet authorities take the view that . . . direct participation in the runnning of affairs is at least as essential an attitute of democracy as voting in occasional elections, it is by no means certain that they are wrong" (*The Soviet Impact on the Western World*, 1946).[1]

Referring to Stalin's description of the 1936 Soviet Constitution as "the only thoroughly democratic constitution in the world", Carr wrote that "it would be a mistake to dismiss such announcements as mere propaganda or humbug".[2] He added: "It would be dangerous to treat Soviet democracy as primarily a Russian phenomenon without roots in the West or without application to Western conditions" (*Soviet Impact*, 1946). A few years later he wrote on the subject of "Western conditions":

> "To speak today of the defence of democracy as if we were defending something which we knew and had possessed for many decades or many centuries is self-deception and sham" (*New Society*).

Referring to Gibbon, Carr wrote that "the point of view of a writer is more likely to reflect the period in which he lives than that about which he writes" (*What is History?*, 1961). But for himself he developed an ingenious scheme by which to escape from the subjective relativities of time and place. It was a scheme which combined a futurological stance with a Mannheimian "sociology of knowledge". The objective historian "has the capacity to rise above the limited vision of his own situation in society and in history". He has "a long term vision over the past and over the future" (*What is History?*).

HOW DOES THE HISTORIAN acquire such a superior perspective? Not just—like Gibbon—by peering into the past, but by looking into the future. He has to diagnose the "historical process" and establish the "historical pattern". This pattern is "determined not so much by the historian's view of the present as by his view of the future" (*New Society*). History does not merely provide information about the past: "History acquires meaning and objectivity only

---

[1] But in the essay of 1967 on "The Russian Revolution: its Place in History", he implicitly contradicted these assertions (of 1946): "The need, with which Lenin wrestled and which Stalin contemptuously dismissed, of reconciling elite leadership with mass democracy has emerged as a key problem in the Soviet Union today."

[2] Writing in 1974 about Bukharin, he praised him for having "rendered honourable service in the campaign against Hitler" (between 1934 and 1936). But he castigated him for being "less impressively . . . one of the principle authors of the famous Stalin Constitution of 1936" (*From Napoleon to Stalin*, 1980).

when it establishes a coherent relation between past and future" (*What is History?*). Good historians, according to Carr, "have the future in their bones".
But how do they get it there? By establishing "the historical pattern". And how do they establish this "pattern"? By looking into the future (and when they see the future, it obviously works . . .).
Here is a circular argument if ever there was one. Clearly, although Carr declared that he did not "believe in laws of history comparable to the laws of science" (*New Society*), his "historical pattern" is related to the Hegelian *Gesetzmässigkeit* and the Leninist *zakonomernost'*. Not for him the warning of Arnaldo Momigliano: "Beware of the historian prophet"!

2. The Futurologist

HOWEVER, WHEN IT CAME to applying his superior insights into the future, or even the present, the contemporary scene, he was not very fortunate in his interpretations. His vaunted knowledge of "the future" more often than not turned out to be simply a combination of prejudices and stereotypes which only clouded his vision.
He felt confident that although "the writing of contemporary history has its pitfalls . . . [they are no] greater than those confronting the historian of the remoter past" (*Bolshevik Revolution*, 1950). Theoretical propositions are matters for dispute, but did Carr avoid such pitfalls in practice? Unlike Gibbon "the moralist", he considered himself "a realist" throughout his life. but in view of his claim to be able to anticipate Clio, has she corroborated his expectations on the major issues of his time? In a recent article in the *London Review of Books* (20 January 1983). Professor Norman Stone reminded us that Carr moved from appeasement of Hitler to support of Stalin. This double record of wrongheadedness was not just a momentary political aberration but a matter of his substantive and enduring views on international relations and on history, with both of which his passing political positions were intimately connected. The fact that Carr's expectations were not fulfilled historically, often leaving him flat on his face, was not cause enough for him to revise his fundamental attitudes. All he did, in the end, was to blur the record. Stone is right in saying that Carr was intellectually "something of a coward". Retrospectively, he would not justify these positions, but he never admitted, in unambiguous terms, to having been wrong. He merely shifted his stance. An intellectual hubris prevented him from re-examining them explicitly.

3. Morality & Power

IN THE CASE OF HITLER, Carr kowtowed before the goddess of power in international relations; in the case of Stalin, he dressed her up as the goddess of history. The factor which underlay Carr's analysis throughout his life was (to paraphrase Spinoza) his *amor potestatis intellectualis*. A clear example of this is provided in *The Twenty Years' Crisis* by the arguments he marshalled to justify "Munich" of 1938:

> ". . . the attempt to make a moral distinction between wars of 'aggression' and wars of 'defence' is misguided. If a change is necessary and desirable, the use or threatened use of force to maintain the *status quo* may be morally more culpable than the use or threatened use of force to alter it. . . . Normally, the threat of war, tacit or overt, seems a necessary condition of important political changes in the international sphere. . . . 'Yielding to threats of force' is a normal part of the process of peaceful change. . . . If the power relations of Europe in 1938 made it inevitable that Czecho-Slovakia should lose part of her territory, and eventually her independence, it was preferable (quite apart from any question of justice or injustice) that this should come about as the result of discussions round a table in Munich rather than as the result either of a war between the Great Powers or of a local war between Germany and Czecho-Slovakia. . . . The negotiations which led up to the Munich Agreement of September 29, 1938, were the nearest approach in recent years to the settlement of a major international issue by a procedure of peaceful change. The element of power was present. The element of morality was also present in the form of the common recognition by the Powers, who effectively decided the issue, of a criterion applicable to the dispute: the principle of self-determination . . . . The change in itself was one which corresponded both to a change in the European equilibrium of forces and to accepted canons of international morality . . . . In practice, we know that peaceful change can only be achieved through a compromise between the utopian conception of a common feeling of right and the realist conception of a mechanical adjustment to a changed equilibrium of forces."

Carr detected indications that "Germany and Italy are already looking forward to the time when, as dominant powers, they will acquire the vested interest in peace recently enjoyed by Great Britain and France". He thought that "since the Munich Agreement, a significant change has occurred in the attitude of the German and Italian dictators". He even stressed (approvingly) an unexpected parallel:

> "When Herr Hitler refuses to believe that 'God has permitted some nations first to acquire a world by force and then to defend this robbery with moralising theories', we have an authentic echo of the Marxist denial of a community of interest between 'haves' and 'have-nots', of the Marxist exposure of the interested character of *'bourgeois* morality' . . . ."

And this is Carr's description of his idea of the relationship between morality and power:

> "It is a basic fact about human nature that human beings do in the long-run reject the doctrine that might makes them right. Oppression sometimes has the effect of strengthening the will, and sharpening the intelligence of its victims, so that it is not universally or absolutely true that a privileged group can control opinion at the expense of the underprivileged. As Herr Hitler says, 'every persecution which lacks a spiritual basis' has to reckon with a 'feeling of opposition to the attempt to crush an idea by brute force' (*Mein Kampf*). And this vital fact gives us another clue to the truth that politics cannot be defined solely in terms of power.

After this, who could accuse him of disregarding morality in politics?

However, the irony of it all is that (as he noted in his Preface to *The Twenty Years' Crisis*) the book "had reached page proof when war broke out on September 3, 1939". Its formulations could only be seen, to put it mildly, as somewhat awkward in the new context; and the unfortunate Carr could do little about it: "To introduce into the text a few verbal modifications hastily made in the light of that event would have served little purpose . . . ." It took over 40 years for the new edition of the book to appear and, not unjustifiably, Carr now described it as a "period-piece". This is surely a more accurate, if still inadequate, description than the reference to it as a "profound and subtle work" (*London Review of Books*, 3 March 1983) by one of his defenders. In any event, this was hardly the work of a historian "who has the capacity to rise above the limited vision of his own situation in society and in history . . . ."

THE CASE OF STALIN provides another illustration of intellectual failure. Carr was no crude whitewasher of Stalin; he was, like Isaac Deutscher, a very subtle apologist. The apologia never took the form of a direct denial of facts, the standard practice of Communists and "fellow-travellers" before Khrushchev's Secret Speech. Some disagreeable facts of Soviet history which were taboo in Soviet historiography were admitted and treated by Carr in his *History*.[3] It was always a matter of what French Communists nowadays call "*le bilan globalement positif*" of Stalin's achievement. (Carr himself said: "The facts of history come into being simultaneously with your diagnosis of the historical process . . . . For me the pattern of history is what is put there by the historian".) But because his arbitrary selection of facts and his emphasis have such a "positive" balance, Carr's work has been rightly perceived by his critics as an apologia.

---

[3] This was unlike, for instance, the Stalinist *History of the USSR* by Andrew Rothstein, published in 1950, the same year as the first volume of Carr's *History*; in his Preface, he thanked Rothstein for "valuable comments and criticisms".

One has only to compare his pronouncements of the 1940s with those of the 1980s—and to contrast the first with the last volume of his *History*—to realize again how his formulations change but his attitudes persist. He concluded in *The Twenty Years' Crisis* that "a successful foreign policy must oscillate between the apparently opposite poles of force and appeasement". This obviously was not very relevant to the new situation after the outbreak of War. But when the Germans launched their attack on the USSR, he again returned to his "oscillation", this time at the opposite pole, the appeasement of Stalin.

4. Errors & Their Compensations

W AS HE COMPENSATING for his previous disappointment? He now went even further and made the rationalization of appeasement not just a matter of pragmatic "mechanical adjustments", but of ideological and historical necessity. As Deputy Editor of *The Times*, he developed his rationale for the Yalta policy in a series of leading articles which advocated (what Professor Abramsky still, rather sanctimoniously, calls) "the need for a better understanding of Russia and its rightful place in the council of nations after the war", i.e., the handing over of Eastern Europe to Stalin.[4] The rationale for this policy was based on the supposed parallel between the situations of 1945 and 1815. The great Allied powers, through their cooperation, will provide security for all after the Second World War, just as the concert of powers "guaranteed the lasting peace" after the Congress of Vienna.

Where was "the principle of self-determination" as "the element of morality" necessary to settle the fate of the Sudeten Germans? Gone. It was no longer needed as an alibi to justify appeasement. The fate of eight European countries and almost 100 million people was to be disregarded and sacrificed to the illusory prospect of post-War harmony between the Western powers and the Soviet Union.

Carr now discovered "a healthy reaction . . . against the principle of self-determination". Wasn't it obsolete? He asserted emphatically that it was, that "the 'national' epoch from which the world is now emerging" is giving way to the "*Grossraum* epoch". He felt that "the expansion of the powers and influence of great multi-national units must encourage the spread of national toleration" (*Nationalism and After*). For instance:

"In the Soviet Union the predominant emphasis is laid—except in the sphere of language and culture—not on the national rights of the Kazbek

---

[4] Abramsky calls these *Times* leaders "the anonymous contribution of Carr to history"; they were deliberately omitted from the bibliography of Carr's works included in the 1974 *Festschrift*. The "anonymous contribution to history" he made through his long association with the *Times Literary Supplement* is another story.

republic [*sic*], but on the equality enjoyed by the Kazbek throughout the Union with the Uzbek or with the Great Russian."

He quoted, as proof, "an emphatic enunciation of this right" in Article 123 of Stalin's Constitution. According to Carr,

"it was Marshal Stalin who, consciously or unconsciously usurping Woodrow Wilson's role in the previous war, once more placed democracy in the forefront of Allied war aims" (*Soviet Impact*).

Internally,

"the degree of moral fervour for the social purposes of Soviet policy which is, according to all observers, generated among the citizens of the Soviet Union is an answer to those critics who used to argue that Marxism could never be successful because it lacked moral appeal".

Comparable to the moral fervour on the home front, externally

"the social and economic system of the Soviet Union, offering—as it does—almost unlimited possibilities of internal development, is hardly subject to those specific stimuli which dictated expansionist policies to capitalist Britain in the 19th century . . . there is nothing in Soviet policy so far to suggest that the east-west movement is likely to take the form of armed aggression or military conquest. The peaceful penetration of the Western world by ideas emanating from the Soviet Union has been, and seems likely to remain, a far more important and conspicuous symptom of the new east-west movement. *Ex Oriente Lux*."

IT IS ONLY AGAINST the background of such writings, published during and immediately after the War, that one can understand not only Carr's decision to write his *History of Soviet Russia*, but the way in which he wrote it. Both his interpretations and his use of sources were affected. Leonard Schapiro summed up the positive side fairly, saying that it "contains a great deal of information assembled with consummate skill and clarity". But he added that "it tends to be overinfluenced by Lenin's outlook in the earlier volumes, and in general deals much more with official policies than with their effects on the population of the country".

Carr was, of course, only one of a number of intellectuals fascinated with power who at the time of its decline in Britain were looking with nostalgic sympathy at the rising new empire. Only a few of them, in identifying themselves with it so irrevocably, went as far as to commit actual treason. But many engaged in *la trahison des clercs*.

Carr's own gigantic rationalization was to be his *History of Soviet Russia*. The first volume provided clear indications. It is only a slight exaggeration to say that in a special note on "The Bolshevik Doctrine of Self-

Determination", Marx, the staunch opponent of the Holy Alliance and an enthusiastic defender of the idea of the restoration of Polish independence, was presented as if he almost shared Carr's own premises concerning Yalta policy. In a note on "Lenin's Theory of the State", Lenin could be seen as if he were well-nigh a consistent follower of Carr's own ideas on the state. But this was only the beginning of what later turned out to be a more complex history "full of cunning passages".

Unlike Schapiro, whose analysis of the relationship between Leninism and Stalinism has been consistently judicious, Carr found difficulty in handling the question—and there is a certain irony here. As a "realist", he tended (unlike Deutscher) to stress the element of continuity between Lenin and Stalin. He echoed Stalin's own self-glorification by exaggerating his role during the early period, and criticized Trotsky, but not Stalin. But after Khrushchev's famous speech, Western "progressives" went into reverse: Stalin was no longer the "Lenin of today". It was now correct to oppose the "good" Lenin to the "bad" Stalin. Once again history had played a trick on Carr.

5. Tricks of History

JUST AS, after the outbreak of the Second World War, he had faced the bankruptcy of his pro-Munich prognosis, and after the end of the War, the crumbling of his pro-Yalta expectations of East-West cooperation, so now he faced a blow to his pro-Stalin orientation. What a cruel fate indeed for a historical "realist"! He could never really extricate himself from this situation. All the factual details which he had so carefully arranged in the earlier volumes of his *History*—especially his discretion with regard to Stalin (sometimes bordering on *omissio veri* and *suggestio falsi*)—were now undermined.

As with *The Twenty Years' Crisis*, there was little the unfortunate Carr could do about it. "The Moving Finger writes; and, having writ Moves on. . . ." He was in the middle of the Way; and his pride and academic propriety, not to mention ideological commitment, forbade any drastic revisions. A subtle, barely detectable, shift did take place. But the de-Stalinization of the general public's perception of Soviet history was not quite matched by a "de-euphemization" in his *History*.

It was 17 years after the publication of the first volume before he made a truly critical reference to the Stalin period—it appears in the eighth volume, on page 451.[5]

---

[5] The reference was still veiled, however. He referred to "the darkest period of Soviet experience" without invoking Stalin's name. A defender of Carr in the *London Review of Books* (17 February 1983) used a garbled quotation from this page of the *History* to prove that "Carr was suprisingly articulate when it came to describing 'Stalin's extreme brutality and indifference to personal dictatorship'. . . ."

We had to wait another 11 years to hear Carr—who only in 1961 first referred (in *What is History?*) to "the grim consequences of the 'cult of personality' "—speak plainly on the subject (in a 1978 interview in the *New Left Review*). Somewhat incongruously, he censured two intellectual categories: "the cold war writers who merely want to blacken Lenin with the sins of Stalin" and "the long blindness of the Left intellectuals in the West to the repressive character of the régime". This was, surely, a breathtaking remark from a man who had done so much to foster this blindness! No reader of Carr's *History* could have inferred what he was now saying in the *New Left Review*:

> "Stalin had no moral authority whatsoever (later he tried to build it up in the crudest ways). He understood nothing but coercion, and from the first employed this openly and brutally. Under Lenin the passage might not have been altogether smooth, but it would have been nothing like what happened. Lenin would not have tolerated the falsification of the record in which Stalin constantly indulged. If failures occurred in Party policy or practice, he would have openly recognized and admitted them as such; he would not, like Stalin, have acclaimed desperate expedients as brilliant victories. The USSR under Lenin would have never become, in Ciliga's phrase, 'the land of the big lie'." (*From Napoleon to Stalin.*)

This is almost too much from an author whose record on the subject is conspicuously less than impressive.

For example, he explained in the Preface to his *History* that he used the 2nd edition of Lenin's works throughout "in preference to the still incomplete 4th edition which omits nearly all the full and informative notes". But what he failed to say was that this omission was due to the systematic re-writing of history in "the Stalinist school of falsification" (although he mentioned this title of a book by Trotsky elsewhere in a footnote to the *History*). This was a lack of candour not uncharacteristic of his handling of other official documents which he used, more or less critically. One has to agree with Norman Stone when he says of the *History* that Carr "never quite said what he meant", but "covered his tracks and never drew recognizable conclusions".

IN THE EARLY VOLUMES of the *History*, Carr's sympathies were obviously with Stalin, not Trotsky. But when after "de-Stalinization" Carr suffered a major reversal he began to develop a more sympathetic attitude towards Trotsky, presumably as compensation for his earlier enthusiasm for Stalin, and praised him, whereas earlier he had stressed his defects. In 1974 he wrote approvingly that

> "on one point his credentials are beyond cavil or challenge . . . . He was

the supreme adversary of Stalin and of everything Stalin stood for" (*From Napoleon to Stalin*).

In his last book, in a special note on "Trotsky and the Rise of Hitler", he stated that "both Trotsky's diagnosis and his foresight [on this point] were astonishingly acute". *C'est le ton qui fait la chanson.* A new tone was introduced into his previous "objectivity"; it could not have been due to his friendship with Deutscher alone.

In her "Personal Memoir" of Carr (*New Left Review*, Jauary–February 1983), Tamara Deutscher described the intellectual friendship of the two:

> "At first sight their personal amity might seem puzzling: on one side, a self-educated former member of the Polish Communist Party—Marxist by conviction, Jewish by origin—who was a refugee from Hitler and Stalin stranded in London; and, on the other side, an English historian who was an unmistakable product of Cambridge, a former member of the Foreign Office, schooled in a diplomatic service famous as a bastion of British traditionalism. . . ."

Since Castor and Pollux, and Don Quixote and Sancho Panza, there have been few such unusual pairs. It was not just a question of the differences in their backgrounds—Edwardian in one case, Talmudic in the other; the one an appeaser of Hitler and Stalin, the other a refugee from them. They had reached their shared "progressive" views via very different routes. (And their views did remain different in certain respects, in spite of their common faith in the Soviet Union and pro-Soviet attitude.)

6. Two Friends

CARR, although he claimed to be a "realist", was no Sancho Panza—he was not able to see the windmills for what they were. Even though towards the end of his life he came closer to recognizing them, he still believed in "progress". And it consisted for him in the replacement of what he called "capitalism" with what he called "socialism". He approved of the direction-of-labour in the East and also advocated it for the West (*New Society*). He believed that "Marx was by temperament and by conviction the sworn enemy of utopianism in any form" (*Soviet Impact*). But he also wrote early in his career that "the dream of an international proletarian revolution has faded" (*Nationalism*), and that "those who believe in world revolution as a short cut to utopia are singularly blind to the lessons of history" (*The Twenty Years' Crisis*).

In his last years he came to the conclusion that "the Russian Revolution, whatever good ultimately came out of it, caused endless misery and devastation"; that "the dictatorship of the proletariat, however one interpreted the phrase, was a pipe-dream", and that Trotsky's "testament" (in which he had expressed some doubt as to the capacity of the proletariat to become the ruling class) had proved to be the correct verdict (*From Napoleon to Stalin*).

All this did not prevent him, to the end, from complaining about "the spirit of carping hostility still characteristic of some Western writing about the revolution . . . the dull and grudging belittlement of its achievements in many current Western accounts" (*1917: Before and After*).

Deutscher, the revolutionary romantic, was even less of a Sancho Panza and he was no Don Quixote either. Like Carr, he lacked the moral sensitivity of the Knight of Rueful Countenance. He was a utopian "true believer" who continued to extol "pristine Marxism", and who believed that, at any moment, the Soviet economy would overtake the Western economy and that a democratization of the Soviet Union was just around the corner. He predicted that the Goddess of Liberty would soon be moving East. In particular, Deutscher rejected as "hyperbole" the doubts expressed in Trotsky's "testament". He supported Trotsky's old idea: the so-called "Thermidor thesis", which postulated that the USSR was "still a workers' state" with no ruling class, that the workers have only to eliminate the "bureaucratic distortions" of Stalinism in order to reveal the path to genuine socialism.

IT IS INTERESTING TO SEE how these two Marxist-inspired authors used the historical documents pertaining to this crucial question. In his review of Volume 2 of Deutscher's biography of Trotsky, Carr was full of extravagant praise. He wrote (*1917*):

"In endless correspondence with other members of the opposition in exile in other parts of eastern Russia and Siberia—notably with Rakovsky, Preobrazhensky and Radek—Trotsky could assert without equivocation the positions which he had failed to defend consistently during the troubled years in Moscow . . . . By and large, the letters of the Alma Ata period—now revealed for the first time from the rich storehouse of the Trotsky Archives in Harvard—are fine examples of Trotsky's powerful intelligence, at grips, without the compromises and inhibitions of the middle 1920s, with the baffling problems of the revolution. By the same token, this is rewarding ground for the biographer . . . . Drawing on the unpublished material of the Archives, he [Deutscher] has given a memorable analysis of the dilemma of Trotsky and of the revolution."

And in the Preface to the second volume of his own *History*, Carr thanked Deutscher for putting at his "disposal the notes made by him of the unpublished Trotsky Archives". What he was presumably unaware of was the way in which Deutscher had used the material on the "Thermidor thesis" from the archives.

As I have since established, Deutscher simply omitted to use a revealing document in the Trotsky Archives—a document which, as it happens, did not fit his ideological stance. I refer to a letter from Trotsky in reply to Karl Radek's criticism of the "Thermidor thesis". The relevant part of the letter reads as follows (Trotsky Archives, T3125):

> "On the theses of comrade Radek, 17 July 1928 [p. 3, note 18] Radek's theses on the problem of the Thermidor say quite unexpectedly: 'I will not analyse here the question of whether the analogy between the Russian and the French revolution is applicable.' What does this mean? . . . . What is the above-mentioned doubt about the applicability of the analogy between the Russian and French revolutions? Are we perhaps sitting in the society of Marxist historians, debating the problems of historical analogies in general? No. We are conducting a political struggle in which we have used the analogy with the Thermidor hundreds of times together with the author of the [present] theses. Analogies should be taken within the strict limits of the ends for which they are being made . . . ."

It is not difficult to see why Deutscher omitted reference to this letter. Were he to have published it, the whole ideological edifice of his biography of Trotsky would have been undermined. It revealed that Trotsky himself did not take seriously the analogy on which the "Thermidor thesis" was built; that he was simply using it as an instrument in the political struggle, leaving it to the Marxist historians (such as Deutscher) to decide whether or not the analogy is basically correct and truly applicable. Deutscher presumably chose not to report the contents of this letter because it would have spoilt his historical analysis and marred his political optimism. These he had based on a seductive analogy, the true appropriateness of which, it appears, left Trotsky indifferent.[6]

How might Carr have reacted to such a disclosure? It could well have accelerated his slow and inconsistent disenchantment and, perhaps, have helped him to realize that his approach to Soviet history (which he shared with Deutscher) was not likely to make his *History* a monument *aere perennius*.

---

[6] Carr's co-author, R. W. Davies, has now posed the following question: "Should we look for more fundamental weaknesses in the political and economic assumptions about the transition to socialism shared by Trotsky and Stalin—and perhaps also by Lenin and Marx?" ("The Debate on Industrialization" in *Pensiero e azione politica di Lev Trockij*, Francesca Gori, ed., Florence: Olschki, 1982, Vol. 1, p. 259).

7. The Year 1929

I T HAS OFTEN been pointed out that Carr's decision to end his *History* with the year 1929 was a peculiar one indeed for a historian of the Soviet Union.

He defended it on the grounds that, by that date, *Foundations of a Planned Economy* (the title of the last six volumes of his work) had already been laid down and the institutional structure of the regime established; and that, after that date, "reliable contemporary material" was no longer available.

But in the Preface to *The Twilight of Comintern* he writes that "thirty years later these arguments need to be qualified", that "what happened in the USSR in the 1930s grew without a break out of what happened in the 1920s. Nor is the documentary landscape as bleak as it seemed in 1950."

The reasons adduced are transparent rationalizations. The real motives for Carr's decision could not have been other than his unwillingness to confront the reality of Stalinist Russia with his "positive" assumptions (quoted above) about the historical accomplishment of the Bolshevik Revolution. These were assumptions with which he had begun the writing of his *History*, and which he would not abandon in spite of the intellectual difficulties he increasingly had to face in his attempt to salvage of them what he could.

It is true that the year 1929 (which Stalin himself called the "year of the great breakthrough") was an important date in Soviet history . . . the end of *NEP*, the beginning of industrialization "at breakneck speed", and the impending introduction of forced collectivization made it a turning-point. The totally centralized state, already in existence, soon became the sole employer, thereby extending immeasurably the network of its control. But this process—and Carr was not enough of a Marxist to believe in economic determinism; he believed rather in the priority of politics—was started with Lenin and continued under Stalin in the 1930s. Institutionally, the system pre-dated Stalin and has continued unchanged until the present day. But Stalin further consolidated its specific features. The imprint of his policies was not just a personal one, although the extent of mass terror (with all its horrific consequences) was undoubtedly shaped by his personality. In this sense, as Adam Ulam has pointed out, "there could have been no Stalinism without Stalin".

But Carr, who at the end of his career at last made open reference to Stalin's special contribution to the *grand guignol* of Soviet history, chose to disregard historical continuity. He refused to deal with the period of Stalin's "high performance" in the 1930s. Only now did he finally admit that "it grew without a break out of what happened in the 1920s", thus retrospectively undercutting his own earlier justification for the time-span covered in his *History*. An additional excuse, that he was too old to embark on another writing project in the 1980s, was offered by one of his recent defenders. But this is hardly a viable excuse since at least the last three volumes of the *History* might well have been devoted to the subject of Stalin in the 1930s, rather than to the Comintern in the 1920s and '30s. But this was evidently not Carr's preference.

WHATEVER ONE'S VIEW of the positive achievements of Carr's *History*, the very fact that it comes to a halt at the brink of the era of high Stalinism undermines its value for the understanding of Soviet history. Leonard Schapiro's *The Communist Party of the Soviet Union*, or Bertram Wolfe's *Three Who Made a Revolution*, are better guides to an understanding of Soviet affairs. With all his factual knowledge and his immense diligence, Carr lacked comparable grasp and insight. He never acquired a genuine feel for his subject. He tended to confine himself to the penumbra of official formulations and of ideological formulas which always concealed, rather than revealed, real Soviet life. Not for him Marx's favourite quotation from Goethe: "*Grau ist alle theorie . . . .*"

An illustration of Carr's lack of what the Germans call *Fingerspitzengefühl* is his introduction to the so-called *Litvinov Diaries*, a forgery which Wolfe spotted immediately and exposed as such. The lack of understanding displayed on this occasion by Carr, the hapless "expert", did not enhance his credibility as an interpreter of Soviet matters in general.

The other reason that Carr offered for ending his *History* in 1929—the paucity of "reliable contemporary material"—appears also to be a lame excuse. After 1956, as he himself admitted, "many documents have been published, as well as crucial articles, by writers having access to party and Soviet archives. . . ." He always preferred to use official documents, but anyway this cannot be a *conditio sine qua non* for the writing of Soviet history. The greatest difficulty is not getting hold of reliable material about what is going on in the Soviet Union, but the ability to distinguish between the reality of the official façade and the "real reality". Carr never quite mastered that particular art. It is for this reason that his *History* is unlikely to survive.

8. Ideology & History

ONE SUSPECTS that ideological difficulties may also be responsible for the thematic meanderings and convoluted construction of the *History*. Carr was a writer who on the whole commanded a style of supreme lucidity. He was gifted with an ability to summarize complicated material and had a talent for producing clear précis.

Yet in his *History*, unlike in the graceful early books *The Romantic Exiles* and *Bakunin*, he is often muscle-bound. The style is at times stilted and the structure of the whole work is so disjointed and weighed down with digressions that it must be very difficult for the general reader to get a clear overall picture. The last two volumes (13 and 14) scarcely deal with Soviet history itself, but, as I have mentioned, are used (under the irrelevant title *Foundations of a Planned Economy*) for an examination of the policies of foreign Communist Parties and their relations with Moscow. The present volume, *The Twilight of Comintern*, is the logical extension, and there would seem to be no reason why it should not have been included (as Volume 15) with the previous volumes—except, of course, that this would have been a violation of Carr's rationale for the magical date of 1929 as the *terminus ad quem* of his *History*. But in effect he violated this himself in the last three volumes.

The Twilight of Comintern is, then, a collection of short histories of various Communist parties between 1929 and 1935, when the Party line changed from the harsh extremism of the "theory of Social Fascism" to the duplicity of more amenable Popular Front tactics. Analytically, it is more critical than Carr's previous writings on the subject; but it still does not convey with sufficient vividness the stolidity and servility of Stalin's foreign accomplices. It relies, again, largely on the texts of official documents, and it attempts to decipher the doctrinal jargon which here (as elsewhere in *History*) defeats Carr's own lucid style.

I FIND IT CURIOUS that Carr does not even mention Franz Borkenau's book on the *Communist International*, published in 1938, which Carr himself praised highly in *The Twenty Years' Crisis*. Of course, Borkenau did not have at his disposal the additional material which accrued in the subsequent four decades; but in my view his book is analytically the better of the two.

In spite of its fame and prestige, most Western historians of Soviet affairs tend to ignore Carr's *History*. Nor, unsurprisingly, is it quoted or referred to in official Soviet publications. Soviet dissidents (Roy Medvedev included) do not mention Carr in their works. The official guardians of Soviet history in the Soviet Union are not happy about Carr because in point of fact he rummages in too many of their "memory holes". They cannot afford to be as cynically "objective" as he, for this would undermine Soviet legitimacy. Like Carr, they can always predict "the future" with ease; but they find it even more difficult to predict their ever-changing past.

Soviet dissidents understandably dislike Carr because his historicism appears to them only a thinly veiled rationalization of the power of their oppressors. They know—contrary to the Hegelian formula of which Carr approved (*What is History?*, p. 100)—that what is real is not necessarily rational. They do not need to read Pasternak or Solzhenitsyn, Akhmatova or Mandelshtam, Shalamov or Ginzburg, in order to comprehend this. They have the past "in their bones".

Ultimately, however, the reasons for Carr's failure do not lie merely in his lack of understanding of the Soviet experience, but in his approach to history in general.

9. Old Times, Modern Times

I N *What is History?* Carr rather sneered at Isaiah Berlin for his concern with moral assessments in history:

> "Sir Isaiah Berlin . . . is terribly worried by the prospect that historians may fail to denounce Genghis Khan and Hitler as bad men. The bad King John and the Good Queen Bess theory is especially rife when we come to more recent times . . . ."

One wonders why Carr mentioned Hitler but not Stalin. Presumably because this is the latterday Carr, the author of *The History of Soviet Russia*, rather than the Carr who wrote *The Twenty Years' Crisis*.

Gibbon compared five good emperors with five bad ones. What would Carr's *History* have been like if his subject had been not Stalin (Pasternak's "pock-marked Caligula"), but Tiberius, Caligula, Nero, Vitellius, or Domitian (and particularly if Carr had been writing as a contemporary)? Confronted with the problem of the limited terror of the Roman Emperors, he most certainly would not have been overconcerned with what Gibbon called the "exquisite sensibility of the sufferers". He would probably have used Imperial Edicts as his main sources, and would have taken at face value their republican terminology, analysing meanings only in terms of what they implied for the power of the rulers concerned.

To compare Carr's approach with Gibbon's is to register the contrast between his moral indifference and Gibbon's human concern, his blinkered pedantry and Gibbon's sovereign achievement in the sifting and validation of evidence.

Carr might have learnt his "realism" about power from Machiavelli. Both stressed that rulers must take into account the moral sentiments of the populace. But Carr saw power to an even greater degree as an exercise in the manipulation of such sentiments. He was not, however, a very thorough pupil: his "realism" was often just a mask for his illusions. In the *Discourses*, Machiavelli wrote that "the great majority of mankind is satisfied with appearances, as if they were realities, and is more often influenced by things that seem than by those that are . . .". More often than not, Carr was among the ranks of those who are "satisfied with appearances". Indeed, he perpetuated the Soviet myth in the name of "realism".

HE WAS THE SPIRITUAL PRODUCT of an earlier era, and in effect he transposed the faith of an Edwardian "progressive" on to Marxist "progressivism". His generation witnessed the collapse of Victorian Britain and experienced the trauma of the First World War. He reacted by rejecting "moralism" and over-investing in the new future.

Did he ever really come to grips with the twentieth century, and was this not at the root of his failure to understand Soviet Russia? In an article published posthumously (*The Guardian*, 7 February 1983), he confessed:

"I must be one of the very few intellectuals still writing who grew up not in the high noon but in the afterglow of the great Victorian age of faith and optimism and it is difficult for me even today to think in terms of a world in permanent and irretrievable decline. . . ."

He still thought of himself as "a moderate optimist"; but this seemed more like compensation and posturing than real conviction. Paradoxically, in the context of the appalling tragedies of the twentieth century, Carr's *History* is, on the whole, a comedy of errors. He tried so hard and so long to be historically "with it". His writings are replete with dogmatic judgments about "outmoded" beliefs. How frantically this 19th-century man strove to be "modern"! This was an adjective he used constantly, turning it into an ideological shibboleth, a litmus test of right and wrong.

Accordingly, Carr had little real feeling for the transitoriness of things in human history, which is the mark of true historical sensibility and which gives a really great historian his historical perspective. Even in his 8th and 9th decades Carr never abandoned his obsessive preoccupation with what he imagined to be "modernity". He thus trivialized his vision by making his postulated (and illusory) future the measure of all things. How much wiser was La Bruyère, who reflected on the occasion of the first dispute about "modernity": "*Nous qui sommes si modernes, serons anciens dans quelques siècles.*"

To judge from various remarks that he made before his death, Carr died a disillusioned man. To the last he tried to put a brave face of declaratory optimism on his disenchantment. Although some of his writings remain impressive, he is unlikely to survive as Gibbon has. His futurological gnosticism made it inevitable that his *History* would be overtaken by history. In fact this has already happened.

5. Chomsky Revisited

STUDENTS OF CASUISTRY should by now be familiar with Noam Chomsky's persistent efforts to prove that the earth is flat. He tries to make us believe that he is motivated in matters of Viet Nam and Cambodia by a scholarly preoccupation with facts and an intellectual "concern for truth". Fiddlesticks. Such declarations are simply a camouflage for his political passions.

How much of it is cant and plain humbug? It is difficult to say. Chomsky lives in a fantasy world in which everything which does not square with his ideological beliefs, no matter how obvious, is instantly dismissed as a product of the "Western propaganda system" and explained away with dialectical logic chopping.

What can one make of an academic linguist who tries to use every channel in the West's free press to propagate his view that the "Free Press" (as he ironically calls it) has deliberately invented and spread the story of "the alleged genocide in Cambodia"? In this nefarious conspiracy aiming to achieve "the reconstruction of imperial ideology" in the West, collusion obviously extends from *The New York Times* to *The Wall Street Journal*, from *Le Monde* to *Le Figaro*, from *Die Zeit* to *Die Welt*.

Does he see much difference between the "Free Press" and the press in the totalitarian countries? Very little (*Working Papers*, May–June 1978):

> "In a totalitarian society the mechanics of indoctrination are simple and transparent. The state determines the official truth. The technocratic and policy-oriented intellectuals parrot official doctrine, which is easily identified. In a curious way this practice frees the mind. Internally, at least, one can identify the propaganda message and reject it. . . . Under capitalist democracy, the situation is considerably more complex. . . . The democratic system of thought control is seductive and compelling. The more vigorous the debate, the better the system of propaganda is served, since the tacit unspoken assumptions are more forcefully implanted."

That's how "the myth of genocide in Cambodia" has been established, with only a few sturdy dissident intellectuals (like Noam Chomsky, Stephen Heder, Ben Kiernan, Torben Retbøll, Laura Summers, Serge Thion, Michael Vickery, Gareth Porter, Edward S. Herman, George Hildebrand, and our own Malcolm Caldwell) seeing through the fraud. But the rest, possessing no such blessedly critical minds, have been seduced by the democratic press (*The Political Economy of Human Rights*, 1979, Vol. II, pp. 299–300):

"The success of the Free Press in reconstructing the imperial ideology since the US withdrawal from Indochina has been spectacular. . . . The system of brainwashing under freedom with mass media voluntary self-censorship in accord with the larger interest of the state, has worked brilliantly. The new propaganda line has been established by endless repetition of the Big Distortions. . . ."

It is against this background that one has to look at Chomsky's latest communication (in *Encounter*, July 1980). For him my article "Myths & Horrors" was, of course, part of "contemporary propaganda" aimed at "reconstructing the imperial ideology" through the brainwashing of hapless readers. How do his arguments stand up to the scrutiny of, admittedly, the perverted pen of an imperial propagandist?

CHOMSKY CLAIMS that I suppressed his "conclusion" that refugees' "reports must be considered seriously" and that I turned it "into its opposite".

This is a good example of his polemical methods: the assertion is totally false. The trick is simple, but still needs to be carefully watched. Chomsky announced the need for "serious consideration" of the refugees' reports . . . but only to deny them any validity. It was a disingenuous way of providing himself with an academic alibi of "objectivity". His conclusion was exactly as I have stated it: that "the refugees from Cambodia were not to be given credence". Contrary to what he says I have correctly rendered his reasoning. I quoted one sentence (italicised below) from a paragraph which, quoted in full, should settle the matter of which of us is misleading readers about Chomsky's attitude to the evidence provided by the Cambodian refugees:

> "*They naturally tend to report what their interlocutors wish to hear.* While their reports must be considered seriously, care and caution are necessary. Specifically, refugees questioned by Westerners and Thais have a vested interest in reporting atrocities on the part of Cambodian revolutionaries. . . ."

Can any reader of Chomsky's letter infer from it what his real point was in his *Nation* (25 June 1977) article?

For good measure he stressed in the same passage "the extreme unreliability of refugee reports" (after "serious consideration"?) and concluded that the Cambodian "executions have numbered at most in thousands".

He presented his conclusion as based on "analysis by highly qualified specialists who have studied the full range of available evidence", dismissing such first-hand studies as the book by Father François Ponchaud. As an Australian writer has pointed out (Robert Manne in *Quadrant*, October 1979), when closely examined, these "highly qualified specialists" and their "full range of evidence" are less than impressive. Chomsky's broad body of scholarly opinion

> "boils down to an unidentified article in a fortnightly news review which has for four years affirmed constantly the Ponchaud analysis; a letter to the editor of a man who now believes that hundreds of thousands of deaths were directly caused by the actions of the Pol Pot régime; and a piece by an ideologically blinkered student [Ben Kiernan] in an undergraduate magazine."

Noam Chomsky now says that he "cited estimates ranging from thousands to hundreds of thousands and even millions killed, concluding that 'We do not pretend to know where the truth lies amidst these sharply conflicting estimates'." He also says that "there has been no 'obfuscation'" on his part.

But he now writes about "thousands *or more* killed" (*Political Economy*, Vol. II, p. 279), and yet, as noted above, he emphatically declared that the "executions numbered *at most* in thousands". He referred ironically to the "alleged human rights violations in Viet Nam" and the "alleged Khmer Rouge atrocities". He derided in general the "tales of communist atrocities". He even scoffed at *The Wall Street Journal* for having "dismissed contemptuously the very idea that the Khmer Rouge could play the constructive role". In his last book (*Political Economy*, Vol. II, p. 347) he sneers at Leo Cherne for having written in 1965 that, after American withdrawal from Viet Nam, "there will be a bloody purge of the non-Communist leaders and intellectuals". Having dismissed such a prospect in his 1973 book, *Counterrevolutionary Violence: Bloodbaths in Fact and Propaganda* (I refer to *Bains de Sang*, the French edition published by Seghers/Laffont in 1975), he is still sarcastic about "the case of the missing bloodbath" in Viet Nam (*The Nation*, 25 June 1977, and *Political Economy*, Vol. II, p. 135).

What has happened in Indochina since the "liberation" makes Chomsky's erroneous perspective painful to recollect. His contemptuous dismissal of "the bloodbath myth" as simply invented by "Washington propaganda" sounds singularly hollow today, as does his prediction that "the movement which tries to gain the support of the peasant masses will certainly not resort to a bloodbath of the rural population" (pp. 31–2 and 102–3). To rescue his earlier assertions he produces some dazzling semantic footwork, but his efforts only indicate obduracy.

HIS SENSE OF REALITY is obviously in inverse proportion to his self-righteousness. The stickler for quantitative precision now plays fast and loose with numbers and magnitudes.

In 1977 he contemptuously rejected the estimated figure of 1.2 million victims. If one now divides it by his uncertainty "factor of 1,000" one obtains a figure similar to that given, apologetically, by the Khmer Rouge leader, Khieu Samphan (10,000), in his recent *Time* (10 March 1980) interview, i.e. "at most in thousands". (If we take 2 million as the basis of division, the result will be similar.) But Khieu Samphan acknowledged the missing Cambodians and conveniently attributed all 2 million victims to the Vietnamese (*they credit him with 3 millions*).

Chomsky has no such escape clause, being stuck, as he is, with his past figures and present obfuscations, for he is not prepared to admit that he was wrong. His "factor of 1,000" simply cannot be tallied with the missing Cambodians. How indignantly Noam Chomsky rejected as a fraud the press report quoting Khieu Samphan's 1976 admission of a missing million in the "liberated" Cambodia! Now he is ready even to quote the "reported" CIA estimates in preference to the figure given by an ideologically less contaminated source (William Shawcross, the *New York Review of Books*, 24 January 1980), 4–5 million surviving Cambodians out of the estimated 7–8 million before the war. In his *Language and Responsibility* Chomsky stressed the need "to look at the facts with an open mind", but his assurances that he is open-minded about the number of victims are unconvincing.

Has ever an open mind been so closed to truth?

IN HIS IDEOLOGICAL fanaticism he constantly shifts his arguments and bends references, quotations and facts, while declaring his "commitment to find the truth". He excoriates the "Free Press", but when it suits his argument, he quotes it extensively. Even his ideological allies sometimes find this hard to swallow. Thus, for instance, the former editor of the radical *Ramparts*, David Horowitz, wrote critically about Chomsky in the Left-wing *Nation* (8 December 1979):

"Consider . . . for a moment, Chomsky's misleading comparison of the Soviet and American presses as 'mirror images'. In fact the ignorance imposed on the Soviet public by Government-controlled media and official censorship is mind-boggling by Western standards. . . .

Why bring this up? Why dwell on the negative features of the Soviet system (or of other Communist states) which in any case are widely reported in the American media? What is the relevance?

These are questions the apologists of the Left raise when they are confronted by the Soviet case. Unfortunately, the consequences of ignoring the flaws of practical Communism are far-ranging and real. To begin with, the credibility of the Left's critique is gravely undermined. Chomsky's article is a good example. The American press does not look inordinately servile when compared with its real world counterparts— and especially its socialist opposites."

Another Chomsky sympathiser, A. J. Langguth, was also critical of Chomsky in his review of *Political Economy* in *The Nation* (16 February 1980):

> "Is there something tinny about the Chomsky–Herman chapters on Cambodia? Perhaps it is the unrelenting insistence that they were right about Indochina and that almost everyone else was wrong. Compared to the recent articles from Shawcross, which concerned the well-being, indeed the survival of the Cambodian people, the passages from Chomsky and Herman represented a high degree of special pleading, which because of our obsession with our sins, ends up slighting the major issue—the present fate of the Cambodians."

Or, in Robert Manne's melancholy reflection:

> "Sad to say [it is not] possible to expect that the political self-confidence of the former supporters of Pol Pot will be in the slightest deflated by the fact that concerning their estimation of him and his odious régime they were wholly, shamefully and ludicrously wrong. Pol Pot has passed; Noam Chomsky, I fear, persisteth."

He persisteth to the point where he is now denying ever having had the slightest intention of pooh-poohing the Cambodian horrors. As he put it in a previous communication to *Encounter* (October 1979):

> "Since authentic defenders of the Khmer Rouge were virtually impossible to find, apart from marginal Maoist groups, it has been necessary to invent them. . . . I have been elected to the post of 'official opponent', so difficult to fill."

Poor misunderstood fellow! He was only concerned with the whole truth about a situation which, as he somewhat belatedly discovered, "was grisly enough". Yet this scholarly solicitude has not met with the milk of human kindness "in the present historical context, when allegations of genocide are being used to whitewash Western imperialism, to distract attention from the 'institutionalized violence' of the expanding system of sub-fascism . . ." (*Political Economy*, Vol. II, p. 150). In such a context, he says, even the figures on the Left began "publishing outlandish falsehoods" about what he refers to as his "alleged views". Many are those among them who have fallen for the Great Imperial Hoax (Sidney H. Schanberg and William Shawcross, Eugene McCarthy and George McGovern, Jean Lacoutre and Claude Roy). Unlike Noam Chomsky they have obviously not realized (p. 149) that

> "To determine the credibility of those who transmit reports is a critical matter for anyone concerned to discover the truth, either about Cambodia or about the current phase of imperial ideology."

Who is the truth-seeker, where is the ideologist?

Consider Father Ponchaud and his "alleged sympathy with the Khmer peasants" which, according to his implacable critic, he invoked "for the benefit of a gullible Western audience". Chomsky called his book "serious and worth reading", but it is difficult to see why, for at the same time he denounced his "deceit", "fakery", and "outright falsehoods" and said that he "plays fast and loose with numbers and is highly unreliable with quotations" (charges which, as we have seen, apply to Chomsky himself).

It is not exactly an unknown psychological phenomenon—attributing to opponents one's own polemical sins. In Chomsky's case it always goes with high moral indignation, and also coincides with a less stringent, not to say callous, attitude to the crimes of one's own side. This type of selective morality is, as Raymond Aron observed a long time ago, a characteristic trait of *gauchistes* in general and is not confined to the apologists of Stalin alone.

I T WOULD TAKE half a lifetime to unravel all the ploys, twists, and other mental acrobatics displayed in Chomsky's writings. Behind the extraordinary technique is a mind-set which is capable of what *The Wall Street Journal* called "intellectual levitation".

Bear with me for a few more examples. Chomsky writes in his letter:

"Labedz claims that I criticised Western intellectuals for giving 'too much "publicity" to the Cambodian genocide', another fabrication."

Here is the editorial introductory note to "An Open Letter to Noam Chomsky" by Claude Roy published in *Le Nouvel Observateur* (3 December 1979):

"In the last issue of the review *Change* (22 March 1979), Noam Chomsky is full of irony in his conversation with Regis Débray about Western intellectuals who gave so much publicity to human rights or to the Cambodian genocide. Our friend Claude Roy finds this irony disturbing and close, very close, to bad faith."

Or take Chomsky's reference to East Timor, his standard argument (but one which, in any event, cannot justify his belittling the horrors in Cambodia). Here also his irony is misplaced: for where did he learn about the East Timor massacres but in the same "Free Press" which he so castigates?

Encounter has not been dealing with the East Timor atrocities, but it was not a case of suppression: it did not cover the Taraki-Amin massacres in Afghanistan either. Or, for that matter, those by the Mengistu régime in Ethiopia. And it came to discuss the horrors of Cambodia themselves only recently.

But whatever the omissions, it really is not a question of conspiracy of the "Free Press", as Chomsky believes. Western newspapers reported the East Timor atrocities. They condemned them with less vehemence than

A Question of Sources

*I*N HIS Political Economy *(Vol. II, p. 343) Noam Chomsky expressed
warm thanks to Ben Kiernan, a left-wing activist from Monash University
in Melbourne, "for important information and very helpful comments".
Approvingly he referred (pp. 226–8) to the studies on Cambodia in which
Kiernan "took issue with the horror stories by refugees", questioned the
assumption "that there was a central direction for atrocities", and rejected the
idea "that the [Pol Pot] government planned and approved a systematic
large-scale purge".*

*A year later this "Australian scholar" (as Chomsky called him) has suddenly
become poacher-turned-gamekeeper in the field of genocide. It happened to be
the same Ben Kiernan who analysed for the* New Statesman *(2 May 1980)
some of the blood-chilling records brought out from Pol Pot's macabre
interrogation centre at Tuol Sleng. Without mentioning his previous
whitewashing of the Pol Pot régime, he wrote:*

**"That Pol Pot ran a violent, repressive régime is something
scarcely open to question."**

*Nimbly confounding the issues, he dissociated himself not only from his own
past, but also from Chomsky:*

**"There is a right-wing argument which suggests that Pol
Pot and his friends, while ferocious, were not more so than
any other rough, tough Third World government. And
there is a left-wing argument—still held, apparently, by
Noam Chomsky—which suggests that, although Pol Pot**

Chomsky, but more explicitly than he leads us to believe. Papers such as the
Wall Street Journal (which, according to Chomsky, has a "disgraceful record
of subservience to state power and apologetics for barbarism") published
articles which also denounced the East Timor atrocities (George Steiner's
"Thinking the Irreparable About Cambodia", 30 November 1979):

"There are no accurate figures as to the number of men, women and
children hounded, gunned, starved to death in Biafra not long ago, or
being eliminated right now by Indonesian policies in East Timor. . . ."

The East Timor outrages may have deserved larger coverage and greater
moral condemnation, but their extent is not comparable to those of
Cambodia. They were assiduously exploited propagandistically by
"progressives" who wanted to "even it up" with Cambodia. As Robert
Conquest wrote (*Daily Telegraph*, 8 March 1980):

made numerous brutal errors, the conception of something especially outlandish about his régime is a chimera bred-up by the Western (and Vietnamese) mass-media."

He concluded, with artless innocence, that "there was something entirely bizarre about the Pol Pot régime. Bizarre, yet disturbingly familiar in parts. . . ."

CHOMSKY IS THUS *not the only one among the dwindling band of Pol Pot apologists who is trying to extricate himself from his past and to cover up its traces. But he does so without renouncing his "outlandish" initial assertions. He may well be surprised by such a sudden turn-about of a "scholar" whom he earlier thanked so profusely for his "evidence"! Ironically, this transformation appeared just after the* New Statesman *(25 April 1980) published an enthusiastic review of Chomsky's* Political Economy—*"this may be the most important contribution to the study of American foreign policy to be published since the Vietnam War ended". A week later, the same* New Statesman *printed a special feature by Ben Kiernan and Chantou Boua: "THE BUREAUCRACY OF DEATH: DOCUMENTS FROM INSIDE POL POT'S TORTURE MACHINE", which occupied eight distinctive central pages of the magazine, with the cover and editorial pages devoted to the same subject. The decision to give it so much space was explained by reference to Santayana's saying that "those who fail to understand history may be condemned to repeat it. . . ."*

Might it not be helpful for this purpose to study the New Statesman's *own history, and its almost unprecedented record of repetitive misunderstandings and chronic failings, from Kingsley Martin to . . . Ben Kiernan?*

"East Timor was until 1974 a Portuguese colony, though ethnically indistinguishable from the Indonesian part of the island. After some fighting, Freitlin, a Communist-front régime, came to power in 1975, and soon afterwards the Indonesians annexed the territory. The story of the supposed super-massacre they carried out was originally based on an administratory telling the Press that 60,000 people had lost their lives or homes (including 40,000 who had fled from the Communists). This was instantly inflated to 60,000 killed, which was gradually put up to '60,000 to 120,000'."

Chomsky now gives in his letter the figure of 100,000 to 200,000.

Professor H. W. Arndt analyzed the story in detail in the Australian magazine *Quadrant* (December 1979), and summed up Noam Chomsky's evidence before the UN Decolonization Committee to the effect that

> "up to half the population of East Timor may have died and that 'the deaths from war, starvation and torture equalled or relatively exceeded those in Kampuchea'. Some Australian newspapers indulged in similarly extravagant statements."

These specious symmetries and counterpoints are nothing new in the history of *gauchisme*. When it was a question of condemning Stalin's genocide, Simone de Beauvoir wrote (in *La Force des Choses*, p. 220) in a way quite similar to Chomsky's argumentation about Cambodia and East Timor:

> "While perfectly indifferent to the 40,000 dead in Sétif, to the 80,000 assassinated in Madagascar, to the hunger and miseries of Algeria, to the burning of villages in Indochina, to the Greeks suffering in the camps, and to the Spaniards being executed by Franco, the bourgeois hearts are suddenly bleeding for the poor Soviet inmates."

The variations on this theme hark back to the time when Arthur Koestler ridiculed in *The Yogi and the Commissar* the standard "progressive" argument about Stalin's forced labour camps: "And what about the lynchings of Negroes in the South? . . ."

No doubt some horrific things happened in East Timor. But it is demagoguery on the part of Chomsky to put the "direct responsibility" for them "in Washington", as it is to say that it bears "basic responsibility" for "the current suffering in Cambodia". Pol Pot had power in Cambodia, whereas the US President did not control East Timor.

THERE IS NO POINT getting into a numbers game, yet the judgment whether there was genocide in Cambodia or East Timor depends on the magnitude of the respective horrors. In this context, just as Chomsky tends to understate the Cambodian atrocities, so he tends to overstate the massacres in East Timor. As usual, he is not too meticulous in his handling of figures.

He refers in his *Political Economy* (Vol. II, p. 139), to the "apparent massacre of something like one-sixth of the population of East Timor". In his present letter the figure becomes "roughly one-fifth of the population". In either case, his assumption of possibly 200,000 victims would make the population of East Timor far higher than it was before the atrocities took place. (It was the 1974 recorded figure of 688,769 which was used by the "progressives" for the charges about the missing East Timorese.) This in no way affects the question of moral condemnation, but it is relevant to his argument about genocide. Although he does not admit it, the percentage of victims in Cambodia is far higher. Nor are the absolute figures in the two cases comparable: in Cambodia they go tragically into millions.

It is not true as he asserts in his letter that for me "it is an incontrovertible fact" that the population there had been reduced "from seven to four million under the Khmer Rouge régime". I did not say this: I just referred to Sidney H. Schanberg's article reporting how his Cambodian journalist friend, Dith Pran, told him about such reduction "by massacre and starvation". But never mind Chomsky's careless use of quotations, references and attributions. Like Father Ponchaud, I do not believe that we can have an exact figure. But I do believe that we can have an idea of the order of magnitude of the Cambodian tragedy, and that it is within the range of millions, not—as Chomsky believes—of "thousands". Thus it falls fully into the terrible category of genocide.

Chomsky's pettifogging becomes easier to understand when one recalls that he has never attributed the responsibility for the Cambodian murders to the policies of *Angka*, the ruling organisation of the Khmer Rouge régime. By now the evidence about its nature and the extent of the Cambodian holocaust is overwhelming. The ghastly story told by Dith Pran to Sidney H. Schanberg led him to the conclusion that

> "the Khmer Rouge terror may have touched a level of cruelty not seen before in our lifetime. It was Cambodians endlessly killing other Cambodians in an orgy of destruction."
>
> (*Sunday Telegraph Magazine*, 13 April 1980)

The evidence is coming not only from the refugees' reports, which Chomsky so cavalierly dismissed, but also from present-day visitors to Cambodia. Chris Mullin described what he saw on-the-spot (in the Left-wing *Tribune*, 11 April 1980):

> "Visitors to Phnom Penh these days are taken on a gruesome little ritual tour of Khmer Rouge handiwork. The highlight is the Tuol Sleng prison (a converted high school) which has records listing over 16,000 inmates, of whom only five are said to have survived. . . . Of course there is no need for the visitor to believe any of this—though it is graphic enough. Instead he or she can take a car along any of the roads out of Phnom Penh. Choose any road, no one will prevent you. Drive until you want to stop at a village, any village, and ask what happened in the Pol Pot time.
>
> I drove one day to Kros, a village 18 kilometres along the road to Battambang. The village I chose at random had a population of around 2,000 before the coming of the Khmer Rouge. Today there are just 853, mostly women."

PERHAPS THE BEST IDEA of Chomsky's warped perceptions can be gauged from his other comparisons. For instance, he contemptuously rejected any parallel between the Pol Pot régime and the Nazi régime, and declared that "a more appropriate comparison is with France after liberation, where 30–40,000 people were massacred with far less motive for revenge. . . ."

(*Political Economy*, Vol. II, p. 149)

And he also declared that, with regard to torture, Israel's "record far exceeds in brutality anything that we know of from Viet Nam" (*Palestine Human Rights Bulletin*, 30 August 1977).

The eeriness of Chomsky's "intellectual levitation" can be judged by his adroit shifts in argument whenever a factual mistake is detected in his writings.

"When we first read Ponchaud's original, we assumed that the Thai journal *Prachachat* must be a right-wing journal giving a criticism of the Khmer Rouge. That is what Ponchaud's account suggests, in particular his final ironic comment, now deleted in the American edition. We wrote in *The Nation* (25 June 1977) that the chain of transmission was too long to be taken very seriously and we raised the following question: 'How seriously would we regard a critical account of the United States in a book by a hostile European leftist based on a report in *Pravda* of a statement allegedly made by an unnamed American official?' . . . Several people (Heder, Ponchaud, Vickery) have pointed out to us that we were mistaken in assuming that *Prachachat* was a right-wing newspaper critical of the Khmer Rouge. The fact is that it was a left-wing newspaper and the actual text is not a criticism of the Khmer Rouge, but a defense of the Khmer Rouge against foreign criticism, something that could hardly be guessed from Ponchaud's account and is certainly worth knowing, in this context.

(*Political Economy*, Vol. II, pp. 263–4)

Well, how does Noam Chomsky get out of his blunder? Very simple. He continues:

"Here then, is an improved version of our original analogy: How seriously would we regard a critical account of the United States in a book by a hostile European leftist based on a report in *Encounter*⋆ of comments by a 'neutral person' who reports statements of an unnamed American official?"

Having discovered the true tribal identity of *Prachachat*, Chomsky added a footnote reflecting his own tribal sympathies:

"⋆Our apologies to the editors of *Prachachat* for this comparison."

Can one take seriously such political infantilism? Why does Noam Chomsky continue to write letters to *Encounter*?[1] Why should he want them to appear in a magazine the comparison with which is a terrible insult to an obscure pro-Pol Pot Thai journal? Why should he expect his stabbing illuminations of dangerous truths to be published in an organ of the "Western propaganda system", exercising "voluntary self-censorship in accordance with the larger interests of state"?

What is our indefatigable publicist up to? And what is his logic? After all, he believes that

> "The democratic system of thought control is seductive and compelling. The more vigorous the debate, the better the system of propaganda is served, since the tacit unspoken assumptions are more forcefully implanted."

He also believes that in the case of Cambodia "critics of US violence" find that

> "their comment is eagerly sought out in the hope that they will deny atrocity reports, so that this denial can be featured as 'proof' that inveterate apologists for Communism will never learn. . . ."

Result: there was no genocide in Cambodia! And the earth remains flat!

NOAM CHOMSKY thinks that he should not be compared with the Nazi and Stalinist apologists. Yet he deals in the same way with Pol Pot's Kampuchea as do other cranky characters with Hitler's Germany and Stalin's Russia when, even now, they deny or minimize the extent of these historic cases of genocide. I can only repeat: I find it indecent in somebody whose own people has been a target of genocide to belittle the tragedy of others who have also suffered it. . . .

During the Stalin–Hitler Pact the US Communists maintained that the refugees from Poland (then occupied by the two partners-in-crime) were not to be given credence. They also attacked the International Rescue Committee (whose chairman, Leo Cherne, is called by Chomsky a "longtime apologist for US violence and oppression") for bringing to the USA European intellectuals, refugees from Nazi-occupied and Vichy France, who were facing the danger of extermination. I wonder if Noam Chomsky is ever troubled by the thought of how unfeeling his attitude toward all these "highly unreliable" Cambodian refugees may appear to them?

---

[1] Every polemical line of Chomsky's communications over more than a decade of argumentative exchanges has been published in the pages of *Encounter* in full, without alteration. Which (and he has privately conceded as much) is more than he has ever enjoyed in his own progressive-Left press.

H E ONCE GAVE US a short, but revealing, description of his political evolution (*New Left Review*, September–October 1969):

> "In the 'forties, when I was a teenager, I would hang around left-wing bookshops and the offices of off-beat groups and periodicals, talking to people—often very perceptive and interesting people who were thinking hard about the problems of social change—and seeing what I could pick up. Then I was much interested in a Jewish organization which was opposed to the Jewish state in Palestine and worked for Arab–Jewish co-operation on a socialist basis. Out of all this, from my relatives and friends, I learned a great deal informally and acquired a certain framework within which my own way of thinking developed. . . . I withdrew during the 'fifties from political involvements, though of course I retained my intellectual interest. I signed petitions, over the Rosenberg case, for instance, and went on occasional demonstrations, but it did not amount to much. Then, in the 'sixties, I began to be more active again."

The rest, as they say, is history. "Chomsky's great intellectual prestige, deservedly obtained in the field of syntax", secured an "undeservedly respectful attention to his political writings" (*New Statesman*, 17 August 1979).

Chomsky likes to quote, as in his last book, both George Orwell and Bertrand Russell. One can imagine what the author of *Homage to Catalonia* would have thought of this particular member of another "generation of unteachables hanging around our necks like a necklace of corpses". Bertrand Russell wrote (in the preface to a book by Gustav Herling, *A World Apart*, 1951) no less relevant words about the then letter-writers who denied the existence of Stalin's forced labour camps:

> "Those who write these letters and those fellow-travellers who allow themselves to believe them share responsibility for the almost unbelievable horrors which are being inflicted upon millions of wretched men and women, slowly done to death by hard labour and starvation in the Arctic cold."

Our letter-writers are still with us.

WHAT CHOMSKY CANNOT ACCEPT is that his opponents were right and he was wrong, that they perceived the nature of the beast; hence all his subsequent rationalizations.

He indignantly denounced (*Political Economy*, Vol. II, p. 163) the *Wall Street Journal* which "has the gall to make the following editorial comment" (23 August 1978):

"Now, having finished the task of destroying [the US presence in Indochina, the American liberals] are shocked and dismayed by the news of the grim and brutal world that resulted. One of the few good things to come out of this sordid end of our Indochina campaign was a period of relative silence from the people who took us through all its painful contortions. They should have had the grace to maintain their quiet at least a while longer."

Perhaps "*they*", but not "*he*". Chomsky would not withdraw—as he should have—from his "political involvements", having lost all credibility. Shouldn't his case be a warning to other progressives who try so hard not to learn from their mistakes?

Malcolm Muggeridge has often written about this problem of intellectual hygiene, and I have his permission to quote a passage from a recent personal letter to me:

"I agree utterly with the last sentence of your 'Myths & Horrors' piece. Ever since my 1932 time in Moscow I've been pondering over the servility and credulity of Western intellectuals *vis-à-vis* the Soviet régime, constantly supposing that such an event—say, Margarete Buber-Neumann's experiences—will put paid to it all, only to find that as the Durantys and the Werths depart, the Chomskys and the Fondas come along. So, I have to conclude it's a death-wish—as my dear and now deceased colleague, Cholerton, used to put it, 'The vomit returns to the dog!' . . ."

So IT IS THAT the radiant guru of the 1960s, Professor Noam Chomsky, is still with us; but the lustre has gone. How eloquent and refreshing he appeared to the militant students of the day, lecturing, writing, protesting, and drawing crowds everywhere!

Now the spirit of '68 is gone. The sobering experiences of the 1970s revealed how blinkered he was and how threadbare his arguments were. But he is still trying to reassert his old ideological doctrines, with his usual aggressive self-righteousness, his familiar polemical tricks. It is all rather unpromising. There are few takers for old illusions.

In the mournful words of Simone Signoret, "Nostalgia is no longer what is used to be. . . ."

(1980)

6. Alexander Werth:

The Story of a Correspondence

IT ALL STARTED with the 50th anniversary of the Soviet revolution. On 29 September 1967, the *New Statesman* published a special article on the subject by Alexander Werth containing some rather unexpected admissions by this "distinguished British correspondent in Moscow".*

Two weeks later the *New Statesman* published my letter to the editor, contrasting some of the critical remarks of Mr Werth in this article about the situation in Russia in the earlier jubilee years—1937 and 1947—with his descriptions at the time. In particular I recalled a discussion about the book by David J. Dallin and Boris Nicolaevsky on Soviet forced labour camps in the correspondence columns of the *New Statesman* in 1948, a discussion in which Mr Werth minimized the number of prisoners and testified that the slave labourers he personally met were "sturdy specimens of humanity".

In his reply Mr Werth admitted that he had been "pulling punches" about Soviet slave labour. He justified it on the grounds that in so doing he was trying to prevent an atomic attack on Moscow. Here are the texts of the exchange:

Sir, As a faithful reader of Alexander Werth for 30 years, I have been struck by his consistently idiosyncratic method of dealing with the Soviet past and present. Writing about the Soviet anniversary year, 1967 (NS, 29 September), he remarks that

"as for the earlier Jubilees, it is better not to think about them: 1947 was a year of acute famine in Russia; and 1937, the year of the greatest mass-arrests and mass-deportations at the height of the Yezhov-Stalin terror, continues to be a byword of horror, fear and insecurity, when no one could be sure that he would not be arrested, deported or shot within a few days. . . . only during very few of the 50 years of the Soviet régime was life at all reasonably tolerable . . . during very few of those 50 years did the Russian people have enough to eat."

Such explicit statements, stripped of apologetics, tend to be retrospective in Mr Werth's writings; criticism, now so boldly applied to Stalin or Krushchev, has been hardly noticeable when they were ruling Russia. Not only at the present anniversary, but at any given time, one usually gets from Mr Werth the impression that, but for the few incidental blemishes in the past, the Russians have never "had it so good". It is only when a ruler is gone that Mr Werth's apologetic tone becomes miraculously transformed into critical spirit. Then, and only then, the previous leader's failing or misdeeds are ruthlessly exposed. (There are, however, exceptions to this rule. On some occasions, when discussing Soviet affairs, Mr Werth still prefers not to display any such critical spirit about the Soviet past. In a recent interview which he gave to

---

* Alexander Werth (1901–1969), author of *Moscow '41* (1942), *The Year of Stalingrad* (1946), *Musical Uproar in Moscow* (1949), *The Khrushchev Phase* (1961), *Russia at War, 1941–1945* (1964), *Russia: Hopes and Fears* (1969), and other works.

Pravda [15 August 1967], he did not say anything about it, limiting himself to the eulogies of present Soviet achievements.) In his book, *Moscow '41* (1942), Mr Werth justified the 1937–38 Purges because, although they "involved thousands of probably innocent people", the purged old Bolsheviks would "have undermined or delayed the growth of Russia's military strength" and "Tukhachevsky was going to sell out to Hitler". It was, said Mr Werth, "a case of smashing opposition in the midst of an extremely dangerous international situation". And he added that anyway the purge "was, clearly, less the work of Stalin than of Yezhov and his gang" (p. 50). This, of course, was written when Stalin was in power.

In his present article Mr Werth informs us that the immediate post-War years were marked by "a new wave of the Stalinist terror". Yet, although he spent those years in Russia, he somehow failed at the time to bring this fact to the attention of his readers in the West. Moreover, it was in that very period that Mr Werth published in the *New Statesman* (19 June 1948) a lengthy extenuation of the Stalinst forced labour camps. In this letter he once again explained away the 1937–38 purges, stating authoritatively that it "did not run into millions" and that, anyway, it affected only the bureaucracy, the political activists, some intellectuals, and part of the officer corps. As to the number of inmates of Stalin's forced labour camps, Mr Werth contemptuously refuted the figure of 8 to 12 million prisoners estimated by Dallin and Nicolaevsky, an estimate which he presented incorrectly in his letter as being of the order of 12 to 15 million. He declared condescendingly that the number of "convicts" "might conceivably amount" to 1½ or 2 million. When Krushchev lifted the veil from the subject, Mr Werth returned to it again in his book, *The Krushchev Phase* (1961), in which (p. 44) he referred to his 1948 letter to the *New Statesman* about Soviet forced labour. Only now he tried to avoid the impression that he was belittling its extent and asserted that the figure he had given in that letter as his estimate was "between 3 and 4 million". In fact, as can be seen, this was double that which he actually gave in the first instance. In a similar fashion he misrepresented the estimates of his opponents, alleging now that they had talked about "20, 30 or even more million slaves" and thus making their estimates appear still more inflated. (Mr Werth evidently has some difficulty in handling figures; in his recent article he stated that "China has nearly *five* times the population of the Soviet Union.")

One can quote many instances of Mr Werth's remarkable hindsight. He applied it not only to Stalin's era, but also to Krushchev. Here is a typical example. In the same jubilee article, Mr Werth states, in a matter-of-fact way, that Krushchev "was notoriously anti-semitic". This is an extraordinary revelation by the "distinguished British correspondent in Moscow", who only a few years before declared in *The Krushchev Phase* (p. 157) that "the stories about Krushchev's anti-semitic sound, to say the least, rather apocryphal". But, of course, this was written when Krushchev was in power. Concluding his October Jubilee article, Mr Werth exclaims: "Soviet Russia should be a very remarkable country indeed when it celebrates its 60th birthday!" One looks forward to Mr Werth's article on that occasion. He will then no doubt fearlessly reveal some of the facts, at present unmentionable, about the Soviet Russia of 1967.

LEOPOLD LABEDZ

ALEXANDER WERTH *writes*: (1) It is not true that I always said that "the Russians never had it so good". In *The Year of Stalingrad*, published in 1946, i.e. during Stalin's lifetime, I speak of the privations, hardships and loss of life the Russian people suffered during the war.

(2) Mr Labedz then says that "it is only when the ruler is gone that Mr Werth's

apologetic tone becomes miraculously transformed into critical spirit". Like *The Year of Stalingrad*, I also published during Stalin's lifetime *Musical Uproar in Moscow*, in which I said all there was to say about the abominable purge in literature, music and the arts generally carried out by Zhdanov, Stalin's right-hand man. Remarkable that, with all his profound study of all my writings, Mr Labedz should somehow have overlooked these two books.

(3) The *Pravda* "interview" last August lasted, in reality, about half-an-hour but *Pravda*, quite rightly no doubt, boiled it all down to a few lines of harmless generalities.

(4) I am now told that I "justified the purges of 1937–38" in *Moscow '41*. This book was written at the height of the war, with the Russians fighting with their backs to the wall at Moscow and Leningrad. It must have been painful for Mr Labedz to admit that, even then, I wrote that "the purges involved thousands of probably innocent people". This is a good deal more than almost anybody else in Britain would have ventured to say then.

(5) I don't know where Mr Labedz was in 1941–42; but if he was in Britain at the time he must remember that people were acutely conscious of the fact that their very existence depended on whether the Russians (under Stalin) held out or not. They were completely starry-eyed about Stalin and the Red Army. That, shortly before the War, "Stalin had a good case for smashing opposition in the midst of an extremely dangerous international situation" seemed obvious enough at the time, though even then, as I readily admitted, "thousands of probably innocent people" had also been destroyed in the process.

(6) As for Tukhachevsky, did Mr Labedz know *at the time* the real facts of the case, any more than I did? If President Benes of Czechoslovakia fell into the *Gestapo* trap, why should less-informed people like Mr Labedz and myself not have fallen into it? As for the story that the purges were less the fault of Stalin than of "Yezhov and his gang", this was a story persistently circulated in Russia between 1938 and 1941. Mr Joseph Davies, the US Ambassador in Moscow, fell for it; not only that: he wrote a book, *Mission to Moscow*, in which he justified the purge trials, which is infinitely more than I ever did.

(7) I was virtually expelled from the Soviet Union in May 1948, after my attacks on Zhdanov and an earlier article in the *Manchester Guardian* in which I had spoken of the near-famine conditions caused in Russia by the drought of 1946. But even so, on returning to Britain, I did "minimise" the number of "slave labourers" in camps, by saying that there were probably "only" 2 million of them, though even this was bad enough. But how many actually were there? Does Mr Labedz know? If so, he might tell us. My estimate was lower than most, I admit. But there was a very good reason for this. In 1948 the Cold War was at its height, and there were no end of people in Britain and especially in the US who were advocating a preventive war against Russia; and the "slave labour" (the more the better) was their pet argument. It was the "hawks" of those days who spoke of 8–30 million "slave labourers" whom it was the Free World's sacred duty to liberate. I remember some distinguished Conservative ex-ministers in London saying quite openly what Churchill was implying in his Llandudno speech of 1948: "Drop the atom bomb on Moscow before it's too late." Yes, I had every reason to pull my punches about "slave labour" because *that* was the Number One argument of all the preventive-war people. And I don't regret it.

(8) It is quite true that in 1959 I did say that "the Russians never had it so good"; it was a plain statement of fact. Krushchev was then at the height of his popularity, and the Virgin Lands had, indeed, proved a success—though only a short-lived success, as it turned out. As for Krushchev's anti-semitism, this is a very small matter; I

underrated it in 1959; since then there has been enough to show (e.g. Krushchev's and his propaganda chief Ilychev's attacks on Ehrenburg in 1963) that he was more anti-semitic than he appeared to be in 1959.

Mr Labedz apparently expects me not to be an intelligent human being who learns from experience, and thus revises some of his opinions from time to time, but a fossil who is never allowed to change his mind about anything, in 10 or even 30 years!

I TOOK UP Alexander Werth's points in a letter sent to the editor of the New Statesman on 16 October 1967. I stressed the implications for the ethos of journalism of Werth's revelation that he was not just ill-informed or biased, but instead of reporting facts as he knew them, he has consciously engaged in pro-Soviet propaganda. I concluded that "as a reporter he damns himself out of his own mouth by his self-admitted readiness to distort facts for political reasons". I asked:

> "It would be interesting to know what the editors of the journals of which he was a correspondent in Moscow, including the Manchester Guardian (as it then was) which has for so many years taken pride in the principle of C. P. Scott that 'opinions are free, but facts are sacred', think about it."

My letter was not published; but the New Statesman (of 20 October 1967) carried another letter—by Mr Robert D. Kempner—which made a similar point. In his reply (27 October 1967) Mr Werth excused himself once again by saying that he "stretched points" about the Soviet slave camps in view of what he considered as an impending danger of a nuclear strike against Moscow, and maintained that he was right in doing so.

THIS WAS THE END of the correspondence in the columns of the New Statesman on the subject. My subsequent letter (of 30 October 1967) was also not published. I wrote in it that Mr Werth was engaged in myth-making and that he was presenting a false dichotomy:

> "Preventive nuclear war was never contemplated by any government in the West; paradoxically, only Lord Bertrand Russell advocated such a course. On a more serious level it was always only a question of deterrence, whatever Soviet propaganda may say. . . ."

It is, of course, entirely up to the editor of a magazine to publish a letter or not. On this occasion the readers of the New Statesman were spared the thought that "the business of a foreign correspondent is to report facts and not send political propaganda".

This is how the matter ended. Alexander Werth had the last word and I forgot about the affair. However, some time later I was jolted by two surprising occurrences, as a result of which I wrote the following letter to the editor of the New Statesman on 18 January 1968.

Dear Sir,

May I call your attention to an extraordinary item recently published in the Soviet press which is relevant to an article by Mr Alexander Werth in your issue of 29 September 1967 and the ensuing debate in your correspondence column.

Mr Werth, you will remember, then confessed (*New Statesman* 13 and 27 October 1967) to having "minimized" the number of the slave labourers in Stalin's concentration camps. He said that he "pulled punches" and "stretched points" about them for political reasons.

If I am reverting now to what another participant in this debate, Mr Robert D. Kempner, referred to as a betrayal by Mr Werth "of his integrity as a journalist" (*New Statesman* 20 October 1967) it is because Mr Werth's original article, in which he described among other things his conversation with the Soviet writer, Valentin Kataev, has now received an interesting comment from rather unexpected sources.

On 10 January 1968, the Soviet *Literary Gazette* published an article entitled "The Belated Repentance of Alexander Werth" which quoted a letter (sent to the editor by Valentin Kataev) referring to Werth's *New Statesman* article: "After its publication in the British and French press, I received a letter from Werth with all kinds of excuses, which included the following paragraph:

'In order to explain better the point of view of the avant-garde writers, i.e. of the real writers, I (and this was the worst stupidity on my part) resorted to a (somewhat doubtful) journalistic trick, attributing to you many things which you did not say, but which I have heard from many other, particularly the young, writers. . . . That I have summarized all this in a half-"invented" conversation with you, was terribly wrong of me.'"

"Comment"—concludes Kataev—"is quite superfluous".

Now, if Mr Werth's letter (translated here from Russian) is not genuine, we will, I imagine, be hearing shortly of his protest and denial. If, however, what Kataev says is true, surely Mr Werth owes an apology not only to Mr Kataev, but also to yourself and your readers.

Perhaps at the same time he may clarify his position on the 1967 Soviet edition of his book *Russia at War*, for which he wrote a special preface. In his introduction the editor, General E. A. Boltin, stated: "The Russian edition of this book was prepared in collaboration with the author, who endorsed it fully, introduced a series of corrections and improvements and, in essence, re-wrote the first part of the book".

As it happened, the "corrections and improvements" consist of changes and omissions in line with current Soviet writing of history, of all passages and chapters on such embarrassing topics as the Soviet-Nazi Pact, the seizure of the Baltic States, Katyn, etc.

Mr Werth's comment on Soviet allegations about him will not be superfluous.

Yours faithfully, etc.

O NE WEEK LATER, on 25 January, Paul Johnson, the editor of the *New Statesman*, telephoned me and explained that Mr Werth, without informing him about it, sent the letter quoted by me to Valentin Kataev, in order to give him a chance to get himself off the hook. Johnson told me that Werth claimed that his original report in the *New Statesman*, attributing various statements to Kataev, was genuine and that his private letter to him, quoted by the Moscow *Literary Gazette*, in which he says that they were not (or only half-invented), was a charitable lie. Johnson said that the publication of my letter in the *New Statesman* may, according to Werth, cause trouble for Valentin Kataev from the Soviet authorities, because if it is published, Werth would have to reveal the truth. Paul Johnson thought therefore that it would be inappropriate to publish it as it might jeopardize Kataev's position. When I pointed out to him that this reasoning certainly does not apply to the second part of the letter, he agreed to publish it if I sent it to him in a modified form, without mentioning the Kataev affair.

On the very same day I sent Paul Johnson a communication in which I again expressed my astonishment at what he told me on the telephone. I said that I was a little bit dizzy on this carousel of revolving explanations by both Kataev and Werth, that I did not know which of them told the truth, but that on one assumption Kataev was acting dishonourably in using Werth's letter by gunning down his friend in the columns of the *Literary Gazette* as a liar, and on another assumption, that the letter was a genuine apology for attributing to Kataev opinions he never voiced, Alexander Werth still stood condemned.

I emphasized that by suppressing the information about the affair and withholding it from the readers of the *New Statesman* its editor would in effect condone the attack in the *Literary Gazette* on "the lies" printed in his magazine. I also pointed out that to conceal the truth about this affair on the excuse that it may be harmful to an eminent senior like Valentin Kataev would not be helpful to all those young Soviet writers who are fighting for the right to tell simple truth and are ready to face prison and labour camps by openly taking a public stand. The contrast between their actions and those of Messrs Kataev and Werth speaks for itself.

I did not see any danger for Kataev in the situation, and I thought that it was "a matter of over-protection misapplied"; but I concluded the letter by saying that "as I do not want to feel responsible for anything that might conceivably happen" I therefore "propose to drop the matter and not deal with it in public. In doing so I am acting against my better judgment." I enclosed the shortened version of my letter, hoping that its 200 words on the two editions of Mr Werth's book would be published, as Johnson said it would be in his telephone conversation with me.

After some delay I received from Paul Johnson a letter (dated 9 February 1968) in which he said:

> "I have now heard from Mr Werth about the points you raise in your letter concerning the Soviet edition of his book *Russia at War*. The matter is infinitely more complicated than you may have realized. You make a generalized charge against Mr Werth which can only be refuted in detail; his reply, I calculate, would take up more than two whole columns of our space, and as the matter to which you refer does not arise from

material published in the *New Statesman* I am not willing to devote this
amount of space to it."

Johnson suggested that I should get in touch directly with Werth, and ask him
for an explanation.

This seemed to me pointless. I had by then read a relevant reply by Mr
Werth to an inquiry by the author of an article comparing the British and
Soviet editions of his book (H. L. Verhaar, in the Dutch magazine
Internationale Spectator, No. 2, 22 January 1968, published by the University
of Amsterdam). In answer to the specific questions raised by Mr Verhaar and
concerned (as was my own letter to the *New Statesman* of 16 January 1968)
with the discrepancies between the two editions of his book, Alexander
Werth wrote:

> "Have a little patience. I am relating the circumstances in which the
> Russian edition of my *Russia at War* was published in *Russia at Peace*, the
> Penguin which will be published in two or three months from now.
> Meantime you can write what you like, and correct your conclusions
> afterwards, if necessary. . . ."

In the circumstances there was obviously no point in repeating the
performance of Verhaar. Anyway, Werth had by then in his hands the texts
of my letters which Paul Johnson had passed on to him. If he wished, he could
have replied. Judging by his answer to Verhaar, he was not too anxious to
provide explanations, private or public.

A LEXANDER WERTH'S BOOK HAS been translated into many
languages and has been sympathetically reviewed.

Corriere della Sera (22 April 1966) described it as "a work which is destined
to last", written by "an honest historian", and other reviews in the
"bourgeois" press (the *New York Times*, *The Observer*, *Die Zeit*, etc.) were on
the whole also quite positive. Yet, interestingly enough, the Soviet "liberal"
Novy Mir (no. 3, 1968) was distinctly dissatisfied with Werth. It could not, of
course, mention the omissions in the Soviet text—this would not be allowed
by the censor—but it did criticize Werth for "a different treatment of material
in the introductions to the Soviet and American editions". This, the reviewer
pointedly said, "causes some surprise"; and he went on to castigate Werth for
trying "to justify the acts of Stalin, the erroneousness of which has been
conclusively proved in Soviet historical and Party literature".

Bernard Levin was more explicit in the *Daily Mail* (10 April 1968). He
referred to "an act of literary self-emasculation that must be almost unique",
and ironically listed the following "insignificant details", omitted from the
Soviet edition of Mr Werth's book:

> "All mention of the secret protocol to the Nazi-Soviet pact; the chapter

on the partition of Poland between Hitler and Stalin; all unfavourable comments on the Soviet seizure of the Baltic States; the chapter on Stalin and the Church; all discussion of Soviet responsibility for the Katyn massacre; all criticism of the Soviet authorities in the reference to the 16 Polish resistance leaders arrested by treachery; the official Soviet condolences to Hitler after the unsuccessful attempt on his life in 1939; the reference to the extermination, in 1949, of the leaders of the defence of Leningrad during the war; the reference to the NKVD units whose purpose during the war was the machine-gunning of Russian soldiers engaged in unauthorised withdrawal. . . ."

Bernard Levin concluded: "I look forward to his [Werth's] discussion in the 1980s, of the deliberate falsification of his own book". Fortunately, our cliff-hanging need not continue as long as that. An inquiry to the Penguin publishers revealed that *Russia at Peace* (which will presumably contain Mr Werth's explanation) is to be published in 1969.[1]

In view of all this, and of other additional elements of public interest in this affair, I no longer had any doubts that it would be right, proper, and useful to publish a summary of the case. But a word about other relevant developments.

IN MOSCOW, THE REACTIONARY EDITOR of the *Literary Gazette*, Alexander Chakovsky, wrote a vicious attack on the young rebel writers in *Sovetskaya Rossiya* (27 January 1968). He reminded them triumphantly that "Valentin Kataev has publicly unmasked the dishonourable act of Alexander Werth". In Hungary, the co-editor of the literary magazine *Kortars*, E. P. Feher, brought the matter to the attention of the Hungarian public in an article "The Ginsburg Case and the Troubles of Soviet Literature" (published in *Elet es Irodalom*, 27 January 1968).

"Kataev favoured his old friend Alexander Werth—the correspondent of the *New Statesman*—with an interview. (Alexander Werth, until now known as a correct British newsman, who has always stuck to the facts, was the Moscow correspondent of the BBC during and after the War, and his interview with Stalin—also published in Moscow—created a sensation.) Werth—as he admitted in his letter to Kataev later—put words into the Soviet writer's mouth which he never said and which could seriously compromise him in his country. . . ."

The article dealt with the Ginsburg-Galanskov trial and Soviet underground literature.

Shortly thereafter, there was also an article on the same subject in the *Times*

---

[1] Published under the title *Russia: Hopes and Fears* (1969) in which Mr Werth engaged in his usual slippery half-truths and evasions.

Literary Supplement (8 February 1968). It was even less sympathetic to the rebellious young writers. Its anonymous author was referred to as "A Special Correspondent". He wrote condescendingly about "*only* some two hundred people [who] assembled outside the court" where Ginsburg and Galanskov were tried. Robert Conquest commented on this in the *Times Literary Supplement* (22 February 1968):

> "Did it not require a certain determination? Not simply that the temperature was −25°C, but that they were, at considerable risk, displaying their faces and identities for the KGB. After all, this is more than your correspondent has done for the readers of the *TLS*."

Robert Conquest also objected to some remarks in the article opposing outside analysts of Soviet affairs to foreign correspondents in Moscow. He pointed out that some of them on their own admission bore false witness:

> "Even Mr Alexander Werth has recently told us that in reporting on the labour camps he 'pulled his punches' for political reasons (see the correspondence columns of the *New Statesman*, 13 October 1967). Now in what conceivable sense is the carefully documented information about the camp system provided by those outside experts Messrs David J. Dallin and Boris Nicolaevsky in their *Forced Labour in Soviet Russia*, published at that time, misleading? It has been confirmed, often in considerable detail, by Soviet sources of the Khrushchev period. Are we seriously to assume that Mr Werth's negatives were superior reporting?
> . . ."

When Robert Conquest wrote his letter he obviously did not know who the "Special Correspondent" of the *Times Literary Supplement* was. But his identity was soon to be discovered. The Russian *émigré* publication *Posev* (no. 5, 1968), which made available to the anonymous "Special Correspondent" of the *Times Literary Supplement* the texts of the Soviet underground literary writings which were the subject of his article, revealed that it was none other than Alexander Werth.

In Stalin's time Werth was pulling punches. In Khrushchev's stretching points. Now under Brezhnev, Werth is obviously the soul of discretion. What price a "Moscow Correspondent"? It may be sometimes difficult for editors to assess; and sometimes they may find it even more difficult to reveal.

(1968)

7. Kolakowski:

On Marxism & Beyond

A T DIFFERENT periods of history, a philosopher comes to reflect in some particularly striking form the human predicament of the age. Leszek Kolakowski may be taken to be such a philosopher. Although his name has become vaguely famous, he is hardly known (at present) in the English-speaking world; and yet his personal career and that of his philosophy deserve the attention of all who are interested in contemporary intellectual life.

In 1956, Leszek Kolakowski, then a young philosopher, epitomized the revolt of his generation against Stalinism. In two essays which remained unpublished in Poland, "What is Socialism" and "The End of the Age of Myths", he summarised the widespread but pent-up feelings which led to the Polish "October". In the first of these essays Kolakowski defined in 72 ironic negations "what socialism is not". Among other things it is not a state

"... in which a person who has committed no crime sits at home waiting for the police. In which there are more spies than nurses and more people in prisons than in hospitals. In which one is forced to resort to lies and compelled to be a thief, in which a person lives better because he does not think at all and which wants all its citizens to have the same opinions in philosophy, foreign policy, economics, literature, and ethics. In which the philosophers and writers always say the same thing as the generals and ministers, but always after them. In which one must each day refute what one affirmed the day before and always believe it to be the same."

Kolakowski concluded by saying that this was "the first point. But now listen attentively, we will tell you what socialism is—well then, socialism is a good thing." In his other essay he wrote about socialism as

"... a society which will abolish the exploitation and oppression of man by man. The conviction that such a society is possible is the main treasure which we are able to rescue from the fire of New Jerusalem, the city of the Great King. This is not little despite appearances; it is not a treasure which it is easy to rescue. One can ask if we are not deluding ourselves again, blinded as always by the myth which we are unable to shed finally. We reply: there are myths which played a great and creative role in human history and contributed more to man's progress than the conviction that it is necessary to live always on the barren land, where man was born. Nobody knows if Colchis really exists, but one can be certain that on the way to it there are better countries than the one we are living in. Yet one thing is more important than anything: that the myths should not be the siren's voice leading nowhere; that they should not paralyse vigilant human reason—the best thing which has emerged on our sad Milky Way."

SINCE THESE SENTIMENTS were expressed (1956) a lot of water has passed under the bridges of the Vistula. The hopes of the Polish "October" were disappointed, and its "conscience", Kolakowski, was made the butt of ideological attacks and withdrew into academic life. He devoted himself to teaching and abstained from any direct political writing. But in his essays written on a more esoteric level, he remained true to his basic convictions. He continued to fight for intellectual freedom within the constantly shrinking limits. He was subject to administrative chicaneries, prevented from travelling abroad, and threatened with expulsion from the Party. The philosophy department of Warsaw University, where he held a chair, was under increasing pressure and eventually its studies were drastically reorganised to curb the heresy of free thought.

On 21 October 1966—the 10th anniversary of the Polish "October"—at a student meeting organised in the history faculty of Warsaw University, Leszek Kolakowski made a speech in which he drew up the balance-sheet of the achievements of "October", and contrasted its hopes with the subsequent developments. He pointed to the restrictions on the freedom of speech, the growing stringency of censorship, the political interference with creative work in the humanities and social sciences, the growing gap between the Party and the public, the arbitrary application of the law.[1] On the following day Kolakowski was expelled from the Polish United Workers' Party.

This decision was followed by a wave of protests in the university and intellectual milieux. Writers and university teachers demanded the reinstatement of Kolakowski as a Party member. The letters of protest were signed by many Party members, some of whom were subsequently suspended by (or resigned from) the Party. At the same time the Central Committee of the Party wished to deprive Kolakowski of his chair of philosophy at the university, but this demand was strongly opposed by the Polish Academy of Sciences (and, in particular, by the distinguished philosopher, Professor Tadeusz Kotarbinski, formerly his university teacher).

KOLAKOWSKI remained at the university. However, it was proposed that its autonomy should be further curtailed through the introduction

---

[1] In saying this, charged the Minister of Education (Henryk Jablonski) who later expelled him from the university, Kolakowski "was not only defying truth, but also in his attitude he violated the principles obligatory to every teacher" (*Nove Drogi*, May 1968).

of new disciplinary commissions. The intellectual life of the country was further stifled and when the authorities banned the performance of the play *Dziady* (*The Forefathers*) by the Polish national poet, Adam Mickiewicz, the Warsaw branch of the Polish Writers' Union held a meeting of protest on 29 February 1968. Professor Kolakowski was only one of the speakers among the most distinguished representatives of Polish literature and cultural life. Once again he spoke about the mechanism of growing repression:

"When the first timid repressive acts are not resisted, they encourage their initiators to an even greater scale of repression, which in practice begins to have no limit. Now in our country the scope of repression has spread so far that in fact all opposition has ceased. Few books are published and their authors no longer have the opportunity of reacting to and effectively counteracting the prohibitions. We observe the constant destruction of scholarship and the hampering of its rate of development, the limitation of the free spirit of investigation. What we have now in our country is not socialism; it has nothing in common with Marxism."

The banning of *Dziady* also led to student disturbances in Poland, which were followed on 25 March 1968 by the expulsion from Warsaw University of six professors, among them Leszek Kolakowski. They had been accused of corrupting the young (no new charge in the history of philosophy). The official communiqué announcing this affirmed that "the highest interests of the state and the nation require that they should be barred from influencing the young" (*Trybuna Ludu*, 26 March 1968).

The general purge made on this occasion particularly affected persons of Jewish origin,[2] but was directed in fact against all those in Polish cultural life tainted not just with "Jewishness" but with liberal attitudes. Kolakowski, who is not a Jew,[3] was the most prominent of them. In the wake of his

---

[2] The head of the cultural section of the Central Committee of the Party, Andrzej Werblan, made the following contribution to the Marxist theory of internationalism:

"No society can tolerate the excessive participation of a national minority in the élite of power . . ." (*Miesiecznik Literacki*, June 1968).

Later on Zenon Kliszko, Gomulka's right-hand man, said (at the 12th plenary session of the Central Committee of the Party) that

"the basic criterion of all the decisions about persons can only be the evaluation of political and ideological attitudes of the Party members. It is alien to our Party to differentiate between the Party members and the citizens of our country by national criteria or criteria of their origin. . . . A false and exaggerated conception of the struggle against Zionism would threaten the Party with a diversion of its attention from the main dangers, which are the forces of reaction and revisionism."

Kliszko indicated that the struggle with revisionism must be the chief target of the Party ideological offensive and singled out Kolakowski as the main culprit in the past "escalation of revisionist pressure" (*Trybuna Ludu*, 9 July, 1968).

[3] But, like Gomulka, he has a wife who is of Jewish origin. In his essay "The Anti-Semites" (*Swiatopoglad i Zycie Codzienne'*, Warsaw, 1957), Kolakowski wrote:

expulsion a great many university teachers including his assistants were deprived of their posts and expelled from the universities and scientific institutes.

ONCE AGAIN Kolakowski has become the target of a vicious press campaign. The official *Trybuna Ludu* (13, 14, 15 April 1968), not normally addicted to the discussion of abstruse problems of epistemology and ontology, devoted an inordinately long article to him, written by his old Stalinist opponent, Henryk Ladosz.

In his article, Ladosz was not concerned with the question of whether Kolakowski was right or wrong in his philosophical evolution; he simply attacked him for no longer being a Marxist. He declared that once he "was able to be a Marxist, but he has gradually lost this ability. This is a process which passes through the stage of philosophical revisionism and ends with anti-Marxism and anti-communism. . . ." History had traced an ironical circle. Kolakowski was originally a good young Stalinist philosopher and in his "revisionist" reaction against "dogmatism" he discovered the "young Marx", whom he used against the Stalinist orthodoxy. Twelve years later, a Stalinist philosopher coming back on the wave of repression praised the "young Kolakowski" in his attack on the mature Kolakowski. There is both political and Hegelian logic in this.

KOLAKOWSKI is not only the most brilliant and original among contemporary philosophers in any communist country, but his evolution is of more than parochial significance. His earlier essays mark some of the stages of his evolution, particularly his "revisionist" *Sturm und Drang* period. His later essays, like "In Praise of Inconsistency" and "The Priest and the Jester", reflect a further development of his philosophy. To give an adequate exposition of his ideas would require a volume; what I can do here is only to sketch his philosophical evolution.

Kolakowski's search began in disillusionment with the doctrinal certainties about historical progress, with a revolt against confusing myths with reality. As he explained in the articles on "Responsibility and History" his contemporaries were taught to believe in the great demiurge of history. However, to use the words of Zbigniew Jordan, "the demiurge turned out to be a figment of imagination created by a secular eschatology, cultivated under the name of scientific history".

Kolakowski was born in 1927 and was a schoolboy when the War broke out. He spent most of the period of the German Occupation in Poland in a

---

"Anti-Semitism is not a theory. . . . It is anti-culture and anti-humanity, anti-theory and anti-science. . . . Anti-Semitism can only be an instrument of reaction. . . . There are no forms of oppression and of national or racial discrimination, which are not at the same time a negation of communism in the very heart of its existence."

KOLAKOWSKI 139

country house with a large library, which he used voraciously. After the war he finished secondary school, became a member of the Communist youth organisation *ZMP*, and later of the Party, entered the philosophical faculty of Lodz University, and graduated in 1950. He was already regarded as a kind of prodigy. He lectured and published philosophical articles even before graduation. He became assistant to Professor Tadeusz Kotarbinski, and later to Professor Adam Schaff, then still the leading orthodox Marxist spokesman in Poland. He received the degree of Candidate of Philosophy, lectured at the Party high school, and became a teacher in the Department of Philosophy at the University of Warsaw. He also became a member of the editorial board of the philosophical journal *Mysl Filozoficzna* (Philosophical Thought). He wrote a good deal, his early publications being mainly concerned with medieval philosophy and contemporary Catholic philosophy. He also published an essay on Avicenna. Later he became interested in Spinoza.

Although these early writings revealed too great an individual philosophical fervour for a good Party philosopher, they bear the marks of orthodoxy. His opinions of the "philosophical class enemies" conformed to Soviet shibboleths.

"With the help of lying formulas [he wrote] such as 'man is the end of society', 'society is for man, not man for society', social–democracy tries to achieve the same purpose as existentialist metaphysics: to oppose the freedom of the individual to the freedom of society, and as a corollary the 'liberation of man' to the liberation of the social class. It tries to demonstrate that the genuine realisation of the rights of man is independent of the class struggle and of the objective laws of social development."

Nor did Kolakowski's disputes with Western analytical students of Marxism deviate from the then familiar pattern:

"Because the old methods of struggle failed and Marxism, drawing strength from the victories of the world revolutionary movement and from the successes of the Soviet Union, and confirmed by scientific developments, was expanding rapidly despite the united action of the police and bourgeois philosophers. . . .

The Atlantic philosophers, recruited to manufacture metaphysical justifications for the activity of the bourgeois police, and relying on the power of verbal mystification, believe that they can keep the working class in the West back from struggle by suggesting that they live in conditions of freedom and welfare and by substituting for the word 'imperialism' the word 'West'. . . .

The idea that a theory can be at the same time class–determined and objective passes the Western comprehension. . . . Every clear idea explained in Marxist writings becomes an obscure puzzle in the mind of an obscurantist. The philosophical opinions express class interest; that it is in the interest of the progressive class to strive for an objective knowledge of the world, that the proletariat is the only class which is interested in an absolutely objective knowledge of the world, without any class limitations deforming the picture of reality; that, in consequence, the ideology of the working class, precisely because of its origin, is free from all mystifications and distortions, and that, in contrast to the 'Atlantic philosophers', the class character of Marxism is the source of and not a fetter on its objectivity—all these are truths familiar to every Marxist. . . .

We know what freedom of science means in bourgois 'democracies'. . . . Everyone can dumbfound and deceive the people, the most anti-human theories are free to circulate. . . ."[4]

At the time these essays were published Kolakowski went to Italy to attend the congress of Thomist philosophers in Rome in 1954 as an observer—an indication of his curiosity and enterprising spirit.

BUT HIS WRITINGS were changing in character. They acquired a double meaning. When he attacked "religious obscurantism" his formulations could be applied to Stalinist dogmas and rituals. He became an early and prominent exponent of the mounting wave of "revisionism" among the young Polish Marxists, when the early Polish "thaw" presented an opportunity for more outspoken criticism. Although Kolakowski's evolution was a step ahead of his milieu, it was fairly representative of the ideological development of other Polish "revisionists". Kolakowski became their most popular exponent, almost a spiritual guide. His philosophical expositions became more subtle and more sophisticated.

In passing through the cycle of disillusionment, he began to grasp and grapple with problems hitherto unsuspected or dismissed without understanding. The central theme of these spiritual struggles was the problems of ethics, and more particularly of conscience and history. His immediate concern was to rescue Marxism from what he termed its institutional degeneration. But at the same time he tried to find out how ethical questions could be solved within its framework.

IN A SERIES OF ESSAYS before "October", Kolakowski dealt with the major ethical and philosophical themes agitating the minds of the young communist intellectuals. "Kolakowski has made the first attempt at a philosophical analysis of the ideological crisis through which a great part of

---

[4] These quotations are taken from Kolakowski's articles written (in Polish) between 1950 and 1954 and collected in *Essays on Catholic Philosophy* (Warsaw, 1955).

the Marxist intelligentsia in our country is passing", said a reviewer of these essays, collected in *Philosophy and Everyday Life*, published in 1957 in Warsaw.

Disenchantment led him, like so many others, to tackle the problem of ends and means. He now discovered that the Kantian phrase that "man should be treated as an end in himself" is not just "a typical bourgeois idea" but that "it can prevent wrongs". Now he thought that

> "the concept of communism embraces also the concept of man under communism, who should develop various moral and intellectual virtues. . . . Communism as an end cannot be reduced, by a misuse of abstraction, to communist property relations. . . . Communism is also an improvement of the moral rules of collective life, which within its framework are *an end in itself*. Communism so understood is an end which justifies the means. It is not difficult to perceive that it cannot be realised by means of political practices which educate the citizens of the socialist society in fear and lies. Because fear and lies are evil in themselves and should be combated as contrary to the ends of socialist construction. . . . The maintenance of power by criminal means is contrary to the ends of socialist construction and fetters its achievement."

Kolakowski's attacks on Thomism took another twist. He condemned it now because in it "the individual's independence of society is compensated by an absolute dependence on the Church. Because of this, philosophy in progressive bourgeois thought, struggling against the theocratic claims of the Church, tried to legitimise the autonomy of man and his recognition as an end in himself. . . ." At the time this essay was written it was already possible to read "Party" for "Church".

Kolakowski's debates with various trends in Christian philosophy also reflected his contemporary preoccupations.

> "Personalist theories, notwithstanding their conservative or sometimes clearly reactionary political content, perceive certain real phenomena in social life, and give them a mythical and absolute shape. Such ideas have social vitality partly because in their ideological activity Marxists today overlook and disregard these phenomena. Therefore it is particularly important that these problems should be dealt with by Marxists, as they are often brought to the attention of people by everyday life. . . . The most important problem among them is that of the relation of the freedom of the individual to the freedom of society in a socialist society.
>
> It was rightly assumed that the human personality, i.e., the sum total of the conscious ways of reacting, is shaped by social environment

(which also includes, indirectly, the influencing of the past social environment, transmitted by heredity). This assumption is clearly false if it is understood in the sense that belonging to a class determines the individual's entire social life and behaviour. It is clear that social situations shaping individual personality differ in many respects for every man and it is true therefore that every individual is in a sense unique. *No individual embodies the essence of social class in its pure form and cannot be reduced to it.*"

It is not surprising that Kolakowski became sceptical of the possibility that conflicts between individual interests and those of society would disappear.

YET HE STILL SEEMED to accept what in Western discussion of ethics came to be called the "naturalistic fallacy", but he was uneasy about it. He already rejected the idea that "moral norms and postulates may determine the content of philosophical knowledge, i.e., that 'practical reason' may in this sense have primacy over speculative reason, not only inspiring it but ordering it. . . . Nor can normative statements give us direct knowledge of the world".

While trying to rescue the rationalist tradition of Marxism, Kolakowski stressed the independence of positive knowledge from normative (and Party) interference. While trying to find the moral roots of behaviour, he identified general outlook (in the sense of *Weltanschauung*) with philosophy itself, unlike the logical positivists, and rejected the restriction of philosophy to logical or linguistic analysis. He defined it as "the sum total of beliefs influencing human behaviour, evaluated morally by society, either praised or condemned (and influencing behaviour according to moral evaluation). . . ."

Kolakowski was not only heretical about Engels' treatment of moral knowledge, but contradicted him directly on knowledge in general. Rejecting the positivistic interpretation of philosophy, he also denied the Marxist contention about its end and its transformation into positive knowledge under full communism. He asked whether "the recognition of the class character of philosophical thinking means the death of philosophy in a classless society?" and gave an emphatically negative answer:

"The social functions of philosophy do not die away when its class functions come to an end. . . . In a society which, in the words of Engels, 'will not only overcome class antagonisms, but also forget about them', and in which 'a truly human morality' will rule, the need for philosophical knowledge cannot wither away, since its proper source, which is the moral life of people, will not dry up. To be sure, we want to transform and revolutionise that life, not only as a means of political, economic, and technical change, but also as an end in itself. The freedom of man is a programme for all spheres of human life."

A LTHOUGH Kolakowski's essays dealt with abstruse philosophical problems, they were very popular. They were probably read by a far wider public than was likely to grasp his argument, because it was felt that in his essays he was striving to give an interpretation of Marxism more in conformity with popular attitudes than the official one. But Kolakowski often descended from abstract theory to a more accessible political level. A particularly strong impression was made by his three essays on the relation of "institutional Marxism" to politics: "Intellectuals and the Communist Movement", "Permanent and Transitory Aspects of Marxism" and "The Concept of the Left".

The first, published in the theoretical organ of the Party on the eve of Gomulka's assumption of power, was a sort of "revisionist" Manifesto against "the impasse which reigns at present in Marxist theory", and against Party control of culture, particularly science:

> "The political inspiration of the communist movement, whose intellectual genealogy is the entire tradition of European rationalism, cannot lead to the deformation of scientific truth for the purpose of proving 'truths' settled beforehand or dished up for belief."

In the second article Kolakowski distinguished between "intellectual" and "institutional" Marxism. In the past, Marxism "meant a doctrine defined purely formally; its content being, in each case, supplied by the decree of the Infallible Institution which, during a certain phase, was the Greatest Philologist, the Greatest Economist, the Greatest Philosopher and the Greatest Historian in the World". He drew the conclusion that "with the gradual refinement of research techniques in the humanities, the concept of Marxism as a separate school of thought will in time become blurred and ultimately disappear altogether—just as there is no 'Newtonism' in physics, no 'Linnaeism' in botany, no 'Harveyism' in physiology, and no 'Guassism' in mathematics. This means that what is permanent in Marx's work will be assimilated in the natural course of scientific development."

In the third article Kolakowski maintained that

> "the Left is not a single political movement, or party, or group of parties. The Left is a characteristic which to a greater or lesser degree can serve particular movements or parties, as well as given individuals, or human activities, attitudes and world outlooks."

He concluded that

> "a communist movement that subordinates its ideology to immediate tactics is destined for degeneration and defeat. It can exist only with the support of the power and the repressive capacity of the state. The intellectual and moral values of communism are not luxurious

ornaments of its activity, but the conditions of its existence. That is why it is difficult to create leftist socialism in a reactionary country. A communist movement whose sole form of existence is sheer tactics and which permits the loss of its original intellectual and moral premises ceases to be a leftist movement. Hence the word 'socialism' has come to have more than one meaning, and is no longer synonymous with the word 'Left'. . . ."

Like other Polish "revisionists" advocating "humanist socialism", Kolakowski has drawn the fire of the guardians of the doctrine, in Poland and abroad. But undaunted by attacks, he wrote in September 1957 a series of articles in *Nowa Kultura*, containing the most thorough and far-reaching polemic with Marxist philosophical fundamentals written by a communist under a communist régime. They were written in a somewhat enigmatic form, but it was clear that Kolakowski's evolution had reached a new stage.

"Responsibility and History" again dealt with the problem of political obligation. The appeal to "History" as the ultimate court of justice was rejected even more radically than before. The relationship between ends and means and facts and values was stated more explicitly and the moral orientation was still more pronounced. In an imaginary conversation between a Clerk (the term is borrowed from Julian Benda) and an anti-Clerk, Kolakowski clearly stated his credo, to which he remained faithful, as the subsequent decade has poignantly shown:

> "I will never believe that the moral and intellectual life of mankind follows the laws of economic investments, that is, the expectation of a better tomorrow by saving today, lying so that truth may triumph, taking advantage of crime to save nobility. I know that sometimes we have to choose between two evils. But when both possibilities are extremely evil, I will do my utmost to refrain from making a choice. In this way, I do choose, be it only man's right to make his own evaluation of the situation in which he finds himself. This is no small matter. . . . Lasting moral values, continuously evolving up till now, are the surest support available if reality demands of us a choice, which after all, is also of a moral nature. In any case, they are more trustworthy than any historiosophy. And that, ultimately, is why I will stick to my opinion."
>
> "Whatever happens?"
>
> "Whatever happens."

KOLAKOWSKI KEPT HIS WORD. During the next decade his philosophical views have undergone a further evolution, but he has not budged from this ethical stance. He remained true to the moral premises of his *Weltanschauung* and stood by them "whatever happened" during the long-drawn process of retreat from the Polish "October".

His essays written at the time show an uneasy mixture of great perspicacity and of somewhat naïve Prometheanism, which results in places in muddled thinking. However, these essays should be taken in their historical context: most of them were written at a time when bitter disillusionment mingled with high hopes.

They are also to be seen as stages in the intellectual self-liberatoin of a very precise mind in the process of growth. At the time of the Polish "October" it was possible to look at Kolakowski mainly in his symptomatic role, as illustrating a tendency, as a mirror of the philosophical anxiety of the communist-educated intellectuals, as a sign of protest against totalitarianism arising from within the system among the younger generation of the intelligentsia, as an indication that critical intelligence survives the Stalinist *Gleichschaltung* of minds.

However, there is little doubt that he deserves a hearing as a philosopher in his own right. His subsequent development has clearly shown not only his rigorous training in logic and philosophy and the wide scope of his interests, but also the growing maturity of his mind.

AFTER THE STALINIST PHASE came the "revisionist" phase in Kolakowski's thought. After "October" he reached the third phase in his intellectual evolution which went beyond Marxist "revisionism". This did not mean the abandonment of all Marxian perspectives, but their transcendence as an exclusive framework of thought. It also meant that the polymathic knowledge of Kolakowski had found a better scope for analytical endeavours and a still more sophisticated way of approaching "the philosophy of man". While in his earlier writings there was little from which a Westerner could learn anything of universal significance, now he has moved from a stage of rediscovery of intellectual landmarks well known in the West to a stage where his search is more original. It is this that makes him, in view of his particular historical experience and individual talents, one of the most interesting contemporary thinkers.[5]

Kolakowski is a philosopher in the somewhat un-modern sense of being concerned with the traditional large questions of philosophy, which began coming back into fashion only when the reaction against logical positivism set in in modern philosophy. He conceives it in the original sense of a quest for wisdom, rather than in the limited sense of logical positivists and linguistic analysts as a technique of precise thinking. He had a thorough analytical training and possesses a solid modern professional competence as a philosopher. This makes his efforts to relate the "unanswerable questions" of a *Weltanschauung* and the "limited questions" of the academic

---

[5] In the ensuing years he has published, among other works, his magisterial *Main Currents of Marxism* (3 Vols., 1978).

philosophy interesting, although they are not always successful. As Anthony Quinton has pointed out, Kolakowski's attempts in "Responsibility and History" to reconcile Marxian social determinism with individual moral responsibility are "more honourable than satisfactory".

His logical training, his political background, and his concern for the autonomy of morals resulted in a characteristic tension, not to say *caesura*, in his philosophy. His passionate interest in individual ethics led him back to the young Marx and to the Hegelian questions, in an attempt to provide Marxism with a humanistic perspective. But his methodology is positivist and this creates both a fertile clash and inconsistency in his writings.

He is quite aware of it. He rejected the idea that value judgments can be deduced from statements of fact and that the moral evaluation of human acts can be derived from historical or sociological generalizations. But he is also very much concerned with positive knowledge. This raises the question of the nature of belief and the nature of knowledge in general almost to the central position in Kolakowski's philosophical thought. In his quest for a clearer view of the middle ground between ontology and epistemology, Kolakowski refuses to abandon an analytical detachment (however often he may sin against it in practice) in favour either of some new "grand synthesis" or one of the traditional philosophical positions. As he put it in his essay on "Hope and History", he tries to avoid a choice between the two attitudes and two visions of reality which derive from the preoccupation either with "*is*" or with "*ought*". Rather he wants to establish a contact between them, even if it is subject to "constant interruptions", a contact which should

> "prevent the alternatives of '*Sollen-Sein*' from becoming polarisations of utopian-opportunism, romanticism-conservatism, purposeless madness *versus* collaboration with crime masquerading as sobriety. . . ."

Like Lukacs, although for quite different reasons, he does not want to settle for a solution (adopted by Max Weber) of a positivist interpretation of Kant, nor for the one adopted by neo-Kantians (like Verlander, Cohen, Naterp) of an ethical emancipation of Socialism from Marxism and scepticism about the possibility of positive knowledge. The reason for this is probably that neither of these positions would be compatible with Kolakowski's "anthropological realism".[6]

In his attempts to overcome "moral solipsism, totalitarian utopias, and petty bourgeois individualism", Kolakowski is trying to preserve (or rescue) in some form historicism, which is combined in him with residual elements

---

[6] Kolakowski's "anthropological realism" is discussed in Z. Jordan, *Philosophy and Ideology* (Dordrecht, 1962). It is expounded by Kolakowski particularly clearly in his essay "Karl Marx and the Classical Definition of Truth" published in a shortened version in *Revisionism* (ed. Labedz, 1962).

of romanticism. Kolakowski is acutely aware of the problem of historical relativity, whether it is seen through the Mannheimian spectacles of the "sociology of knowledge", or whether the conceptual apparatus of the historian is seen through phenomenological spectacles. With his experience of historiography permanently falsified by the Party, he is also very conscious of the distinction between the cultural or anthropological problem of the relativity of historical perception, and the political problem of its deliberate falsification.

There is a sharp distinction between the question involved in the rewriting of history à la Stalin in his *Short Course* and the Bergsonian question of conceptual *découpage* which affects historical understanding. Kolakowski explains this point in general terms:[7]

> "In its relationship to its material the science of the history of ideas then finds itself in the same situation as that of the human species *vis-à-vis* the world. Not creating it *ex nihilo*, it imposes its limited system of divisions and makes a choice among factors which it tends, unconsciously, to judge as thus or otherwise differentiated according to their pertinence.

> This is a simple statement of fact, and not an expression of intent to see history as a projection of the present into the past. For the intentional application of such a rule can risk shocking distortions. In any case, it provides disastrous justifications for arbitrary choices of facts and for the ignoring of facts incompatible with a previously accepted hypothesis. This changeable system of divisions we are speaking about is a function of conditions never defined by the researcher according to his will—as opposed to a painter, for example, who can never be accused of painting false pictures.

> If, therefore, we can reasonably say that the historian like the painter creates objects which do not exist in 'nature' still the former is always bound by the principle of non-contradiction toward known data— whereas the latter does not bear this responsibility, though he knows the material from which he ultimately produces his world. It is also certain that there exist limits to the similarity between scientific historical creativity and that which the human species as a whole creates out of its material 'substance'. The conditions that determine a historian in his use thus, and not otherwise, of a conceptual apparatus in the analysis of his object change not only depending on historical eras, but also on different views of the world which in the same era create different environments, classes and social groups.

> If, then, the countless different pictures of the same collection of facts

---

[7] Cf. "*Cogito*, Historical Materialism, and the Expressive Interpretation of Personality", in *Kultura i Fetysze* [Culture and Fetishes] (Warsaw, 1967).

co-exist and if all are approximately compatible with accepted technical rules of work, then the choice among them is defined by a more general choice, one of a certain view of the world, which constitutes an integral part of historical interpretation."

Kolakowski developed an ingenious way of handling the relation between the ontological problem of "metaphysical certainty" and the epistemological problem of positive knowledge in history. It is contained in his essay on "Historical Understanding and the Understanding of an Historical Event". He argued there that it is impossible to find in history any immanent meaning, but that meaning can be attributed to it by an act of faith. There are two ineluctable alternatives.

"We can either accept the point of view of an authentic historicism and in doing so make the history totally meaningless, but gain by it a feeling of consciousness without illusions, of consciousness free from faith. Or we can take the idea of a history which is meaningful through a conscious design which when it is projected into the past makes it understandable. Such a design contains at the same time an act of hope and an act of faith; of hope that it is possible in reality, of faith that this possibility supports a certain pre-historical *eidos* of humanity, the difficult implementation of which we observe in history. But this design is a decision, not an act legitimised scientifically."

What Kolakowski has done here is in effect to secularize Pascal. Historical belief, like religious belief, becomes an act of faith, and an act of faith of a special nature, a risk to be taken. Only here its object is not God, but history. It is, like that of Pascal, a wager, but a secular not a religious wager. Thus "anthropological realism" makes possible for Kolakowski historical knowledge through an act of faith. It is a rationalist faith, not a secular version of Tertullian's *credo quia absurdum*, but it hinges on some fragile assumptions about the historical "design".

WHERE ARE THESE ASSUMPTIONS to come from?
They cannot come from historical knowledge because of Kolakowski's own definition of the problem. (It would also be circular reasoning.) They can only derive directly from an existentialist choice. This choice, Kolakowski thinks,[8] has been reduced in the philosophical work of our day under the influence of positivist criticism, to two alternatives, and he does not like either of them.
One alternative is the so-called philosophy of life (*Lebensphilosophie*), which in its extreme form presupposes that man's intellectual life is evidence

---

[8] Cf. *Filozofia Pozytywistyczna, Od Hume'a do Koła Wiedeńskiego* (Warsaw, 1966), published in English translation as *The Alienation of Reason* (New York, 1968).

of his biological decadence. The other is "a lurid Manichean vision" which can be formulated "without recourse to religious ideas" and which presupposes "that our biological life and our metaphysical explorations spring from two incompatible and even hostile existential sources". Kolakowski feels that both involve a positivistic reduction of philosophy to a biological level.

"Positivism, when it is radical, renounces the transcendental meaning of truth, and reduces logical values to a feature of biological behaviour. The rejection of the possibility of synthetic judgments *a priori*—the fundamental act constituting positivism as a doctrine—can be justified with the reduction of all knowledge to biological responses. . . ."

The conclusion which Kolakowski draws from this is that although one has to take cognisance "of the positivist critiques of synthetic judgments *a priori*, of the validity of induction, of 'essentialist' metaphysics, and of value judgments", it is not necessary to accept such a critique in the sense "that it reduces every metaphysical investigation and quest for certainty to mere 'error' "—but only in the limited sense that it makes it necessary "to renounce once and for all claims to 'scientific' status" for all ontological endeavours. He refuses to accept the positivist proposition that all genuine knowledge is to be identified with the results of scientific method.

LIKE OTHER GOOD PHILOSOPHERS, Kolakowski is caught between the necessity for ontological choice and the impossibility of epistemological proof. He has been called a philosopher of life, but this does not reflect adequately his philosophical quest, although it calls attention to an important aspect of it.

His favourite philosopher, whose influence can be traced throughout his writings, is Spinoza. Like Spinoza, Kolakowski faces philosophical dichotomies which are for him a Procrustean bed. Idealism and materialism, monism and dualism, individual and infinity, ethics and determinism, these traditional antinomies are so many stations of the cross in Kolakowski's philosophical *via dolorosa*. Like that of Spinoza's, his own thought is in its ultimate effect internally divided.

The parallel goes further. Like Spinoza, Kolakowski faces the problem of *la condition humaine* in that special way which blends desperation with hope, and affirmation of life with the scepticism of wisdom. And like Spinoza, he not only made moral orientation the linchpin of his philosophy, but faced the political and social orthodoxy of his own time and place with courage and ethical determination. He illuminated his own attitude to general philosophy in his comment on Spinoza. In a book on his favourite philosopher, he refers to a "*via spinoza*, a thorny path where one engages in a stubborn struggle with the finiteness of one's thought".

Spinoza, says Kolakowski, tried to overcome the thought of death without recourse to the illusion of immortality. An individual has to find a way to keep company with infinity "as an organism keeps company with its heart".

> "Only if the two can live together, and only through such co-habitation, can human solitude be overcome. It cannot be really overcome by links with any finite being. Man only *seems* to become rooted in existence because he has his own family, his own country, his own nation, his own religion, and his own god. In its ultimate conclusion, Spinozism reveals that man does not have either family, country, nation, god, or religion. But only Spinoza, because of his own life, could live through the ultimate awareness of this situation, which is a universal human situation masked by the appearances of daily life. . . . If this [i.e. Spinoza's] solution of two main problems of life to which philosophy has to give an open or concealed answer—the problem of freedom and the problem of death—is fictitious, it is the most beautiful fiction of the many with which philosophy feeds human minds through the ages."

Kolakowski considers the position of Spinoza as not really pantheistic or in any sense religious. This is so for two reasons: because it is not transcendental and because Spinoza's ethics is not heteronomous and is secular. Kolakowski argues that if these two conditions are not satisfied, but "every quest for happiness through the cognition of the absolute" is considered a religion, the term "becomes a misleading psuedonym for the type of thought which is common to almost all 'grand systems' in philosophy".

Clearly, his own philosophical longing is somehow reminiscent of what Spinoza called "the intellectual love of God".

KOLAKOWSKI'S ATTITUDE TO RELIGION has undergone a further change.[9] He has radically departed from any vulgar type of criticism of religion, and has been castigated for this in the article by Ladosz I have quoted above. It said that "this once excellent critic of Christian philosophical doctrines" has turned into his opposite, and that he brought into question the fundamental and elementary theses "not only of the Marxist, but of any materialist theory of religion" by expressing doubt about the idea that "religious conceptions reflect man's helplessness *vis-à-vis* nature".

It is not true that Kolakowski "has turned into his opposite" in his attitude to religion. But his philosophical evolution undoubtedly shows a shift away from what for Ladosz is a "materialist theory of religion". The essay under attack was a very subtle analysis of the role of religious symbols and of the significance of religion for the faithful. Kolakowski rejects in it various conventional empirical interpretations of the function of religion. He argues that if religious symbols can be used to reflect or organize non-religious

---

[9] I wrote this before Kolakowski presented his views in his small book on *Religion* (1982).

values, it is only because they "must inevitably possess their own special value, irreducible and *sui generis*". Otherwise they would not be able to perform this function, and the question why they are used to reflect and satisfy other values would remain unintelligible.

Kolakowski asks why, if religious symbols are only objects for projections or channels for expression of various social, economic, or libidinal needs, are they at all necessary? Why are such needs not expressed directly? He considers and rejects one after another, Marxist, rationalist, Freudian, Jungian, and phenomenological arguments about the genesis of religion. He concludes that there is no indication of any historical tendency towards the weakening of the religious impulses; that there is no correlation between the fall of religion and the rise of education (as postulated by rationalists), or between religious belief and social control (as postulated by psycho-analysis); that technololgical civilisation weakens the vitality of religious symbols but only by permitting people to escape from the fundamental questions of life.

> "In this way there comes into being a false irreligiosity which arises not from the overcoming of religious symbols as a way of thought, but from stifling the self-awareness of the situation which gives birth to religious symbols. For that reason this type of influence of contemporary civilisation on religious faith is deceptive and short-lived. Like religiosity, irreligiosity can be false or authentic. . . ."

If religious symbols are "irresolvable" and "religion really exists", the only way to confront the "irreplaceable values" which they provide, is to show that "they promise the fulfilment of the impossible".

> "Authentic irreligiosity always arises from an awareness of the need to which religious symbols are an answer, and from a conscious rejection of acceptance of the religious satisfaction of these needs. . . . It is a resignation from illusions, with a simultaneous knowledge about the situation which gives birth to such illusions. . . . This kind of self-awareness is only possible in a humanistic culture. . . ."

This is a far cry from the young Kolakowski writing at the time when he has not yet lost his secular faith, that the function of religion is:

> "to promise the exploited the rights which are to be given in the other world, while asking them to renounce their worldly rights."

EQUALLY STRIKING IS THE CONTRAST between the past and present evaluation by Kolakowski of the cultural role of Christianity in history. In his early essay on Avicenna he wrote that his neglect by "bourgeois philosophical historiography"

> ". . . probably resulted mainly from a programmatic arrangement of

the history of philosophy in cosmopolitan categories of 'European culture'. . . . Such a conception of 'Aryan' or 'Christian' philosophy was in fact one of the manifestations of the contempt disseminated by the bourgeoisie of the metropolitan countries towards the colonial and oppressed nations. . . ."

In a more recent essay, "Jesus Christ, Prophet and Reformer", Kolakowski analysed the values "that, thanks to the teaching of Jesus, permanently entered the spiritual substance of Europe, and of the world". These reflections on the subject are very different in tone from his early ones.

"One can, justly, find similar points in the religions of Asia. However, in the circle of the Mediterranean culture, to which we belong by birth, these values are connected with the teachings of Jesus and with his name. It is the spiritual supply which he introduced and to which he gave an impetus. Hence, any attempt to 'invalidate Jesus', to eliminate him from our culture on the basis that we don't believe in the God in which he believed, is ridiculous and fruitless. Such an attempt is the deed only of unenlightened people who imagine that a crudely formulated atheism can suffice as the view of the world and can also justify someone's curtailing the cultural tradition according to his own doctrinaire plan and by that taking away from it the most vital saps."[10]

KOLAKOWSKI'S social philosophy has also undergone a perceptible evolution since his "revisionist" phase. When he was not in a position to discuss explicitly contemporary cultural, social, and political problems, there were direct indications of his attitudes and reflections which have contemporary relevance.

It is difficult not to detect contemporary undertones in his historical studies in which he is preoccupied with such problems as the relation between beliefs and organization, the evolution of ideologies, and the role of myths. In his major work, *Religious Consciousness and the Church Affiliation* (Warsaw, 1965),[11] which is a study of the fate of the (mainly) Dutch sects in the 17th century, Kolakowski comes to some pessimistic conclusions about the chances of resuscitation of the true faith by the fundamentalists who inevitably must face its corruption in any organized community of believers.

"Historically, the attempts to create a non-denominational Christianity appear to us as purely negative phenomena. Their existence can only be perceived in relation to the organized religion against which they rose. They cannot basically transform the collective and hierarchical forms

[10] *Argumenty* (December 1965), published in English translation in *Tri-Quarterly* (No. 1, Spring 1967).
[11] French edition: *Chrétiens sans Église* (Gallimard, 1969).

of religious life in line with their own ideas, which would signify (and, in some cases, does in fact signify) the adoption of a realistic, rational structure denying the very premise of their protest. Consequently, the non-denominational Christians are at best able to create inside (or parallel to) the church communities, pressure groups which force their opponents to assimilate some of their ideas in an emasculated form, leading to some modification of organized religion. Non-denominational Christianity, to the extent that it means anything in social life, was a negative force influencing the integration of positive Christianity. But it had no real power to disintegrate the Churches.

Favourable circumstances can shake it into an effective reform movement. But it can take social root only if it accepts the principle of organization, that is if it denies its principles. . . .''

Kolakowski's main concern in this book was "unsuccessful radicalism". He noticed the repeated failures of religious radicals to arrive at an "authenticated" and "cleaned-up" faith, and traced the destinies of their activities against the "betrayal" of religions by the Church. He describes the ideas of one such heretical thinker, Dirk Rafaelszoon Camphuysen, in a way which inevitably brings to mind his own predicament.

"The thought of Camphuysen is the thought of Erasmus after a century of disappointments. . . .''

There is a melancholy reflection and a warning, both of contemporary significance, in Kolakowski's essay on Erasmus.[12]

"The Catholic Counter-Reformation, directed in the same measure against the great reform and against the Erasmian humanism, was successful only because it had assimilated the slogans of its critics, thus neutralising their anti-Church consequences.

The reform aimed practically at the institution of the Church was transformed in this way into an internal reform, to a great extent a verbal one, and thus it rendered harmless the subversive slogans, assimilating them without any detriment to the institution. . . .

The old subversive slogans became inoffensive truisms. In the history of the Church this method proved to be the most effective in dealing with criticism. It consisted of taking over the criticism and its reduction to banality—emasculation through assimilation. This explains also why the reformist slogans which have a slender chance of immediate realisation, cannot be formulated once and for all, but need a constant recreation in new versions, if they are not going to rot in the antique

---

[12] "On the Defeats of the Religious Reformers", in *Notaki o Wspolczesnej Kontrreformacji* (Warsaw, 1962).

shop of trivialities, to be accepted by all, but to have no practical consequences. . . ."

This *cri de cœur* is particularly poignant when one remembers Kolakowski's own fate.

He is a rationalist who knows the limitations of pure reason and realizes the importance of practical reason. He accepted the Marxist tradition, but rejected its teleology (despite some residual faith in the Hegelian "cunning of reason" in history). He not only disregards the Leninist critique of "fideism" in philosophy but postulates an act of faith as a necessary precondition of historical thinking. He destroys contemporary myths, while realizing the role of myths in history. He is positivistic in his methods of analysis, but rejects the identification of scientific and philosophical goals.

Man is the centre of his philosophical concern, but he makes metaphysics the basis of his ethics, although he does not accept religious assumptions for his metaphysical beliefs. He makes "anthropological realism" his philosophical platform, yet considers that "infinity is the only fatherland of man".

He is a truly tragic philosopher who does not however surrender to despair. He is in the line of Stoic philosophers and, like Seneca and Spinoza, embodies their honourable tradition.

(1969)

DoB. 26/6/ 1903 D. 21/Jan 1950
INDIA.

8. Will George Orwell Survive 1984?

"When you lie, it's much to know you're lying."
George Orwell

"It is a most encouraging thing to hear a human voice when fifty thousand gramophones are playing the same tune."
George Orwell

"How fascinating to live long enough to meet one's own world as history, and find it barely recognisable!"
Malcolm Muggeridge

ORWELLIAN orgy . . . Orwellian overkill . . . the tedium of 1984"—these are just a few descriptions of the extraordinary explosion of articles, reports, plays, conferences and books on the occasion of the advent of the Orwellian year. As Paul Johnson put it in *The Spectator* (7 January 1984):

> "The excesses of the Orwell industry became a kind of Orwellian nightmare in themselves. Big Brother, in the shape of Big Crick and other senior entrepreneurs in the industry, filled our TV screens, dominated the radio waves and overflowed the newspaper columns. . . . The Orwell industry will end by destroying Orwell's work. He has already been turned upside down and stood, as it were, on his short-back-and-sides head."

Orwell fever isn't always Big Business; sometimes it is cottage industry. The following small financial note appeared in the *Daily Telegraph* (16 November 1983):

> "Six weeks to 1984, George Orwell's definitive biographer Prof. Crick yesterday predicted a solid 12 months of commercialization, on a scale approaching that of *Star Wars*.
> Everything from T-shirts to popcorn and stuffed toys, are dreaded by Crick, who tells me *1984* fever is sweeping the world 'like the black plague'.
> Crick, however, is not allowing the Orwellian bandwagon to pass him by: 'to rip off the Yanks—or rather provide something responsible for the Americans',—he is staging a five day 'George Orwell Summer School' in London at up to £180 a ticket. Included is a curious music hall show at the Players Theatre of songs 'mentioned in Orwell's work'.
> This follows a tour of 20 *1984* conferences in America, starting in January, where I trust Crick's hosts will be more receptive than those in Brussels last weekend, *Les Amis de Science Fiction et Fantasie*. He tells me

few of the 'freaks' turned up because they considered *1984* neither fiction nor fantasy."

Reading the unending stream of commentaries on Orwell and "his" year, it is indeed obvious that, more often than not, he has been misunderstood and generally trivialized, and his insights wilfully distorted. Irving Kristol rightly remarked in *The Wall Street Journal* (19 December 1983) that

"George Orwell must be slowly spinning in his grave. Throughout the Western world a substantial segment of the media and academia is gearing to 'appreciate' his ideas in ways that would have confirmed his worst apprehensions."

What happened to Orwell can be precisely described as the application to himself of the mechanism of Orwellian inversion of meaning. Like Winston Smith, he became its innocent victim. More than that: not only have his perceptions been corrupted and perverted, but he has been adopted by some of the very people whose mentality and attitudes he despised most.

How did this operation, this Orwellian lobotomy on Orwell, come about? Once upon a time (i.e. when Orwell was still alive) things were "normal". Orwell, democrat and libertarian, would criticize communism and the "progressive" intelligentsia. *The Daily Worker* would castigate him as a reactionary servant of imperialism, as its "running dog". The fellow-travellers considered him unclean. The editor of the *New Statesman*, Kingsley Martin, disapproved of him, and Orwell in turn despised Kingsley Martin.

"Once when he and I were lunching at a favourite Greek restaurant of his in Percy Street [Malcolm Muggeridge recalls], suddenly out of the blue he asked me to change places with him, which I of course agreed to do. He explained that the reason he wanted to change places was that from where he had been sitting, he found himself looking straight at Kingsley Martin lunching at a nearby table. The spectacle of so corrupt a face, he said, would assuredly spoil his luncheon. . . ."

(*Sunday Telegraph*, 18 December 1983)

As for attitudes to Orwell, they were clear-cut: from the Stalinist *Pravda* which described him as "a lackey of the bourgeoisie", to the "anti-Stalinist" Isaac Deutscher who described Orwell as a "fanatic" sowing the seeds of McCarthyism, and *1984* as the "ideological super-weapon in the Cold War".

With the passing of time things became more complicated. The "era of the Cult of Personality" (an Orwellism if ever there was one) was denounced by Khrushchev, causing disarray among Western pro-Soviet men of the Left. While Stalin's victims were being "rehabilitated" in the Soviet Union (in an Orwellian way), Orwell, by then long since dead, was beginning to be "reassessed" by "progressives". Their appropriation and expropriation of

Orwell began. He was by now already being called "a great teacher" in the *New Statesman* itself.

It seemed to presage a great puzzlement, and at that time (in *Survey*, October 1968) I referred to the "Orwellization" of Orwell:

"How would George Orwell regard the general consensus which his writings evoke today? What would he think about some of his recent admirers? How would he view the present scene if he were alive?

There is no doubt, as *Time* magazine pointed out, that 'today he would be equally unpopular'. In his time he was made into a political pariah by the 'progressive' *bien-pensants* for his lucid exposition of their cant and their 'smelly little orthodoxies'. Now, reading the reviews of *The Collected Essays, Journalism and Letters of George Orwell* makes one realize that, like so many others before him, he is safely on the way to emasculation through canonization (the actual ceremony will take place in 1984). Particularly striking is the change in the ostensible attitude towards him of the same 'progressive' *bien-pensants* whose type of mentality he despised most and who displayed such marked antipathy towards him in the past. They snubbed him then, they embrace him now.

In fact, to entertain the idea that Orwell would have been pleased with the 'progressive' intelligentsia of today would require a double 'doublethink'. The elderly subjects of Orwell's scorn are still with us: his unmasking of the humbug of the pacifist and fellow-travelling Old Left has not prevented the passing-on of some of its mental attitudes to the younger generation. Its shibboleths and pieties have crept into the spirit of the age. One has only to contrast the refreshing, cant-proof individual style of Orwell with the thoughtless imitativeness, the sanctimonious 'revolutionary' clichés, and the stereotyped 'non-conformism' of the New Left.

Twenty-eight years ago [in 1940] Orwell wrote: 'The thing that frightens me about the modern intelligentsia is their inability to see that human society must be based on common decency, whatever the political and economic forms may be.' . . . In 1948 he wrote in his essay *Writers and Leviathan*: 'Obviously, for about fifteen years past, the dominant orthodoxy, especially among the young, has been Left. The key words are: progressive, democratic and revolutionary, while the labels which you must at all costs avoid having gummed upon you are bourgeois, reactionary and Fascist.' . . ."

What has changed? How, and why?

1. The Case of Raymond Williams, or
Going Doublethink One Better

IN THE 1970s the "recovery" of Orwell by the "progressives" advanced substantially. Raymond Williams published a book on Orwell in the Fontana *Modern Masters* series (1970) in which he "reinterpreted" Orwell in a way which actually made him a precursor of the New Left. This ideological surgery was performed by using very selective quotations and leaving aside what was obviously essential in the evolution of Orwell's thought.

According to Raymond Williams, Orwell's "anticipations of *1984* are primarily responses to fascism". He contends that "long after his controversies with what he saw as the official lying of the Communist press, it was still fascism that he saw as the totalitarian danger. . . ." The sophistry of this "reinterpretation" consists in avoiding Orwell's preoccupation with the concept of totalitarianism which led him (unlike Raymond Williams) to see not only the historical differences between Nazism and Communism, but also the real similarities between the two. Williams' pious diagnosis of Orwell as "a complex man" even manages to exclude some of his most characteristic concerns—for example the tendency of the "progressive" intelligentsia to be single-minded while holding fast to incompatible ideas; to doublethink. This, of course, is more than understandable since Raymond Williams belongs to the species himself.

On one split level of thought Raymond Williams must know perfectly well that after the defeat of the Axis powers in 1945 it was *not* "still fascism that [Orwell] saw as a totalitarian danger", but communism, and that the novel *1984* is *not* "primarily a response to fascism". Elsewhere in his book, he says so himself; but evidently he has a deep need to explain away the main thrust of *Animal Farm* and of *1984*. He attempts to dilute Orwell's concern with communism and criticizes him at the same time for "cutting out the spring of hope" by creating in the novel "the conditions for defeat and despair . . . the revival of the Socialist movement, which [Orwell] said he wanted, is met by the sad ghost of his late imagination". At one point Williams admits that "in understanding his last work . . . the key element . . . was the substitution of Communism for Fascism as the totalitarian threat", and thus explicitly contradicts himself.

He even concedes that "there is a clear line, certainly, from Orwell's *Inside the Whale* and *Nineteen Eighty-Four* to an orthodox North Atlantic mood"; but he also confers "Orwell's effective inheritance" on the New Left which "respected Orwell directly, especially in its early years". What happened, then, in later years? Down the memory hole?

Williams points out Orwell's contradictions, but why does he curiously refuse to look at "these different tendencies" as part of Orwell's political evolution? He admits that "there are phases of Orwell's development"—but this obvious observation is given a very special twist:

> "Evidence for each of the positions can be drawn from each of the periods, though of course with differences of emphasis."

This turns into a remarkable exercise in sophistry in which one stresses only what it is convenient to emphasize. In order to protect the faith from doubts and doubters, Williams looks at Orwell not as shedding various illusions over time, but as maintaining contradictory positions, only "with differences of emphasis".

Thus, even before the likeness of Orwell was officially made into a wax figure in Madame Tussaud's gallery, Williams exhibits him as being permanently fixed in a state of doublethink ("the power of holding two contradictory beliefs in one's mind simultaneously, and accepting both of them"). This ideological "one-upmanship", amounting to "treblethink", is given a spurious air of ideological detachment:

> "It would be easy but pointless to start a quarrel over Orwell's inheritance: body snatching or mantle snatching. . . . Instead of flattening out contradictions by choosing this or that tendency as the 'real Orwell', or fragmenting them by separating this or that period or this or that genre, we ought to say that it is the paradoxes which are finally significant."

One can almost sympathize with Raymond Williams' difficulty. Unlike him, Orwell was not "a true believer"; he had the audacity to learn from experience. His intellectual history is the history of his gradual emancipation from the fog of "progressive" attitudes and stereotypes, although he died before he had quite shed them all.

O RWELL was never a Communist, but his evolution was not dissimilar to that of the prominent ex-Communists of the era: Boris Souvarine, Ignazio Silone, Franz Borkenau, Manès Sperber, Arthur Koestler, Bertram D. Wolfe. In his short life he moved from the mental horizons of a Kingsley Martin *milieu* to the intellectual world of a Koestler (who was similarly ostracized by "progressive" circles).

Williams regrets that "in [Orwell's] criticism of people who went on holding or who came to hold positions identical or close to his own between 1937 and 1939, there is some lively polemic, but also a good deal of rancour or random abuse". He does not seem to want to understand the basic reason why Orwell, having gone through the "lively" ideological historical experience of the late 1930s, abandoned these positions, and nowhere does he quote or refer to a basic conclusion of "the real Orwell":

"The sin of nearly all left-wingers from 1933 onward is that they have wanted to be anti-fascist without being anti-totalitarian."

For the lesson Orwell learned on his return from Catalonia was that defence of political liberties had to be consistent, alert to tyrannous militant tendencies on both Left and Right; that freedom was indivisible; and that false friends behind the lines could purge you as quickly as open enemies on the front.

Orwell was a left-winger, but he always resolutely rejected communism and I have little doubt that, were he alive, he would be branded today as "a vulgar anti-Communist" and, even worse, "a cold warrior". His political opposition to communism was firmly based on ethical grounds: he insisted that "all the people who are morally sound have known since about 1931 that the Russian régime stinks". Intellectually, communism was for him "a form of Socialism that makes mental honesty impossible".

He made his position particularly clear in his attack on W. H. Auden's notorious notion of "the necessary murder" (in *Inside the Whale*, 1940):

"Personally I would not speak so lightly of murder. It so happens that I have seen the bodies of numbers of murdered men—I don't mean killed in battle, I mean murdered. Therefore I have some conception of what murder means—the terror, the hatred, the howling relatives, the post-mortems, the blood, the smells. To me, murder is something to be avoided. So it is to any ordinary person. The Hitlers and Stalins find murder necessary, but they don't advertise their callousness, and they don't speak of it as murder; it is 'liquidation', 'elimination' or some such soothing phrase. . . . The huge tribe known as 'the right Left people' found it easy to condone the purge-and-*OGPU* side of the Russian régime and the horrors of the first Five-Year Plan."

Intellectually, Orwell was no less emphatic in his condemnation of Communist practices and of those who justify them:

"Fifteen years ago, when one defended the freedom of the intellect, one had to defend it against Conservatives, against Catholics, and to some extent—for they were not of great importance in England—against Fascists. Today one has to defend it against Communists and 'fellow-travellers'. One ought not to exaggerate the direct influence of the small English Communist Party, but there can be no question about the poisonous effect of the Russian *mythos* on English intellectual life. Because of it, known facts are suppressed and distorted to such an extent as to make it doubtful whether a true history of our times can ever be written.

Let me give just one instance out of the hundreds that could be cited. When Germany collapsed, it was found that very large numbers of

THEIR

Soviet Russians—mostly, no doubt, from non-political motives—had changed sides and were fighting for the Germans. Also, a small but not negligible proportion of the Russian prisoners and Displaced Persons refused to go back to the U.S.S.R., and some of them, at least, were repatriated against her will. These facts, known to many journalists on the spot, went almost unmentioned in the British press, while at the same time russophile publicists in England continued to justify the purges and deportation of 1936–8 by claiming that the U.S.S.R. 'had no quislings'. The fog of lies and misinformation that surrounds such subjects as the Ukraine famine, the Spanish Civil War, Russian policy in Poland, and so forth, is not due entirely to conscious dishonesty, but any writer or journalist who is fully sympathetic to the U.S.S.R.— sympathetic, that is, in the way the Russians themselves would want him to be—does have to acquiesce in deliberate falsification on important issues. . . ." (*Collected Essays*, Vol. 4, pp. 84–85)

2. Orwell and the "right Left people"

NOT THAT George Orwell was always that consistent. But, unlike other men of the Left, his intellectual integrity impelled him not to indulge in tortuous rationalizations, to face refractory realities, to call a spade a spade, rather than engage in the usual face- and faith-saving euphemisms and semantic acrobatics. In the process, "the crystal spirit" which Orwell invoked early on (in a short poem written in 1939) clarified his own mind and those of many other people. Inevitably, this entailed eliminating various contradictory beliefs of his own. Between 1937 and 1939 Orwell was, no doubt about it, involved in a bit of "doublethink" himself.

The best example is perhaps his attitude in the late 1930s to the international question of War and Foreign Policy. In the period between his return from Spain and the outbreak of the Second World War, Orwell belonged to both the pacifist Peace Pledge Union and the ILP (the splintered Independent Labour Party) which advocated "a revolutionary war". At a time when the official Labour Party was advocating "resistance to the dictators" but opposing rearmament, he expressed the following ideas:

31 July 1937: "It is evident that people can be deceived by the anti-Fascist stuff exactly as they were deceived by the gallant little Belgium stuff, and when war comes they will walk straight into it. I don't, however, agree with the pacifist attitude. . . . I still think that one must fight Socialism against Fascism. I mean fight physically with weapons. . . ."

28 August 1937: "War against a foreign country only happens when the moneyed classes think they are going to profit from it. . . . Every war when it comes, or before it comes, is represented not as war but as an act of self-defence against a homicidal maniac ('militarist' Germany in 1914, 'Fascist' Germany next year or the year after). The essential job is to get people to recognise war propaganda when they see it, especially when it is disguised as peace propaganda."

15 September 1937: "Everyone with any imagination can forsee that Fascism, not of course called Fascism, will be imposed on us as soon as the war starts. . . . If one collaborates with a capitalist-imperialist government in a struggle 'against Fascism', i.e. against rival imperialism, one is simply letting Fascism in by the back door."

5 February 1938: "If someone drops a bomb on your mother, go and drop two bombs on his mother. The only apparant alternatives are to smash dwelling houses to powder, blow out human entrails and burn holes in children with lumps of thermite, or to be enslaved by people who are oddly more ready to do these things than you are yourself; as yet no one has suggested a practicable way out."

26 May 1938: "Pacifism is so far from being fashionable, or acceptable to the possessing class, that all the big daily newspapers unite to boycott all news of pacifist activities. . . . Meanwhile there is considerable possibility of producing an effective anti-war movement in England. It is a question of mobilizing the dislike of war that undoubtedly exists in ordinary decent people, as opposed to the hack journalist and the pansy left."

12 October 1938: "The policy of simultaneously shouting for a war policy and pretending to denounce conscription, rearmament etc. is utter nonsense and the general public aren't such bloody fools as not to see it."

4 January 1939: ". . . that Britain and France ought to have gone to war [to defend the Czechs] . . . I don't believe to be true."

ONCE THE WAR started, however, Orwell cleared his mind.

10 January 1940: "It seems to me that now we are in this bloody war we have got to win it and I would like to lend a hand."

8 June 1940: "Since 1934 I have known war between England and Germany was coming, and since 1936 I have known it with complete certainty. I could feel it in my belly, and the chatter of the pacifists on the one hand and of the Popular Front people who pretended to fear that Britain was preparing for war against Russia on the other, never deceived me."

12 July 1942: "In so far as it takes effect at all, pacifist propaganda can only be effective *against* those countries where a certain amount of freedom of speech is still permitted; in other words it is helpful to totalitarianism. . . . Despotic governments can stand 'moral force' till the cows come home; what they fear is physical force."

This is not exactly a tale full of consistency. But is shows Orwell's characteristic evolution. His common sense told him, increasingly, as his subsequent positions demonstrated, to abandon confused ideological clichés cherished by the Left and make responsible choices by looking steadily at realities in the light of experience.

THE PATH Orwell traversed can be gauged by one dramatic comparison. Here is what he said in his article "Why I Joined the Independent Labour Party", in *The New Leader* (24 June 1938):

> "We know the terrible temptation of the present moment—the temptation to fling every principle overboard in order to prepare for an imperialist war. . . . I believe that the ILP is the only party which, as a party, is likely to take the right line against imperialist war or against Fascism when this appears in its British form . . . the only party I could join with at least the certainty that I would never be led up the garden path in the name of capitalist democracy."

And here is what Orwell said in his "Notes on Nationalism" (*Polemic*, No. 1, October 1945):

> "There is a minority of intellectual pacifists whose real though unadmitted motive appears to be hatred of western democracy and admiration for totalitarianism. Pacifist propaganda usually boils down to saying that one side is as bad as the other, but if one looks closely at the writings of the younger intellectual pacifists, one finds that they do not by any means express impartial disapproval but are directed almost entirely against Britain and the United States. Moreover they do not as a rule condemn violence as such, but only violence used in the defence of the Western countries. The Russians, unlike the British, are not blamed for defending themselves by warlike means. . . ."

It is not surprising that Raymond Williams does not dwell on such points; but fudging them is not always possible. The deep, ill-concealed hostility to "the real Orwell" often surfaces in ideological censure. Having earlier praised Orwell as "a generous, inquiring, truthful man", Williams then charges him with having made "an accommodation to capitalism"; and wearily concludes that "the thing to do with his work, his history, is to read it, not imitate it".

In an additional chapter, "*Nineteen Eighty-Four* in 1984", recently written for the new edition of his book (1984), Williams condemned what he calls "the use and abuse of the novel during the cold war". He also reproached Orwell for the "error" of excluding from the novel "the national liberation and revolutionary movements of what he knew as the colonial world". In his article in the Communist *Morning Star* (3 January 1984)[1] he made his point even more explicit, arguing in tortuous prose that the fact that Orwell's vision

> "has been at least partly verified . . . including within Socialism and the labour movement, cannot outweigh the more important cancellation of all significant political struggles and hopes.
>
> But this was the cancellation that was steadily worked for, in the period from the Cold War—the (Communist) God that failed—through the propagation of the End of Ideology to the so-called New Philosophers who see the struggle for freedom as opening the door to tyranny."

It is not difficult to see the cat slipping out of the bag. Williams' attitude here is, unmistakably, the very opposite of Orwell's. Sidney Hook once wrote ironically about people "who always tried to keep in delicate balance their appreciation of both totalitarianism and democracy". Williams clearly tips even this "delicate balance". But after all, he comes to praise Orwell, not to bury him.

In his book Williams displays a kind of fearful symmetrism, so characteristic of the "progressive" intelligentsia.[2] Almost all his examples of Orwellisms, from "doublethink" through "*Newspeak*" to "the memory hole", refer to what he sees as their manifestations in the West, while references to Soviet and Communist practices are shrouded in "delicate" obfuscation. The crime of the Western "oligarchy" resides in

> "identifying as public enemies, in its newspapers, dissenting political figures: not the 'proper official Opposition', but the 'unofficial' Reds, Wreckers, Extremists who in good *1984* style are seen as either mad or guilty of 'thoughtcrime'. . . . "

By contrast, Williams' comments on Communist practices are full of polite, cautious restraint. He writes about "socialist order which under long historical pressures had become authoritarian". He magnanimously admits—*quelle finesse de sentiments!*—that "reservations could be made about the nature of Soviet communism", but refers to its all-embracing falsehoods as "official simplifications". He sedulously avoids mentioning the crimes: the omnipresent systematic lying from the Moscow Trials to the nasty little war in Afghanistan; the Gulag slave-labour camps, the psychiatric prisons; the

---

[1] Excerpts from Raymond Williams' chapter on "*Nineteen Eighty-Four* in 1984" appeared simultaneously in the "Euro-Communist" *Marxism Today* (January 1984), which is at loggerheads with the pro-Soviet *Morning Star*.

[2] Koestler described this form of *trahison des clercs* as follows:

> "It showed a forgiving attitude towards totalitarian terror, but denounced with unforgiving venom any failing or injustice in the West." (*The Yogi and the Commisar*, 1945.)

persecution of writers, artists, religious and national minorities; the subjection of countries to satellite status; the ugly militarization of society combined with hypocritical "peace" propaganda; and all the rest of the temporary deviations from shining ideals for the radiant future. His rare references to such unpleasantnesses are indirect and euphemistic: he certainly is no follower of unflinching Orwellian realism when it comes to *Soviet affairs*.[3] The net result is a complete travesty of Orwell in this pathetic attempt at "reinterpretation".

3. Emasculation through Canonization

ALTHOUGH the "official" biography of Orwell by Bernard Crick (Secker & Warburg 1980)[4] does not suffer from the same excesses as the Williams book, it has also contributed to the misinterpretation of Orwell and to his false "new image".

It is certainly a more solid and professional piece of work; but Crick's "progressive" mentality is so different from Orwell's that he had somehow to rationalize the divergence of his attitudes from those of his subject, who was the scourge of the *bien-pensants* of his day. He accordingly invented the concept of "empathetic fallacy" in order to refashion his "hero". The end result is rather more subtle than in the case of Williams' "reinterpretation", but is none the less problematical. Edward Crankshaw rightly pointed out in his *Times Literary Supplement* review (26 December 1980) that while Orwell's life history is conscientiously recorded and extolled, Crick's Orwell is devoid of all his essential human characteristics.

> "Because Professor Crick is so bent on avoiding what he calls the 'empathetic fallacy', he has devised a method of exposition, a sort of laboratory demonstrator's method, unfit for application to any organism more complex than a newt. . . . There is no shape, no light, no shade. . . . Above all what is lacking from beginning to end of this book is life and warmth."

---

[3] Without invoking the "economic interpretation", one might say that Williams has invested too much in Utopia to be able to renounce it emotionally after its bankruptcy has become intellectually obvious. As the reviewer of his latest book, *Towards 2000* (1983), remarked in the *London Review of Books* (2–15 February 1984): "Williams does not know where to stand: the book is the tragedy of a man who can't any longer make up his mind."

[4] Bernard Crick expressed his thanks to "the late Mrs Sonia Orwell who in 1972 granted me unrestricted access to all of George Orwell's papers", but he stressed that "in no sense is this an official biography". What he did not mention in his "Acknowledgements" was the fact—revealed by Julian Symons—that, having invited Bernard Crick to write Orwell's biography, Sonia Orwell (for reasons which are not made explicit) "later tried vainly to retract" the invitation (*Times Literary Supplement*, 27 January 1984). Afterwards Crick disclosed that Sonia Orwell was "breathing down my neck with a deadline on a contract which would have removed my absolute right to quote and say what I pleased—a deadline that by the end she was hoping, almost predictably, I would not meet" (*Times Higher Education Supplement*, 20 April 1984).

Still, many reviewers "approved" the biography, and not a few were highly complimentary.[5] The book certainly helped to prepare the ground for subsequent attempts at the "Orwellization" of Orwell.

It was when 1984 itself was approaching that the "emasculation through canonization" of Orwell finally occurred. This is not, of course, to say that there weren't many highly perceptive and intelligent articles and essays on Orwell, but many were so thoroughly misconceived that the public was left with an even greater disorientation than before. Or, as General Jaruzelski's *Trybuna Ludu* (28–29 January 1984) put it:

> "For over 30 years the anti-Communist propagandists tried in every way to identify Orwell's novel (*1984*) with the reality of the USSR and other socialist countries. Today, however, this is not so easy for them as at the height of the cold war. In 1984 the arch-conservative politicians, the spokesmen of Big Capital and the anti-Communist crusaders in the USA have to conduct polemics with the opinions of other well-known Americans—the activists for Human Rights, Racial Equality, and Peace who are comparing the realities of the United States with the Orwellian vision of '*Big Brother is Watching You*'. Similar voices were widespread in West Germany, Great Britain, and the Scandinavian countries."

If one disregards the Orwellian character of this passage, its second part refers to something that has actually happened, and indeed reached an astonishing degree of intensity. The "widespread voices" not only confused the great issues and Orwell's attitude to them, their scale and persistence testified to a serious decline of common sense and sense of proportion in the West. They ranged from muddled assertions that 1984 was aimed both at the (totalitarian) East and at the (democratic) West to the brazen relocation of Orwell's target: not the USSR but the USA. The spectrum of this "reinterpretation" of Orwell ranged from, say, the minimum of $2 + 2 = 4\frac{1}{2}$ to the maximum of $2 + 2 = 5$. The final—lunatic—touch to this Pirandellesque situation was the triumphal reclamation of Orwell by the Soviet press.

AMERICAN WRITERS were not without their own surrealistic touches. In the US symposium *1984 Revised* (edited by Irving Howe), Marc Crispin Miller proclaimed that "we should not read *1984* as a bitter allegory on the evils of Stalinism", since the novel is really concerned with the horrors of Consumer Society:

> "Under the influence of television, the consumer is intended to end up

---

[5] Julian Symons even called it (in the *Sunday Times*, 23 November 1980) "the definitive biography", which it most definitely is not. Nigel Dennis was more discerning (in the *Sunday Telegraph*, 23 November 1980): "Orwell asked that no biography be written of him—an impossible request, considering the importance of his life. But he may have envisaged falling into the hands of a writer like Professor Crick . . . a fate worse than death."

gasping wide-eyed and open-mouthed at his advertising supplements and video-screens, turned just as infantile as those Party members at the end of the Two Minutes of Hate, with their 'deep, slow, rhythmical chant of B-B! . . . B-B! . . . B-B! . . .'"

Another contributor to Professor Howe's symposium, Bernard Avishai, produced a no less profound reflection:

"Who can read Orwell's account of Oceania's violent and pornographic telecasts without thinking about American crime shows, the soaps, the Big Events and the commercials that interrupt them?"

In his special two-hour TV programme on *1984* (also shown on BBC 1), Walter Cronkite, the famous American newscaster, did not even mention the phenomenon of communism. Instead, he used the internment of the American Japanese during the Second World War as an example of government by "Big Brother". Like so many others, he presented *1984* today as a problem of the threat to freedom by technology—computers, lie-detectors, and all that—as if Orwell was concerned with inanimate robots in a science fiction and not with flesh-and-bone villains wielding totalitarian power. For Orwell the problem was the technology of power rather than the power of technology.

This dehydrated view of politics—it is, naturally, the favourite of the popular press and media, so drawn to the "telescreen"—could not be further from Orwell's view. He knew that it is people who move machines, not the other way round; and he saw the threat not in the wickedness of robots, those bloodless technical vampires, but primarily in the danger of political totalitarianism to the individual and to civil society. Big Brother is not a Dalek and *1984* is not a science-fiction.

There was little in Orwell's early background (Eton, the Raj in Burma, down-and-out in Paris) to provide him with a key to the understanding of totalitarianism, but anybody with personal experience of it is amazed by his uncanny intuitive powers. Contemporary writings, those of Franz Borkenau and others, helped intellectually; but imaginatively he understood the wider picture from being acquainted with British "progressives" (and their "doublethink") and with the Communist terror in Catalonia. His personal familiarity with "censorship in Britain"—so often invoked to distort and blur his message by suggesting that his discomfiting BBC and published experiences were somehow relevant to his *1984* vision—nearly always involved his anti-communist writings, whether he was censored "from below" (Kingsley Martin, Victor Gollancz, T. S. Eliot) or "from above" (in the "Good Uncle Joe" period during the Second World War). To pretend that Orwell's message is not basically rooted in his revulsion against communist and pro-communist practices is to shred the evidence and doctor the tapes. He repeatedly complained about being hampered by editors and publishers, referring to "the kind of censorship under which we are now suffering and of which the Left Book Club is a symptom".

Erich Fromm, in his preface to the 1961 New American Library edition of *1984*, declared that "it would be most unfortunate if the reader smugly interpreted *1984* as another description of Stalinist barbarism, and if he does not see that it means us, too". (Walter Cronkite's "*Afterword*" to the 1983 edition repeats this theme.)

I N HIS BIOGRAPHY Bernard Crick rejected what he severely called "the *Encounter* view of Orwell"[6] and those critics who "saw the satire as applicable only to the Soviets, and their sympathizers, and not also to the Western way of life". With the Orwellian year looming ahead, Crick tried to deflate with pinprick after penprick all who did not share this view. In particular, he criticized Conor Cruise O'Brien for saying (in *The Observer*, 18 December 1983) that *1984*

> ". . . is about . . . something which can only be Communism as it developed in the Soviet Union. . . . Where, as often, a parallel with a particular system suggests itself, it is always a parallel with the Soviet system, under Stalin. Big Brother's familiar style . . . is Stalin's unmistakable style . . . The Party is a Communist party, not a Nazi one. . . . The forced labour camps described are of Communist, not Nazi type. And so on, it is all of a piece. The brilliant inventions of *Newspeak* and *Doublethink* are Orwellian extrapolations of Soviet practice, not of any other."

When Conor Cruise O'Brien, referring to Crick's assertions, ironically exclaimed that "If *1984* is even partially any kind of satire on our Western way of life, I'm a Chinaman", Crick replied (*Financial Times*, 31 December 1983):

> "O'Brien is a Chinaman. His anti-Communism is myopic (therefore not likely to be effective). . . . To deny that [*1984*] satirizes ourselves as well as the Russians is simply to distance it, to see only the mote in the other's eye and not the beam in our own. Orwell was expert in seeing double."

Crick is obviously not very expert in seeing single. Unable to provide a

---

[6] Among the critics who published articles on Orwell in *Encounter* were Rayner Heppenstall ("A Blurred Portrait", February–March 1981); Dennis J. O'Keefe and James McNamara ("Waiting for 1984", December 1982); and John Wain ("Orwell & the Intelligentsia" and "Koestler & Orwell on the Totalitarian Mind", December 1968 and September–October 1983). In his Introduction (p. 107) to *1984* Bernard Crick actually refers quite favourably to John Wain's essay on Orwell, which suggests that his allegations about "the *Encounter* view of Orwell" are perhaps only *minitrue*. . . .

reasoned reply to O'Brien's point, he offered incoherent double-talk. The "progressive" intelligentsia which Orwell came to dispute still cannot live without their portion of "doublethink"; but why do they have to dabble in this particular subject, get excited about it, tie themselves into knots about it? Orwell obviously got under their skin, not just at the time but now and, perhaps, forever. With their symmetrism they still *prefer* to see "the beam" in our eyes rather than "the mote" in Soviet eyes.

Bernard Crick referred to O'Brien again, if in some hectic ethnic confusion, in an article in *Tribune* (6 January 1984):

> "If it was a satire of conditions in the West, [O'Brien] said, I'm a Dutchman. That explains a lot. But a bit much for everyone's favourite bull-in-a-china-shop to miss even the significance of Orwell giving Winston's Thought Police torturer the name of O'Brien."

The mind boggles. Is, then, O'Brien a Dutchman in a China shop or a Chinaman talking double-Dutch? Such careless shooting-from-the-hip is characteristic of Crick, and so, as Nigel Dennis (true enough, a former *Encounter* editor) noticed, is the quality of his style, puerility being its essential hallmark. The Crick biography of Orwell provides a number of examples of both.

Giving the impression that Orwell somehow became his personal property, and with single-minded obsessiveness, Crick was double-quick in accusing all and sundry— "the radical Right" in his *Tribune* article, *The Times* in his letter-to-the-editor (6 January 1983)—of "body-snatching" Orwell. In *The Financial Times* he wrote:

> "Body-snatchers from almost all points of the political compass descend on the long-dead Orwell: only the Communists remain consistent in rejecting him completely."

In this he could not be more mistaken.

As it happens, while Bernard Crick, Raymond Williams, and other Left forward-lookers were doing their best to "reinterpret" *1984* by refocusing its message, the Italian Communists were carrying out their own analogous operation on Orwell, published as a special supplement to *l'Unità* (18 December 1983). The leader of the PCI, the late Enrico Berlinguer, criticized Orwell's "false prophecies", and went on to reject firmly the idea that in *1984* "the great English humanist" intended to depict the USSR and Stalin. This was simply an invention of "cold warriors" who wanted to manipulate the novel for their own nefarious propaganda purposes (an argument not unfamiliar to the readers of Williams, Crick, and the British Communists).

4. Up from The Memory Hole

A LL THESE half-hearted "reinterpretations" pale into insignificance in comparison with the bold stroke performed by the Soviet press, which simply declared that *1984* is solely about . . . England and America.

This clearly put Moscow one up on the Western "progressives". Orwell, at first vilified and made into an "unperson", has now been uplifted from the "memory hole". His books have not, to be sure, been published in the Soviet Union, nor are copies of foreign editions allowed into the country. On the contrary, Soviet dissidents found in possession of *1984* (like Gunnars Astra and Valery Senderov in 1983) were sentenced to 12 years' "deprivation of liberty". (Senderov, who distributed it, even received an additional five years' imprisonment on the basis of a new law which allows the Gulag camp directors to extend sentences arbitrarily.) Yet in a peculiar way George Orwell has been, if not exactly "rehabilitated", at least resurrected or reclaimed.

Operation "Rehab" began last year when *Foreign Literature* and *Literaturnaya Gazeta* published the first Soviet articles to suggest that the novel actually pertains to the West. A number of other articles followed quickly (in *Komsomolskaya Pravda, Moscow News, Novoe Vremya*, and *Izvestiya*). The last two published very long texts with detailed argumentation about some aspects of the work.

According to *Novoe Vremya* (1 January 1984), Orwell recognized "the falsehoods of bourgeois democracy" which extinguishes and "vaporizes" the individual. The anti-Communists have been trying "to fit the tight suit of totalitarianism tailored by Orwell to the body of really existing socialism; but in fact it is just the right cut for capitalism. . . ." The author of the article, Victor Tsopi, argued that the book was quite misunderstood. It was intended only as an anticipation by Orwell of what lay ahead for the capitalist West:

> "This novel is a grim warning precisely to bourgeois society, bourgeois civilization, bourgeois democracy in which, as he feared, the poisonous roots of anti-humanism, all-devouring militarism and oppression have today thrust up truly monstrous shoots. . . ."

Tsopi stressed that Orwell had been a member of the militant ILP and had fought in Spain against Franco, thus intimating that he was a sympathetic "progressive" figure, although "it would be an exaggeration to suggest that he was a convinced adherent to the Communist outlook". Even so Orwell had correctly anticipated the rule of "Big Brother"—who is none other than Ronald Reagan applying Orwellian policies in the USA of 1984, to which *Moscow News* added with humour that "Reagan invests the slogan '*Ignorance is Strength*' with his own literal meaning". While *Komsomolskaya Pravda* noticed that Orwell's view of totalitarian controls "is actually in line with present-day Britain", *Izvestiya* (15 and 16 January) devoted two articles by its American correspondent Melor Sturua[7] to pointing out that they are no less applicable to present-day America:

> "Every year from 1949 to 1984 has shown, more and more palpably and persuasively, that Orwell, unintentionally and without being aware of it (though perhaps that is questionable), painted not a caricature of Socialism and Communism, but a fully realistic picture of contemporary Capitalism–Imperialism. The subject of Orwell's gloomy fantasy became the reality of the Western world, and primarily of the United States of America, which is a genuine and not an imaginary centre of evil in our time. . . ."

The cover of the New Year issue of the *New Statesman* (16–23 December 1983) carried the same inverted perception. It presented Orwell looking at a party in Room 101 where Margaret Thatcher stands with Ronald Reagan, the Queen, Michael Heseltine ("Ministry of Peace") and others, under the inscription "despite Everything Doubleplusgood 1984 to All Our Readers".

A word here, although there is very little new to say, about the *New Statesman*. Just as at the time of *Homage to Catalonia* (1938) the *Statesman* did not want to see Stalin for what he was, so in 1983–84 it did not want to see Andropov for what he was. Instead, with the usual ideological self-indulgence, it preferred to see Ronald Reagan (and Margaret Thatcher) as "Big Brother" (and "Big Sister"). The only difference is that now it does not censor the subject but puts Orwell on the front page.

The "progressive" mentality evidently changes precious little with the change of generations. The past is an unchanging scenario of progressive good opposed to reactionary evil, heroes of the future versus villains who are all yesterday's men. The real drama of the present, its new twists and tragic turns, leaves them unmoved. The Bourbons of the Left have learnt nothing since 1917, and appear to have forgotten everything between Chernavin ("I Speak for the Silent") and Chernenko (who silences those who speak). Why do they prefer to put a Khrushchev (with his *Secret Report*) or a Solzhenitsyn (with his *Gulag Archipelago*) at least half-way down the "memory hole"? What drives them to apply the same characteristic selective indignation and double standards to current East and West afflictions as they always did in the past? Is it so intellectually difficult, or ethically problematic, to establish as obvious that in 1984 Winston Smith would in the USSR be sent to a psychiatric prison or a labour camp for "slandering the Soviet state"—while in the USA he would be able to read and write as he pleased? I suspect he

---

[7] His first name, "Melor", is fashionably (lingering Bolshevik modishness) made up from the initials of Marx, Engels, Lenin, October Revolution.

would even be able to get hold of Emmanuel Goldstein's famous secret treatise about Oceania, with the support of the *Washington Post*, by invoking the US "Freedom of Information" Act.

Like the poor, will the *"progressives"* always be with us? Although the word has a special meaning in our time, historically, the concept derives from the 18th-century belief in inevitable amelioration which dominated the Western mind from Condorcet, Paine and Jefferson until the beginning of the 20th century, when J. B. Bury analysed "the idea of progress" in a book which became its epitaph. The First World War undermined the belief in history as an upward escalator, the Second gave it a *coup de grâce*. From then on the belief was retained only by those sects who were committed to the idea of "the historical inevitability of socialism". The horrors of the 20th century even led many socialists to abandon this deterministic version of their faith, but they continued to divide mankind into "progressives" on the Left and "reactionaries" on the Right.

The Communists have their own version of the concept. It covers the entire spectrum of their friends, ranging from ideological sympathizers to those whom Lenin called "deaf mutes" and who were later renamed "useful idiots". When Stalin was alive, he was always described as "the Leader of All Progressive Humanity". Once dead, he may have been pushed down a "memory hole", but in the Soviet vocabulary the word "progressive" continued to be used even more frequently. International usage increasingly resembled Soviet usage. I am using the word in the same sense in which the "progressives" use it, and to make this clear I apply inverted commas to it. (Raymond Aron used for the same purpose the French word *sinistrisme*.)

The Orwell celebrations provided many manifestations of the "progressives'" evergreen conventional wisdom. Perhaps the archetypal example is the much-decorated veteran of a thousand struggles between Progress and Reaction, James Cameron, who, writing in *The Guardian* (3 January 1984), proclaimed:

> "Let me denounce the year, the book, the image, the cliché 1984 . . . George Orwell was a great and good man, and also shrewd enough to die soon thereafter [i.e. after 1948], so that 1984 would haunt us, not him.
>
> I always thought that his prophesy was rather mild anyway. Big Brother was more daunting but less boring than Small Sister, and I believe I would rather be bullied by a brute than patronized by a prig."

Such perverse choices have a long history on the Left. Another worldly-wise "progressive", G. D. H. Cole (Bernard Crick depicts him as being in the same political lineage as Orwell), put it somewhat differently in 1942: "much better be ruled by Stalin than by a pack of half-witted and half-hearted Social Democrats. . . ."[8] He would prefer that, would he?

As Orwell said: "One has to belong to the intelligentsia to believe things like that, no ordinary man could be such a fool".

5. *Ex Oriente Lux*

W HO can be listened to on the subject today? Not the twisters who just can't bear to concede a point which Orwell himself insisted upon a dozen times; and certainly not the Soviet "Rehab" corps. I recommend the East European dissidents, the "Winston Smiths" who survived Stalin's brain washings and post-Stalin "rehabilitations", and who are talking to us with the chastened voice of historical experience. None of them is on record as preferring to be bullied by a brute than patronized by a prig. They know where Big Brother has his headquarters.

Thus the fate of Orwell's last book is perhaps best guaged by the juxtaposition of the reaction to it by "progressive" commentators in the West and by unofficial commentators in the East. Among those in the Communist countries who happen to have read it, it is difficult to find any who fail to be struck by its perceptiveness and its painful relevance to their own life. In Stalin's time, Czeslaw Milosz (the future Nobel Prize winner) wrote that Orwell's Party readers "are amazed that a writer who never lived in Russia should have so keen a perception of its life", an observation Crick himself quotes. This year, a Czech sociologist, Milan Simecka, writes in the Introduction to the *samizdat* edition of *1984*:

> "When I read the story of Winston Smith, I received a shock, because all of a sudden I realized that this was my own story I was reading. . . . Those living in Eastern Europe, and especially those who were born here and who have lived through all the 'victories' and defeats of real socialism, are struck, when reading *1984*, by many astounding similarities. . . . The similarity to our everyday life comes as a physical shock, neither pleasant nor amusing. The prophetic accuracy of the book arouses in us feelings that are difficult to describe . . . a numbing sense of *déjà vu*. . . . I have grown up in a world of forbidden books, a world of omnipresent indoctrination, where the past was being rewritten all the time. . . . Can you wonder, given all this, that Winston Smith came to seem to me like my own brother?"
> (*Index on Censorship*, February 1984)

It is not so difficult for Czechoslovaks to "imagine a boot stamping on a

---

[8] The Fabian Society pamphlet *100 years of Fabian Socialism, 1884–1984* (March 1984) has the following reference: "The Coles understood the danger of totalitarianism, kept clear of the Communist Party without ever being anti-Communist. . . ."

human face" after their experience between 1948 and 1984 and the military suppression of all hopes for "socialism with a human face".

IN POLAND during the *Solidarity* period (1980–81), an "underground" publisher (Miroslaw Chojecki, now an exile in Paris) organized—with official permission—a book exhibition in Warsaw which included "illegally" published works, and among them Orwell's *1984*. Since General Jaruzelski's *coup*, Polish underground publications again frequently refer to Orwell,[9] whose influence can also be seen in the fact that some of his phrases have found their way into everyday Polish language, just as they did into English. There is even a scholarly book, published in *samizdat* in 1982 (under the imprint of the University in Cracow), entitled *Newspeak* and devoted to the "Orwellization" of the Polish language. As the editors explain, the work is based on the proceedings of a scholarly conference held at the University in January 1981, when (as they say) "truth was being restored to words".

> "To the organizers of the conference the question of language seemed to be one of the most important elements in the social ferment, in the struggle to achieve a decent basis for our everyday life and a right to live in a reality which is not falsified and constantly redefined, in which language has been transformed into an instrument for enslavement instead of being an instrument serving human communication."

Adam Michnik took up the same theme:

> "I believe that a dispute about language has been the central element of Polish intellectual life for the last 35 years. It concerns our ability to defend reality and to communicate with each other. In that period a great many people have lost the ability to communicate because of the language foisted upon them."

The most succinct formulation of the problem was by Stanislaw J. Lec: "Does surrealism cease to be surrealism if it becomes reality?" This goes to the heart of the matter—which has been precisely described by Leszek Kolakowski (*Trialogue*, December 1983):

> "The intolerable aspect of Sovietism is the open mendacity of public language. The adjective 'open' needs to be stressed here. The point is not that the official verbiage is full of lies, but that its ostensible content is not

---

[9] An article entitled "Ignorance is Strength" (in the underground publication *Promienisci*, November 1983) describes, in Orwellian terminology, official propaganda under Jaruzelski. Another *samizdat* publication, *Solidarity Information* (Mazowzse Region, No. 159), discloses under the title "Orwell Reborn" the confidential Party instruction to the press which is quite similar to the secret recommendations by the Control Office for the media contained in the famous *Black Book on Censorship* published in *samizdat* in 1977. Cf. my articles in *The Times* (26 and 27 September 1977) and *The Washington Post* (6 November 1977).

really supposed to have semantic value in the first place; it belongs to a
realm of reality which has little to do with daily life or daily speech; its
function is not to inform but always to order, to regulate human
behaviour, to threaten, to encourage, to forbid, etc. People who have
properly assimilated the usage of '*Newspeak*' are not even expected to
believe that it is conveying something that might be true or false in the
normal sense: they are expected to behave according to the rulers'
wishes. The language of politics in the Western world may of course be
infected with lies, be hypocritical, stupid, or brutal; it still remains a
language with a normal function. The language of Sovietism has
changed ontologically, as it were: it has become an element of the
practical execution of power and has nearly lost other functions; it has
become as a-semantic as music. . . ."

The genius of Orwell was best manifested in his having imaginatively
understood and conveyed this, although the people on the Left whom he
tried to instruct are still completely missing the point.

IN ITS FATHERLAND the use of "*Newspeak*" is as pervasive as ever. As
usual, the recent "elections" (99·9 per cent in favour) to the Supreme
Soviet were described by headlines like THE REALITY OF OUR DEMOCRACY
(*Izvestiya*, 31 January 1984).

A report in *Izvestiya* (25 February 1984) of the meeting of similar
"parliamentary representatives" from Communist countries held in Hanoi
was entitled THE NOBLE MISSION OF PARLIAMENTARIANS (they also regularly
attended the meetings of the "Inter-Parliamentary" Union. . .). The horrors
of "the capitalist world" are depicted with familiar and routinized
deceitfulness. One example among myriad instances of the continuing use
of the Orwellian "reversal" technique is an article on the US media in
Literaturnaya Gazeta (29 February 1984): GENOCIDE THROUGH CENSORSHIP.

Orwell explained it presciently when he wrote that "if thought corrupts
language, language can also corrupt thought", and he made this point (in
1946) with reference to totalitarian "cultures":

"I should expect to find—this is a guess which I have not sufficient
knowledge to verify—that the German, Russian and Italian languages
have all deteriorated in the last ten or fifteen years, as a result of
dictatorship."

In Italy and West Germany, the blighted languages, sturdy plants that they
are, have recovered their normal character in democratic and open societies.
In Communist states Orwell's insight has been confirmed. The only
exception was Yugoslavia, where a translation of *1984* was officially
permitted to be published (by *BIGZ* Publications).

B UT THIS IS a reminder that *"Newspeak"* did not start with Stalin. It was Lenin who spoke first about the necessity of "conquering the language", even if it reached its totalitarian zenith under Stalin. The ideological codification of *"Newspeak"* continues, and its vocabulary is constantly adapted and applied to new circumstances. (Shi'ites in Iran are no longer "progressive", those in Lebanon still are; pacifist Christians are "progressive", Lebanese Christians are not, etc.) Current usage is organized and dictated by ideological instruments of the Party—as Alain Besançon has remarked: in totalitarian logocracies, power is exercised "at the tip of the tongue". Soviet linguists confirm this Orwellian perspective:

> "The great task of the mass media in socialist society is to develop and bring to perfection the consciousness of its members in the desired direction."

Orwell pointed out that the function of *"Newspeak"* was to try to render impossible any other mode of thinking.

He also knew that it was not limited to Communist countries—it is, quite voluntarily, embraced in non-Communist countries. The same Soviet linguists stress that "certain traits inherent in the socialist language can also be found in the progressive press of the capitalist world".[10] Orwell described it pithily in "Politics and the English Language" (1946).

> "People are imprisoned for years without trial, or shot in the back of the neck or sent to die of scurvy in Arctic labour camps: this is called *elimination of unreliable elements*. Such phraseology is needed if one wants to name things without calling up mental pictures of them. . . . The great enemy of clear language is insincerity. When there is a gap between one's real and one's declared aims, one turns as it were instinctively to long words and exhausted idioms, like a cuttlefish squirting ink."

The phraseology continues to flourish, the cuttlefish are still squirting.

Indeed, the infiltration of *"Newspeak"* into democratic countries, and the adoption of some of its aspects by the media, is probably the most glaring yet

---

[10] *Language in the Developed Socialist Society, A Symposium by the Academy of Science* (Moscow, 1982), pp. 15, 88.

In his review of *1984* in *Partisan Review* (July 1949), Philip Rahv (of whom Crick is critical) wrote:

> "Now what is 'double-think', actually, if not the technique continuously practised by the Communists and their liberal collaborators, dupes and apologists. Nor is it a technique available exclusively to Soviet citizens. Right here in New York any issue of the *Daily Worker* or of *The Daily Compass* will provide you with illustrations of it as vicious and ludicrous as any you will come across in Orwell's story. . . ."

Crick wrote that, "unfortunately, Rahv's reading of Orwell proved very influential: the Right accepted it and many of the Left reacted against Orwell because of the popularity of this well-meant but most partial and crude reading".

the least noticed contemporary phenomenon. One of the few who do refer to it, Richard Pipes, writes in his new book, *Survival is Not Enough*:

"The vocabulary of East–West relations, shared by Western 'liberals' and the Soviet apparatus, serves the same purpose as the official jargon inside the Soviet Union. It focuses the discussion on matters which are desired but often do not exist, and places out of bounds subjects which exist but are deemed best unmentioned. It perverts one's perception of phenomena by attaching to them pejorative words when they are considered inimical, and positive ones when they are useful. . . . Because 'Communism' evokes negative images in the West, it has been gradually supplanted with 'socialism'. For some time now, Moscow has been calling its bloc the 'Socialist camp', and this usage, too, has spread to Western media. . . . 'Liberal' journalists have not only assimilated much of this vocabulary but introduced refinements of their own, which are promptly borrowed by Moscow. They routinely call someone critical of the Soviet Union a 'hard-line anti-Communist', but never refer to anyone as a 'soft-line pro-Communist', even though every adjective demands its opposite. An 'extremist', when applied to a person's views on the Soviet Union, invariably means an anti-Communist, pro-Soviet 'extremist' being unknown to journalism: the latter is a 'moderate'.

Linguistic manipulation causes mental confusion and as such it is extremely dangerous. It enables Soviet political strategists to dominate the intellectual climate of East–West relations and to insinuate themselves into Western political discussions. It allows them to project false identities of interest between the two systems and to incite internecine conflicts of opinion as well as of interest within the Western community. It blurs the line between fiction and reality. . . ."

WHILE IN Eastern Europe there is a demotic linguistic resistance to *"Newspeak"*, in the West the "Finlandization" of language is perceptibly progressing.

The mainline Western media allowed the "progressives" to capture the word *"Peace"*, and now they can safely use the Soviet ideological concept of "Peaceful Coexistence" as a substitute. In the 1940s and '50s, the term "Cold War" was generally understood as the Soviet method of political warfare. Now its derivative, "Cold Warrior", is a term of abuse applied to those who advocate resistance to the Soviet Union and not appeasement. Examples can, alas, be multiplied, in the unthinking acceptance of the stereotypes which increasingly pollute our language. The term *"Newspeak"* is more and more applied only to Western usages. *A Dictionary of Newspeak* (compiled by Johnathan Green) has been published recently, and it is concerned with

Western jargon, not with the Communist perversions of language. The same applies to the *Quarterly Journal of Doublespeak* edited by William Lutz of Rutgers University's English department. The *Morning Star* now calls Britain "Airstrip One", and is certain that "Big Brother is alive and well in the US".

What Western journalists and broadcasters, statesmen and diplomats often seem not to realize is that the climate of opinion created by the confusing use, if not adoption, of Soviet terms and their frequent acceptance at face value considerably undermines the Western position. This not only disarms the West politically, but because of it even the negotiations with the Soviet Union are "loaded against the West".

The encroachments on our languages cripple the Western case by smuggling Soviet premises into the very framework of the debate. At the time of Yalta the expression "Soviet democracy" was not considered oxymoronic; now it is "peaceful coexistence" which is taken at face value. Obviously the attempts to reverse Orwell's message are part of a wider process of meaning-reversal which is affecting the whole of the West.

This applies not only to the present but also to the past: "Who controls the past, controls the future." Raymond Williams, obsessed with his fearful symmetrism, provides an undifferentiated and equidistant amalgam of Soviet and Western historical writing. Looking "beyond [the] differences of systems", he takes up

". . . the point [which] bears most closely on the notorious 'memory hole'. For if there is one thing that has not proved necessary in manipulating majority opinion, it is systematically rewriting the past. On the contrary, the past in itself becomes a kind of memory hole, from which only a few scholars and researchers bother to uncover and recover the facts. Why were the first atom bombs dropped on Japan *after* its government had proposed the outline of peace? What really happened in the Gulf of Tonkin? Which way and during what peace negotiations was the *General Belgrano* sailing? These are questions (none, in their whole context, with very simple answers) which with a thousand of others, from the role of Trotsky in the Russian Revolution to the policy of Mao and the Red Guards in China, are still intensely inquired into by small minorities, while the dominant public stance, in one social order after another, is to go blithely on with the news of the day, leaving the past to the obsessive and to the dry-as-dust. . . ."

Is this a case of "ignorance is strength", or of weakness through ignorance? To identify Western controversies on contemporary history with systematic Soviet rewriting of history is a casuistic amalgam. In the 1960s and '70s, American "revisionist" historians—a spectrum which ranged from the old William Appleton Williams to his younger New Left pupils—worked hard to put the blame on the West for the onset of the "Cold War". They lost the debate, I think, although, notably enough, it was conducted with open arguments and references to authentic historical sources.

Footnotes were the weapons, not Gulag camps. But the symmetrical imperative calls for putting Western patterns of historical controversy on a par with the sub-standard Soviet practices of historical falsification.

T HE BASIC DIFFERENCES between the Soviet and Western historiography are as clear as they are deep. Michel Heller has remarked:

"Soviet citizens under 25 may know who Assurbanipal is (they've heard of him from school), but not who Khrushchev was: the name of the former First Secretary of the Central Committee and Prime Minister has been completely eliminated from newspapers, textbooks, and historical monographs. Lack of memory, for the historian too, becomes a virtue in socialist countries. In certain conditions it is even a guarantee of security. It is easier to predict the future than the past.

The permanent transformation of the past makes lies absolutely necessary. It turns deceit into a fundamental element of idelogy. George Orwell, first in the West to have understood the essence of the Soviet system, remarked that 'organized lying is something integral to totalitarianism', and he forecast that 'it would continue even if concentration camps and secret police forces ceased to be necessary'. 'The really frightening thing about totalitarianism', wrote Orwell, 'is not that it commits "atrocities", but that it attacks the concept of objective truth'. . . ."[11]

All this will be amply illustrated in a comparison of successive editions of the Soviet Party *History* and *The Great Soviet Encyclopaedia* (of which the 7th and the 3rd editions were respectively published and completed this year). These are the institutional monuments to Soviet historiographical "vaporization". For those who, unlike Soviet citizens, have access to previous editions they provide an observation point on the Soviet "memory hole". Perhaps the finest example of the post-Stalinist Orwellian "memory hole" technique was the circular sent out to all subscribers to the 3rd edition of *The Great Soviet Encyclopaedia* requesting them to replace—"with scissors and glue"—the page containing the biographical note on *Lavrenti Beria* by a new page with an entry on the *Bering Straits*. The new page was enclosed with the circular. It would be difficult for Raymond Williams in his symmetrical frenzy to find an example to match this in the *Encyclopaedia Britannica*.

---

[11] Michel Heller, "History as Contraband" in *Survey* (No. 2, 1982). Cf. also *Contemporary History in the Soviet Mirror* (1964), ed. John Keep; Leopold Labedz, "Rehabilitation and Perdition" in *Problems of Communism* (No. 2, 1963); J. P. Shapiro, "Soviet Historiography and the Moscow Trials" in *Russian Review* (No. 1, 1968); A. P. van Gondoever, *Angst voor het verleden* (Fear of the Past), (Utrecht, 1983).

Since the scrapping of the celebrated Stalinist bible, *The Short Course of Party History* (1938), Khrushchev and Brezhnev managed to denounce their predecessors in their own textbooks of Party history. For whatever reasons, Andropov did not succeed in doing this before he died, and only time will tell whether Chernenko will have sufficient power and time to obliterate the memory of his old rival. But, although the falsifications are somewhat less blatant today, they remain the same in principle: Soviet historiography is still contemporary politics projected into the past. The fact that it is now conducted in a more sophisticated way does not basically change its Orwellian character. The Moscow Trials are still non-existent, and so is the "secret protocol" of the Stalin–Hitler Pact. A counterfeit history does not cease to be counterfeit if additional details are provided, just as a false banknote does not become legal currency if the counterfeiter's techniques improve.

I T IS REVEALING that those who refuse to recognize the difference in principle between Soviet and Western history-writing, and prefer to apply the metaphor of the Orwellian "memory hole" to both, are so oblivious to the misdemeanours of their own comrades. One example among many is particularly relevant to the story of the "re-interpretation" of Orwell.

Writing in *Tribune* (6 January 1984) about *1984*, Bernard Crick asserted that Orwell was "a pretty typical *Tribune* socialist, in other words of the kind of young Michael Foot and the middle-aged Aneurin Bevan". Was Crick being serious, or merely blinkered? Orwell was certainly *not* a "typical" *Tribune* socialist. As a "fervent anti-Communist" (Crick's own description) Orwell wrote his *Tribune* column, "As I Please", in a way which was very untypical of the rest of the paper.

Early in 1948, Orwell wrote an open letter to *Tribune* about their persistent differences. It is reproduced in *The Collected Essays, Journalism and Letters* (Vol. 4, pp. 449–455), but is not referred to by Crick. (In his biography he only quotes, strangely enough, Orwell's congratulatory remark from his piece published in *Tribune* on its 10th anniversary.) In his letter "In Defence of Comrade Zilliacus" (which was *not* published), Orwell wrote that *Tribune* was

> "sitting on the fence, uttering contradictory slogans and getting nowhere. . . . *Tribune* has consistently, over a period of years, failed to make its position clear. He [Zilliacus] knows that the only big political questions today are: for Russia—against Russia, for America—against America, for democracy—against democracy. . . . To be anti-American, to recall that the Americans helped us in 1940 when the Russians were supplying the Germans with oil and setting on their Communist Parties to sabotage the war effort, is to be branded as a

'reactionary'. And I suspect that when *Tribune* joins in the chorus it is more from fear of this label than from genuine conviction.

Surely, if one is going to write about foreign policy at all, there is one question that should be answered plainly. It is: 'If you *had* to choose between Russia and America, which would you choose?' It will not do to give the usual quibbling answer, 'I refuse to choose'. In the end the choice may be forced upon us. . . . And in spite of all the fashionable chatter of the moment, everyone knows in his heart that we should choose America."

One looks in vain in Crick or Williams for this clear-cut reflection of Orwell's political attitude in the last period of his life, the years when he wrote *1984*.

6. Orwell and the "*Tribune*" Legend

W HAT OF *Tribune* itself? It too has consigned such recollections to a "memory hole" (together with other reminiscences of its political past).

With the advent of the Orwellian year, *Tribune* tried to squeeze the last ounce of glory from its association with Orwell. On 30 December 1983, it reproduced his "As I Please" column of 2 February 1945; and in early 1984, for several weeks, it printed a number of articles on *1984* by "commentators of both Left and Right".

This was an unusual display of editorial tolerance, since *Tribune* would not normally touch certain writers of the Right (such as Alfred Sherman or Peregrine Worsthorne) with a barge-pole. Somehow this was supposed to imply that today's *Tribune* has a special claim on Orwell, and its aim was "to provide some perspective".

Curiously enough, the first article in the series (by Bernard Crick) was printed alongside an excerpt from a book by the late Wilfred Burchett, the Communist propagandist famous for his "reports" on alleged US "bacteriological warfare" in Korea. This in itself was an indication of how far the sensitivities of *Tribune* are from Orwell's own. But it is really the whole history of *Tribune* that "provides some perspective" on the question of Orwell in 1984. It is, I am convinced, fair to say that during the 47 years of its existence its editorial line, with all its vicissitudes, never once coincided with Orwell's own attitude to such problems as communism, the Soviet Union, and foreign policy, even—as his unpublished letter quoted above testifies—at the time he was writing for it. For most of the time, and in particular in its pre-War period (and especially so at present), *Tribune* was and is in striking contrast to Orwell's own position.

Before the Second World War *Tribune* advocated a "Popular Front" with the Communists. (Orwell was against it.) Its editorial of 25 August 1939 was a classic of fellow-travellerish political obtuseness, an immortal boob in the annals of quotable nonsense:

"A pact of non-aggression between Russia and Germany, if it is signed, will be a great reinforcement for peace in Eastern Europe. At the same time it is a lie to suggest that it leaves Germany a free hand against Poland or anyone else."

On 1 September 1939, the day Hitler attacked Poland, *Tribune* was unlucky enough to publish another editorial still stressing that "the non-aggression pact signed by Stalin with Hitler had strongly reinforced the power for peace in Europe". In an article called "Stalin—Architect for Peace" it reiterated that "only malicious or ignorant commentators could pretend that the Soviet-German Pact is an arrangement to give Germany a free hand in Europe". This "contemptible lie" was also criticized by Konni Zilliacus (Orwell later castigated him as a "crypto-Communist"):

"Let us dismiss the tales of a secret Nazi-Soviet alliance for the partition of Poland."

During the Second World War *Tribune* changed its position. Orwell was a shade naive about this when he wrote, after the War, that *Tribune*'s anti-Americanism is not sincere but is an attempt to keep in with fashionable opinion. . . ." This surely was wishful thinking on his part: in fact, the continuity of the Left was reasserting itself. If he were alive in 1984 he would see that *Tribune* has almost come full circle during the post-War period, moving from the initial "*Keep Left*" to its present "hard Left" position.

It was, to be sure, not possible simply to return to the fellow-travellerish position of the 1930s. Too much embarrassing Soviet dirt had come to the surface in between to make this politically respectable. For the same reason, the two anniversary anthologies of selected *Tribune* writings published in book form (*Tribune 21* and *Tribune 40*) carefully omitted embarrassing pre-War texts such as those quoted above. But on its 45th anniversary *Tribune* came close to an apologia for its stand in the 1930s. In an editorial (1 January 1982) reviewing its own history, it censured the pro-rearmament stand of its opponents before the outbreak of the war with Hitler:

"Governments, industrialists and financiers were clamouring for rearmament—reviving the spectre of war. . . . *Tribune* attacked the Government's pro-Franco indifference to the Republican plight in Spain. It attacked the plunge towards another war in which the working man would be called upon to die to make the world safe for capitalism."

Oblivious to any inconsistency, the editorial continued:

"When war was declared in September 1939, *Tribune* flung itself into its own contribution to the struggle against fascism, underlining the duties of all socialists within that struggle."

Readers were kindly spared the telling details of what actually happened. But the post-War *Tribune* position which Orwell had criticized was now (in 1982) criticized in the *Tribune* editorial . . . from the very opposite standpoint:

"As the cold war grew more glacial . . . the paper tended then to over-react from the rejection of Stalinist communism into what seemed to be a fervent pro-American position—so that at first, it could even make supporting noises over American ('United Nations') intervention in Korea. . . . The leanings towards America diminished sharply later, when the full reality of Dulles's anti-communist crusade emerged."

IN THAT SAME ISSUE, as I have noted, Orwell's column on the 10th anniversary of *Tribune* was reproduced, but to avoid telling the whole truth about its schizoid past, *Tribune* omitted the *first* paragraph, which contained the following passage:

"*Tribune* in its short life has been two distinct papers, if not three, and my own contacts with it have varied sharply, starting off, if I remember rightly, with a rap on the knuckles."

It also omitted a passage (italicized below) from another paragraph:

"With the outbreak of war [*Tribune's*] circulation had taken a severe knock, because the Communists and near-Communists who had been among its warmest supporters now refused to help in distributing it. *Some of them went on writing for it, however, and the futile controversy between 'supporters' and 'opposers' of the war continued to rumble in its columns while the German armies gathered for the spring offensives. . . .*"

Tribune's claim was that its "views of the Stalin dictatorship" were justified "by the Khrushchev revelations". This scarcely amounted to an adequate description of *Tribune's* ambiguities. In any case, the "revelations" merely led it to become (like many other papers of the "radical left") not anti-Soviet, but more anti-American. They may have been frustrated Utopians, but they remained "true believers". They found in a shrill anti-Americanism a compensatory factor for their inability to extol "the country with a Hope and a Plan".

This was the very opposite of Orwell's own evolution. The contrasts and contradictions made it necessary for the "progressives" to suppress into their subconscious, or to drop into a "memory hole", all those embarrassing elements of their past. Recollection might undermine their present political positions. Looking at 1984 with "some perspective", it is obvious why *Tribune* was so concerned. *Tribune* is clearly not in "the Orwell tradition", yet claims him for its own: a strange case of "Orwellians" tiptoeing around the skeletons still rattling in the closet—the skeletons of Stalin and . . . Orwell.

7. The Question of Orwell's Socialism

IN THE "progressive" rites for St Orwell the *leitmotif* was that he was a "socialist", and therefore the present representatives of the "socialist tradition" are his legitimate heirs. The putative body-snatchers' foul deed consisted of claiming spiritual affinity with Orwell. But the "progressives" made no attempt (with one exception, to which I'll return in a moment) to substantiate the charges. Why not falsify the "body-snatchers'" claim by contrasting it with the authentic voice of Orwell *on specific issues?* Not on your life. Instead there were selective quotations, general labels, and conventional Left stereotypes.

In fact, no one among the mysterious corps of "body-snatchers", whoever they were, ever denied that Orwell considered himself "a socialist". This did not prevent his latter-day "followers" from triumphantly proving it with a well-known quotation about *1984*:

> "My recent novel is *not* intended as an attack on Socialism or on the British Labour Party (of which I am a supporter) but as a show-up of the perversions to which a centralised economy is liable and which have already been partly realised in Communism and Fascism. . . . The scene of the book is laid in Britain in order to emphasize that the English-speaking races are not innately better than anyone else and that totalitarianism, *if not fought against*, could triumph anywhere."

If this remark points to anything, it is to the need to fight totalitarianism (the italics are Orwell's own), but this is not the point emphasized by those who quote it so frequently. By claiming the "socialist" Orwell as their patron-saint they provide an alibi for themselves.

In the same passage Orwell stressed that "totalitarian ideas have taken root in the minds of intellectuals everywhere". It is a supreme irony that those who, following his advice and example, are fighting totalitarianism are denounced as "Cold Warriors" and "body-snatchers" by those who concentrate on *anti*-anti-Communism. It is, of course, their right to reject anti-Communism; but to invoke the anti-Communist Orwell for that purpose is an intellectual fraud.

Anyway, what is in the "socialist" name? When Orwell used it 35 years ago it was still possible to adopt the label and be "a fervent anti-Communist". But like so many other words, concepts, and ideas, "socialism" no longer signifies today what it signified for Orwell. Would he believe today that (as he put it on joining the ILP) "the only régime which in the long run will permit freedom of speech is a socialist régime"? At that time (as well as now), the believers in a socialist Utopia were, as Sidney Hook put it, "judging capitalism by its operations and socialism by its hopes and aspirations". The difference is that today the experience of "the perversions of the centralized economy" (and of centralized power in the hands of the Party-State) is far wider, deeper, and better known.

It is, naturally, impossible to say whether Orwell would still use the term "socialist" in the present circumstances, after an additional 35 years of historical experience. His attachment to equality—his belief in the common decency and common sense of the common man—might or might not be represented for him by the same label now. But if we cannot say what Orwell would call himself today, we can be quite certain that he would not be a *"progressive"*.

Except for a very short period of time, he never was. And it is because he abandoned the Left's "smelly little orthodoxies" of the "progressive" stance that he achieved his greatness. Had he not, Orwell would not be Orwell, but yet another conventional Utopian. Without his contempt for the conventional wisdom of the day, and his anti-totalitarian passion and understanding, he would have written neither *Animal Farm* nor *1984*; and he would have been forgotten.

I HAVE NO DOUBT THAT Orwell would never have shared the post-War illusions which he has done so much to dispel. Can one imagine him falling for all those self-renewing fallacies which marked the deceptive expectations of the Left (and, often, also of the Right) about the Soviet Union? Can one visualize the author of *Animal Farm* subscribing to the "theory of Convergence" of Western and Soviet societies in the imminent "liberalization" of the USSR after "the Thaw"? (More than 20 years ago Isaac Deutscher assured us that "the Goddess of Liberty" would soon be moving from the West to the East. . . .) Would Orwell enthuse in the 1980s, as each new "Big Brother" generates Western "liberal" expectations for fundamental reform? Would he affirm, with Michael Walzer and Richard Lowenthal (in Irving Howe's *1984 Revisited* anthology), that the Soviet Union is no longer totalitarian? Would he hold with Roy Medvedev, writing in *l'Unità* (18 December 1983), that computerization would facilitate liberalization in the USSR, but would produce only a "Great Fear" in the USA?

In 1984, sad to record, Big Brother still loves his Winston Smiths in all the Communist countries. In the USSR dissidents are in mental prisons or in Gulag labour camps. In Poland *Solidarity* has been suppressed. In Czechoslovakia the voluble hopes of 1968 have given way to the silence of the grave. And nobody (as Senator Moynihan put it) "swims through shark-infested waters to reach the shores of East Germany. . . ."

As early as 1940, Orwell referred to "the squalid farce of left-wing politics". Can one imagine the author of *1984* calling massacre a "liberation" as so many "progressives" did in respect of Vietnam and Cambodia? Or adopting a pacifist position—which he never did when he was alive? Saying "Better Red than Dead" rather than pointing out that "peace" propaganda "is helpful to totalitarianism"?

In short, embracing those whom he denounced and who, poor impoverished spirits, are so eager to embrace him now? All this because he was a "socialist"? He was never that kind of "socialist".

8. The Case of Simon Leys

ONE AUTHOR, Simon Leys (Pierre Ryckmans), who unlike the Williamses and the Cricks must be taken with intellectual seriousness, has presented a view somewhat similar to theirs on this point.[12]

Simon Leys was the single most important source describing the real character of the Chinese "Cultural Revolution" in his reports and books. He saw and analyzed the operation of Orwell's mechanisms—"Big Brother" and "Two Minutes' Hate" with *The Little Red Book*. At the time when Maoism was becoming fashionable among the "revolutionary" romantics in California and France, he brought realities into sharp focus. In his splendid polemic against Han Suyin[13] he performed the same valuable service in dissecting Chinese propaganda techniques as his predecessors did in Stalin's time in exposing the "Red Dean", Hewlett Johnson, or D. N. Pritt, QC. He certainly needs no introduction to Orwell either in print or in reality.

I find it, therefore, all the more inexplicable that his book on Orwell is marred by a certain incomprehension of the wider, larger issues involved, even though it displays at the same time a highly perceptive analysis of Orwell's writings. Stressing Orwell's conversion to "socialism", he goes so far as to contend that:

> "His socialist 'illumination' was as sudden and absolute as the *satori* experienced by a Zen adept, or one could say that *The Road to Wigan Pier* was his Way to Damascus."

One "could say" many things, but some of them obviously trouble Simon Leys, for in the very next sentence he tries to handle the possible objections to this rather fanciful portrait of Orwell, whose "Englishness" and commonsense empiricism escape him. He indulges in some mystagogic flights of imagination:

---

[12] In his new book called *Orwell ou l'Horreur de la Politique* (Paris, Hermann, 1984). Excerpts from it were published in *Commentaire* (Paris, No. 24 & No. 25), in *Le Monde* (30 December 1983), and in *Quadrant* (Sydney, December 1983).

[13] Simon Leys, "The Double Vision of Han Suyin", *Encounter* (November 1980).

"The metaphors may appear inappropriate when we consider his innate allergy to all forms of religion (and more particularly he felt an even stronger revulsion for a certain form of socialist mystique that used 'to draw with magnetic force every fruit-juice drinker, nudist, sandal-wearer, sex-maniac, Quaker, "Nature-cure" quack, pacifist and feminist in England'); and yet it seems that only a reference to a religious experience could adequately account for the instantaneous, total and unshakeable character of his new commitment. . . ."

Total and unshakeable? Leys makes Orwell into a "true believer" which he emphatically was not. His socialism was demonstrably not a form of religious experience (as Leys' comparison of Orwell with Simone Weil seems to imply).

ON a more down-to-earth level Simon Leys maintains that "For Orwell, socialism provided the final solution of a very personal problem: how to communicate with the oppressed". Judging by his last novel which was not a socialist communication, it was hardly a solution, much less the "final" one.

All Leys' quotations from Orwell, showing his concern for "the underdog" and his attachment to "justice and liberty" as fundamental values of socialism, merely underline the fact that the nature of his political commitment to "socialism" was pretty vague, that there was a certain incongruity between the concrete character of his specific reactions to the political events of his epoch and the rather general nature of his socialist commitment. Contrary to what Bernard Crick tries to make of Orwell, he was not really a systematic political thinker (and Crick's comparison with Hobbes is wildly out of place). His genius lay in giving imaginative expression to the understanding of the *sui generis* experience of the epoch: the totalitarian system.

This was a remarkable achievement, considering that even now, after so many decades, there is so little understanding of it among those who have no direct personal knowledge of it. Still, this is no reason to make Orwell into a theoretician, or to portray him as a saint or a knight *sans peur et sans reproche*.[14] One must be especially wary of drawing any "progressive" conclusions for today about "socialist countries", or socialism in general, from his commitment at a time when "Left anti-Communism" was a powerful ideological force (and the Socialist International was still a hostile target of Communist *Agitprop* rather than a venue for a "dialogue" between Willy Brandt and Boris Ponomarev).

Simon Leys writes about Orwell's "socialism" as if it were a self-

---

[14] For a sceptical view of Orwell, see Herb Greer's sharp analysis, "Orwell in Perspective", *Commentary* (March 1983).

explanatory concept and its meaning self-evident. Yet this, as we know, is not exactly the case. Seen in historical perspective, there are only three ways to approaching the problem of Orwell's "socialism".

One is to treat it as a belief in Utopia; but Orwell, a gritty commonsensical fellow, was not a Utopian.

The second is to take the historical experience of the "socialist" (i.e. Communist) countries and analyze their institutional evolution—what it has been and might be. This is what Orwell did, 35 years ago, in *1984*.

The third approach is to bypass both the dream and the nightmare, to offer a realistic programme of social and institutional development. What kind of transformation of historic societies would satisfy certain ideals and socialist desiderata (including Orwell's own)? How would it deal with the problem that many such values may be incompatible in practice? Orwell might well have subscribed to Leszek Kolakowski's manifesto, "How to Be a Conservative-Liberal Socialist".[15]

In short, it is not enough to apply in the 1984 discussion of Orwell's "socialism" the old fallacy, nailed down by Sidney Hook of "judging capitalism by its operations and socialism by its hopes and aspirations". For somebody like Orwell, with his common sense and *penchant* for the concrete, and his abhorrence of the loose use of words, it is only right and just to apply such standards to his own ideas, rather than take them out of historical context as if they had only a sentimental and not an intellectual content.

But that is just what Simon Leys does, as if to show that what appeared *desirable* (his italics) to Orwell at an early state of his political evolution is to be decisive in the analysis of his relevance today. Leys writes:

> "Of course, no one could deny that Orwell's socialism presented a few paradoxes. He entirely ignored Marxist theory; he had total (and fully justified) contempt for a large part of the socialist intelligentsia; he cursed the communist experiment in its entirety; he believed that 'all revolutions are failures'. With all that, the fact that he persisted with such obstinacy in affirming that he was a 'socialist' may indeed appear somewhat disconcerting. . . . Actually, he wanted to rediscover what he considered the fundamental values of socialism—the ideal of 'justice and liberty' that was being 'buried beneath layer after layer of doctrinaire priggishness, party squabbles and half-baked "progressivism" until it is like a diamond hidden under a mountain of dung. The job of the Socialist is to get it out again.'. . ."

If this is what Orwell thought (at one or another stage of his political development), still Simon Leys loyally admits that

---

[15] Leszek Kolakowski, "how to Be a Conservative–Liberal Socialist", *Encounter* (October 1978).

"In all other respects, he entertained no illusions: 'Collectivism leads to concentration camps, leader worship and war. There is no way out of this unless a planned economy can be somehow combined with the freedom of the intellect, which can only happen if the concept of right and wrong is restored to politics.' He perceived clearly that a centralized economy could become a grave menace for individual freedom and that, in this situation 'the State may come to mean no more than a self-elected political party, and oligarchy and privilege can return, based on power rather than on money.'. . ."

L EYS maintains that "the interpretation according to which Orwell's political stand would have drastically shifted had he lived long enough does not withstand analysis" because "in the realm of *principles* his convictions never wavered". He admits that Orwell changed, for instance, his belief that "it would be pointless to try resisting Fascism without first achieving a socialist revolution"—he "effectively ceased to believe in the imminent *possibility* of such revolutionary upheavals". But he argues (a shade ambivalently, in my view) that "there is nothing in his writings that would allow us to conclude that he actually ceased to consider these *desirable*".

Does all this mean that while Orwell did not believe in "Utopia", he would not give up his belief in "Revolution"? Here it comes—

". . . when a political movement that dissociates the cause of liberty from that of justice, now attempts to press-gang his dead body into its ranks, the abuse seems enormous. Orwell always faced his enemies with much equanimity; one wonders, however, if he could have kept his cool, had he been confronted with his latter-day admirers."

Unlike Raymond Williams, Leys does give a specific reference:

"An outrageous example of this kind of manipulation can be provided by a recent article by N. Podhoretz."

The article in question, "If Orwell Were Alive Today", was published in the American monthly, *Harpers* (January 1983). Its author, Norman Podhoretz (the editor of *Commentary*), made many points similar to my own. He went on to say:

"Despite Crick's sophistical protestations, there can be no doubt that Orwell did belong in 'the camp of the Cold War' while he was still alive. Nor can there be much doubt that if he were alive today he would have felt a greater kinship with the neo-conservatives who are calling for resistance to Soviet imperialism than with either the socialist supporters of *détente* or the coalition of neutralists and pacifists who dominate the 'peace movement' in Europe and their neo-isolationist allies in the United States. . . ."

Podhoretz does not actually assert that Orwell would have become a neo-conservative—only that if he were alive today "he would be taking his stand with neo-conservatives and against the Left" in the context of the post-War struggle between totalitarianism and democracy, that he is not certain about Orwell's "socialism", as "there is no way of knowing whether and to what extent he would have changed his views in response to a changing world" in spite of Orwell's pride in his "power of facing unpleasant facts".

ORWELL in his lifetime underwent a political evolution from "Tory anarchist" to revolutionary militant who then turned libertarian-democrat-socialist. Would he today be a neo-conservative or a social democrat? This is not, I feel, as significant as what his attitude would have been towards the international conflict which he faced unequivocally. About that there can indeed be little doubt.

There is nothing, in my view, "outrageous" or "manipulatory" about Podhoretz's article. One may or may not agree with its thesis, but it is a reasoned argument; and Simon Leys himself has "lost his cool" by describing it in these terms without providing specific evidence for such harsh and summary dismissal. A certain special ideological animus perhaps accounts for it. The incongruity of his position can be seen in his mournful comment on

> "the persisting stupidity of the progressives, who, instead of applying themselves at last to reading and understanding [Orwell], are allowing the enemy to confiscate their best writer."

I am afraid that the scourge of the Maoist revolutionaries is showing here the same *naïveté* as the scourge of the progressive intelligentsia did in his alibi for *Tribune*. How long might Simon Leys have to wait before his appeal for the "progressives" genuinely to outdo the "enemy" on Orwell is answered? Orwell died too early to see the outcome of such naive and confused hopes.

What has happened since is that the Left became frightened at its move to the "Centre" and retreated to its threadbare illusions about making "fundamental changes" to a bourgeois-capitalist society (rather than consolidating all forces in free societies in the face of a threatening totalitarian system). Simon Leys can still face the difficult and disagreeable issues squarely. He has shown in China, as no one else did, an Orwellian "power of facing unpleasant facts".

9. Body Language

ARE THESE battles about Orwell merely about "body-snatching"? Not at all. They are really about the historical significance of politics in our epoch: and for this, Orwell dead is as relevant as Orwell alive. His emasculators seem to feel that "he who possesses Orwell possesses the future". They merely demonstrate that he who misunderstands the past misunderstands the present.

Orwell once referred to a "generation of unteachables who hang around us like a necklace of corpses". One would have thought that a number of myths believed by "progressives" would have been abandoned by now, when most human links in Orwell's "necklace of corpses" are literally dead. But it is not whole generations which are unteachable, but a section of the intelligentsia in each generation. Their present treatment of Orwell is only one example of their mythopoetic frame of mind.

Another is the perpetuation of old myths among the children—and grandchildren—of Orwell's generation of "progressives". They wanted so much at the time to believe in the guilt of the accused in the Moscow Trials; but they hotly defended the thesis of the innocence of Alger Hiss and the Rosenbergs. After Khrushchev's "secret speech" it is no longer possible to perpetuate the first myth, but that, as it happens, is only an additional motive for perpetuating the second. "Innocence" persists, in spite of all the Philbys and Blunts, and all the comprehensive evidence sifted and analyzed by the authors of historical books on the two cases—*Perjury* by Alan Weinstein and *The Rosenberg File* by Ronald Radosh and Joyce Milton. These authors were not "anti-Communists". Weinstein was a "progressive" when he began his book, Radosh and Milton probably still are. To perpetuate the myths of the innocence of Hiss and of the Rosenbergs may not make much sense in terms of argument and logic; but it does make it easier, psychologically, to preserve a certain kind of political faith.

We have here again the familiar mechanism of symmetrism: Stalin was certainly evil (nobody can deny that he got rid of a number of innocent people; but then so did the Americans). As against "the Great Terror" (Robert Conquest) in the USSR under Stalin, there was "the Great Fear" (David Caute) in the USA under Joseph McCarthy. Bukharin was innocent, but then so was Hiss. There were, perhaps, some differences in scale and even, possibly, in character between the Soviet deportation of nationalities and the American wartime internment of the *Nisei*, just as there might be no exact parallel between the fate of the scores of millions of Gulag victims and the fate of Miss Lillian Hellman and "the Hollywood Ten". But is it all not similar "in principle"?

Given this psychological predisposition, contemporary "progressives" show little inclination to ask themselves difficult questions. They concentrate their energy on American misdemeanours to improve the balance. They try desperately, for instance, to rehabilitate Alger Hiss and the Rosenbergs.[16]

---

[16] When Hiss was interviewed on BBC TV his innocence was taken for granted: he was treated as a victim of a self-evident frame-up. The case of the Rosenbergs is still considered

$\longrightarrow$

The result is the perpetuation of myths which should have died long ago. It is the attitude behind such myths which provides the motives for the present operation on Orwell.

CONSIDER THIS recent episode in *The Guardian*.[17] It published on 17 December 1983 an article by R. W. Johnson, "007: Licence to Kill". The author, an Oxford don, developed a conspiracy theory for the shooting down of the Korean airliner. He put the blame for it on the Americans. This fantasy was promptly reproduced in *Literaturnaya Gazeta* (18 January) and summarized in detail by *Trybuna Ludu* (13 January). It was criticized by Professor R. V. Jones (*The Guardian*, 20 January), who referred to Johnson's assertion that in 1940 "Churchill had had foreknowledge of which cities were to be attacked by *Luftwaffe* and had deliberately withheld such information from Fighter Command". Professor Jones—a scientist and, as author of *Most Secret War* (1978), the authority on the subject—characterized this as "a monstrous travesty of fact". He concluded that "Mr Johnson's readiness to misrepresent the facts in this instance is so blatant that it disqualifies him as an analyst of such an international tragedy as the Korean airliner".

In his rejoinder, "KAL 007 conspiracy theory that shouldn't be sidetracked" (*The Guardian*, 25 January), R. W. Johnson lamely replied by expressing his hope that Professor Jones "will not persist in jumping from the scarcely connected facts of the Coventry raid to the confident assertion that all was just as the US told us it was in the case of the KAL tragedy. . . ."

Such flights of ideological fancy would not be worth mentioning except for the fact that they illustrate the persistence of myth-making tendencies in the present-day Left. The political attitude behind it is not all that different

---

"controversial". It constantly crops up in the correspondence columns of various magazines (e.g. *The Spectator* in England, *The Nation* in the USA). Hardly a year has gone by without a new book, TV programme, film, or play on Hiss or the Rosenbergs.

For instance, reviewing one such attempted "rehabilitation"—the film *Daniel*—in *The Times* (13 January 1984). David Robinson wrote with a snappiness that defied a thousand years of jurisprudence:

"The probability now seems to be that they were innocent, but that is hardly relevant."

The statement that the question of guilt in atomic spying "is hardly relevant" is staggering. Robinson also mentioned the Barbican retrospective, "Thoughtcrimes", which "is designed to show the need for vigilance in warding off the nightmares like Orwell's *1984* or McCarthy's 1950. . . ."

[17] Just how far the present *Guardian* has strayed from the tradition of the old *Manchester Guardian* has been documented by Peter Deli, "The *Manchester Guardian* and the Soviet Purges 1936–38", *Survey* (Spring 1984). Its current symmetrism—possible only if real and fundamental distinctions get blurred by calling them "irrelevant" or "immaterial"—is constantly manifested:

"Whether George Orwell had set *1984* in the Soviet Union, the USA or Ruritania, is immaterial; what matters is his prediction of the progressive loss of civil liberties, the centralisation of power and the increasing ability of this power to manipulate"
(Martin Ryle in *The Guardian*, 23 April 1984).

from the hatred of the West which motivated their "progressive" forefathers. R. W. Johnson, in his article "Churchill Airstrip" (*New Society*, 19 January), writes:

> "Less than three weeks into 1984, most of us are already terminally bored by discussions of whether the age of Big Brother has/will/might arrive. This is a pity. If you think about it, Big Brother was just a personalized flourish at the summit of the society Orwell envisaged. The far more fundamental fact was the division of the world into the three great competing blocks, Oceania, Eurasia and Eastasia."

According to Johnson, Churchill not only cold-bloodedly sacrificed Coventry, but his foolishly-based foreign policy rested on a fundamental error:

> "The problem which all British governments have had since 1945 was that Churchill's grand design was wrong, indeed a disaster—but that it has been legitimated forever by the quixotic triumph of 1940. Accordingly they have tried to sidle away from the Churchill heritage obliquely, without facing up to the need to deal with that heritage in the same way that the Russians needed to confront the legacy of Stalinism with a positive campaign of de-stalinisation. For Britain's future now clearly lies with Eurasia, not with Oceania."

For Johnson, Britain's future now clearly lies with the East not with the West. It is this which explains Mr Johnson's myth-making about the Korean airliner and the anti-Americanism of his conspiracy theory (though it does not excuse the waywardness of his "de-stalinisation" reference). But why drag the anti-Soviet Orwell into a pro-Soviet argument?

What accounts for the strange mixture? How is it—why should it be—that attitudes directly contrary to Orwell's own on Soviet and Communist affairs are coupled with his ostensible endorsement by the new generation of "progressives"?

The answer seems to lie in the contemporary history of the Left, and especially in the evolution of the New Left during the quarter-of-a-century since its inception. When it emerged after Khrushchev's 1956 speech and the Soviet suppression of the Hungarian Revolution it was, under the impact of these two shocks, at its most critical about Soviet actions. (That is why Raymond Williams could write that it respected Orwell "*especially* in its early years".) But gradually the New Left shifted its position. It moved from its early "anti-Stalinist" stance to an attitude which is not antagonistic to, or is helpful to, Soviet policies. The conservative enemy at home, not the totalitarian enemy abroad, is the main enemy!

The old "progressive" impulse slowly but surely reasserted itself, and resulted in an increasing obliteration of the original distinctions between the

Old and the New Left. This political evolution could be observed from the time of the *Universities and Left Review* to the present, when its successor, *New Left Review*, exhibits how the old *"Newspeak"* of the Old Left has merged with the new *"Newspeak"* of the New Left.[18]

T HE adaptation of *"Newspeak"* to current realities also goes on in the Soviet Union and other communist countries. The necessity of "conquering the language" has been a continuous consideration ever since Lenin expressed the idea. At present Soviet linguists have been given the task of preparing a monumental "Leninist Dictionary" which is supposed to provide an authoritive interpretation of the philological legacy of the Soviet founding father. The editor of this "Dictionary", Pyotr Denisov of the Soviet Academy of Science, explained:

> "Lenin was a great innovator not only in politics but also in linguistics. . . . The Leninist word had a beneficial influence on the language of Soviet publications and official documents. . . . The writings of Lenin are in many respects the culmination of the development of the classical Russian language of the nineteenth century associated with the flourishing of Russian *belles lettres*, materialist philosophy and political publications. Lenin's writings begin the new—Soviet—phase. . . ."

Denisov provided some information about the "Dictionary" in an interview given to Edward Krustkaln from the Novosti Press Agency (*Trybuna Ludu*, 4 May 1984):

> "The work of the index has demonstrated again the wealth of Lenin's language. For instance, Lenin used 12,000 words once only, while the overall number of words used by him amounts to 37,500. I would like to add by way of a comparison that Shakespeare used only 15,000 words, Cervantes and Pushkin—about 20,000."

Almost every word used by Lenin in the 5th edition of his *Collected Works* (over 50 volumes) will have a special entry in the five volumes of the new "Dictionary". The publication of the 1st volume is scheduled for 1984. Clearly the enterprise "overtakes and surpasses" even the Orwellian imagination.

In the fatherland of Czeslaw Milosz no such monumental works are planned, but Milosz's classic "Murti-bing" is being brushed up in the Poland of General Jaruzelski. The official *Trybuna Ludu* now regularly runs a special column entitled "Words We Are Using". Polishing up the old vocabulary, it offers a new *duckspeak* for "the masses" whose semantic sensitivities have,

---

[18] See my article, "Of Myths and Horrors", *Encounter* (February 1980).

after all, been profoundly affected by the *Solidarity* era. In order to restore some credibility and lustre to the old *Newspeak*, it gives seemingly rational definitions for such concepts as "Socialism . . . Imperialism . . . Liberalism . . . Conservatism . . . Anarchism . . . Dialectics", etc. This last concept is described (*Trybuna Ludu*, 21–22 January 1984) as providing "the ground for a better understanding and explanation of reality". A better, neo-Orwellian definition might be that it represents the phenomenon of double-talk rationalizing "Doublethink".

An entry on "Democracy" (*Trybuna Ludu*, 14–15 April 1984) is a good example of these attempts to make "*Newspeak*" "viable" again. "The contemporary bourgeoisie reduces democracy to the general right to vote for politicians." By contrast: "the provision of real political and economic power for the people is the fundamental purpose of the socialist revolution". The benefits of "social democracy" are the superior fruits of "really existing socialism", while the choices offered in the Western countries are a contemptible substitute for genuine people's power.

An even more striking example was provided in "Words We Are Using", in an entry on "Totalitarianism" (a word which *Trybuna Ludu* does not normally use) which claimed that:

> "In the '30s and '40s the concept had—rightly—an unambiguous meaning: it became a synonym for state terror, fascist genocide, and the violation of human rights. In the '50s, however, the concept began a new career. In the period of Cold War the experts on anti-Communist propaganda began applying the term to socialist countries. . . . For 30 years, the whole powerful machinery of Western propaganda has been used to identify the concept with really existing socialism."

The column, nicely combining "dialectics" with historical falsification, went on to say that this was a "distorting picture" and that it is the USA which was founded through the employment of totalitarian methods, methods which are used in its various genocidal client states.

The fact that the column was published on April Fool's Day, 1984, is probably of no dialectical significance.

O NE FURTHER Western example, the last and, perhaps, the least. In some respects, young Christopher Hitchens is not quite representative of the New Left's evolution; nevertheless he reflects it, both in its "progressive" regression and in its contradictoriness about Orwell.

In his early "Trotskyist" period, at the beginning of his journalistic career, Christopher Hitchens was very censorious about things Soviet (that hopelessly degenerated "workers' state", that monstrously bureaucratic collectivism, etc.)—conspiciously more so than other members of the New

Left. In his more recent writings one can detect an increasing ambiguity in his attitudes to pro- and anti-Soviet writings.

Take, for example, his review in the *New Statesman* (22 May 1981) of the book *Cockburn Sums Up* (Quartet, 1981), by the late (and to the end unreconstructed) Stalinist Claud Cockburn, who was an ingenious representative of Soviet viewpoints in the 1930s (in the *Daily Worker* and in *The Week*,[19] the influential disinformation bulletin which he produced). Hitchens considered him something of a father figure in spite of his having been a "rank Stalinist" who remained "proud of having told lies for his propaganda causes". Although, as Hitchens tells us, he had "some vicious arguments" with him "about Spain, Orwell, the Molotov-Ribbentrop Pact", etc., he considered him "a great journalist" who reminded him "of Orwell's description of Dickens—a man generously angry. . . ." His generous anger, like that of Wilfred Burchett, was somewhat narrowly selective. It did not include communist atrocities. And we know what Orwell thought of the Cockburns in the 1930s.

The incongruity of Hitchens' enthusiasm both for the apostle of intellectual integrity and for the cynical liar who even in the 1970s continued to produce reminiscences which were still full of palpable fabrications tells us volumes about Hitchens' ambivalences. The juxtaposition of the two figures—Orwell and Cockburn, the opponent and the supporter of the Moscow Trials, both of whom he described as *"Dreyfusards"*—tells us something about Hitchens' deficient perception of Orwellian values.

All this fatuity becomes understandable in the light of what I have referred to as the recidivism of the New Left. What the experience of the 1930s taught the then "progressive" poet W. H. Auden, later found expression in his celebrated reference to it as a "low, dishonest decade". But Hitchens—in his thrillingly vicarious, if belated, adolescent excitement—describes them as "the stirring Thirties", a remark which may offer a clue to the psychological sources of his political muddle. Whom will it surprise that in a polemic with Norman Podhoretz (*Harpers*, February 1983), he tried to rescue Orwell from the reactionary clutches of this neo-conservative monster? Or that in his friendly review of Bernard Crick's biography of Orwell (*New Statesman*, 28 November 1980), Hitchens declared that "its chief strength lies in its thoroughness and its honesty"?

It may only be a case of one left hand washing the other.

10. Eggs, Omelettes, and Good Cheer

B ERNARD CRICK, to crown his Orwellian labours, has just produced a new edition of *1984* with his own introduction and annotations (Clarendon Press, Oxford). It is quite beyond my critical powers to describe

---

[19] See Donald Watt's documented critique, "The Week That Was", *Encounter* (May 1972).

the triviality of its textual analysis, the meandering obfuscations of its arguments, and the pedantic tedium of its Lit. Crit.-cum-Pol. Sci. style. When Nigel Dennis cracked that Crick's writing on the late George Orwell was "a fate worse than death", he had not then read Crick's new introduction to *1984*. It is difficult to imagine that anyone who has read all 136 pages of it (154 with annotations) will have enough stamina left to read the novel itself.

In Crick's introduction Orwell becomes a convenient ventriloquist's dummy. The squeaking message is simple: the novel is just a satire. The "Seven Satiric Thrusts"—Crick's *summa* of the novel—are a *mélange* of the obvious and the flat, at the border of the ridiculous. Like a long explanatory footnote to a joke, they most surely deprive the reader of any joy in savouring the novel or understanding its significance. Needless to say, there is also the obsessive standard reference to "body-snatching" and inconsequential sophistries about Orwell's critique of the Left:

> "He was expert in the art of rubbing his own cat's fur backwards and he enjoyed doing just that. Not to be explicitly socialist is not the same as being implicitly anti-socialist, as body-snatchers for neo-conservatism now argue. . . ."

The text was described in *The Observer* (25 March 1984) by Conor Cruise O'Brien as "a classical example of misplaced and excessive ingenuity, obfuscating the text it is intended to illuminate".

Somehow, for Crick, *1984* is intended not only to "warn" and to "rally", but also to "cheer us up". To assist the cheerfulness, he even manages to give it almost a happy ending:

> "The real ending of the book is not on the note of sado-masochistic horror of the scene in room 101; nor on the picture of a gin-soaked, broken man loving an imaginary leader, but on the words 'so late a date as 2050'. That is the date for the final translation of everything into Newspeak. What has held it up so long, we are authoritatively told by *The Times*, is 'the difficulty' (i.e. the impossibility) of translating writers like 'Shakespeare, Swift, Byron, Dickens'. May clear language and good literature sustain us."

So "the real ending" of *1984* is after all not so gloomy. We can remain cheerful. Professor Crick assures us that Orwell himself meant it so. For Crick, *1984* is a "satire" which is "harsh but good-humoured"—an echo of the blurb on its 1951 edition which first presented it under the obtuse description: "*A good-natured satire on dictatorship*".

The shallowness of so many comments on Orwell is perhaps best highlighted by the words of a Russian dissident. Natalya Hesse emigrated to the West, and she described her last meeting with the Sakharovs:

"Between questions about the life of our dear ones—who has been arrested? whose homes have been searched?—we recalled Orwell, and I think this was not coincidental. We have lived to see the year predicted by Orwell—1984. And it may seem strange to a Western person, it may seem that Orwell has nothing to do with a real life, that this terrible utopia still remains a utopia or maybe an anti-utopia. However, the Soviet authorities—our dear KGB—have overtaken Orwell by four whole years. In 1980, Andrei Dmitrievich Sakharov and Elena Georgievna Bonner were plunged into a world that surpassed Orwell's nightmarish fantasies . . ."

(*The Times*, 9 April 1984,
and *New York Review of Books*, 12 April 1984)

For the Sakharovs, cut off from the world and fighting for their lives, 1984 has indeed been a nightmare. The spectacle of Big Brother's deadly spite towards perhaps the greatest living Russian provided no occasion for Western good cheer.

11. The Ideology of Rubbish

THE "Orwellization" of Orwell continues. The number of examples of rubbish I have inflicted on the reader are just a small portion of the proliferation of "Orwellian" folly occasioned by the advent of 1984.

Who can follow it all? It is, alas, a part of a wider phenomenon involving the general political contamination of our cultural scene and of the "*Newspeak*" pollution of language. In all of this the traditional analytical distinctions between "Right" and "Left" are increasingly difficult to maintain. This seems only too obvious to those who write about the totalitarian experience they have personally undergone. A recent Polish exile in Paris, Kazimierz Brandys, reiterates in *Le Monde* (26 March 1984):

"The writer who arrives [in Western Europe] from Warsaw, Prague, or Budapest . . . is struck by the absence of new ideas. The ideological divisions between Right and Left seem to him to have been overtaken by the experience of his country. He had got used to dividing countries between democratic and totalitarian ones."

This, however, the contemporary Western Left is reluctant to accept. Why? Doubtless during this period the influence of "progressives" on the evolution of the Left has been growing. This can be seen in the evolution of the parties and organizations of the "Left" in the West. In the United States the Democratic Party shifted from Truman, Kennedy and Johnson to Edward Kennedy, Walter Mondale, and Gary Hart (and the "Americans for Democratic Action" shifted from anti-Communism to McGovernism). In

Britain the Labour Party moved from the Attlee and Gaitskell to Foot and Kinnock (while the secession of the SDP weakened its moderate wing). In Germany the Social Democratic Party shifted from Kurt Schumacher and Ernst Reuter to Brandt and Vogel; in Sweden Erlander was replaced by Palme; in Greece there was the rise of *Pasok* and Papandreou.

In other Western countries, like France and Italy, the shift was not so pronounced; but everywhere there was a new polarization reflected in the labels differentiating "socialists" and "social democrats". The Socialist International itself evolved from an organization of an anti-Communist Left (under Braunthal and de Broûckere) to an *anti*-anti-Communist one which, under Brandt and Palme, came close to neutralism. The marked change in the climate of opinion on the Left found its expression not only in the emergence of the so-called "Hard Left" (in Britain, Tony Benn; in France, Jean-Pierre Chevènement), but also in the opportunistic behaviour of such right-wing Labour politicians with formerly strong anti-Communist credentials as Denis Healey and Roy Hattersley.

WOULD Orwell be able to recognize the Labour Party he once supported? It is now officially committed to unilateral nuclear disarmament. Would he recognize the *Tribune* group which while he was alive still supported, however reluctantly, British membership of NATO?

Was Orwell a "pre-nuclear" visionary? Clearly, one new ideological event has occurred: the splitting of the atom has led to the splitting of the "progressive" soul. Some are now more concerned with the vision of the Apocalypse (the End is near) than with the vision of Utopia (Paradise is near). Others, like Raymond Williams and E. P. Thompson, try to combine the two. It is a position logically more appropriate for good Christians than for good Marxists.

In the Soviet Union the post-Khrushchev leaders abandoned the Utopian perspective of the Third Party Programme of 1961 (which proclaimed that Communism would be achieved by 1980) and codified the new ideological line in the formula of "really existing socialism", i.e. the consecration of the internal *status quo*, and the relegation of the classless Utopia to an ever more distant future. That freezing of Utopia also entails a freeze on dialectics: no new theoretical propositions are offered.

In the West the ideological bankruptcy of the Communist movement is matched by the ideological sterility of the "progressives". In all their theoretical dissertations and debates there are no specific proposals as to how the socialist society is, at long last, supposed to work in terms of political organization and economic planning, motives and incentives, distribution and limitations of power, the role of the free or "liberated" individual and of the market. The debates between the "theoreticians" of the New Left are even more vague and abstract than those of their ancestors. The current, very abstract discussions among "progressives", which at the moment divide "Socialists" from "Coalitionists",[20] are entirely devoted to strategy and tactics in "the struggle for power". One can still find Williams tirelessly repeating the monotonous petition for the Left "to develop contemporary (including new) analyses and policies" (*The Guardian*, 20 February 1984)— without himself, of course, offering any such original insights.

In France, the Communists and the Left socialists from CERES vote for Mitterrand in the Chamber of Deputies and criticize him outside it, while the former *gauchiste* professor of sociology Alain Touraine declares that "the essential merit of the government of the Left is to have relieved us of the embarrassment of the socialist ideology".

Thus, the old theories of "socialist transformation" are no longer usable, and no new ideas are available. The "Soviet model" (with its political oppression and Stalinist rigidities of planning) is no longer attractive. The Yugoslav model (with its "market socialism") is in economic trouble; its "workers' self-management" is increasingly seen as an empty ideological alibi, for in practice it does not at all mean "Workers' Control" as in the Western progressive dream. What remains is the allure of power for the activists, who use ideological rationalizations for their "idealistic" motives. In a new "socialist" society the militant trade-union leader Arthur Scargill may well drive a Rolls-Royce instead of a mere Jaguar, but miners will not have the right to strike.

What then is the meaning of "socialism" for those who reject the "really existing" models? If there is no clear answer to this question in 1984, how can one talk about Orwell's "socialism" in the context of 1984 as if it were a proposition which had real meaning? There is no doubt, as everyone admits, that he did consider himself a "socialist" and "a man of the Left". But it is difficult to imagine what these labels would mean to Orwell in the present, now that they have become even more hazy (even in his own time he was unclear about them).

In his article on "Catastrophic Gradualism" (1945) he rejected the definition of socialism as "common ownership of the means of production", as leading to "centralized control" and "a new form of oligarchy". He also condemned "catastrophic gradualism" as the standard justification for "progressive" terror ("you can't make an omelette without breaking eggs") and went on to attack Kingsley Martin for using it:

> "Stalin, he admitted, had done terrible things, but on balance he had served the cause of 'progress' and a few million 'liquidations' cannot obscure this fact. . . ."

[20] See, in particular, Eric Hobsbawm in *Marxism Today* (March 1983) and Raymond Williams in *New Socialist* (March/April 1983).

To the question of "Yes, but where is the omelette?" Orwell wrote, the answer "is likely to be: 'Oh well, you can't expect everything to happen all in a moment.'. . .''

12. The Transvaluation of Values

FORTY YEARS have passed and it is no longer a question of "a moment", but of an epochal experience. Orwell in 1984 would have to ask himself, therefore, whether this point of reference (in another passage about socialism, in the same essay) was sufficient:

> "In the name of Socialism the Russian régime has committed almost every crime that can be imagined, but at the same time its evolution is away from Socialism, unless one redefines that word in terms that no Socialist of 1917 would have accepted."

But in 1984, surely, a "1917" definition of socialism which does not take into account the experience of two-thirds of the century would seem woefully inadequate.

Orwell was at the time still satisfied with the easy formula about the need to combine "planning with freedom". But there were some seeds of doubt in his mind about it, as his review (*The Observer*, 9 April 1944) of F. A. Hayek's *The Road to Serfdom* indicates. Although he criticized its propositions, he also wrote:

> "In the negative part of Professor Hayek's thesis there is a great deal of truth. It cannot be said too often—at any rate, it is not being said nearly often enough—that collectivism is not inherently democratic, but, on the contrary, gives to a tyrannical minority such powers as the Spanish Inquisitors never dreamed of."

Nor, of course, did the author of *Animal Farm* have any illusions about widening privileges in a Soviet-type society. But he did move from the "Revolution Betrayed" type of perception implied by *Animal Farm* (and by the reference to the 1917 socialists) to a more sophisticated argument in *1984*—where it is not just a question of a privileged new ruling class, but of a totalitarian organization of society according to the needs of power, its exercise and its perpetuation.

> "The Party is not a class in the old sense of the word. . . . The older kind of Socialist, who had been trained to fight against something called 'class privilege', assumed that what is not hereditary cannot be permanent. He did not . . . pause to reflect that hereditary aristocracies have always been short-lived, whereas adoptive organizations such as the Catholic Church have sometimes lasted for hundreds or thousands of years."

Crick who asserts that *1984* is "neither wholly nor obsessively concerned with a totalitarian future", has produced a characteristically confused account of Orwell's analysis of it:

> "Most previous writers on totalitarianism, including Orwell himself in essays, had stressed its revolutionary and restless character, its creation of societies in a perpetual state of mobilization for change—what Trotsky had called (encouragingly) 'permanent revolution'. The general view was also that totalitarian parties in power would seek to enrol more members rather than less. Orwell, prompted by Burnham, sees that cold war and atomic stalemate could lead instead to 'stability', or rather a ghastly freezing of human aspiration and social change into a caste, not even a class, society. . . ."

This comment indicates that Crick (*a*) has still not grasped Orwell's meaning; (*b*) does not understand totalitarianism; (*c*) does not know what Trotsky's theory of "permanent revolution" is specifically about. (It is, as every undergraduate Marxist knows, about the telescoping of "bourgeois" and "socialist" revolutions in backward countries, and *not* about the creation of societies in a perpetual state of mobilization for change".)

As for a programme of equality, promising "fair shares" for all and actually banishing economic inequalities, Orwell wrote:

> "Ingsoc, which grew out of the earlier Socialist movement and inherited its phraseology, has in fact carried out the main item in the Socialist programme; with the result, forseen and intended beforehand, that economic inequality has been made permanent."

Crick's annotation to this disturbing passage is the bland apologetic assurance to the reader that "Orwell is not attacking socialism, but a simplistic version. . . ."

Orwell was quite unambiguous about a certain naive purism so often invoked by disappointed "true believers". He approvingly paraphrased Arthur Koestler on this "notion that so-and-so has 'betrayed' . . . [which] is ever present in left-wing thought":

> "It is not merely that 'power corrupts'; so also do the ways of attaining power. Therefore all efforts to regenerate society *by violent means* leads to the cellars of the *OGPU*, Lenin leads to Stalin, and would have come to resemble Stalin if he had happened to survive."
>
> (*Collected Essays*, Vol. 3, p. 278)

Similarly he made this trenchant comment on Trotsky:

> "Trotsky, in exile, denounces the Russian dictatorship, but he is probably as much responsible for it as any man now living and there is

no certainty that as a dictator he would be preferable to Stalin, though undoubtedly he has a much more interesting mind. The essential act is the rejection of democracy—that is, of the underlying values of democracy; once you have decided upon that, Stalin—or at any rate someone *like* Stalin—is already under way."

(Collected Essays, Vol. 1, p. 418)

O RWELL IS NOT THE FIRST (and one presumes not the last) major writer who has been subject to misinterpretation. But it is difficult to find a comparable case of ideological "reinterpretation" where the message of the author has undergone such a degree of distortion and corruption so soon—such a total reversal so early on.

The ideological need for it must be very great indeed because the process continues. Reviewing in *Tribune* (23 March 1984) the new edition of Raymond Williams' *Orwell*, Oliver Whitehead approves his thesis that:

> "Orwell actually moved to the Left as he developed politically, not, as is often supposed, in the other direction. The Cold War warriors who claim Orwell for themselves are profoundly wrong. . . . 'In England', Orwell wrote towards the end of his life, 'the immediate enemies of truthfulness, and hence of freedom of thought, are the press lords, the film magnates and the bureaucrats' and it is this insight which shaped some of the most significant sections of *1984*."

And in "a collection of radical essays" entitled *Nineteen Eighty-Four in 1984* (Comedia), David Widgery busies himself with "reclaiming" Orwell "from the Cold War fanatics".

Faced with this whirligig of absurdity, one can only recall Orwell's remark that "*to be corrupted by totalitarianism one does not have to live in a totalitarian country. The mere prevalence of certain ideas can spread a kind of poison. . . .*" But surely Orwell would not have imagined that he himself would be adopted by the "progressives", and used to spread the poison.

LOOKING AT THE WHOLE STORY OF Orwell between *1984* and 1984, one cannot help but feel a certain relief in reading a letter to the Editor of the *New Statesman* (6 January 1984) which honestly expresses, in "*Oldspeak*", an old straightforward sentiment:

> "1984 is the year for socialists to consign Orwell to the dustbin of history."

Alas, this is unlikely to happen. The "progressives" may well explore still other possibilities of "Orwellian transvaluation". What, for instance, should prevent them from "Orwellizing" *Darkness at Noon*, now that Arthur Koestler is safely dead? The "Cold Warriors" could again be accused of "body-snatching". One could almost hear the argument that what Koestler really had in mind was "Midnight in Manhattan"—Rubashov being modelled on Rosenberg, and Gletkin on Judge Irving Kaufman. . . .

In a recent book (*Headbirths, or the Germans are Dying Out*) Günter Grass raised the question: "How will Sisyphus react to Orwell's decade?" The answer is now obvious. Judging by this mid-year history of Orwell in 1984, it will be the same old Sisyphean story all over again.

IT IS A DISPIRITING SPECTACLE to see so many of our Western contemporaries (who enjoy freedom) wailing that Orwell predicted their present terrible enslavement.

Yet we can take heart at the stirring effort of so many libertarian dissidents (who are actually enslaved) as they turn to the message of a writer who offers them the spiritual weapons of clarity and integrity. George Orwell will survive 1984.

(1984)

9. Appreciating Milosz

*"[An article] . . . provoked my anger, as always happens when
someone uncovers our painful secret"*
Czeslaw Milosz, NATIVE REALM (1968)
*". . . Our respect for someone's justifiable anger does not exempt
us from critical objectivity."*
Czeslaw Milosz, THE LAND OF ULRO (1977)

C ZESLAW MILOSZ'S poetry, essays, and novels have been translated
into many languages, but for a Nobel laureate his literary audience is not
very wide. ★ This is not, it seems, only because (as Paul Valéry said) "poetry is
the thing which is lost in translation . . ." Milosz pointed out the deeper
reason in his Nobel Prize lecture. He said that a newcomer from Eastern
Europe, "wherever he finds himself, notices that he is separated from his new
environment by the store of his experience. . . ." There is, inevitably, a gap
between Milosz's vision, images and reflections, his references and allusions,
and their reception by readers with a quite different "store of experience".
In *The Land of Ulro* Milosz asked the question:

"How to accept that what is obvious to us may not be so for others?
How many ways, on how many levels, do we discover the
inaccessibility of another mind? And this makes for unease: if behind the
words uttered in conversation lies another perception, another wisdom,
then the words, although the same, must connote something different."

In his pessimism on intercommunication—which may be realistic on a
mass level, but which his own books can only undermine—Milosz is saying
in effect that every national experience is an island unto itself and cannot be
approached from outside:

"I do not believe in the possibility of communing outside a shared
language, a shared history. . . . One of the most serious and frustrating
dilemmas resulting from prolonged residence abroad is having to
repress the constantly intruding thought: How would this sound in
English? How constructed by a foreign reader? I cannot stand writing in
a foreign language."

In this, and in many other respects, he is obviously the opposite of Joseph
Conrad (except, perhaps, in their perception of Russia, as can be seen from a
comparison of *Under Western Eyes* and of Conrad's essay "Autocracy and

---

★ *Czeslaw Milosz* recently celebrated his 75th birthday. The 1980 Polish Nobel Prize-winner
for Literature has been living in California since 1961 (where until his retirement he was
Professor of Slavic Languages and Literatures at Berkeley).

War" with the chapter on the subject in *Native Realm*). Unlike Conrad, Milosz decided that:

> ". . . if I am to nourish the hope of writing with a free hand, with gaiety, and not under pressure, then I must proceed by keeping only a few Polish readers in mind. . . . I belong to the estate of Polish literature and to no other."

It is, of course, possible for a writer of Milosz's intellectual breadth to bridge the gap to some extent, to be understood not only by his compatriots. Indeed, while remaining rooted in his particular experience, Milosz tries after all to give it a universal significance. And in this respect it is not just his influential political book of 1953, *The Captive Mind*, which is of relevance.

The role of memory in Milosz's writings cannot be overstressed. In his words, "For me memory is mother of all the Muses." He remains "an exile", as have so many fine European writers ever since Dante; but for him memory is not just a question of nostalgia—even though, as he has remarked, the number of "Florences" has grown enormously since Dante's time.

> "The exile of a poet is today a function of a relatively recent discovery: today those in power may also control the language, not only through censorship, but by changing the meaning of words."

THIS ORWELLIAN CONNECTION between the manipulation of language and the nature of the totalitarian state was the subject of *The Captive Mind* (1953), and it powerfully supplemented *1984*; for, after all, it was a non-fictional report on a really *lived* experience. Milosz recollects that "The Marxists . . . had attracted me as a young man because I sensed in them something vital and bracing." He says that for him "the Russian Revolution was personified not by Lenin, but by Vladimir Mayakovsky". With his strong Manichean predisposition, he felt an affinity with the Communists, who "were bolstered by a variant of a belief in the fundamental hidden rationality of the historical process. . . ." Eventually, however, he obviously found that Mayakovsky (who committed suicide before Milosz exhibited enthusiasm for him) had played, after all, a less important role than Lenin in shaping Communist reality. As a writer Milosz had discovered the "socialist-realist" compulsion to pretend that this reality is not what it is.

Like so many other disappointed intellectuals, Milosz realized that the most important defence against the Communist denial of "the right to reality" is memory, both for the poet and for the people: they all need to retain their identity. Hence, the primary task of a writer is to preserve memory as the first line of resistance against the enforced falsification of words, images, and ideas. Whatever his subject, and whatever his mood, authenticity is his first duty. His individual awareness inevitably clashes with the fraudulent "truth" forced upon him by the state. The pressure is strong, and the temptation to submit great.

Milosz analysed the mechanism of the intellectual rationalization of such submission in *The Captive Mind* in a way that made it comprehensible to a Western audience at a time when very few people in the West were aware of such phenomena in any detail. He pointed out that totalitarianism is not just the sombre drama of horror and purges, that it has more humdrum but no less far-reaching consequences:

> "Terror is not, as Western intellectuals imagine, monumental; it is abject, it has a furtive glance, it destroys the fabric of human society and changes the relationships of millions of individuals into channels of blackmail. . . ."

Apart from his insight into Stalinized Poland, the other themes of Milosz's poetic memory are his youth in Wilno, the multi-ethnic town in pre-War north-eastern Poland, and his wartime experiences under the Nazi occupation in Warsaw. With the exception of some of his lyrical poems and literary essays, all his writings, in one way or another, echo these three themes. As with all his generation, the basic trauma which divides his memory is the clash between the innocence (and "normality") of his youth before the Second World War and the ensuing horrors during and after it.

A S A STUDENT, Milosz belonged to a left-wing group opposing the ruling régime in pre-War Poland.[1] As a young poet, he sensed the approaching disaster (he belonged to a poetic school described as "the Catastrophists"). Under the Nazis the reality surpassed anything he may have vaguely feared in his "anti-fascist" imagination. His experiences of the Hitler occupation in Poland were shattering:

> "For a study of human madness, the history of the Vistula basin, during the time it bore the curious name of '*Government General*', makes excellent material. Yet the enormity of the crimes committed here paralyses the imagination, and this, no doubt, is why the massacres in the small Czech town of Lidice and in the small French town of Oradour are given more notice in the annals of Nazi-dominated Europe than the region where there were hundreds of Lidices and Oradours. . . ."

Milosz gave poetic testimony to one of these horrors in a poem entitled "Campo dei Fiori", written at the time of the liquidation by the Germans of the Warsaw Ghetto in 1943. Its last stanza conveys his awe-stricken dread:

---

[1] The subsequent destiny of other members of this group is of interest. One was executed during the Occupation by the Polish Underground for helping the Soviet secret police. Two were killed by the Russians in Katyn in 1940. Two others became very prominent figures in Communist Poland after the War.

Those dying here, the lonely
forgotten by the world,
their tongue becomes for us
the language of an ancient planet.
Until when all is legend,
and many years have passed,
on a new Campo dei Fiori
rage will kindle at a poet's word.

Milosz knows only too well that certain experiences cannot be adequately transmitted through words in any language:

> "Had I been given the choice, perhaps, I would have blown the country to bits, so that the grass would no longer grow over the ashes of Treblinka and Maidanek and Auschwitz, so that the notes of a harmonica played under a gnarled pine tree would no longer float over the nightmarish pits and dunes on the city outskirts. Because there is a kind of pity that is unbearable. And so one blows it all up, at least in one's mind, that is, one is possessed by one single desire: not to look. . . ."

AFTER THE WAR, Milosz joined the Communist régime, less out of ideological enthusiasm for "the New Faith" than from a belief that the victory of the Soviet juggernaut was "historically inevitable". To justify this he accepted a type of philosophical rationalization elaborated by his friend, the philosopher Tadeusz Kronski—"Tiger", He described him in his essays as sharing the mental affliction which came to be called "being bitten by Hegel", a Polish counterpart to Schopenhauer's remark that "Whoever becomes infected by '*Hegelei und Schleiermacherei*' will never be cured."

Tiger, who died in 1958, was his intellectual guru, and Milosz describes him with great warmth. At the same time, the retrospective apologia for Tiger helps Milosz to defend himself from accusations of simple opportunism:

> "Words cannot describe the fascination with someone's personality or an intellectual friendship. . . . When Tiger spoke of 'Christians', it was understood he meant Communists. The allegory was justified in so far as the idea of the inevitable progress or of a hidden force behind the scenes—implacable toward all who disobeyed the Teacher's commands—took its origins from Christianity: without Christianity, after all, there would have been no Hegel or Marx. The sacred merely underwent secularization, the immanent replaced the transcendent.
>
> In any case, should not the wise man have drawn conclusions from the inevitable?"

Rationalizations know no limits in history. Reflecting on the decline of the Roman Empire, the Greek poet C. P. Cavafy wrote about Roman citizens 'waiting for the barbarians'', and he concluded his poem with the line: "The barbarians were a kind of solution.'' Milosz also found for himself a kind of solution.

"In the teaching of 'Ketman' practised by Mohammedan heretics in Persia (it was not unlike the Jesuit *reservatio mentalis*), a distinction was made between the goal toward which we fervently and passionately strive and the veils by which the prudent screen it from view. . . . Wear a mask, throw them off the scent—you will be forgiven if you preserve the love of Good within you.''

But although Milosz realized that "there is no immanent divinity that guarantees the moral glory of what is irreversible'', he still insists:

"I was right in rejecting the light from the East, but the Communists were also right. Thanks to the Red Army, they soon seized power [in Poland] and then I had to serve them. Whoever claims that force cannot suffice as an argument overlooks the character of politics, where winner takes all. . . . From the dreams of 19th-century Socialists about a perfect society, nothing had really been salvaged. Instead, the foreground was dominated by the Hegelian conviction that certain phases will be victorious over others: that things are as they are, and we are not responsible.''

MILOSZ DID NOT TRY to make a virtue out of "historical necessity'', but, as is his wont, he tried to avoid making a choice: he would not, as he loftily says, "lapse into the comfort of moral intransigency'', nor did he "attach himself solely to the present by writing for the Party''. His attitude was reminiscent of Joyce's maxim: "Silence, exile and cunning.'' As the present was both unpleasant and inevitable, the Hegelian snake-bite became for Tiger and Milosz an ideological rationale for moral as well as political impotence. Milosz reflects, however, that:

". . . the problem with choosing madness (a refusal to recognise necessity) and servility (an acknowledgement of our complete powerlessness) is that one act of obedience can be the start of a downward slide.''

He adds that his (imagined) "freedom of manoeuvre remained intact only as long as I lived abroad behind the screen of diplomatic service''. But he felt that he was "threatened with sliding because we are drawn into compromise almost without our being aware of it. . . .''

It is, to be sure, a moot point when the "sliding'' begins. But although Hegel idealized the Prussian state, and the Russian writer Belinsky "made use of Hegel during a certain period of his life to deify Czardom", Milosz still thought that "History's course is not something to be discarded easily." He referred to his religious instructor, a Catholic priest at his school, as "Naphta". But his guru now was Tiger, who perhaps fitted Thomas Mann's description even better.[2] According to Milosz, Tiger "had persuaded himself that in the last analysis his deceit served the truth". Milosz continued to cultivate his "dialectical" garden:

> "Immobility or resistance to historical changes that time brings with it in the name of unchangeable moral commandments and a stable structure of the universe is deserving of respect. However, those who armour themselves in this way risk punishment, because sooner or later the Spirit of History will appear, 'His face large as ten moons, a chain of freshly cut heads around his neck. . . .' I refused simply to slip out of the antinomy between the divine and the historical that was poisoning my life."

OTHER "ANTINOMIES" were also present. As a Communist diplomat he had to confront constantly the hypocrisy of living on two levels of reality. His private thoughts clashed sharply with his official duties, as he recalls in *Native Realm*:

> "At many a reception in Washington or in Paris, where enthusiastic ladies would approach a Red with a delicious shiver . . . I felt that I was only half present. . . ."

He ironically describes "those lady enthusiasts at our receptions at the Embassy, admirers of progress in the East, hens pleading for a few kernels of lying propaganda. . . . One of them gravely asked us how we intend to solve the Negro problem in our country." But at the time—the time when Orwell and Koestler were trying to dispel the illusions of the Western intelligentsia— this was not Milosz's concern.

> "I munched *hors d'oeuvres* while exchanging polite clichés with a crowd of progressive writers at various receptions, but I did not attempt to break down the wall that stood between me and them. Their warmed-

---

[2] Milosz writes about Tiger:

"When the unpleasant subject of concentration camps [in the Soviet Union] cropped up in our conversation, there were always two stages in his response. First he would wither and contract: although he was splendidly informed about the millions of people behind barbed wire, he did not want to 'weaken'; that is to imagine the extent of their suffering. Then he would break into yells: he accused me of common sense (which is reactionary), of sympathy for fools. . . . It seemed as if cruelty, if it is abstract enough, strengthened his convictions: the more shadow a thing makes, the greater and the more powerful it is. But if he kept himself pumped up with the lives of the saints—Thorez's autobiography, *Le Fils du Peuple*, lay on his night table—for balance he read Arthur Koestler and Orwell's *1984*. . . ."

over Jacobin ideas did not coincide with any reality; they were social diversions. It was not my place to enlighten them or to betray what I thought of them."

But he was very unhappy about it.

"Standing with my glass of vodka at receptions in the Soviet Embassy, I watched how Leftist luminaires of French literature and art minced around a [Soviet] diplomat, seizing upon his every word, nodding approval—polite little boys in front of their teacher. The magic unguent of power must have rubbed off upon me too, a new arrival from the East, with my broad non-Western face, but I was ashamed of it."

After his service as a cultural attaché in the Polish Embassies in France and the USA, Milosz had eventually had enough of self-deception. In 1951 he "chose freedom". He expounded the reasons for his decision at a press conference chaired by Ignazio Silone (organized in Paris by the Congress for Cultural Freedom), and in an article, "No", published in the Polish émigré magazine *Kultura*. There he stated that a writer in the People's Democracies "has to renounce the truth completely" even though "he witnesses every day human tragedies in comparison with which the tragedies of antiquity pale into insignificance".

HIS DECISION and his explanations provoked furious attacks on him in the Polish official press (including one by the poet Antoni Slonimski, who later renounced his own opportunism and became the literary patron of the dissident opposition).[3]

Polish émigrés in the West were divided. Some criticized Milosz for "belated discovery of the obvious" after supporting the Communist régime for years, and particularly for becoming its official representative; others welcomed him and demanded tolerance for a writer who had undergone "an honest disillusionment".

Milosz was clearly very wounded by these attacks and polemics (especially from émigrés) about his motives, and replied to them with acerbity. They eventually died down. He became accepted by the Poles, both inside the country and abroad, as a leading contemporary Polish poet. During the period of *Solidarity* he was officially rehabilitated, belatedly published, and even personally fêted during his visit to Poland in 1981. The workers from

---

[3] In 1980—in his last poem, "The Trial of Don Quixote", which became his testament— Slonimski wrote:

> Here, only yesterday, brother would send
> brother to rot in jail, would humiliate and
> torture him on a Procrustean bed
> Then he'd put a jester's cap on his bloody head.

the Gdansk shipyard put a quotation from a Milosz poem on the monument
they built for their murdered colleagues. He became, again, a target of
censorship under General Jaruzelski.[4] The Serbian Academy of Arts and
Sciences, which made Milosz (in 1986) "a corresponding member abroad",
was sharply attacked in the Polish press, and Yugoslav journals were
criticized for praising that reprehensible (but still unforgotten) book, *The
Captive Mind*.

Milosz is an intellectual poet; also a metaphysical poet, and one of passion.
Each of these elements inevitably clashes with the others, and this becomes a
source of a creative tension and of certain problems for his philosophy.
Poetry seems to help him clarify his feelings, but philosophy only tends
to obfuscate them. While his emotions are always rather obvious, his
philosophical attitudes are more often than not equivocal. He almost made
the cultivation of *ambivalence* into a programmatic philosophical premise;
nothing seems more painful to him than the intellectual necessity of *choice*.
This is revealed in the description of his early attitudes both to Marxism and
to religion. He indicates that he found it impossible to make up his mind
about them:

> "Marxists dismissed their opponents by treating them en masse as
> 'idealists'. Although such an indictment embraced too many elements to
> be philosophically correct, it did contain a particle of truth. I was
> stretched, therefore, between two poles: the contemplation of a
> motionless point and the command to participate actively in history; in
> other words, between transcendence and becoming. I did not manage to
> bring these elements into unity, but I did not want to give either of them
> up."

The roots of the dichotomy go back to his school education where the
Catholic priest and the Latin teacher presented him with opposite
philosophical positions:

> "The mere presence of such a Naphta and such a Settembrini gave us an
> option. My rebellion against the priest weighted the scale in favour of

---

[4] In 1985 the Literary Publishing House in Cracow published an anthology—*Poznawanie
Milosza (Getting to Know Milosz)*, edited by Jerzy Kwiatkowski—on many aspects of Milosz's
literary work, written by Polish admirers of the poet. The book, published in a limited edition, is
a collection of essays most of which had appeared during the earlier period when Milosz's
writings were more accessible in Poland. A review of the anthology by Joanna Gramek, in the
Catholic journal *Znak* (No. 1, 1986), was heavily cut by the censors.

The planned Polish edition of Milosz's works has not so far materialized, and its chances have
not increased now that he has written an introduction to the English translation of Adam
Michnik's *Letters from Prison* (translated by Maya Latynski, University of California Press), in
which he extols this hero of KOR, *Solidarity*, and the (non-violent) resistance to the Jaruzelski
régime.

the Latinist. But my religious crisis was not a final thing; it did not end in a clear 'yes' or 'no'. . . ."

In his writings Milosz refers very often to the wisdom of various Biblical sayings. But "Let your communication be, Yea, yea; Nay, nay . . ." is not one of them. He is well aware of this psychological trait. Commenting on his intellectual and political evolution, he wrote:

"The official anti-Communism of the West was false, as is every frozen thought, but many a time its representatives closed their eyes to what they did not wish to see in my works. In that Tower of Babel, language was confounded because the levels of consciousness were different. I had to consent in advance to defeat, which is dangerous, because then we are tempted to exult in our inner readiness to accept the cross. . . . Many of my contemporaries may regard such thrashing about as the neurotic unhinging of a modern Hamlet. Their jobs and their amusements prevent them from seeing what is really at stake. I was not a philosopher. Events themselves threw me into my century's towering philosophical pressures, into the vortex of its hardest and most essential questions. Perhaps these exceeded my grasp, but they mobilised all my energies."

Milosz thinks that in his work "the song of innocence and the song of experience share a common theme". Perhaps. But one cannot help listening to the songs, noting how often he has changed his tune. In the poetic programme of his youth he exclaimed that "one does not wear short pants forever"; in Communist Poland he considers his poetry "a kind of higher politics, an unpolitical politics"; and now he says that "in poetry, I wanted to save my childhood". It is easier to see here the fortuitous continuity of a poet than the serene wisdom of a philosopher.[5]

He is particularly fascinated by the mystical and religious poets and writers: Blake and Swedenborg; Shestov and Dostoevsky; the French poet Oscar Milosz (his cousin) and Simone Weil. He has also been particularly affected by his reading of the Bible, and has even learned Hebrew in order to make a new translation of the Book of Job and the Psalms into Polish.

THE RELIGIOUS, IF NOT MYSTICAL, motifs are particularly developed in his *Land of Ulro*; the autobiographical background is described in his novel *The Issa Valley* (1955). In a recent interview for *La Stampa* (5 July 1986) Milosz explained:

---

[5] Writing in his diary (*Fragments d'un journal*, Gallimard, 1973), Mircea Eliade reflected on 25 August 1947:

"They tell me that . . . one has to respond, in one way or another, to the historical time one lives in. Agreed, but I would respond to it as did Buddha or Socrates: by transcending my historical time, creating a new one, or preparing it."

"The Lithuania of my youth is for me very much alive because the forests, the valleys and the rivers which I saw in my childhood possess for me a strong evocative force. But, as happened with Proust, childhood also for me became separated from time. If I talk in my writings about Lithuania, it is not out of nostalgia for the past, the nostalgia of an exile, but for artistic purposes, for writer's reasons. Already this landscape has become for me mixed in my memory with the landscapes of other countries I have seen since; California, and elsewhere. Thus my poems are both 'Lithuanian' and 'Californian' at the same time. . . ."

He has also declared, "A poet carries his land within him. I never left Poland."

Facing the problem of national identity presents Milosz with one of his crucifying choices. He often refers to his mixed ethnic background. His mother was of Lithuanian ancestry, and in describing her he says that she was responsible for "the tangle of contradictions I see in myself".

"Another trait of hers was patriotism, but not toward the nation or the state—she responded rather coolly to that brand. Instead, she taught me a partiotism of 'home'; i.e., of my native province."

This is undoubtedly one of the reasons why Milosz is so attached to the realm of his youth. It also accounts for his local "patriotism".

Another person who strongly influenced him was his cousin Oscar Milosz, who faced a similar problem. He opted for Lithuania, and represented its interests at a Paris Peace Conference in 1919. Czeslaw Milosz has described his native Wilno with its ethnically mixed environment in an anthropological symposium,[6] in an essay which could serve as a model for a *verstehende* approach in cultural anthropology. It also reflects his ethnic dilemmas.

"Today, if I call this city the capital of the Lithuanian Soviet Republic, Vilnius, I give a hint of my Lithuanian identity. If I call it Wilno, I present myself to the Lithuanians as probably a Pole or a Russian. Behind the double names lie the complex historical events of several centuries."

In all his other writings Milosz uses the word "Wilno". But this is hardly a reflection of Polish nationalism: he has made quite clear his hatred of the Polish "nationalist party", and particularly to the xenophobic "radical nationalists".

"My allergy to everything that smacks of the 'national' and an almost

---

[6] Czeslaw Milosz, "Vilnius, Lithuania: An Ethnic Agglomerate", in *Ethnic Identity, Cultural Continuities and Change* (ed. George de Vos and Lola Romanucci-Ross, Palo Alto, 1975), pp. 339–352.

physical disgust for people who transmit such [xenophobic] signals have weighed heavily upon my destiny."

The national strife over Wilno/Vilnius evoked in Milosz some melancholy thoughts:

> "The Poles maintained that Wilno should belong to Poland, the Lithuanians that Vilnius has always been and would be a part of Lithuania. Perhaps those sardines fighting each other in the mouth of a whale are not untypical of the relations between humans when they search for self-assertion through ethnic values magnified into absolutes."

A NUMBER OF Milosz's philosophical reflections and literary essays can be read in *Emperor of the Earth: Modes of Eccentric Vision* (1977). His poetry, translated into English by himself and others, has been published in several volumes; and his autobiographical self-definition against the East European background and that of Western civilization is most vividly expressed in his *Native Realm* and in *The Land of Ulro*. This short list of his works in English gives perhaps an idea of his range. Some of his writings in Polish are not yet available in translation, but what has appeared in English provides, I think, the Western reader with enough material to appreciate Milosz's stature as a writer and a witness for the times. He has touchingly summarized his life and work in *The Land of Ulro*:

> "In a cruel and mean century, 'catastrophism' entertained dreams of an idyllic earth where 'the hay smells of the dream', where tree, man, animal are joined in praise of the Garden's beauty. By recalling that the boy and the poet 'catastrophist' and the old professor at Berkeley are the same man, I am merely observing the guiding principle of this book, a book both childish and adult, both ethereal and earthbound. Reader, be tolerant of me."

For all his philosophical and political peregrinations, East and West, one cannot but be impressed by Milosz's intact poetic and literary sensibility. From his "store of experience" he has vividly conveyed the meaning of contemporary tragedies and personal dilemmas.

At 75 Milosz remains as intensely puzzled by the world as when he was a child. In his novel *The Issa Valley*, he wrote that his birthplace "has the distinction of being inhabited by an unusually large number of devils", and he concluded that "there is no denying the cunning of the demons":

> "How ingenious of them to undermine the confidence of Thomas [his childhood *alter ego* in the novel] in his own internal voice, to rob him of his peace of mind by appealing to his scrupulosity. No longer could he implore God for illumination; genuflecting, he would always have the

feeling he was kneeling before himself. Thomas wanted to confide in the Real, not in a cloud that, nourished by what is inside us, hangs overhead."

"Tiger" (who bestowed on Milosz "the glorious title of dialectician") argued that "evil is a test of what is *real*". This is evidently a question which does not at all bother the poet, but to which the philosopher cannot get the answer from the dialectician. That is, perhaps, why Milosz is such an elusive personality and such an open book.

(1986)

10. Raymond Aron's "Vindication"

R AYMOND ARON'S *Plaidoyer pour l'Europe décadente*,[1] was written as a
tract for the French elections of March 1978. But it deals not just with the
political issues and electoral risks; it provides a sharp focus on the general
historical implications of current European weaknesses and confusions. The
West Europeans, preoccupied as they are with the immediate home-front
problems of their countries, seem unable or unwilling to recognize the
dangers involved in the choices facing them at the moment, choices which
might be decisive for liberal values in Western Europe.

In his defence of "our decadent Europe", Raymond Aron gives a
magisterial analysis of the cultural, political and economic problems facing us
in the fourth decade after the Second World War. He reflects on the historic
tribulations of the Communist countries, on the present economic crisis in
the West, on so-called North–South relations, on Soviet dissidence, and on
the Euro-Communists. He draws lessons from 20th-century experience and
presents his conclusions—Aron's own political *summa* of contemporary
history—not just for France, but for the West as a whole. The volume has not
yet been published in English, but excerpts from the book (in *Encounter*) give
an idea of its scope, its depth and its cool reasonableness, so characteristic of
Aron's writings. Raymond Aron's position can be ignored by the West only
at its peril.

Plaidoyer pour l'Europe décadente can also be seen against the background of a
particularly ironical juxtaposition. Aron writes that during the last French
electoral campaign (in 1974) he was struck by the overwhelming support
given by the French intelligentsia to the Socialist-Communist coalition.
Paradoxically, although the French "progressive" intellectuals still support
it, they are undergoing an ideological upheaval at the very moment when
l'Union de la Gauche is poised to win the election under the banner of the
Programme Commun. After decades of sophisticated self-deception about the
harsh realities in Communist countries and of the double standards applied
to them, the ritualistic passions, mental stereotypes, and cherished myths
composing what Aron calls *le sinistrisme* (inadequately translated as
"Leftism") have suddenly been challenged from within the *gauchist* milieu
itself.

THE IDEOLOGICAL EARTHQUAKE started with Solzhenitsyn. He found
defenders not only among the "visceral anti-Communists" but also among

---

[1] *Plaidoyer pour l'Europe décadente*, by Raymond Aron (Robert Laffont, 1977).

the old radical Left—the editor of the now defunct *Les Lettres Françaises*, the (then) Communist Pierre Daix; the editor of *Le Nouvel Observateur*, Jean Daniel; its regular contributor, Maurice Clavel; and many others.

Soon younger intellectuals from among the *contestataires* of May 1968 appeared on the scene. One of them, the ex-Maoist André Glucksmann, wrote a passionate defence of Solzhenitsyn in the press and then published an equally passionate *cri de coeur* about his disillusion in two books: *La Cuisinière et le Mangeur d'Hommes* (subtitled "Essay on the State, Marxism and the Concentration Camps"), and *Les Maîtres Penseurs* in which he rejected both Marxist theories and Communist practices.

After the publication of *The Gulag Archipelago* a number of young French writers and philosophers suddenly discovered the problem of totalitarianism. The children of 1968 saw in Solzhenitsyn "the Shakespeare of our age". *"Gulag"* entered their vocabulary and the *Archipelago* texts (as François Bondy put it) "became their political Bible", replete with testaments of suffering and courage. They refused to see Stalin simply as an historical aberration, and began to search for the explanation of the totalitarian phenomenon in Marx's own ideas. Even the somewhat older philosopher, the former editor of *Socialisme ou Barbarie*, Claude Lefort in *Un Homme Fort* (subtitled "Reflections on *The Gulag Archipelago*") subjected his own Marxist assumptions to a critical examination, and concluded that it was Marx himself who in a contradictory way was nevertheless the source of the totalitarian practices of his disciples as they become the masters of the state. Marcel Gauchet, in his essay "The Totalitarian Experience and Political Thought" (*Esprit*, July–August 1976), asserted that the common trait of both Fascist and Communist states is their claim of a total identification with society. Bernard-Henri Lévy made another dent in the Marxist domination of the post-War intellectual scene in France. He asked himself the puzzling question how it was possible for "scientific socialism" to permit the emergence of "Gulag" and for the "proletarian consciousness" embodied in the Communist Party to tolerate the tyranny of Stalin. In his painfully pessimistic book, Lévy criticized not just Marxism but also *le progressisme* and, in effect, French revolutionary rhetoric itself. He warned that the promises of *les lendemains qui chantent* made by the Left may lead, as they did elsewhere, to *l'univers concentrationnaire*.

THE NEW PHILOSOPHY, as this tendency was dubbed, has evoked an extraordinary response among Left intellectuals, including some of the most famous archetypal progressives. But it was subjected to bitter attacks from those among them who remained attached to their revolutionary utopias. They accused the young gurus (as *Le Nouvel Observateur* called the "New Philosophers") of having become "the tool of reaction" and of undermining the electoral chances of *l'Union de la Gauche*. They were even labelled "the

New Right"—although they evidently derive from the radical mainstream of the French Left and still proclaim their attachment to it. We observe here an evolution not just of separate individuals, but of a whole milieu. Between 1966 and 1968 Bernard-Henri Lévy, Philippe Nemo, Christian Jambet, Guy Lardreau, Michel Guérin (and some other future New Philosophers) attended the seminars at the famous Louis-le-Grand *lycée*. They were influenced by Lacan and Althusser. Later, some of them collaborated with the Maoist and New Left journals (e.g. *La Cause du Peuple* and *l'Idiot International*).

The New Philosophers were censured by a number of critics. Maurice Duverger stressed their "confusion" (*Le Monde*, 10 June), which is true enough, but (as Raymond Aron emphasizes) Duverger himself is far from being free from related ambiguities. It is also true that they have not originated any essentially new ideas. They began to elaborate certain old truths which had been expressed often before by successive European generations of disillusioned utopians and revolutionaries. But they have done so with authentic passion, and there was indeed an evident freshness in their discovery of liberty. Attacks on them were mainly concerned with their effect on the already crumbling myths of the "progressive" intelligentsia, on the fading hold of Marxism (once described by Sartre as "the unsurpassable philosophy of our time") in the present intellectual climate of France. They have changed it to a point where references to David Rousset (who even in the 1940s tried to convince the French Left intelligentsia that Stalinist forced labour camps *did* exist) and to Viktor Kravchenko (whose *I Chose Freedom* was the centrepiece in a famous Paris libel trial) are no longer taboo.

Raymond Aron's point in his latest book is very apposite:

"The essence of a certain *sinistrisme* is the systematic application of double standards. I happened to be listening to a Paris radio broadcast on the day when Andrei Sakharov was awarded the Nobel Peace Prize. '*Une petite bombe*', the journalist remarked in a superior tone, as if to remind his listeners that the physicist had played a big part in the manufacture of the H-bomb. Yes, this champion of human rights whom the Norwegian judges were honouring had indeed helped to perfect the thermonuclear missile. But when Robert Oppenheimer, who had been head of the Los Alamos team, was persecuted during the McCarthyite 'witch-hunt' period, the intelligentsia throughout the world rushed to his defence. And what did the persecution consist of? He was denied access to US secret documents on the ground that he was a 'security risk'. But he retained the confidence of the trustees of the Institute for Advanced Study at Princeton, and remained Director of that prestigious institution.

Sakharov has spent years struggling for the cause of human rights in the Soviet Union, a matter of concern for the whole of humanity, for which he has sacrificed his peace and security, and his privileges. Why react with reserve, as if with embarrassment, to a tribute rendered to a hero of non-violent resistance? Andrei Sakharov, that anonymous Paris broadcaster said, often joined up with 'the professionals' of anti-Communism. Should we include among these 'professionals' N. S. Khrushchev, who made the famous speech to the Twentieth Congress which has never been disavowed by those who attack 'Cold War anti-Communists'? Shouldn't the real charge be that these 'professionals' were for so long a time the only ones in the West or East to speak the truth? . . ."

THE COUNTER-OFFENSIVE of *le sinistrisme* soon got under way. Regis Debray—the pupil of Louis Althusser, the theoretician of the revolutionary *foco* in guerrilla warfare (*Revolution in the Revolution*), who moved from Che Guevara to François Mitterand by way of Salvador Allende—has violently castigated the New Philosophers for "mechanically identifying the Gulag with real socialism" ("Les Pleureuses du Printemps", *Le Nouvel Observateur*, 13 June). Others accused them of indulging in a "new obscurantism", of "*un travail de cochon*" (*cf.* François Aubral and Xavier Delcourt, *Contre La Nouvelle Philosophie*, Gallimard, 1977, and Gilles Deleuze in *Le Monde*, 19–20 June).

Replying to the critics, Jean-Marie Benoist defined the issue (in *Le Monde*, 3–4 July) as one in which what is at stake is the possibility that wherever the Communist Party came to power "Marxism would become a monopolistic state religion, barbaric and even more bloodthirsty than the Christianity of the Inquisition." Bernard-Henri Lévy was no less emphatic in *Le Nouvel Observateur* (27 June 1977):

> "When I published my *Barbarie à visage humain* a few weeks ago I did not anticipate that it would generate so much hatred and bad faith, so much meanness and stupidity. . . . I have never believed that I personally possess 'the truth' or even that I am 'in the right'; but, facing such a concert of accusations, I begin to ask myself whether I have not touched some very sensitive point. Which one? . . . Some of us think that to 'resist' today means to dare to say 'no' to the murderous visions of the omniscient savants who claim to know the way to happiness. Today some of us realise that such false claims in politics frequently end in a blood-bath, though unfortunately the blood spilled is always that of others."

In his editorial in the same journal, Jean Daniel formulated the thought in a less abstract form:

> "The belief in Marxist prophecy remains intact in the French Communist Party, and it could produce a totalitarian trend. . . ."

THE CURRENT DEBATE on the French Left indicates that some of its members have got cold feet at the prospect of *la Gauche* coming to power in a coalition which includes the Communists. They have evidently had second thoughts about what the victory of *l'Union de la Gauche* in its present form may imply in its eventual outcome. It has also been a remarkable indication that Raymond Aron has been right all along—ever since he formulated his critique of Marxism and of the French "progressives" more than a quarter-of-a-century ago! Some of them are only now recovering from the mental effects of being for so long addicted to "the opium of the intellectuals".

Their extraordinary twists and turns are a matter of record. Sartre is no longer saying that one must not reveal the truth about Stalin's camps for fear of depriving the French workers of socialist hopes: "*Il ne faut pas désespérer Billancourt.*" He now appeals for the support of the Polish workers and Soviet dissidents. One remembers how he once reproached Albert Camus for his criticism of the Soviet concentration camps:[2] "Like you, I find them inadmissible, but I also find inadmissible the usage which is daily made of them by the bourgeois press. . . ."

But although Sartre has never admitted that he was demonstrably wrong in the past (and because of this Solzhenitsyn refused to meet him in Moscow), he is now publicly associating with people whom not so long ago he would have dismissed as "vulgar anti-Communists".[3] While Brezhnev dined with Giscard d'Estaing at the Elysée palace on 21 June 1977, Sartre attended the solidarity meeting at the Théâtre Récamier alongside Soviet dissidents, among them Maximov, Bukovsky, Amalrik, Sinyavsky, and other much "anti-Soviet elements" (e.g. Eugène Ionesco) with whom in the past Sartre would not have been seen dead, much less called them by the honourable name of *résistants*! Not difficult to imagine what his old critic and erstwhile friend, Raymond Aron (whom Simone de Beauvoir had caricatured in *Les Mandarins*), must have thought about it. . . .

IS IT EVER ANY GOOD being prematurely right? Doesn't it always result in even greater animus from those who were wrong and prefer never to be reminded of it? But despite such embarrassments and inhibitions of the non-expiatory progressives, the emergence of the New Philosophers has been called "Aron's Vindication" (by Alain Gerard Slama in *Il Giornale*, 23 June). The "liberal" Communist historian Jean Elleinstein sensed it when he reproached the New Philosophers in *Le Monde* (27 May 1977):

---

[2] On Sartre, Solzhenitsyn, and the political record, see *Encounter* (July 1975), p. 94.
[3] Perhaps to compensate for this, Sartre indulges in new political fantasies by protesting against repression . . . in Italy. His "Appeal" has been roundly derided by the Italians from Right to Left.

"With André Glucksmann and Bernard-Henri Lévy we are already at the entrance to the universe of Raymond Aron, of his analysis of *une Europe décadente* which, we believe, only socialism will regenerate. . . ."

Among the French Communists, Jean Elleinstein is the most explicit critic of Stalinist crimes. Aron, who preceded Elleinstein in his basic (but much more thorough and consistent) diagnosis by some 25 years, now warns his compatriots (*"Etrange nation! La plus intelligente ou la plus déraisonnable du monde"*) not to believe that what resulted in degeneration in the East could ever bring regeneration in the West. In his concern with "decadent" Europe, Raymond Aron prefers to trust historical experience rather than Euro-Communist "dialectics of history". One can only hope that his French compatriots will heed his council. That also goes for the other Europeans— and indeed for the Americans too.

(1977)

11. The Two Minds of George Kennan

How To Un-Learn from Experience

"My feelings change; my judgment does not."
Montaigne
*"Nothing is more tiresome than to have to explain what everybody
should know."*
Baudelaire

T HE IDEAS and arguments of George Kennan on contemporary
international problems have been reaching the public for 30 years; he has
been developing them for 50 years. Government dispatches and memoranda,
articles and interviews, lectures and broadcasts, and many, many books have
made Kennan's views widely familiar. His opinions on the current situation
formulated in detail in his most recent work, *The Cloud of Danger* (1977) were
conveniently summarized in the speech delivered at a November 1977
meeting of the Council of Foreign Relations.

In the past George Kennan has been attacked from the most diverse
quarters. The Soviet and East European press referred to him regularly as
"the architect of the Cold War"; our own Communist daily, *Morning Star*,
reviewing his *Memoirs* (on 15 March 1973), still called him "a true servant and
ideologue of American imperialism"; Professor Anatol Rapoport, an
American academic scientist, likened his views to those of Fred Schwartz, the
leader of the "Christian Anti-Communist Crusade". But he was also
severely criticized by John Foster Dulles and William Buckley's conservative
National Review.

At present, no less curiously, his writings have been praised as "wise" by
such diverse commentators as James Reston in the *New York Times* and
Georgi Ratiani in *Pravda* (21 January 1978). Another *Pravda* commentator,
G. Gerasimov, wrote (12 July 1977) that "Kennan's views have substantially
evolved in the direction of common sense" and that many pages of his latest
book

> "are devoted to convincingly showing the utter groundlessness, lies and
> malice of constant statements by the Western bourgeois press that the
> Soviet Union is nurturing plans to attack Western Europe and America
> and that it is generally striving for 'world hegemony'."

The book "can be recommended for the reference libraries of the State

Department and of the White House itself". Coming from *Pravda* it is quite a commendation for the author of the once-notorious "Containment" policy!

George Kennan denies inconsistency. When confronted by some of his own contrasting statements (for instance by George Urban in the *Encounter* interview "From Containment to Self-Containment", September 1976) he either refuses to admit their contradictory character or belittles its significance: "All Russian reality is contradictory, and so perhaps are some of my attitudes to Russia" (the first proposition cannot be taken as logically countenancing the second). Presented with the two opposite recommendations which he made in 1946 and 1952 respectively, Kennan explains it all away by arguing that "each of the two, seemingly irreconcilable, strands of my argument were entirely justified in the context in which it was put forward". Or again:

> "For the purposes of the argument, I am given to overstating a case; and that is one of the reasons why you accuse me of contradiction. If one wants to see both sides of a coin, one has, momentarily at least, to bring out each side in exaggerated relief."

Rereading George Kennan's numerous writings (including his dispatches from pre-War Czechoslovakia and the Soviet Union) makes one realize that there is nothing "momentary" about his contradictions, that in spite of his profound conviction that he has been basically right throughout the four decades covered by these writings, they betray very clearly the fact that over a period of time his attitudes and counsels have reflected not a balanced judgment, but an almost schizoid political dualism; and it is this which has made him a butt of such diametrically opposite criticism. No amount of logic-chopping can reconcile these flagrant contradictions; the only consistency one can detect—with some difficulty—is not logical, but psychological.

This may sound harsh and it is painful to have to say it so bluntly in view of the sterling qualities of George Kennan's intellect and character. Those who have criticized him (and with whom he has disagreed)—Dean Acheson and Paul Nitze, Raymond Aron and Hugh Seton-Watson, Adam Ulam and Richard Pipes—have all been highly complimentary about his talents, historical knowledge, and sophistication. And these were not just conventional tributes. They were deservedly given and I can only endorse them.[1] This makes an inquest on George Kennan's political writings a

---

[1] In his *Memoirs* (Part II, p. 237) George Kennan puzzles about a similar juxtaposition (occasioned by his Reith Lectures, 1957):

> "The criticisms, almost without exception, were cast in terms respectful of myself as a person and designed to spare, if possible, my own feelings. . . . Never, surely, has anyone been so widely and generously forgiven as a person for what were, in the eyes of his critics, such grievous errors as a thinker."

$\rightarrow$

melancholy occasion: one is aware of how right and perspicacious he has been on many subjects. Not only Kennan *Mark I*, but occasionally even Kennan *Mark II*, Yet *amicus Plato*. . . .

The Strategy of Containment: Mark I

K ENNAN *MARK I* is of course "Mr X", the man who articulated the "Containment" idea. Kennan *Mark II* is the man who evolved from his original position of advising resistance to Soviet expansionism to the present one of advocating its accommodation. This evolution was punctuated by occasional relapses, i.e. when he said after Prague 1968: "I have never understood this talk about *détente*. I have never seen any evidence of *détente* and I wouldn't trust any so-called *détente* if it is not supported by free contacts between governments and peoples." But the overall direction of his evolution is unmistakable (which explains why *Pravda* endorses him now). Here is Kennan *Mark I*:

> "It is not our lack of knowledge which causes us to be puzzled by Russia. It is that we are incapable of understanding the truth about Russia when we see it." *(September 1944)*

> "It is no concern of the Soviet government to disabuse the American public of prejudices highly favourable to Soviet interests. It is entirely agreeable to Moscow that Americans should be indulged in a series of illusions which lead them to put pressure on their government to accomplish the impossible and to go always one step further in pursuit of the illusive favour of the Soviet government. They observe with gratification that in this way a great people can be led, like an ever-hopeful suitor, to perform one act of ingratiation after the other without ever reaching the goal which would satisfy its ardour and allay its generosity. . . . No English or American politician can pass up any half-way adequate opportunity for claiming that he has been successful in gaining Russian confidence and committing the Russians to a more moderate course of action. In other words, they consider that Anglo-Saxon opinion can always be easily appeased in a pinch by a single generous gesture, or even in all probability by a few promising words, and that Western statesmen can always be depended upon to collaborate enthusiastically in this appeasement." *(May 1945)*

Kennan believes that such reaction was due "to the happenings and the atmostphere of the day". In fact, it has been repeated by friendly critics again and again for a quarter-of-a-century. There is nothing paradoxical or strange about admiring Kennan's attainments and considering his political judgment wrong on many occasions.

"I have no hesitation in saying quite categorically, in the light of some eleven years' experience with Russian matters, that it would be highly dangerous to our security if the Russians were to develop the use of atomic energy. . . . It is thus my profound conviction that to reveal to the Soviet government any knowledge which might be vital to the defense of the United States, without adequate guarantees for the control of its use in the Soviet Union, would constitute a frivolous neglect of vital interests of our people." *(September 1945)*

"The Soviet régime is a police régime par excellence, reared in the dim half-world of Tsarist police intrigue, accustomed to think primarily in terms of police power. This should never be lost sight of in gauging Soviet motives. Soviet power, unlike that of Hitlerite Germany, is neither schematic nor adventuristic. It does not take unnecessary risks. Impervious to logic of reason, it is highly sensitive to logic of force." *(February 1946)*

"I think there can be no more dangerous tendency in American public opinion than one which places on our government an obligation to accomplish the impossible by gestures of good will and conciliation towards a political entity constitutionally incapable of being conciliated." *(March 1946)*

"It is clear that the main element of any US policy towards the Soviet Union must be that of a long-term, patient but firm and vigilant containment of Russian expansive tendencies." *(July 1947)*[2]

Ever since then George Kennan has kept explaining that "Mr X" has been misunderstood. In his *Memoirs* he maintains that this was largely his own fault. He confesses to responsibility for the "misunderstandings" because of the three "serious deficiencies" of the article: (1) the failure to mention "the difficulties with which the Soviet leaders were faced in their attempt to exercise political dominion over Eastern Europe"; (2) "the failure to make clear that what I was talking about when I mentioned the containment of Soviet power was not the containment by military means of a military threat, but the political containment of a political threat"; (3) the failure "to make clear that the "containment" of which I was speaking was not something that I thought we could, necessarily, do everywhere successfully, or even needed to do everywhere successfully, in order to serve the purpose that I had in mind".

---

[2] The above quotations are from Kennan's dispatches from Moscow. Cf. *Foreign Relations of the United States*, Vol. V (1945) & Vol. VI (1946), Department of State (Washington, 1967 & 1969). The concluding one is from: "The Sources of Soviet Conduct", *Foreign Affairs* (July 1947).

At least partly as a result of what he calls these "egregious errors", Mr Kennan sadly reflects, "the myth of the 'doctrine of containment' has never fully lost its spell". He has (as he put it in the interview with George Urban) "oversold his bill of goods". Thirty years after the publication of the "Mr X" article, Kennan complained that it has dogged his "footsteps ever since, like a faithful but unwanted and somewhat embarrassing animal", a remark triumphantly quoted in *Pravda* (21 January 1978).

But like the Shakespearean lady (whom he himself invokes), George Kennan doth protest too much. This can be seen not only from the ambiguities and contradictions accompanying his arguments, but also from the shifting premises of such arguments in the course of his political evolution. It can be gauged from the comparison of the tenor of his earlier pronouncements with those being made by Kennan *Mark II*.

IN HIS *Memoirs* Mr Kennan describes his frustration at trying to explain to American officials and politicians the nature of the problem presented by post-War Soviet Russia.

> "For eighteen long months I had done little else but pluck people's sleeves, trying to make them understand the nature of the phenomenon with which we in the Moscow embassy were daily confronted and which our government and people had to learn to understand if they were to have any chance of coping successfully with the problems of the post-war world. So far as official Washington was concerned, it had been to all intents and purposes like talking to a stone. . . . Now, suddenly, my opinion was being asked. . . . Here was a case where nothing but the whole truth would do. Now, by God, they would have it." (Vol. I, p. 293)

The result was a "long telegram" (of 22 February 1946, quoted above) in which Kennan analysed the basic features of the "post-War Soviet outlook" and which, he says, established his reputation. "My voice now carried."

It is more than ironical that Kennan now considers the "long telegram" as hardly justifying such an outcome:

> "I read it over today [1967] with a horrified amusement. Much of it reads exactly like one of those primers put out by alarmed Congressional committees or by the Daughters of the American Revolution, designed to arouse the citizenry to the dangers of the Communist conspiracy." (p. 294)

Actually, it does not. Kennan exaggerates his anti-Bolshevik self-criticism. If he were in fact wrong then he should say so plainly, instead of building an elaborate edifice of rationalizations for his basic change of political position.

To attribute it solely to a change in the (objective) situation only indicates that Kennan has not the courage of his (changed) convictions.

When revisionist historians or ideologues of the New Left or *Pravda* dismiss the Soviet danger to the West, an attitude towards which George Kennan has increasingly gravitated during the last 30 years, they themselves have at least some measure of consistency. Kennan has none. He knows from personal experience that the revisionist historians indulge in myth-making. There is no anti-Soviet Western conspiracy which started the Cold War. If anything, the "Good Uncle Joe" era of illusions in the West contributed to that appeasement of Stalin against which Kennan himself warned. He has never had any sympathy for the *enragé* New Revolutionaries of the 1960s, with their fanaticism, violence, shallow millenarianism and historical ignorance.[3] He has always been repelled by "progressive" double standards:

> "Any régime that chooses to call itself Marxist can be sure that its brutalities and oppression will be forgiven, whereas any régime that does not is stamped as being of the Right, in which case the slightest invasion of the rights or liberties on *its* territory at once becomes the object of intense indignation."

Nor was he ever tempted by Marxism. Indeed, he considers that "its irrelevance has been amply demonstrated at every turn". As for *Pravda*, he has never had anything but contempt for Soviet mendacity. In his Reith Lectures (1953) he said:

> "From the time of their seizure of power, forty years ago, the Russian Communists have always been characterised by their extraordinary ability to cultivate falsehood as a deliberate weapon of policy. . . . Their habitual carelessness about the truth has tended to obliterate in their minds the distinction between what they do believe and what they merely find it convenient to say. . . . A wise Western policy will insist that no single falsehood or distortion from the Soviet side should ever go unanswered . . . would make it harder for them to ignore the distinction between the real and the unreal, and would place limitations—thus far not visible—on their use of falsehood as a weapon of political policy."

Today, 20 years later, *Pravda* and *Izvestia* (and Soviet Communists in general) are as mendacious as ever. Whatever other changes might have occurred in the Soviet Union, this particular official habit of mind has endured and, even now, as Kennan wrote in 1946, "Soviet people are fed by Soviet government and Party propaganda a distorted and often vicious picture of the USA. . . ."

---

[3] Cf. George Kennan, *Democracy and the Student Left* (1968). Also his "Rebels Without a Program", *New York Times Magazine* (21 January 1968).

The Art of Repudiation: Mark II

THE CONTRAST WITH the attitudes of Kennan *Mark II* cannot be more pronounced, even though he is too sophisticated and intelligent a person not to soften it by introducing qualifications, conditional clauses, and other eristic ploys to rationalize the shift in his attitude towards Western policy.

His fundamental premise is, of course, the argument that the Soviet Union has changed.

> "[With] some people the trouble seems to be that they are unaware of the changes . . . between 1947 and 1977, [people] who talk of the problems of Soviet-American relations in terms identical with those used at the height of the Cold War—who sometimes seem in fact unaware that Stalin is dead."[4]

His subordinate premise is that during that period the Western world has "not at all been able to make the pretence [of a higher moral departure-point] valid". Kennan *Mark II* concluded, therefore, that "as things are, I can see very little merit in organizing ourselves to defend from the Russians the porno-shops in central Washington".[5] As a dismaying indication of Western decadence it may be a legitimate reflection; as a logical argument about the defence of Western civilization it is absurd.

Is the question of changes in post-Stalin Russia something which the serious critics of Kennan have in fact truly over-looked? Some of these critics have been following the "thaws", the "liberalisation", and "bourgeoisification" problems as closely as he did himself. Ulam, Pipes, Seton-Watson, Laqueur, Schapiro, Conquest, Grossman, or myself cannot really be charged with ignorance in this respect; so George Kennan is, to use his own expression, creating a dummy only "to treat it as if it were real". The question is not whether there were changes—no sane person, no open-eyed student of society, would deny it. But what is their character and significance, how relevant are they to the problem of Soviet expansionism and *a fortiori* to Western policy? Not *any* change is sufficient to diminish the Soviet danger to Europe and America. There was relaxation under Khrushchev, but it did not prevent Soviet intervention in Hungary after the 20th CPSU "de-Stalinisation" Congress nor did it hinder the placing of missiles in Cuba after the 22nd "de-Stalinisation" Congress. And under Brezhnev Stalin became less dead than before.

---

[4] Kennan, "Mr *X* Reconsiders: A Current Assessment of Soviet-American Relations", *Encounter* (March 1978), reprinted in *Encounters With Kennan: The Great Debate* (with an introduction by Daniel P. Moynihan, London, 1979).
[5] George Kennan and George Urban, "From Containment to Self-Containment", *Encounter* (September 1976), reprinted in *Encounters With Kennan: The Great Debate*.

In 1945 Kennan *Mark I* expressed his deep concern that because of the illusions

> "kept alive among large sections of the American public, the Kremlin will not give up the hope that the Western democracies may, for the time being, be used as the greatest and most powerful auxiliary instrument in the establishment of Russian power in Eastern and Central Europe."

In 1946 he wrote to the Secretary of State:

> "We must see that our public is educated to the realities of the Russian situation, I cannot overemphasise the importance of this."[6]

In 1977, when America has lost its military superiority and the Soviet Union is fighting proxy wars in Africa, Kennan *Mark II* writes that "the creation of the satellite area of Eastern and Central Europe . . . was in reality a revival [*sic*] of traditional Russian power in that region", that "the tendency to border expansion . . . does not play a prominent role in the motivation of Soviet leaders today", that their "motivation is essentially defensive and . . . riveted primarily to the unsolved problems of economic development within their own country".[7] The Soviet government's action in Angola may have demonstrated "its newly acquired ability to project its military presence to distant and peripheral points", but that *Mark I* insight does not bother Kennan *Mark II*:

> "The effort to assist to the seats of power in distant countries factions whose aims seem reasonably compatible with one's own is, as I have already noted, not foreign to the normal practice of great powers, including the United States. Why it should cause such great surprise or alarm when it proceeds from the Soviet Union I fail to understand."[8]

There is, therefore, no need to worry about all those Cubans on African battlefields and the Soviet billion-dollar arms-airlift to embattled Ethiopia. After all, the Russians "have not even sent their own forces abroad into other countries", says Kennan *Mark II*.

Thus I do not find it unduly surprising that he now repudiates the lessons which once upon a time he learnt in Moscow.

In his *Memoirs* (Vol. 1, pp. 291–2) he already "partly" retracted his famous 1946 rules of conduct *vis-à-vis* the Russians which now (in 1967) he claimed to be only "a useful set of rules for dealing with the Stalin régime":

> "Don't act chummy with them. . . . Don't assume a community of aims with them which does not really exist. . . . Don't make fatuous

---

[6] *Foreign Relations*, Vol. V (1945), p. 858; Vol. VI (1946), p. 708.
[7] *The Cloud of Danger*, pp. 176, 177–8.   [8] *The Cloud of Danger*, pp. 154, 179.

gestures of good will. .... Do not be afraid to use heavy weapons for what seem to us to be minor matters .... Do not be afraid of unpleasantness and public airing of differences . . ." etc.

Ten years later he has gone on to forget them altogether. In his last book he declared that no Soviet objectives which are in conflict with those of the United States

"seem to be of such nature as to challenge any vital interest of ours—the only possible exception being Berlin."

The growing Soviet strategic proximity to the Western sources of oil and the life-lines to them are pooh-poohed, but then Kennan *Mark II* has become rather solicitous about *Soviet* strategic interests. He is very much concerned about the Soviet leaders'

"feelings [which] must be supplemented with a new element of alarm as they sit and watch the pouring of these unconscionable quantities of American weaponry into Saudi Arabia and, more disturbing still, into the neighbouring Iran."

They are, presumably, worried about the threat from the Shah and the Saudi King to "the security of their sensitive southern border" which Kennan solemnly invokes in this context.

Nor is it very surprising, given this new Kennan *Mark II* attitude, to hear him concluding that there is no cause for alarm for the West although, as we have just seen, this is not necessarily true for the Soviet leaders who do have sensitive causes for alarm. Our own Western apprehensions,

"which have been used to justify appeals for a totally negative, hostile, and militaristic attitude towards the Soviet Union, have little substance behind them and are not responsive to the real profile of the problem which the existence of the Communist power in Russia presents for American statesmanship."[9]

What can one conclude from this but that Mr Kennan's equanimity has increased *pari passu* with the rise of the Soviet Union as a global power and the shrinkage of American power?

Elements of "Peace"

IT TOOK Kennan 20 years to learn about Russian and Soviet expansionism and 30 subsequent years of experience to unlearn it. When it comes to China, he wisely reminds us in his latest book

---

[9] *The Cloud of Danger*, pp. 179, 180.

"of the danger of building too extensively, in our foreign relations, on individual personalities at the head of a foreign state. These come and go; the state remains. When it comes to laying out American policies designed to stand the test of time, it is better to look at the long-term interests, and the long-term behaviour, of a state than at the personalities who momentarily head it."

But when it comes to Russia this is forgotten by Kennan *Mark II*. "Stalin is dead"—as some of us have evidently failed to notice—and

"the régime is headed by a moderate, in fact, conservative man; a man who, whatever failings of outlook he may have, is a man of the middle, a skilled balancer among political forces—a man confidently regarded by all who know him as a man of peace."

Apart from disregarding his own analytical precepts, this kind of assertion raises the simple question: How does George F. Kennan know that Brezhnev "is a man of peace"? And what does he mean by it? Stalin too was "a man of the middle, a skilled balancer among political forces", and neither Stalin nor Khrushchev wanted a global war. Brezhnev does not want it either. But does that make him "a man of peace"? Czechoslovakia, Angola, Somalia, and Ethiopia (as well as Afghanistan 1979–) remind us of the contrary. Nor do they indicate, as Kennan asserts, that "as this leadership looks abroad, it sees more dangers than inviting opportunities. Its reactions and purposes are therefore much more defensive than aggressive."[10] He can tell that to the marines—of Admiral Gorshkov operating along the shores of the Red Sea and the Indian Ocean.

One can only applaud Mr Kennan when he calls for an act of humility— "the confession that none of us knows too much about what we are talking about". But I do not find it reassuring to hear him telling us, in a curious passage, that the present elderly Soviet leadership wants to end

"its own days peacefully—its members going down in history as constructive leaders who contributed, more much than Stalin and at least as much as Khrushchev, to the advancement of the glory of the Soviet Union and the cause of world communism."[11]

Kennan reiterates in "A Current Assessment of Soviet-American Relations"[12] the argument about the "peaceful" character of Soviet gerontocrats. He sees them "as highly conservative men, perhaps the most conservative ruling group to be found anywhere in the world, markedly advanced in age, approaching the end of their tenure, and given to everything else but rash adventure. . . ." This may be true as far as it goes, but does it go

---

[10] *The Cloud of Danger*, pp. 100, 200.
[11] *The Cloud of Danger*, p. 200.   [12] *Encounters With Kennan: The Great Debate*.

far enough? Stalin was over 70 at the time of the Korean war; and in any case, as Kennan himself says, the Leaders come and go but the State remains. Surely the argument about age as an indicator of the "peacefulness" of post-Stalin Russia is just a rationalization of an older George Kennan's wishful thinking. I remember him at a seminar in Switzerland (which I also attended) expressing similar convictions about Khrushchevian Russia on the basis of the exactly opposite premise: the impending inevitable *rejuvenation* of the Soviet political élite. . . .![13] It is, I fear, no less incongruous to hear Kennan *Mark II* arguing that the Soviet Union is today only concerned with its security:

> "Just as the security (not the expansion) of their own power is the prime consideration for the Soviet leaders when they face their own country, so it is when they face the outside world."

This was the standard argument at the time of the Teheran, Yalta, and Potsdam conferences of those men of illusions whom Kennan *Mark I* criticized so harshly in his diplomatic dispatches and who were ready, therefore, to sacrifice to the Russians Eastern Europe which, as Kennan (sarcastically, and inappositely for him today) puts it, "we, by our tacit consent, assigned to their good graces in 1945 . . . ."[14] But it was clear then, as it is clear now, that expansion creates new security problems for the Soviet Union and new "sensitive borders" in turn prompt further expansion. This is another lesson which George Kennan has somehow consigned to the memory-hole.

Resistance & Appeasement

DESPITE HIS APPEALS for a "detached" and "unemotional" analysis of Soviet developments, he is himself rather emotional; it is a not unendearing human trait, but one that results in some vagaries and inconsistencies. I offer only a few additional examples: one where his sentiments vitiate his *Realpolitik*, and another one where his *Realpolitik* vitiates his Puritan conscience. (Someone has, I think rightly, called him a Preacher and a Machiavellian at the same time.)

It is clear from Kennan's *Memoirs* that he does not like the Chinese (who seem to him "lacking in the capacity for pity and the sense of sin") and that he does like the Russians for whom he feels a special affinity ("a spontaneous meeting of minds and temperaments . . . a kinship that comes from being a

---

[13] Cf. R. Aron; G. F. Kennan; R. Oppenheimer, et al., *Les colloques de Rheinfelden* (Calmann-Lévy, Paris, 1959). Kennan also emphasized his hopes about the "coming generation" in the Soviet Union in his conversation with Melvin J. Lasky, *Encounter* (March 1960), reprinted in *Encounters With Kennan: The Great Debate*.

[14] *The Cloud of Danger*, pp. 179, 186.

citizen of a large continental country".) But although China is also "a large continental country", Kennan feels no kinship with it, which is understandable enough; but the sentiments of the kin of Russia lead the *Realpolitiker* to get smothered under the "sense of sin" of a moralist.

> "A real aberration of American thinking about the future of our relations with China is the view that we should 'tilt' our relations with China against the Soviet Union, should try, in other words, to make use of China as an instrument for the advancement of our interests, and the reduction of the Soviet ones, in the Soviet-American relationship. I find it difficult to say how strongly I disapprove of any such suggestion. . . . The Western community must find other, more solid and more positive ways than this of improving its relationship to the Soviet Union than by trying to play China off against it, if the catastrophe we all fear is to be averted and if the great constructive possibilities of the Soviet-American relationship are ultimately to be realized."[15]

Is, then, a balance-of-power policy today just too sinful? Only yesterday "containment" and its ensuing balance for peace were both realistic and moral. Again, it is not surprising that Moscow Radio (on 9 July 1977) quoted these Kennan *Mark II* remarks with satisfaction.

What about the "human rights" question? Here Kennan *Mark II* has strange inhibitions for such an upright man with such a decent record of public and private support for the humane cause of liberalism. This time it is the Moralist who gets smothered by a *Realpolitiker*.

> "The Soviet government asked for trouble, of course, when it signed the Helsinki declarations on human rights. The Western governments are formally on good ground in making this an issue of their relations with Moscow, if they care to do so. But the question remains whether it is wise for them to proceed much further along this path. . . . I should perhaps explain that I yield to no one in my admiration for such men as Solzhenitsyn and Sakharov; I would place them among the greatest Russians of the modern age. Were I a Russian, they would have my deepest gratitude and . . . support. But I am not a Russian." (p. 215)

What is he then? Mr Kennan now admits that he is an American Isolationist, a tag he does not like because of "its extreme connotations". He still advocates the defence of Europe and Japan, and he even grudgingly concedes the need to strengthen the conventional forces of NATO. But he is quite ready to give up all kinds of strategic and military positions. He wants to induce Greece and Turkey to withdraw from NATO; he wants to abandon Korea and the Philippines; and above all he wants to give up the nuclear

---

[15] *The Cloud of Danger*, p. 106.

deterrent by signing an agreement with Russia about the "non-first use of nuclear weapons". Faced with the overwhelming Soviet conventional superiority the Europeans are offered only the advice to strengthen their conventional defences—and to be prepared for civil action and guerrilla warfare . . . under Occupation. A wise counsel? A "realistic" prospect? Kennan refers to the heroic resistance during the last War, but forgets that it was only sustained by the hope of an Allied military victory.

In his 1938–1940 dispatches from occupied Prague,[16] Kennan records his sympathies with those "more responsible Czech leaders" who felt that "the cornerstone of any long-term Czech policy must be a *modus vivendi* with the Germans". He deplored "the tendency to romanticism in political thought" among the Czechs (of all people!), and he rejected "the romantic solution of hopeless resistance rather than the humiliating but truly heroic one of realism".[17]

Today Kennan is "not sure that Hacha and the Czechs were wise to yield".[18] But in the wider context it is his original reaction to the consequences of Munich (1938) (which he characterises in his *Memoirs* as one of "temperate optimism" and "not devoid of hope") which underlies his present position. In his dispatch from Prague after Munich, he expressed hope that

"such changes as occur will lead in the direction of greater economic security and greater racial tolerance for [the Czechoslovak] people sadly in need of both. . . ."

Kennan's evolution is a clean example that *"On revient toujours à ses premiers amours. . . ."* After a life of foreign experience and the emergence of global problems, George Kennan wants to return home to the Middle West, to the homely illusion that America (even with Europe and Japan feeling increasingly abandoned) could withstand the slings and arrows of outrageous fortune in a hostile world. No less illusory is his assertion that Western Europe has no reason to fear "Finlandization". He even thinks that "today the Finns enjoy complete freedom in their internal affairs", which is palpably untrue.

He advocated in 1947 as "Mr X" an "adroit and vigilant application of counterforce" against Soviet expansionism. In 1966 in his testimony before the Senate Foreign Relations Committee, although he emphasised his objections to the way "Containment" was applied, he still thought it

---

[16] Kennan, *From Prague after Munich* (Princeton, 1968), pp. 5, 240.
[17] *Memoirs*, Vol. I, p. 96. I cannot help comparing Kennan's reaction to the Czech events with that of Dorothy Thompson at the time: "I for one believe that if ever the time comes that the antennae of this country are not sensitive to assaults on liberty, wherever these assaults may occur, then this country will have degenerated into an unvirtuous and defeatist senility." *Let the Record Speak* (London, 1939), p. 381.
[18] See "From Containment to Self-Containment".

necessary. Now, he has in effect given it up. For all practical purposes he has replaced the idea of resistance to Soviet expansionism by appeasement and isolationism.

The Psychology of Withdrawal

HOW DID THIS strange evolution from Containment to Isolationism come about? What led him to such a curiously "unvirtuous and defeatist" attitude? What turned Hamlet into a King Lear who despite his age and experience could not know which of his three daughters was truly attached to him?

He was not altogether wrong about his "self-criticisms" of the three "grievous errors" of "Mr X", even though they were afterthoughts rather than (as he implied) disclaimers. There was indeed little real thought (as against rhetoric) about Eastern Europe. But so-called "Disengagement", which he proposed, was not a practical solution.

I would be the first to agree that there was indeed an underestimation of the political—as against the military—factor. But Kennan, as Dean Acheson said, "never grasped the realities of power relationships", and he still cannot comprehend the political function of military and strategic factors. At any rate, the increased emphasis on the *political* element in the Containment policy would have intensified rather than diminished what the Russians call "the ideological struggle" (which they have never renounced, unlike George Kennan). Nor can Western strategy be safely reduced to Kennan's simple withdrawal-to-the-industrial-heartland scheme. The price of this isolationist luxury—unprompted declarations of territorial disinterestedness (as in Dean Acheson's ill-fated Korea statement)—is that defence becomes at once more difficult and more expensive, not easier and cheaper.

I would agree with Kennan that there was indeed an error in "globalism": not in the idea of military resistance where necessary, but in the mindless schematism which prevented flexibility and a clear-eyed choice of global strategic priorities.

But George Kennan has thrown the baby out with the bath-water. His frustrations led him increasingly to abandon his original concern about the Soviet danger which he began "to wish away" concurrently (as I have pointed out) with the rise of Soviet strength. Yet he cannot explain, in terms of his own arguments, why the Soviet Union spends more on "defence" than the USA—out of a Gross National Product which is half of the American GNP—if the military factor ceases to be effective above a certain level of destructiveness ("overkill"). He attributes to Soviet policy changes which have not occurred and good will which it does not possess.

He is also preoccupied with the search for scapegoats. He admits that at least some people critical of the pseudo-*Détente* policy are "honourable people", indeed his "friends"; and he does "not suspect or disrespect their motives". But he still lumps them all as "the Right". He caricatures their views and cannot conceive "in the bowels of Christ" (in spite of his professed humility) that *he* may be mistaken. He mentions no names, but it behoves him to distinguish between the "chauvinist Right Deviation" and the people whom I mentioned earlier and who differ with George Kennan in their reasoned assessment of the world problems and risks. He even produces a spurious symmetry between "Mr *X*"-Kennan *Mark I*'s criticism of the Left Deviation and Kennan *Mark II*'s criticism of the Right Deviation. In fact, the Yalta appeasement was not just a matter of the Left, unless he includes therein all his official Establishment superiors in Washington; and the intellectual anti-pseudo-*Détente* critique is not at all just a matter of the Right, unless the word is used in its Orwellian sense and one becomes Right by definition if one is not "friendly to the Soviet Union". (In this sense Kennan *Mark II* moved to the Left but in no other respect, as New Left ideologues would be the first to recognize.)

Without mentioning any names, George Kennan constantly attacks those who, according to him, think that a war with the USSR is "inevitable". But who are they? Only the official Chinese thesis maintains it (and now only in a somewhat diluted form). None of Kennan's serious critics whom he deplores believes it. Why, then, the imputation?

Because originally "Containment" contained two elements: resistance to Soviet expansionism *and* the avoidance of war. George Kennan knows this only too well. But now that he has abandoned one of the elements, he feels impelled to stress the other one against his critics. But why should he doubt that they are every bit as much concerned with the survival of humanity as he is? They do not believe, however, that appeasement is the way to do it. If it leads to the defeat of the West the nuclear danger will not disappear.[19] The prospect of peaceful world-politics in a world of Nuclear Communist powers is not exactly hopeful, as the Sino-Soviet, Vietnamese–Cambodian, and Somali–Ethiopian military clashes indicate. Lenin used to say "Capitalism brings with it war as the cloud brings with it the storm". It is not true today, if it ever was.

---

[19] See "From Containment to Self-Containment", where George Kennan said that "no one in his right senses would yield to any such thing as nuclear blackmail", that it cannot "be used for gaining political advantage except against people who, as Stalin said, have weak nerves". He evidently rates European nerves very highly. But he seems to have forgotten European reaction to the Cuban 1962 missile crisis and the 1973 oil embargo, not to mention the possible impact of the Soviet projection of *both* nuclear and conventional power. In a game of "nuclear chess" defeat can be conceded without playing all the moves to the bitter end.

Kennan himself reminded us how the Chinese used to fight their battles. "When they had figured out which side had the stronger forces, victory would be conceded to that side without shooting." In any case, if there is no reason to fear nuclear blackmail, why is Kennan so apprehensive about the possibility of nuclear war and so denunciatory about the bogey-men who allegedly maintain that it is "inevitable"?

George Kennan has misjudged "the cloud of danger". The survival of Western civilization is a necessary pre-condition of holding back "the cloud", and his proposals would only undermine the chance of such survival. His assessment of the world situation tells us more about his psychological evolution than about the real historical perils which the policy of Containment, however inadequate, has so far contributed to avoid. After all, we should not forget the Berlin Blockade (1948–9) and Cuba (1962) when Soviet military threats were decisively frustrated and indeed *contained*. Nor should we forget that Japan is as closely related, geopolitically, to Korea as Western Europe is to the Middle East. That Containment worked in all these contexts, but above all that it worked in the overall context of the global balance of power, is no mean achievement. There is certainly no reason moodily and irascibly to abandon it when new perils arise and the balance has already been altered to the West's disadvantage.

On Learning from Experience

KENNAN'S EVOLUTION, as I said at the outset, was rooted in a dualism which he obviously could not overcome.[20] The Preacher and the Machiavellian, the diplomat and the intellectual, the official and the non-conformist, the nostalgic conservative and the liberal "progressive", the sophisticated cosmopolitan and the embarrassed isolationist—all these and other dualities have created an imbalance in his political judgment. Dean Acheson was right when he characterized one of his memoranda as

> "typical of its gifted author, beautifully expressed, sometimes contradictory, in which were mingled flashes of prophetic insight and suggestions, as the document itself conceded, of total impracticality."[21]

This applies to the whole political evolution of George Kennan. He has now made a full circle.

He is still under the illusion that "it is much easier for some Americans to understand the Soviet Union than it is for most qualified Continental Europeans and Englishmen. . . ." It would, of course, be silly to generalize about such matters; they are best assessed on the basis of individual performance. But if there is a valid element of the "sociology of knowledge" in the assessment of the evolution of East–West attitudes and views, perhaps I may be permitted to surmise that it is not without significance that George Kennan comes from the Middle West, the cradle of America's traditional

---

[20] The two roles are interestingly juxtaposed in the incident of Mr Kennan's expulsion from the Moscow ambassadorship (1952). When he compared the conditions of foreign diplomats there with those in Nazi Germany, he was declared *persona non grata*. In his *Memoirs* he criticizes himself for being foolish. As a diplomat he undoubtedly was; but as a person and as an intellectual he had only told the truth.

[21] *Present at the Creation* (1969), p. 446.

isolationism. Even so, his evolution is a very personal matter, and it is deplorable that he has un-learned the lessons of Russian and European history. He seems no longer concerned with the need to learn from history.

For a politician this is a weakness, for a diplomat an error, for an historian a sin.

(*1979*)

12. Holocaust: Myths & Horrors

> *"Go, go, go, said the bird: human kind*
> *Cannot bear very much reality."*
> **T. S. Eliot**, Four Quartets
>
> *"Illusions, dead, continue to rot within us."*
> **Dmitri Shostakovich**, Memoirs

A S A SEMANTIC LEGACY of Hitler's and Stalin's practices, our vocabulary has been enriched by *"Genocide"* and *"Gulag"*. Unfortunately, even though the two dictators are long since dead, these terms are not just of historical interest.

Originally, *"genocide"*—a concept formulated by Rafael Lemkin in connection with the Holocaust—was defined as the deliberate destruction of an ethnic group. But it has come to mean the wholesale extermination of any category of people by a political authority controlling them; thus it applies not only to the annihilation of Jews by Nazis, but also to the victims of the Pol Pot régime in Cambodia.

"Gulag" is a term which did not originate as a concept. It was an acronym of the Main Administration of the Camps (*Glavnoe Upravlenye Lagerey*) in Stalin's Russia. But when Solzhenitsyn gave it general currency in the West, it came to be applied to other cases of what David Rousset had defined as *l'univers concentrationnaire*. In France, a recent book about the Vietnamese "re-education camps" is called *Le Goulag Vietnamien*; and Charles Sternberg (the executive director of the International Rescue Committee) has called them a contemporary version of the Gulag Archipelago.

The two terms evoke, more vividly than anything else in the language, the specific form of man's inhumanity to man in our time: the gas ovens of Auschwitz and Treblinka, the white hell of Vorkuta and Kolyma, the macabre mass "evacuation" of the capital city of Phnom Penh and the subsequent *Khmer Rouge* bestialities. What was involved in all these 20th-century horrors was not only torture, starvation, and violent death inflicted upon defenceless people, but also the fact that they were committed not as acts of war, but as civil actions in which the question of personal or individual guilt had not even arisen. For the individual it is not a matter of "having done something", but simply of being something (or being so accused). For him there is no way out; no alternative behaviour can help him avoid his fate. At the time of the Inquisition, Jews could at least convert to becoming *Marranos*. Under Hitler they were unconditionally condemned to perdition on racial grounds. Under Stalin "enemies of the people" were extirpated according to such general categories as "kulaks", "Trotskyist wreckers", or "rootless cosmopolitans". Under Pol Pot, people ("the intellectuals") were killed simply for being literate (often "proved" by their wearing spectacles).

One day, perhaps, we will have a comparative study of Genocide, and the story would be incomplete without a picture of the international reactions in the outside world to these atrocities. It is striking what great, evidently deep-seated, reluctance there was in each historical case of genocide to accept the hard facts and recognize them for what they were.[1] Universal condemnation was delayed on each occasion by a tendency to ignore, obfuscate, or rationalize the facts. Were those who denied them anything but moral accomplices?

WILFUL BLINDNESS is not so visible today, but we are dismally confronted by many forms of moral insensitivity about the problem at present. For one thing, the term "genocide" is increasingly used as a trivial metaphor. For instance, at a recent Labour Party Conference, Neil Kinnock MP referred to the Government's school policy as "Tory educational genocide", while another delegate, objecting to rising unemployment, spoke of "industrial genocide in the North" (the Communist *Morning Star* of 5 October 1979 published a photograph of a shipyard worker carrying a placard with the words "*Industrial genicide* [sic] *on Tayside*"). But the Labour Party's Conference resolution on Cambodia actually managed to avoid mentioning the horrors in "liberated" Indo-China. . . .

Denying the Undeniable

THERE SEEMS TO BE a virtual consensus on the subject of "Genocide"—yet although everybody duly abhors it, how often this is accompanied by ambiguities and inconsistencies! The skeletons in the mega-closets are so ideologically embarrassing that it is frequently difficult to distinguish between the process of selective amnesia and an onset of new myth-making, between cranks and non-cranks, even between Left and Right.

The former US Attorney-General, Ramsey Clark, a leading American "progressive", has called Israeli actions in South Lebanon—"genocidal". James Baldwin declared in *The Nation* (29 September 1979), after the dismissal of Ambassador Andrew Young, that he had "attempted to ward off a holocaust" and he added quickly, lest he be suspected of harbouring ethical or humanitarian sentiments, that "the state of Israel was not created for the salvation of the Jews: it was created for the salvation of the Western interests. . . ."

---

[1] The most striking case is that of Jews themselves, cf. Walter Laqueur, "Jewish Denial and The Holocaust", *Commentary* (December 1979).

The Rev. Jesse Jackson, the American Black activist who went to the Middle East on a "peace mission", has declared that he is "sick and tired of hearing about the Holocaust. . . ." After visiting Israel's Yad Vashem memorial he said that "in all, the Nazis had killed more non-Jews than Jews"—and, after all, "60 million blacks had been exterminated during the slavery era" (*Newsweek*, 8 October). The point of this preposterously inaccurate comparison is presumably to indicate that Blacks suffered more than Jews. *Roots—si, Holocaust—no*. But why should even those who learn their history from the TV soap-operas want to weigh up the beastliness of chattel slavery against the gas-chamber horrors of genocide?

Like the Rev. Jesse Jackson, Vanessa Redgrave also embraced the PLO's Yasir Arafat. When she received her "*Oscar*" award for fighting the Nazis in the Hollywood film on (and by) Lillian Hellman, the local American Nazis demonstrated to support her against the protesting Jews. Unlike the Rev. Jackson, she obviously is not "sick and tired of hearing about the Holocaust"—in her next film she is playing the role of Fania Fénelon who happened to survive Auschwitz because she was a violinist in the camp orchestra.

Quelle finesse de sentiments! And what an admirable combination—a Trotskyite and a Christian; Vanessa and Jesse; *Rouge et Noir*; white cant and black hypocrisy (or vice versa); Nazi genocide and soul-food for thought. But not a murmur yet about the (red) graves in Cambodia.

A NXIETIES have recently been expressed that the German wave of interest in Adolf Hitler, manifested a generation after his downfall, may possibly reflect a desire to vindicate some of his policies, even though the neo-Nazis have remained a tiny and insignificant group. The phenomenal interest in the TV showing of *Holocaust* (seen by over 53 million German viewers) has put paid to such speculations. Whatever its artistic demerits, the series made it more difficult to cast doubts on the Nazi atrocities.

Who could now dismiss Hitler's genocide of the Jews as "a Zionist myth"? This, after all, was a permanent theme of neo-Nazi propaganda in its attempt to exploit the universal reluctance to believe the horrors and, indeed, the specifically German reluctance to face the *Schuldfrage*. It is ironical that so many of the specious efforts to whitewash Hitler, contributing to the perpetuation of the *unbewältigte Vergangenheit*, the Germans' "unmastered past", have come from outside Germany.

In Britain the pseudonymous Richard Harwood published a pamphlet, *Did Six Million Really Die?*, an attempt to "revise" the established image of the Nazi murders by declaring them to be *Greuelpropaganda* spread by Jews and Communists. According to Gitta Sereny (in the *New Statesman* of 2 November 1979), the real name of the author is Richard Verrall, the editor of the National Front monthly, *Spearhead*. The pamphlet has now been translated into German and French, reprinted in Great Britain, and serialized in the USA by a Louisiana monthly, *Christian Vanguard*.

ANOTHER CONTRIBUTION to the myth-making about Hitler, also coming to Germany from abroad, is the book by David Irving, *Hitler's War*. Irving, who exculpates Hitler from complicity in "the Final Solution", has been soundly thrashed by the leading British specialists on the subject, such as Alan Bullock and Hugh Trevor-Roper; and his book has been dismissed by serious journals such as *The Economist* as "a masterpiece of disinformation". But it has undoubtedly helped spread confusion and has provided the German neo-Nazis with welcome succour.

In the USA the associate professor of electrical engineering at Northwestern University in Evanston, Illinois, Arthur R. Butz, has written a pseudo-scientific book (with 444 footnotes!), *The Hoax of the Twentieth Century*, in which it is claimed, yet again, that the Holocaust was a "Zionist" and "Marxist" propaganda invention. It has been published in German translation as *Der Jahrhundert-Betrug* and has evidently also influenced a number of cranks in Britain, France, and Australia. In a letter to the *New Statesman* (4 August), the author "strongly objects" to the characterization of his book as "neo-Nazi". But it was put out by the same publisher as Harwood's pamphlet and has been used by the neo-Nazis here and elsewhere to "demonstrate" that the Holocaust is "a fairy tale". The neo-Nazi weekly *Deutsche National-Zeitung* published excerpts from it, with a red banner headline above the masthead: "WER ERFAND DEN SCHWINDEL VON 6 MILLIONEN VERGASTEN JUDEN? (*Who Invented the Hoax of 6 Million Gassed Jews?*)"

Another academic crank in America, a former professor of economics, Lyndon H. LaRouche, Jr., provides a spectacular example of effortless transition from New Left to New Right, if such labels still retain any significance.

As in other manifestations of the Commu-Nazi syndrome, anti-Semitism today plays a prominent role. LaRouche is the chairman of the so-called "US Labour Party" and its candidate for President in the 1980 elections. He has been politically active since 1966, but first appeared as a leader of the Marxist National Caucus of Labour Committees during the 1968 Columbia University "student revolution". In 1972, after a visit to Germany, LaRouche turned his party on a new path, preaching an economic policy based on a "corrected" Marxist "theory of value", a "humanist outlook"— and anti-Semitism. He does not whitewash Hitler, but considers that the monetarist economic policy *à la* Milton Friedman must also lead to "slave labour and death camps". He declares that "the current monetary and economic policies of the Carter Administration are fascist", and that "the Zionist lobby in the USA is a fascist political formation". As a *New York*

Times editorial (10 October) noted, he warned "a thousand well-organized followers that he is a target for assassination by conspiracies involving the Rockefeller family, the Carter Administration, the Israeli secret police and even the Queen of England. . . ."

IS ANYONE STILL under the impression that Cartesian *clarté* must be less blind than Anglo-Saxon empiricism?

In France, two academic figures have tried assiduously to deny the existence of the Holocaust. One of them, the late Paul Rassinier (from the *Académie de Besançon*), was himself imprisoned in Buchenwald. He wrote some four books (*Le Mensonge d'Ulysse*; *Ulysse Trahi par les Siens*; *Le Véritable Procès Eichmann*; *Le Drame des Juifs Européens*—all also published in Germany) in which he vehemently attacked "the legend of Nazi diabolism". Another French academic who rejected "the myth of the Nazi gas-chambers" is the associate professor of literature at the University of Lyon, Robert Faurisson. In his lectures and communications (*Le Monde*, 16 and 29 December 1978) he referred to 20 books (among them the aforementioned) which established this "fact". His allegations were immediately refuted by a number of surviving eye-witnesses and qualified historians; but who can tell how many gullible innocents may drink from this well?

THE LIES OF THE MYTH-MAKERS confuse the ignorant and poison the memory of humanity. And when the contemporary witnesses are dead, who knows what effect such obnoxious and cranky falsifications may have in undermining the historical truth about the genocidal abominations? With the passage of time the traumatic impact of such crimes and their memories fades, and myths will increasingly encroach on authentic history.

In Australia, the Melbourne lawyer John Bennett (the secretary of the liberal Victorian Council for Civil Liberties) created a sensation by publishing a letter in the Melbourne *Age* (22 January 1979) and in the *News-Weekly* (31 January 1979) which repeated the assertions of A. R. Butz. His letter has been followed by yet another media "debate" in which the deranged ravings of a mythomaniac manage to achieve the status of "controversial" opinions.

The "controversy" in the respectable organs of the Australian press raged more intensely than the one with Harwood in the London *Daily Telegraph* and with Faurisson in the Paris *Le Monde*. It flourished in the *National Times* and *The Age* in January–April, and again in June–July 1979 in the Australian *National Review*. Bennett declared that he "had been conned for 30 years by the Holocaust propaganda" and said that "the idea of Holocaust is a spill-over from wartime propaganda". His odd mentality produced a peculiar "progressive–reactionary" symbiosis whitewashing all genocidal régimes:

"The Holocaust legend is extensively used for propaganda reasons to support the diplomatic position of Israel. The legend is no more reliable than the atrocity stories about genocide in Kampuchea and Uganda, or the 20 million killed by Stalin legend."

This kind of Right–Left symbiosis reminds one of the German "libertarian" terrorist Ulrike Meinhof, who did not deny the fact of the Holocaust, but argued during her trial (*Frankfurter Allgemeine Zeitung*, 15 December 1972) that

"Auschwitz meant that six million Jews were killed, and thrown on to the waste-heap of Europe, for what they were: money-Jews (*Geldjuden*). . . ."

Specific beliefs about the significance of genocide, or indeed about its extent, may differ; yet there is no mistaking the remarkable confluence of attitudes reflected in the ideological prejudices and political stereotypes of the mythomaniacs, on both the Right and the Left.

In matters of genocide also, *les extrèmes se touchent*.

Holocaust & Gulag

IN THE SOVIET UNION there is constant harping on the theme of "neo-Nazism", but not on the theme of the Holocaust. Soviet propaganda has always tried to obscure the fact that Jews were a special target of Hitler's "Final Solution". That Hitler singled out European Jewry for "special treatment" is glossed over. When, after resisting for decades the proposal to erect a local memorial to the massacred victims of Babi Yar, the Soviet government finally built one there, there was simply no reference at all to the slaughter of Jews! Until recently, the term "genocide" was scarcely used in Soviet publications; but it suddenly was very current when it became necessary to justify the Vietnamese invasion of Cambodia.

Occasional references to the Jewish tragedy may appear when they are used to lend credibility to the alarm over "the neo-Nazi menace". It was quite exceptional when *Literaturnaya Gazeta* (20 September 1978), reporting on the Richard Harwood pamphlet, wrote that "he tries to deny the fact, known to the whole world, of the extermination of millions of Jews in the Nazi concentration camps". It seemed almost a slip of censorship control, for such statements are practically never encountered in Soviet publications. They would run counter to the open and official anti-Semitic campaign which is being increasingly conducted in the Soviet Union. The campaign is based on the familiar stereotypes recalling Streicher's *Der Stuermer* and the infamous *Protocols of the Elders of Zion*. A recent book, *International Zionism: History and Politics* (published in 1977 under the auspices of no less an institution than the

Soviet Academy of Sciences), asserts that "the Jewish bourgeoisie", using such firms as Lazard Frères, Lehman Brothers, Kuhn Loeb, Loeb Rhoades, Bache & Co., and Goldman Sachs, pursues its ancient goal of world domination by seeking "the expansion of their positions in the economy of the largest capitalist states . . . and in the economic system of world capitalism as a whole".

It is but a small step from this accusation to the charge that Jews actually "collaborated" in the Nazi genocide. A recent exhibition of Soviet art featured a painting showing a Nazi soldier and a Jewish prisoner with a Star of David, and both grinning over a pile of corpses!

Yet not even a whisper can be uttered in the official media of Brezhnev's Russia about the millions who perished in Stalin's genocide. There are corpses, and corpses.

Varlam Shalamov, a Soviet writer with even greater experience of corpses in Stalin's concentration camps than Solzhenitsyn, has written:

> "Kolyma was a great test of the moral strength of man . . . of ordinary human morality, and 99% of the people have not passed that test."

This sober conclusion about human behaviour in an extreme situation evokes melancholy reminiscences about those of us who observed it from the outside. Can one ever forget how a great part of the Left passed that test during "the low, dishonest decade" of the 1930s, when a *Daily Worker* headline on the Moscow Trial screamed: SHOOT THE REPTILES! Khrushchev's speech came as a shock to the "progressives". What has happened since to their *unbewältigte Vergangenheit*, their own "unmastered past"?

ON THE FACE OF IT, this past may seem to have been overcome on the Left. European Social Democracy was, on the whole, never pro-Soviet. With the emergence of "the New Left" and "Euro-Communism" practically everybody seems to be condemning the Stalinism of yesterday. French Communists, who first denounced Khrushchev's speech as "a bourgeois falsification" and then maintained that they were not "aware" of its authenticity because their delegates at the 20th Congress of the CPSU had just "not been told about it", finally admitted in *l'Humanité* that this threadbare excuse was indeed a lie. British Communists have denounced the Nazi–Soviet Pact for its "disastrous consequences" (which, as the *Morning Star* of 23 August admitted, included "handing over German Communists who had sought political asylum in the Soviet Union").[2] Those Communists

---

[2] The article also referred, without making clear what it was about, to "the secret protocol" of the Pact which divided Poland between Nazi Germany and the Soviet Union. The existence of this protocol has never been admitted by Soviet historians. They continue to denounce those who "spread an utterly false argument that the Soviet–German Pact gave Hitler the 'green light' to attack Poland". (P. Zhilin, "The Lessons of the Past Must Not Be Forgotten", *Pravda*, 21 August 1979.)

who disagreed with such bold criticism said that the "Soviet–Nazi Pact [was] no crime" (*Morning Star*, 31 August). But although they added that "of course we should remember the crimes and mistakes committed by Stalin", their real attitude is better reflected in a remark by one of the disgruntled delegates at the '79 Party congress: "Let's stop picking our sores. . . ." (*The Guardian*, 12 November).

S UCH "PICKING" has always been extremely private. The neo-Stalinists within the Euro-Communist parties (like the Soviet *apparatchiki* themselves) are hypersensitive about it. None of the Communist parties, in Europe or elsewhere, has treated Stalin's genocide in anything like a forthright manner. The reality of these crimes is avoided by euphemisms, circumlocutions, evasions, and, above all, when an actual Orwellian "memory hole" is not involved, by making historical references as unspecific as possible.

Is it just a question of a few unreconstructed Stalinists and fellow-travellers (like the late D. N. Pritt who until his death still retained his belief in the veracity of the Moscow Trials)?

Even the "critical" Communists only hint at what they know, without making it explicit. Previously they did not want to face the facts, now they do not like to live with them, although, in one form or another, they cannot help admitting them retrospectively. Any reader who had to rely on Western Communist publications would find it very difficult indeed to comprehend what happened in Russia under Stalin. He would know about "certain negative phenomena" or even crimes. But even though a reference to "millions of prisoners" in Stalin labour camps was once made in the *Morning Star*, its significance could not make much impact on the imagination of its readers, who are so sheltered from such themes that they can hardly visualize what it was all about.

ANY SUCH "anti-Soviet" writings are seduously ignored. Solzhenitsyn is dismissed as "a reactionary". Neither his *Gulag Archipelago* nor any other book on the subject was ever reviewed, even negatively, in the *Morning Star*. Instead one can read pathetic (and euphemistic) little homilies, such as the assurance of the Party secretary, Gordon McLennan, that "We have always made clear that our disagreement with some actions taken in Socialist countries is from the point of view of principle . . ." (12 November). Nor are the French or Italian Communists more candid in this respect. Truth is contraband, to be smuggled in when the dark opportunity presents itself. But then it serves only as another apologetic rationalization. The pieces of such black-market "truth" only confuse spirits rather than make them free.

The official verdict of the French Communist Party that Stalin's Russia was on balance a factor for progress is a dismal illustration of this. (Even so, the book *l'URSS et Nous*, dealing in part with the Communist "unmastered past", was attacked in the Soviet press, in spite of its restrained character and the French Party blessing.) The real psychological background to the ideological reluctance to settle scores with the past squarely can be seen in the intellectual meandering of the French palaeo- and ex- "true believers". More than in any other country, the scene in France is full of ex-Stalinists baring their souls; by now their memoirs could fill several bookshelves.

Their belated discovery of the obvious throws light on one phenomenon only: the varieties of self-deception.

Who Lied about the Camps?

THE LATEST TWO SUCH MEMOIRS have a particular bearing on the problem of reactions in the West to Stalin's genocide. Claude Morgan and André Wurmser were the two principal protagonists of the memorable 1949 trial in Paris—the libel suit brought by a Soviet Russian defector, Victor Kravchenko, against the Communist weekly, *Les Lettres Françaises* (of which Morgan was then the editor and Wurmser one of the chief contributors). It was the first occasion on which "the Gulag Archipelago" received world-wide publicity. Kravchenko, whose best-selling book *I Chose Freedom*, published in 1946, described the Stalinist terror, the purges, and the system of forced labour camps, produced a number of witnesses who testified from their own experience to the truth of his assertions. Among them was Margarete Buber-Neumann, the author of *Under Two Dictators*, who had been imprisoned in both Stalin's and Hitler's concentration camps, and Alex Weissberg, who had had a somewhat similar experience and had described it in his book *Conspiracy of Silence* (in the USA entitled *The Witches' Sabbath*). Both of them had been handed over by the *NKVD* to the *Gestapo* in 1940. David Rousset, a former inmate of a German concentration camp, found himself ostracized by all his "progressive" friends because of his support for Kravchenko.

The defence mobilized some of the best-known names of the French intellectual Left: Joliot-Curie, Vercors, d'Astier de la Vigerie, Pierre Cot, Roger Garaudy, using them as witnesses to discredit Kravchenko and his outrageous assertions about "the Fatherland of all progressive humanity" and its "great Leader and Teacher". They all declared that Kravchenko's book was a tissue of lies and that the testimonies of the eye-witnesses were the anti-Soviet inventions of reactionary émigrés manipulated by the US State Department and intelligence services. Pierre Daix, Morgan's successor as editor of *Les Lettres Françaises*, wrote a special pamphlet for the occasion: *Les Camps Concentrationnaires Sovietiques n'Existent Pas* ("Soviet Concentration Camps Do Not Exist"). And the lawyer of *Les Lettres Françaises*, Joe

Nordmann, even paid homage in his concluding speech to the "objective manner" in which the notorious prosecutor in the Moscow Trials, Andrei Vyshinsky, had conducted the cross-examination of the accused.

SUCH WAS THE ATMOSPHERE in post-War France that Kravchenko, despite the documentary evidence presented on the Soviet camps, was awarded only the symbolic minimum damages of "*un franc*", a judgment which *Le Monde* (25 September 1979) characterizes even today as "a homage rendered to the character and the past of the Communist writers who led the attack on Kravchenko". And such is the persistence of "progressive" stereotypes that when 17 years later Victor Kravchenko tragically took his own life, the London *Times* (26 February 1966) published an obituary which was full of cheap ironies and hostility. It did not mention his suicide. It characterized him as "one of the noisiest and most controversial figures at the height of the 'Cold War'," serving "cold-war propaganda". As it came after Khrushchev's and Solzhenitsyn's "revelations", the *Times* obituary archly admitted that "there was, for all its exaggeration, a strong basis of truth in Kravchenko's autobiography, *I Chose Freedom*, with its lurid stories of the Stalin purges in the 1930s, with its harrowing accounts of the police terror in Russia. . . ." Far from being any kind of "exaggeration", Kravchenko's account was actually something of an understatement of the extent of Stalin's genocide. In reality the Gulag was even more "harrowing", as not only Solzhenitsyn, but also Nadezhda Mandelshtam, Shalamov and so many others have testified. Kravchenko had no comparable literary talent, but he did have an important message for which he was vilified in the West, not yet ready for "premature truth". If he was "lurid", so was Anna Akhmatova's *Requiem*. However, it was not a question of literary quality, but of the unwillingness of the "progressive intelligentsia" at that time to face the truth about Soviet reality.

TODAY, 30 YEARS AFTER the trial, Claude Morgan has finally admitted in his autobiography, *Don Quichotte et les Autres*, that "Kravchenko was right"! He confesses that after Kravchenko's suicide he wanted "to pay him homage, but it was as yet too early. . . ." He reveals that the original article, "How Kravchenko was Fabricated", published in *Les Lettres Françaises* under the signature of "Sim Thomas" (presented as a US journalist), was in fact written by André Ulmann, a French contributor to the journal. Morgan and Wurmser had claimed that Kravchenko "was not even the author of his book".

André Wurmser, however, has evidently refused to do a *mea culpa* in his recent autobiography, *Fidèlement Vôtre*. For him, "Kravchenko was not telling the truth, he was deforming it. . . ." Answering Morgan, who reproached him for upholding his old charges against Kravchenko ("One must know how to admit being in the wrong; I am afraid he is not sincere"),[3] Wurmser now explains in *l'Humanité* (20 September) that Kravchenko's

> "book, or rather the book which he signed . . . reduced the whole history of the USSR to Stalinist arbitrary measures. He mixed fiction with one aspect of Soviet reality about which the Communists were ignorant at that time. . . . We were unfortunately mistaken in asserting, as all progressives did the world over (contrary to what the 20th Congress of the CPSU later revealed to be the truth), that the camps did not exist in the Soviet Union. The condemnation which our Party pronounced, confirmed, and repeated against the methods of Stalin needs no reminders. . . ."

So much for Kravchenko, so much for genocide. . . .

Unlike Claude Morgan, who still considers himself a Communist although he has left the Party, Pierre Daix has made a radical break with his past, as his books (*J'ai cru au matin* and *Les Chemins du Printemps*) testify. He became an early advocate of Solzhenitsyn in France and was prepared to admit his past errors. The other protagonist of the Kravchenko affair, Roger Garaudy, left the Party after the invasion of Czechoslovakia in 1968, although he declared that "Khrushchev's [1956] speech was a turning point of my dreams" (*Le Nouvel Observateur*, 29 October). Until then, he confessed, "I could not imagine that Stalin was a dictator".[4]

IRONICALLY ENOUGH, if their past presents a problem to the Communists, their present practices no longer provoke such censure from the Socialists and the New Left as they did in olden times. They show themselves increasingly reluctant to condemn in a clear and outspoken manner even such barbaric Communist actions as those which have occurred in Cambodia and Viet Nam. As one Social Democrat, Carl Gershman (*Commentary*, October 1979), reminds us: "On these questions, as on all others regarding brutality by Communist régimes, the Socialist International has remained silent. . . ."

Similarly, the New Left, whose emergence was influenced by a reaction to Khrushchev's "revelations" about Stalin, has become less unfriendly towards the Brezhnev régime which has ended "de-Stalinisation". The closing of the circle of confusion can be seen in a *New Left Review* editorial (September–October 1979):

---

[3] In an astonishing sentence Wurmser wrote: "One should not judge what some of us thought by what we have said."

[4] George Bernard Shaw observed (in November 1934), quite without his wonted Shavian wit, that Stalin is "a simple secretary of the supreme organ of control who is liable to be dismissed from his position in ten minutes if his performance is not satisfactory. . . ."

"One of the most salient features of the later '70s has been a widespread recrudescence of Cold War politics in the West. The relative novelty of this second round of orchestrated international reaction has been its overwhelming concentration on the USSR as a target . . . it has become an increasing vogue among sections of the Left as well, which in their frustration at the impasse of the labour movement in the West, have taken to discharging their aggression upon the USSR."

Poor Workers' Paradise, still being set upon by malefic scribblers! Thus not only do we have ex-Communists and ex-Stalinists, we also now have ex-New Leftists and we are even beginning to get new Old Leftists. The lessons of Genocide and Gulag are lost on secular salvationists and their fellow-travellers, old and new. In his conversation with Régis Debray (published in the French journal, *Change*), Noam Chomsky has been ironical about Western intellectuals who, according to him, gave too much "publicity" to the Cambodian genocide. He detected conspiracy (*Le Monde*, 22 March 1979):

"It is striking that the discovery of Gulag was made at the end of the Vietnam war, when it was convenient to deflect attention to other things."

The conspiratorial ways of the Western press are indeed far-reaching! For Régis Debray Western perversion of truth goes even further: for him Gulag "is a word imposed by imperialism". . . .

Cults & Crimes

SANTAYANA'S acute characterization of "those who do not learn from history" (being condemned to repeat it) and Hegel's melancholy reflection on "the only thing we learn from history" (that we never learn from history) do not go far enough. It may be that each generation fails to learn from the experience of its predecessors; but some generations, one suspects, even fail to learn from their own experience.

When the generation of the 1930s was replaced by the generation of the 1960s, and the cult of "good Uncle Joe" was replaced by the cult of good "Uncle Ho", perhaps the most infuriating aspect of the new decade for those who remembered the old one was not just the feeling of *déjà vu* and the re-emergence of daft political attitudes, but the fact that so many people who should have known better were ready to embrace them and join the Gadarene rush. The naïve "revolutionary" utopianism of "the kids" has been matched by the postures of their elders trying to re-acquire political virginity. As Norman Podhoretz recollects in his memoir, *Breaking Ranks*:

"To be pro-American in the '60s was like being anti-Soviet in the '30s,

252 HOLOCAUST: MYTHS & HORRORS

for just as radicalism then had been tied to support of the Soviet Union as the centre of Socialist hope, so radicalism now increasingly defined itself in opposition to the United States as the major obstacle to the birth of a better world."

For the New Left intelligentsia, America became "the moral equivalent of Nazi Germany". Its whole history was "obscene", said Susan Sontag, based as it was on genocide. The war in Viet Nam was not a defence of South Viet Nam against the communist expansionism of Hanoi, but an imperialist action of *Amerika*. The respectable sympathizers of the "Movement" among the "radical rich", the media, and the political élite—and even many who did not share such jejune political perspectives—had little critical, sceptical awareness of the possible consequences of their attitudes. The "kids" were chanting

> *"Hey, hey, hey, LBJ*
> *How many kids you killed today?"*

Their elders pooh-poohed any danger of the "domino effect" following American defeat in Viet Nam. Warnings that there might be a bloodbath when the Communists took over (and other unpleasant consequences for the inhabitants of Indochinese states) were derided and firmly rejected as the scaremongering of the "hawks". The intelligentsia and its leading ladies began to make their tours to Hanoi. Mary McCarthy and Jane Fonda symbolized the merger of the '30s and the '60s. Once again a "brave new world" was in the offing.

Où sont les neiges d'antan? Where are all those self-righteous expectations and blithely complacent predictions of the "progressives" and the "doves"? There was not just a bloodbath, there was *genocide* in Cambodia. There was an "oceanic Holocaust" in Viet Nam. There was an invasion of Cambodia by Viet Nam. The moment the "Boat People" disappeared from the television screens, the emaciated bodies of Cambodian children made their horrific appearance.

AND WHAT HAPPENED to the "progressive" journalists and singers engaged in the anti-Viet Nam war movement? Once again, as in the aftermath of the 1930s, some discovered the consequences of their illusions, others persisted in them.

Five days before the *Khmer Rouge* troops entered Phnom Penh, the *New York Times* reporter there, Sydney H. Schanberg, wrote that "it is difficult to imagine how [the] lives [of ordinary people] could be anything but better with the Americans gone". He explained that

> "Wars nourish brutality and sadism and sometime certain people are
> executed by the victors, but it would be tendentious to forecast such

abnormal behaviour as a national policy under a Communist government once the war is over. Cambodia, being a country blessed with rich agricultural land and a relatively small population, can be revived without any major reconstruction program. . . ."

Shortly after, having witnessed the brutal removal of the whole population from Phnom Penh by the victorious *Khmer Rouge*, Mr Schanberg became (to his credit) the first reporter to describe the horrors of the "evacuation", literally the first step on the road to genocide in Cambodia. Four-and-a-half years later (on 12 October 1979), he reported the story of his colleague, a Cambodian journalist, Dith Pran, employed by the *New York Times*, who reached Bangkok and told him about the "true hell" he had been through— the reduction of his country's population from seven to four million by massacres and starvation.

None So Blind . . .

D URING THE FOUR-AND-A-HALF YEARS between these two dispatches the world has gradually learned and generally recognized the bestial behaviour of the *Khmer Rouge* and the magnitude of their crimes. But the "progressive intelligentsia" was at first reluctant to acknowledge them. In America, Leo Cherne and his colleagues from the International Rescue Committee and Freedom House were the first who went to Thailand to investigate the case and to produce an authoritative report based on extensive interviews with the Cambodian refugees. It was, however, totally disregarded by the secular "progressives" from *The Nation* and the "progressive" Catholics from the *Commonweal*.

Similarly in Britain, it was Bernard Levin, and not John Pilger with his Hanoi sympathies, who was writing articles attacking the chief apologist of the Pol Pot régime in this country, Dr Malcolm Caldwell.

At that time, in the liberal *Guardian* and the socialist *Tribune*, Dr Caldwell tried hard to deny or minimize testimony about the catastrophe. He contemptuously rejected Levin's accusations. He did not feel that "those who did not subscribe to his [Levin's] fantasy [are] in effect mentally ill and comparable to blind apologists for Hitler and Stalin". He would not commit himself to any particular figure, but with a great display of moral indignation argued that there were only "scores, or hundreds of thousands" killed and not a million or more. He quoted approvingly an American "delegate" (*Tribune*, 8 September 1978):

"The new Government, fighting for its survival against all this counter-revolutionary activity, had to deal swiftly and sternly with every instance of sabotage and subversion. Undoubtedly, this was a bloody process that may well have entailed some excesses and mistakes.

But without revolutionary violence against the enemy, the revolution itself would have been crushed in its infancy."

You can't make an omelette. . . .

Dr Caldwell was killed in Phnom Penh while visiting the land of Pol Pot. We do not know who shot him. During his travels he was reported to have paraphrased the remark of Lincoln Steffens about the Soviet Union by saying: "I have seen the past and it works" (*International Herald Tribune*, 27 December 1978). *Tribune* (29 December 1978) published an obituary on the "tragic death of Cambodia's friend", a warm tribute to Malcolm Caldwell by his CND friend, Peggy Duff. An obituary note by John Gittings in that once distinguished bastion of humane liberalism, *The Guardian* (27 December 1978) said:

> "Caldwell attempted (notably in an article in the *Guardian* on 8 May) to understand the stories (often exaggerated) of mass executions and an enforced return to the land in Cambodia after the revolutionary victory of April 1975. And in a reply to a harsh attack on him by Bernard Levin in the *Times*, he argued first that retribution against collaboration with the US-backed Lon Nol régime of 1970–75 was understandable, and secondly that the new policy of 'taking agriculture as the base' made good economic sense. . . . Caldwell was an irreplaceable teacher and comrade whose work will undoubtedly suffer the customary fate of being better appreciated after his death."

Christopher Hitchens was rather more critical in the *New Statesman* (5 January 1979), arguing that "the access to power of the *Khmer Rouge* has been the excuse for a truly epoch-making bloodbath" and that "Caldwell, in some of his sallies into print, was reduced to haggling over the exact number of those killed". But he almost found an extenuating circumstance in the fact that "the more he was attacked by the Bernard Levins of this world, the more certain he became that he was right (a dangerous logic, as students of the 1930s will know)".

And there was the inevitable rationalization, which anticipated the "documentary proof" later to be provided by William Shawcross: "The genocidal American bombing was also, it need hardly be added, a midwife to the Cambodian régime." When *Tribune* also came out against the Pol Pot régime on this "controversial" problem, Dr Caldwell's sister, Isobel Colquhoun, protested vigorously (*Tribune*, 19 January 1979):

> "I was deeply shocked when I read both your editorial and Chris Mullin's article on Cambodia (*Tribune*, January 12). They were both written as though my brother, Malcolm Caldwell, had never existed. The same well-worn clichéd themes (that the Khmer Rouge Government ruled by terror, that there were large-scale government

directed massacres and that there were no desperate reasons for evacuating Phnom Penh) were trundled out with no reference whatever to what Malcolm had written questioning these hypotheses. . . . You might have given some indication that there was another side to the story, particularly as Malcolm had written on the subject in your columns not so long ago."

Are there no limits to brazenness?

Soon *Tribune* (16 November 1979) was waxing indignant on the basis of a premise which not so long ago it had treated as controversial. Now it mustered enough anger to condemn

". . . one of the more cynical episodes in the recent history of British foreign policy where Britain—in common with most other Western governments—has continued to recognize a régime which is openly acknowledged to be responsible for mass murder and which controls less than 10% of Kampuchea."

The pattern is not unfamiliar. We have seen it in the belated anti-Stalinism of old fellow-travellers and in the belated recognition of the horrors of new genocides. As it happens, three weeks later the British government had withdrawn recognition of the Pol Pot régime (without recognizing the puppet Government of Heng Samrin).

CONFUSING A TIGER WITH AN UNDERDOG has been a perennial tendency among "the progressives". One is reminded not only how many of them supported Stalin's "legitimate" ambitions, but also how others, in spite of ideological antipathy, tended to feel that one should not be beastly to Hitler, because of his "legitimate" concerns with the "wicked" Versailles Treaty.[5]

Before the Second World War, *Tribune* (under William Mellor and H. J. Hartshorn) and the *New Statesman* (under Kingsley Martin) supported the Stalin régime, endorsing the Moscow Trials and the Soviet–Nazi Pact. Later, they at least had the excuse (also used by repentant Nazis) that they simply "did not know about" genocide. (The repentant French Stalinists, like Claude Morgan, just could not believe in the existence of the Soviet concentration camps.) But this time the genocide was not unprecedented, therefore there were no similar barriers to the imagination.

For the pro-Vietnamese Communists truth-telling became expedient only

---

[5] Commenting in a letter (of 22 January 1935) to Robert Vansittart about the pilgrimages to Hitler of the British Labour "progressives" like George Lansbury and Clifford Allen, the British ambassador in Berlin, Sir Eric Phipps, wrote:

". . . One of the very odd features of a very odd situation is the anxiety of Hitler's political opponents in all countries to interview and negotiate with him. . . . The more German pacifists he throws into his concentration camps the more of that ilk arrive from abroad to see him."

when the Vietnamese began their propaganda offensive against the Pol Pot
régime. The veteran Stalinist propagandist, Wilfred Burchett—who had
concocted the stories about US "germ warfare" in Korea—described
Cambodian atrocities (in *The Guardian*, 11 May 1979) and estimated the
genocide's victims at 2–3 million. Even the French Communists, never
strong on veracity, began to publish true stories: for instance, the account by
Lola Sivath, cousin of Prince Sihanouk, describing how she lost her husband
and three daughters:

> "Seeing her father standing beneath the mango tree, my daughter began
> running. One of the Pol Pot soldiers fired from his rifle and shot her in
> the head. She fell on the ground. Then they shot my husband before my
> eyes. . . . What wanton cruelty! Had I not been a witness and a victim I
> would not have believed it was possible. Earlier, when I saw films about
> the Nazi concentration camps, they had seemed incredible to me. . . ."

This appeared in *l'Humanité* on 15 September 1979. A few days later it carried
the reply of André Wurmser to Claude Morgan about Kravchenko having
"deformed the truth".

The Party-line can change; but some lines stay hard and fast.

T HE SOVIET UNION has not for a long time shown any concern about
what was happening in Cambodia. Until well into 1978 (i.e. for three
years) there was not a squeak in the Soviet press on Cambodian atrocities. On
the contrary, as long as Moscow hoped that it could regain some influence
with the *Khmer Rouge* régime to counter that of Peking, it was perfectly ready
to disregard such trifles.

In 1976, when Pol Pot became a prime minister of "democratic
Kampuchea", Kosygin sent a congratulatory telegram (published in *Pravda*).
In October 1977, the Soviet foreign-affairs weekly, *New Times*, acclaimed
Pol Pot's "progressive social and economic reforms" in an approving article.
In 1978 the Central Committee of the CPSU welcomed the formal
announcement of the existence of the Communist Party of Kampuchea.
Only later in that year did the Soviet press begin to attack the "monster
régime" of Pol Pot and to discover its genocidal character. So it is not
surprising that the Soviet book on the subject, called *Kampuchea: From
Tragedy to Revival* (Politizdat, 1979) contains Soviet press material from 1978
and 1979 only.

Belated "indignation" about *Khmer Rouge* massacres is a purely political
function of Soviet foreign policy interests. It would not have been expressed
if "Democratic Kampuchea" had chosen neutrality or a pro-Soviet position
in the Sino-Soviet conflict. When it comes to genocide, the Soviet Union
must first confront its own past, before it can have any title to condemn the
imitators of its own paradigmatic original.

Eggs & Omelettes

FACED WITH THE MORAL PROBLEM presented by the sequel to their own victory, the members and sympathizers of the anti-Viet Nam war movement in the USA began to adopt different positions.

One of its singing bards, Pete Seeger, an enthusiastic Stalinist in the past, has "found Jesus" (without apparently losing Stalin). Joan Baez, another singer who played an important part in opposing the Viet Nam war, condemned Hanoi for its violations of human rights and invited many prominent participants in the "movement" to sign her letter of protest. 84 "celebrities" signed, but others refused: William Kunstler wrote in the *Village Voice* that he "would never join in a public denunciation of a socialist country". And Jane Fonda refused to associate herself with the protest, saying that the charges against Hanoi are "inaccurate" and "not substantiated". She wrote to Joan Baez:

> "Your action only aligns you with the most narrow and negative elements in our country who continue to believe that Communism is worse than death."

The ensuing "battle of advertisements" between the two show-biz political gurus would have been comic if the subject was not so tragic.

Shortly before, there was a "battle of posters" in Italy in which the terrorist organization, *La Prima Linea*, accused the official Italian Communist Party of supporting the genocide attempt of the Vietnamese invading Cambodia, while the PCI of course made the reverse—better substantiated—charge. It was, I believe, the very first time in history that Communists had accused each other of genocide.

Both proved right. After the genocidal outrages of Pol Pot, the Vietnamese "liberators" of Cambodia contributed to the calamity of mass starvation by confiscating seed grains and damaging agriculture. Later, they faced the hunger catastrophe quite cynically, making acceptance of Western aid conditional on their control of its distribution. They also began to settle tens of thousands of Vietnamese in the depopulated Cambodia.

One celebrity who travelled to Hanoi in the past, Mary McCarthy, said that she "might have signed the Joan Baez protest about the boat people, but I was not asked" (*The Observer*, 14 October 1979). However, she did offer some regrets about her trip to Hanoi:

> "I'm ashamed to say, for instance, how many suitcases containing clothes I took to North Viet Nam. . . ."

Let's hope that Miss McCarthy will in future have less embarrassment with her Left luggage. The dress rehearsals of the 1930s and the '60s should be of some help.

IN BRITAIN THE BATTLE among the ex-"Vietniks" was fought out between Richard Gott, the features editor of *The Guardian*, and John Pilger from the *Daily Mirror*. Richard Gott regretted that the Pol Pot régime "has been so fiercely pilloried abroad", that he had been compared to Adolf Hitler, and that his own paper had called Pol Pot's actions "monstrous". Like Professor Noam Chomsky in America, he expressed doubts about the extent of the slaughter and quoted a figure of "something between 100,000 and 300,000 [who] could have been killed" (*The Guardian*, 12 November 1979). John Pilger easily disposed of these arguments and, for good measure, added a reminder about "Henry Kissinger's lethal complicity in Cambodia's ordeal" (14 November).

Ever since the appearance of William Shawcross' book, *Sideshow* this last assertion has become an ideological life-belt for both Old and New Leftists. They were perplexed, confused, and somewhat uneasy about the organized murder of the "gentle people". They needed a new rationalization to retain their self-righteousness. Shawcross provided it; hence the popular notoriety of his book.

His fundamental argument is that by bombing and invading the Viet Minh bases in Cambodia, the US "destabilized" it, ended its precarious "neutrality", and by "brutalising" the *Khmer Rouge* indirectly contributed to the genocide. "Cambodia was not a mistake; it was a crime." All the dispirited protesters who not so long ago were marching with posters demanding *Stop the Killing!* could breathe more easily—without, however, applying the slogan to the new, unexpectedly more murderous situation. This would have been ideologically very awkward indeed.

Sympathetic reviewers hailed the Shawcross book for its scholarly qualities and the sophistication of its arguments. Irving Howe described it in *Dissent* (Fall 1979) as an "overpowering and meticulous study". Unfortunately, the compliments are exaggerated; the reasoning is specious, and, as some reviewers discovered, the scholarship is not flawless either.

On Shawcross's logic, one could attribute moral responsibility for the Nazi Holocaust to "Bomber" Harris rather than to Hitler. The alleged causative connection is a myth. It was the Viet Minh who first violated the neutrality of Cambodia; the Americans only reacted against attacks from the military sanctuaries established there and tolerated by the "neutral" Prince Sihanouk. The general conclusion of the book is not based on the specific documentary material which is paraded as establishing it, but only illustrates its *a priori* character. As Charles Fairbanks Jr. demonstrated (in the *Wall Street Journal* of 2 November 1979), Shawcross applied for the Pentagon documents under the Freedom of Information Act not earlier than March 1977. But already in December 1976,

"[he] had published in the *Sunday Times* of London a long piece

('Cambodia: the Blame') in which he makes exactly the same argument about American guilt that appears later in the book. . . . Thus he could not have developed his thesis in response to the newly obtained documents. . . ."

Dr Kissinger's assistant, Peter Rodman, has found that Shawcross used these documents very selectively. For instance, he omitted many references to the detailed descriptions of *Khmer Rouge* totalitarian practices in the areas controlled by them in 1971, i.e. well before US action in Cambodia could have affected it.

In fact the starting-point of Shawcross's reasoning is wrong. If he had a more experienced understanding of totalitarian mentality, he would have put the blame for genocide where it belongs: on the ideological fanaticism of the *Khmer Rouge*, whose leaders learned their revolutionary theory in Paris and applied it ruthlessly and primitively by "wiping the slate clean" and starting a whole new society from scratch. In his book on *Utopia and Revolution*, Melvin J. Lasky provides a variety of historical examples of this revolutionary utopianism. This time the lunacy has gone even further than ever before. As François Ponchaud put it in his *Cambodia, Year Zero* (Penguin, 1978, pp. 16, 214):

> "Their ideology has led them to invent a radically new kind of man in a radically new society. . . . It [was] a perfect application of an ideology pushed to the furthest limit of its own internal logic."

They were not "brutalized"—they were brutal. They had to make a brand-new omelette. So, once again, what matter if a few million eggs get broken in the process?

THERE IS NO NEED for rationalization, just as previously there was no reason for false expectations. It is only "the cuckolds of history" who are always surprised when their expectations of a new utopia end in a new catastrophe, their permanent hopes leading to repeated genocides. *Le Nouvel Observateur* (5 November 1979) reflected:

> "One would have liked to believe that this striking abandonment of the critical spirit is only an exceptional momentary aberration. But it is nothing of the sort. On the contrary, it is a structural trait, a constant in the behaviour of intellectuals. . . ."

A melancholy thought.

Some of our "best and brightest" minds tried to love Stalin (even, like Anthony Blunt, becoming *NKVD* agents in "good conscience") and then were confounded by the Gulag. And when they tried to revere Uncle Ho (shouting his name in praise in Western capitals), they were surprised by millions of dead and dying refugees in Indo-China—a land that was supposed to have been "liberated" at long last from the iniquities of American "imperialism".

It was an uncanny repetition of the self-induced blindness of earlier Communists and fellow-travellers. The same mentality, "born again", manifested itself among "progressives" in the new period. Just as in the past they denied the existence of Stalin's *Gulag*, so now they denied Pol Pot's genocide. No argument was too thin to be used, no régime too obnoxious to be defended, if it was anti-Western.

Again, the best available evidence was rejected on the same spurious grounds that victims' testimonies are "unreliable". Like those who refused to listen to the reports from Soviet Russia and Nazi Germany, Noam Chomsky now argued that the refugees from Cambodia were not to be given credence, that they "tend to report what they believe their interlocutors wish to hear" (*The Nation*, 25 June 1977). Quoting profusely from odd and misleading sources, he presented a "scholarly" conclusion that "highly qualified specialists who have studied the full range of evidence available . . . concluded that executions [in Cambodia] have numbered at most in thousands."

The same line was taken by George C. Hildebrand and Gareth Porter in their book *Cambodia, Starvation and Revolution* (Monthly Review Press, 1976) and many others in the USA. The parallel with the 1930s and '40s is striking. The new "progressives", while rejecting the attitude to Stalin of their predecessors, the Pritts and the Webbs, displayed the same credulousness. In this historical encore, a "true believer's" faith once more replaced critical intelligence. As François Ponchaud pointed out in his book, "Their only sources of evaluation [of the situation in Cambodia] are deliberately chosen official statements. . . ."

WHY WAS THERE no instinctive resonance among "progressives" to the horrors of genocide? Was it just a general reluctance to face appalling realities?

No, the blinkers were in their ideological prejudices. Their ideologies inhibited them, stopped them from recognizing the horrors, prevented a humane concern with the skeletal figures who could only remind one painfully of the haggard *KZ-niks* and *Zeks* of the Nazi and Soviet concentration camps.

What a miserable irony of closed minds joined to hardened hearts!—that those who were so often branded "bleeding hearts" were so cold-bloodedly inclined to disregard the crimes of genocide.

All the *post hoc* casuistries and rationalizations cannot disguise this failure in the supreme test of professed humanitarianism. The elementary rules of intellectual hygiene require that this should be remembered in the 1980s.

A FINAL WORD about the pitfalls of myths and horrors in our day. In his Column *(Encounter,* October 1979) Goronwy Rees wrote: "Dr Kissinger can murder a few million Cambodians on the Machiavellian principle that the end justifies the means. . . ."

I was never very well disposed to Dr Kissinger's policies, but I find this allegation monstrous. It is of the type which naturally finds its way to the *New Statesman* rather than *Encounter.* It echoes, of course, William Shawcross who in *Sideshow* attributes moral responsibility for the genocide in Cambodia under Pol Pot to Dr Kissinger. Shawcross' emotions about Cambodia are understandable, but his moral judgment is confused. His is a familiar kind of reasoning which manages to shift the blame for the crimes of totalitarian régimes on to their victims or their opponents.[6]

It was not surprising that in the USA (where it appeared first) his book was eagerly seized by the ideological orphans of the Viet Nam war. As I have said above, it was a time when some of them began having second thoughts about their "Vietnik" expectations and their own role during this war. Joan Baez and Jane Fonda were locked in fierce polemic about the behaviour of Hanoi after the "liberation", and so were their "progressive" followers. They had been neither impressed nor distressed by earlier Viet Cong atrocities. After all, terrible things do happen during a war (such as the cold-blooded Hué murders—but there were no "excuses" for My Lai).

Yet now, the sheer size of the horror—the millions liquidated in Communist Cambodia, the fleeing mass of Vietnamese "boat people"—has made them distinctly uneasy. Even Noam Chomsky, as his letter in the same issue of *Encounter* testifies, finds it necessary to obfuscate his own position on the matter.[7] His concern about the *exact number* of the victims of genocide in

---

[6] After the occupation of Warsaw in 1939 the Germans put up posters with a photograph of destruction caused in the Polish capital by their own bombing. The caption read: *"England, This Is Your Doing!"*

[7] In the "Introduction" to his interview with Chomsky (*Men of Ideas,* BBC Publications, 1979, p. 204) Bryan Magee wrote:

"Noam Chomsky has made two international reputations in apparently unrelated fields. The widest is as one of the national leaders of resistance to the Vietnam war. The deepest is as a Professor of Linguistics who, before he was 40 years old, had transformed the nature of his subject."

Whether his "wider reputation" will survive him is doubtful.

Ever since the genocide in Cambodia, he has tried hard to refuse to acknowledge the facts and to minimize the extent of their horror in a series of polemics with François Ponchaud, Jean Lacouture, and Dennis Duncanson. I find something indecent in somebody whose own people have been a target of genocide belittling the tragedy of others who have undergone it too. He makes heavy weather of "scholarship" and "scientific doubt" about the number of victims of the Pol Pot régime; but as Jean Lacouture pointed out in *Le Nouvel Observateur* (20 November 1978):

"Is it necessary in order to condemn Nazism to prove that it has killed millions (1945) or tens of thousands (1935). . . . Must Chomsky know about one [concentration] camp or a hundred camps in order to denounce Stalinism?" →

Cambodia reminds one of the Nazi apologists, like Rassinier, who argue that Hitler killed "only" 1.2 million Jews, not 6 million. . . .

FOR THIS TYPE OF MENTALITY Shawcross' book was a godsend. It was enthusiastically received in the USA by the "liberal" *Nation*, and excerpts from it were reproduced in London's *New Statesman*. It provided a Freudian "defence mechanism" for the troubled simpletons on the Left. The blame for the whole Cambodian nightmare could now be put where it belonged: on Dr Kissinger! He was presented as a butcher, with axe and hands dripping with blood (in the best *Pravda* or *Krokodil* style) on the cover cartoon of the *New Statesman*. After that, all good and true progressives had their doubts assuaged—as if the specific wartime US bombings of the "Ho Chi Minh trail" were somehow part-and-parcel of a Communist régime's peacetime genocidal purge of its own population. They could now proceed on their usual ideological course with lily-white consciences.

Such scapegoating and such reversals are not exactly new. In answer to Mr James Fenton who had argued (in the *New Statesman* of 6 January 1978) that "it was America that set the process going in Cambodia", the Editor of *Encounter* (May 1978), put the matter forcefully:

> "So the Americans are guilty! And who is guilty of the Gulag Archipelago? Presumably Winston Churchill and the Allied Intervention 'that set the process going'. And who was guilty of the Hitlerian Holocaust? Presumably the vindictive Men of Versailles with their harsh anti-German peace that set the process going'. And who is guilty of Idi Amin's massacres in East Africa? Who but the white British Imperialists, the men of the Black Hole of Calcutta and Amritsar and the Hola camps who 'set the process going.'. . . How 'crass' to think, with typical anti-communist McCarthyite hysteria, that the Communists are, truly and deep down, really responsible for the inhumanities

---

Chomsky's sophistries are increasingly shrill and inconsistent. He now claims that his writings "contain harsh criticisms of Marxist–Leninist ideology and practice" (*International Affairs*, October 1979, p. 595). But here is what he said in an interview which he gave to the *New Left Review* (September–October 1969):

> "It would be a grotesque error to say that Stalin was simply the realization of Leninist principles. . . . There are different strands in Lenin's theories. On the one hand, there is *State and Revolution*, which is basically fine, and on the other hand, there is effective dismantling of the Soviets, there is Kronstadt and the suppression of the Workers' Opposition, which was under Lenin's aegis at least."

The "harsh criticism of Marxist–Leninist ideology and practice" happened to be a naive fundamentalist dissent from a few aspects of Leninism. This is hardly what his readers might infer from his letter to *International Affairs*. They may also be less than clear about his real position on the Cambodian genocide.

All in all, this "Einstein of linguistics", the author of *Language and Responsibility*, converts linguistic energy into a mass of casuistic irresponsibilities.

committed! How deceptively 'attractive' it is to think that the politicians who commit a specific crime are not the actual criminals!"

In a long letter to *The Economist* (8 September 1979), in his TV talk with David Frost, and in his *Memoirs*, Dr Kissinger tried to refute this type of reasoning, in which William Shawcross confounds front-line military action with non-combative atrocities, and attributes the latter to the former. But will such protests stop the slurs?

"Progressive" rationalizations give one the best idea of infinity. The making of ideological myths is, alas, endless.

(*1980*)

13. The Student Revolt of the 1960s

*"The time is fast approaching when freedom, public peace, and
social order will not be able to exist without education."*

Alexis de Tocqueville (1835)

T O SAY THAT the world has been bewildered by the Student Revolt is
to state something embarrassingly obvious. What is not so obvious is
the contention that the answer to the question: "Why is it bewildered?" is
more important than the answer to the question: "Why do the students
revolt?" This is not just because of the recent events in France, but because it
is the wider context of this revolt which is of greater importance.

In a series of articles on the subject in *The Times* (27 May–1 June 1968),
Richard Davy attributed the Student Revolt to a "distress over modern
society", and drew the following conclusion:

> "If you want to synthesize a student revolt in your laboratory proceed as
> follows. Take several thousand students of sociology and make them
> attend lectures in a hall that holds a hundred. Tell them that even if they
> pass their examinations there will probably be no jobs for them.
> Surround them with a society that does not practise what it preaches and
> is run by political parties that do not represent the students' ideas.
>
> Tell them to think about what is wrong with society and how to put it
> right. As soon as they become actively interested in the subject send in
> the police to beat them up. Then stand well clear of the bang and affect an
> attitude of confused surprise.
>
> This is, of course, a crude simplification, but it does at least hint at the
> pattern of some of the student trouble in the Western world—a
> combination of educational grievances, political disillusion, moral
> concern, frustration, boredom, enthusiasm, and a certain amount of
> imitativeness."

The hint is suggestive, but not sufficient. "A society that does not practise
what it preaches" is too vague a description which, if taken literally, applies
to all known societies in history (excepting, possibly, some small monastic
groups). On the other hand, if the expression refers to the gap between the
professed values and social practice, it is not necessarily wider in the countries
witnessing Student Revolt than in others where it has not occurred.

The most striking thing about it is the contradictory character of some of
the reasons which have been advanced for its supposed general causes.

It has been said that the students revolt because they are becoming cogs in the "knowledge factories", cogs facing the anonymous "multiversity" in the big lecture halls of Berkeley University ("I'm only a number"). But in Berlin they revolt, it has been suggested, because they want a wider *Gemeinschaft* than they have in small seminars. There is revolt at Columbia University as a result of the American *"permissive education"*. There is revolt in Hamburg and Frankfurt because of the alleged authoritarian character of the German educational system.

There is revolt in Naples and Turin because the Italian professors do not fulfil their teaching duties; indeed some of them do not. But this cannot be said about the German professors who were driven by the German students to resign.

Students revolt in Paris and Rome where there is in fact scandalous overcrowding of lecture halls and libraries. They also revolt in New York and other American cities where there is no such overcrowding.

In Columbia University they use the issue of the building of a new gymnasium, which might have been taken as an act of racial segregation against Harlem Negroes. At Northwestern University the Negro students forced the authorities to provide them with segregated housing on racist lines.

There is revolt in California against the Affluent society and the prospect of living (like their philistine fathers) in the "ticky-tacky houses" of the Pete Seeger song. In Paris though, there is revolt against bad housing conditions.

In Tokyo there is revolt because after competitive entrance examinations students find themselves available for politics, with a degree virtually guaranteed because of the traditionally easy grading in the Japanese universities. Yet in Paris, we are told, there is revolt because of the examination neurosis induced by the harshness of the French examination system.

There is revolt in Rome, where life is exciting (and Italian students are easily excitable). But there is also revolt in Stockholm, where life is boring and the students are cool-blooded Scandinavians.

In Paris the middle-class university rebels say that more students of working-class origin should be admitted, and the same is said in Belgrade, where such students form a more sizable part of the university. But the Paris revolt started with a protest against the non-admittance of male students to the women students' quarters in Nanterre; and the Belgrade revolt with a protest against the system of distribution of tickets to a pop show which gave high priority to industrial and farm workers.

The students at the London School of Economics staged a sit-down to win participation in the running of the university, and the same is demanded by students at the Universities of Leeds and Essex, not to mention the French students and their demands for *cogestion*. But the students also revolt in Santiago where they do have a system of *cogobierno* in the university and in

Berlin where they have had their *Mitbestimmung* from the very beginning of
the Free University.

Last but not least, there is the contrast between the prevalent ideological
posture of the students in the Communist and Western countries. In Warsaw
and Prague they demand political freedom. In Paris, Rome, and Berlin, they
invoke Ho, Mao, and Marcuse.

I N SHORT, THE ONLY COMMON FEATURE of the Student Revolt
is the students' rebellious mood, and its historical originality is that it
appeared in the highly industrialized countries. Neither its practice nor its
"theory" are coherent enough to be seen as an attempt to seek rational goals
by rational means.

Rather, we are faced here with all kinds of ideological rationalizations of
emotional drives which are contradictory. For such complexes, genuine
problems of social and educational change can provide stimuli or
justification; but they are only instrumental in providing outlets for other
motives, as can be seen from the fact that such students' demands which are
fulfilled are immediately followed by *another* set of demands. This is not just a
matter of revolutionary tactics. It is a classical pattern of all movements
which manifest political *"transference neuroses"*. In such movements realizable
goals are irrelevant, and Utopia (i.e. fantasy) is the only satisfactory symbol.
This is the emotional background behind the current ideological hotch-potch
in which the "one-dimensional pessimism" of Marcuse is combined with the
"revolutionary optimism" of Mao. It is a mixture in which, ironically, élitist
philosophy and dictatorial practice are supposed to serve as a guide to a
"participatory democracy" in a permissive society.

This is not to suggest that the problems which the students' movement
reflects are often not genuine, and sometimes even serious. It is only to point
out that the "philosophy" with which they confront them is jejune and
confused. Many of the postures and fads displayed in them look like a parody
of similar manifestations in the past, in a situation which is very different; and
the young actors seem insufficiently aware of this. If some of them were more
concerned with the extension of their historical knowledge, they could not
but have the feeling of *déjà vu*.

There is, for instance, nothing new in the bohemian attitude to sex, except
that it has now become an Anglo-Saxon phenomenon, after the belated
discovery that Queen Victoria is dead. As long ago as 1832 Barthelemy
Prosper Enfantin created a commune in Menilmontant based on the theory of
sexual permissiveness (and it led to a split amongst the Saint-Simonists).
Since then, there have been the views of Engels; the "glass of water" theory
of Alexandra Kollontai; and, finally, the advent of the Pill. What we are
witnessing now, however, is not just the changing pattern of sexual mores,
but also an extraordinary ideological confusion accompanying it. At one and

the same time there is the use of the slogan "*Make Love not War!*" and the acceptance of Mao's thought that "*Political power grows out of the barrel of a gun*". The sympathy for the Chinese "cultural revolution" is not seen as incompatible with the fact that Mao does not endorse sexual per-missiveness—but discourages love as a bourgeois indulgence—and (for good demographic reasons) prohibits early marriage among the Red Guards.

There is certainly nothing new in the attitude to power among the politically-minded revolutionary students. They see themselves as the vanguard of Total Change.[1] Their attitude is reminiscent of Bakunin's idea that pan-destruction is "constructive". Pure secular chiliasm, unsullied by secular experience, is manifested in the constant reiteration that it is necessary to destroy totally "the dominant system" and that no partial changes, smacking of reformism, can be envisaged. As to the alternative arrangements which are to replace the present ones, history and sociology might just as well not exist for many of the students of these subjects. Apart from some nebulous ideas about "Workers' Control" (which hardly dovetail with Dr Marcuse's idea that the working class has been increasingly integrated into the capitalist system), there are no indications about the political, social, and economic organization which is to issue from the "total change".[2] As Dr Marcuse said last year at the Free University of Berlin: "*For the moment the concrete alternative is still only the negation.*"

WITH HIS CONCEPTUAL CATEGORIES divorced from empirical questions in a special type of *a priori* analysis, Marcuse seems to be the latest product of what Marx called "the decomposition of the Hegelian philosophy". He has been emerging as a caricature of the Young Hegelians, whom Marx, concerned as he was with "empirical history", ridiculed in *The German Ideology* and criticized for using "speculative-idealistic, i.e. fantastic terms".

---

[1] One of the student leaders in France made the following, not untypical, point:
"Soviet society has not accomplished a real mutation in comparison with the bourgeois societies. The communist Soviet man is not in fact fundamentally different. The idea of a total man which was the point of departure of Marxism has not been realized. It has been more or less tried, more in China than in the Soviet Union; it has been tried in Cuba. But the experience has been a failure from the point of view of civilization. It is necessary to make a cultural revolution, a sexual revolution. We do not want only 'to change the world', but also 'to transform life'. . . ." (*Magazine Litteraire*, Paris, May 1968.)

[2] "What they all want is the world of free men" (*Magazine Litteraire*, May 1968)—such was the romantic notion about the French Student Revolt. Yet Daniel Cohn-Bendit proposed only two "concrete demands":
"We demand the suppression of the university canteens. They should become canteens for youth, where all the young people could eat at 1·40 francs . . . ." (*Le Nouvel Observateur*, 20 May 1968.)
"The resources of a technological society are vast. I can't see why only a few people should go to the Café Royale for coffee. It should be for everybody. . . ." (*The Sunday Times*, 16 June 1968.)

Marcuse's *One-Dimensional Man* is closer in spirit to Max Stirner's *Der Einzige und sein Eigentum* (1845) than to Marx's critique of "Saint Max", and that is why it appeals to the present, anarchistic type of rebelliousness. In his book, *Szkice o ideologiach* (Instytut Literacki, Paris, 1967), Alexander Hertz noted that Stirner wrote in an atmosphere of German romanticism, when it was stirred by the revolutionary dreams before 1848. He was as repelled by his time as Marcuse is by the present one. But his is a case of cultural, not yet of technological alienation. Unlike Marcuse, he is, intellectually, profoundly anti-ideological, rejecting all *Begriffe* (abstractions, general ideas, and cultural values) of which, according to him, the unique individual is but a slave. However, *emotionally* Stirner is profoundly ideological, displaying all the familiar traits of the bohemian intelligentsia which wants "the privilege of the whore: power without responsibility": permissiveness without order, privileges without duties. His is the most extreme case of the philosophy of the *Id*, which would be totally unconstrained. Writing long before Freud, Stirner is of course not aware of the "subconscious" dimension; but like Rousseau, from whom he stems, he wants a man unsullied by civilization. Like Rousseau's "noble savage", his *Einzige* is itself an abstract a-historical construct devoid of any concrete sociological characteristics which connect man with society and culture.

Stirner wrote in *Der Einzige und sein Eigentum*: "A people cannot be free otherwise than at the individuals' expense." Marcuse expressed a similar idea in Freudian terms in the *One-Dimensional Man*: "The greater liberty involves a contradiction rather than extension and development of instinctual needs. . . ." This refers to "advanced industrial society", but in fact comes close to a rejection of civilization as such (which in Freudian schemes is always based on some sort of sexual repression). Similarly, Stirner's critique is concerned not with any particular form of society, but with society as such, which for him means inevitable constraints. He rejects all of them in his quest for the absolute freedom of a solipsistic individual. Marcuse does not go so far. But he engages in an equally absolutist critique of "institutional desublimation" in the "advanced industrial society". He calls for "a new anthropology, not only as a theory, but [as] a form of existence". Is it not an anthropology which would express, in Reichian terms, Rousseau's idea of a "noble savage"?[3]

I T IS NOT SURPRISING that those who want to return to Arcadia or to Utopia are afraid of "empirical history" as the devil is of holy water. But what about their libertarianism? It appears very shallow in spite of all the

---

[3] Marcuse's earlier book, *Soviet Marxism* (1958), is for a self-declared follower of Marx a most un-Marxian study! The topic is discussed historically *in vacuo*, and the author would have done well to sit for a while in the British Museum to acquire a necessary minimum of knowledge on the subject.

indignation against the "Organization Man", the despotic bureaucracy, the "over-developed society".[4]

Bakunin rejected Marx's authoritarianism, but was himself an authoritarian. Daniel Cohn-Bendit or Alan Geismar sound more like Bakunin than Prince Kropotkin, and the same applies to some of the German student leaders. Among their followers there is no doubt a certain libertarian potential, but a sceptical observer cannot fail to notice the ambiguous elements of manipulation in the student movement. In the past, those who propagated the necessity of violence as a "midwife of history" did not call their organizations "non-violent co-ordinating committees". While itching for the cobble-stones, if not for the "purifying fire", they would not cover revolutionary impulse with the fig-leaf of pacifist intentions. It may be good revolutionary tactics nowadays, but it is hardly *authenticité*.

Hypocrisy is no less striking if Tartuffe appears to be youthful (especially when the argument is against the insincerity of the older generation). The dilemma of ends-and-means catches up with the revolutionaries[5] even when they are too young to realize it, and too ill-informed to understand the lessons of Nechayev. Their libertarianism is suspect not only because of their choice of some very *non-libertarian* political heroes as symbols of their hopes. There is also the associated concomitant condemnation of "repressive tolerance" in the West and the idealization of the revolutionary intolerance in China, North Vietnam, or Cuba—as well as the evident lack of sympathy for the students in the Communist countries among many of the Western adherents of the student New Left. The more revolutionary among them condemn them outright as "reactionary". Others express solidarity only very grudgingly, or not at all. Only the Belgrade and Prague students protested against the police maltreatment of the Warsaw students. In the West, apart from the Trotskyites and some Berlin students, there were no similar declarations of support for them.[6] During more than a decade of the existence

---

[4] Marcuse argues that one should be tolerant towards the Left, but intolerant towards the Right. Daniel Cohn-Bendit said: "We demand freedom of expression inside the family, but we refuse it to the pro-Americans" (*Le Nouvel Observateur*, 8 May 1968).

Five hundred students of Rome University refused to take part in an examination, in which they were asked to translate from Latin some of the "thoughts of Chairman Mao". They considered the choice "provocative" and demanded the abolition of Latin. The text ran:

"Omnes questiones non possunt valide perstringi, nisi ratione inquirendi adhibita (All questions can only be resolved by methods of discussion). . . ."

(*Corriere della Sera*, 14 May 1968.)

[5] *Time* Magazine (7 June 1968) quoted a Columbia student: "How can you use your ends to justify your means? Well, as my philosophy teacher used to say, what else can you possibly use to justify your means? There is nothing else!"

[6] In the discussion programme, *Students in Revolt*, shown by BBC television, Daniel Cohn-Bendit objected to the word "liberalization" used in respect of Czechoslovak developments. But in an interview given to *Magazine Littéraire* (May 1968) he said:

"In Prague, liberalization took place because the Czechoslovak economy was completely dead. Liberalization took place there because there is a revival of the 'capitalist basis'. . . ."

$\rightarrow$

of the revolutionary New Left publications, they have shown a marked disregard for the fate of the young East European "revisionists".

Why should this be so?

After all, in the beginning the New Left stressed that one of the factors in its emergence was disillusionment with Stalinism after Hungary 1956. After that, the evolution in Eastern Europe and the evolution of the New Left have been divergent. Since the Hungarian Revolution there have been many other cases of repression in Eastern Europe calling for similar condemnation, but the New Left remained indifferent.[7]

Its evolution was obviously dictated by the psychological need of its adherents for Utopia. It was no longer possible to locate it in the Soviet Union, as their ancestors were doing in the 1930s so substitutes had to be found elsewhere. Revolutionary romanticism in search of a love-object had now a variety of choices in the polycentric communist world, but clearly some of them could better fulfil the role than others. Cuba is obviously at the head of the messianic queue (and Che Guevara the best symbol of revolutionary romanticism). On the other hand, the Soviet Union and the countries of Eastern Europe no longer qualify. After all that is known about their Stalinist past and their bureaucratic present, it is difficult to go on believing that they embody Utopia-in-the-making, that they correspond to the romantic notion expressed half a century ago by Lincoln Steffens: "I have seen the future and it works." The old faithful may still stick to it, but the New Romantics are quite unconcerned whether it *works* or *not*. They cannot see it as *the* future. The glamour which "the fatherland of the proletariat" had for their forebearers is gone. They had to move to new pastures—from the revolution of rising expectations to the expectation of rising revolutions.

IT IS THUS NOT AT ALL SURPRISING that those who are now longing for Utopia turn away from those who had a long experience of living with it. They feel uncomfortable when faced with the historical evidence which may adduce a sceptical corrective to their messianic fervour and deflate their ideological perspective.

Conversely, it is only natural that those who had the experience of how Utopia works in practise (e.g. the Polish or Czech students) are aware of the

---

There is an outlandish political "free for all" here. Cohn-Bendit, who declared himself an "anti-Trotskyite", criticized the cult of Mao and called the French Communists "*les crapules staliniennes*". Yuri Zhukov called him in *Pravda* (30 May 1968) a "werewolf" and a CIA agent. When the Yugoslav student, Dragana Stavijel, praised Tito on the same BBC programme, she was later critized by Cohn-Bendit and branded by Tariq Ali as a "Titoist stooge". The Yugoslav demonstrators were first praised in the Chinese press and later supported by Tito, who (according to the Chinese) "smeared the students' struggle" (*Peking Review*, 14 June 1968).

[7] "They simultaneously refused to identify with the Soviet Union or to be greatly concerned about injustice in any of the Communist societies." (Paul Jacobs & Saul Landau, *The New Radicals*, 1966, p. 12.)

yawning chasm between the ideological abstractions and the personal lessons of their daily life, and regard those who still approach secular political problems in the chiliastic perspective as politically infantile. For them such an attitude can only be another illustration of Santayana's dictum that those who do not learn from history are bound to repeat it. For them "Repressive Tolerance" would be an improvement on the intolerant repression which they are facing. The "Consumer Society" would be a preferable progressive alternative to the shortage of goods. Even a slow change in the right direction would be acceptable, although they have infinitely more reason than those who demand "total change" in the West to talk about "the System", "the Military-Industrial complex", and "the structures of power" (which, in their case, are based on the Party's monopoly and not on political pluralism). They are concerned with their own countries, rather than a projection of their hopes on revolutions elsewhere.

Occasionally a self-critical insight breaks through in the West. Here is the recent reaction of one New Left sympathizer to his meetings with Czechoslovak students. Writing in the *New Statesman* (21 June 1968), David Caute reflected:

> "... these observations, both now and at the time, reveal to me a certain perversity in my own attitude. Nostalgia for student riots, clashes with the police, and totally exposed thighs suggests a false romanticism, an irritable desire to inflict on an ostensibly sane society a form of chaos which, as a way of life, is superficial and nihilistic. The manner in which the young Czechs are conducting themselves is really a model of civic control and enlightenment, whereas we have become alcoholic on sensation and violence."

FEW GENERALIZATIONS about student revolutions apply to the majority of students. It has often been pointed out that radical attitudes, particularly in their political form, are not representative of the student body as a whole, and reflect only the position of an "activist" minority.[8] However, such small but organized minorities have demonstrated their ability "to set student populations in motion and to define the issues".[9] After the French "Student Revolution" the question is not only how much revolutionary potential can be tapped by them in the student body, but in the population as a whole.

---

[8] Cf. Seymour Martin Lipset, *Student Politics* (1967).
[9] Lipset, pp. 199–201. Cf. also Frank A. Pinner, "Tradition and Transgression" in a special issue of *Daedalus* (Winter 1968) on "Students and Politics", pp. 139 and 151. An academic observer in sympathy with 'the Movement' argued that it is basically irrelevant "to point out that the alienated activists of the New Left [in the United States] represent only a few thousand people on all the campuses combined [out of 6,000,000 students]. What is relevant is that in some inchoate manner they articulated what many others felt." (*Dissent*, May–June 1968.)

Obviously the situation is different in different countries, and it would be quite wrong to generalize. Consider the conclusion drawn by Edgar Morin in *Le Monde* (5–6 June 1968):

> "It has happened for the first time in Western society of the 20th century, economically developed and politically liberal, that a specifically student and youth movement has triggered off a vast movement throughout all society. This permits a forecast of the role which can be played in future by (*a*) the youth as a force of disruption, rebellion, and innovation . . . in modern society; (*b*) the University, grown to a point where it will soon comprise half of the juvenile population and will find itself, as Alain Touraine has indicated, at the very centre of social problems; (*c*) the intelligentsia which reacts more and more virulently on the one hand against the techno-bureaucratic organization to which it is partially chained, and on the other against bourgeois life itself. The motive force of future changes seems therefore to be in the alliance of the intelligentsia and of the youth in the vast university concentrations. . . ."

For the revolutionary romantics the Working Class ceased to be a chosen class. When they noticed that it was not fulfilling the task "given to it by history", they began to look elsewhere.[10] Both the prophets of the New Left—the neo-populist C. Wright Mills and the paleo-Hegelian Marcuse—located the new revolutionary syndrome in the Intelligentsia and among "the popular masses" of the underdeveloped countries. However, when the intelligentsia in the industrial countries began showing the symptoms of "alienation", the youth and students in the industrial countries became the centre of attention. Some even argued that in the United States

> ". . . the new, potentially revolutionary, exploited class is no longer the working class as a whole, [but that the young] form the new proletariat, are undergoing impoverishment, and can become the new revolutionary class. . . . As happens when a class is exploited, young people are beginning to become aware of their exploitation. Many have taken the essential step to consciousness, the rejection of the present system, and are available to develop a consciousness of themselves as a class. . . ."[11]

---

[10] Among the old hands, Paul Sweezy diagnosed "the degeneration of a Western working class" which led it "into open collaboration with the bourgeoisie" as a result of its "natural tendency" towards reformism (*National Guardian*, 16 September 1967).

[11] John and Margaret Rowntree, "Youth as a Class", *International Socialist Journal* (February 1968). The authors criticize Marcuse and argue that their analysis "does not depend on the development of a disembodied anti-consumer consciousness on the part of the youth, but instead finds a real revolutionary potential in the youth arising out of their role in production".

Thus Marxist method is used to prove that class war between the Workers and the Capitalists has been replaced by the class war between the Young and the capitalist system. No attempt is

→

The gap between generations, which is now so acute, has been the subject of many comments which help to explain its existence, but not its present form. It has often been pointed out that youth tends to be idealistic; that it wants to assert its identity; and that its sexual drives are stronger and more easily sublimated through abstract identifications. Yet if students' libidos tend to be unanchored this may account for similarities in their behaviour over time, but not for its variations.

It has also been stressed[12] that as the young now experience the world in the shadow of a possible nuclear catastrophe, history has become contingent for them, and therefore ideological certainties and historical necessities of the old systems are no longer relevant or appealing. Although this applies to all who entered the nuclear age, it can be argued that the older generation is incapable of transcending its set mental habits, while youth is more sensitive to the new aspects of the historical situation.

Yet, what we have witnessed is not the rise of a sceptical generation, but of a romantic one, a situation in which "cynical idealists" are elevating, as has been said, "the ill-digested compound of primitive Marxism, Anarchism, Maoism, etc., to the dignity of a philosophy", in which ideological certainties and historical necessities are once again replacing thought. A new fascination with violence is thus introduced into the combustion chamber of the nuclear age.[13] *Furor ideologicus* has been given a new lease of life. After "Race" comes "Youth"; after Fanon—Marcuse. It has been pointed out triumphantly that "the bankruptcy of the 'end of ideology' school has been amply demonstrated by recent history". There is little doubt that at present the *Zeitgeist* shows a resuscitation of the ideological temper.

---

made to explain the ferment of youth in the Communist countries by this original application of the method of analysis based on economic determinism.

In *Pravda* (30 May 1968), Yuri Zhukov violently attacked Marcuse, suggesting that he had been "catapulted from far-away San Diego to Paris" in order "to sow confusion" and "to oppose the youth, and the students in particular, to the fundamental forces of the working class".

A more sophisticated critique of Marcuse appeared in the Polish *Trybuna Ludu* (9 June 1968). The pro-Chinese *La Voix du Peuple* (31 May 1968) declared that it is necessary to dispel "confusionism": "The student community does not constitute a social class." The pro-Chinese *Progressive Labour* (June 1968) added sternly: "The students in Eastern Europe are being used by the reactionary ruling cliques to move to the right and unite with US imperialism. . . . Students in Poland . . . can hardly be considered in the vanguard of anything but reaction."

[12] Donald G. MacRae, *Ideology and Society* (1961).

[13] One example among many of this attitude is given by a sympathetic observer of the French student movement in *Magazine Litteraire* (May 1968), who wrote about "our society which makes the exclusion of all violence the alpha and omega of all its political mini-ideas". He contrasted this with the attitude of the students "who have discovered that one should not obtusely oppose violence and dialogue, that violence is a condition of the introduction of all true dialogue. The right to the word is won on the field of battle." Raymond Aron quoted in *Figaro L'Arc*: "The philosophy of tomorrow will be the philosophy of terror . . . linked up with the practice of political terror." Both Marcuse and Dutschke quoted Rousseau on the necessity for making slaves conscious of their slavery and forcing people to be free.

D ANIEL BELL wrote that at the end of the 1950s, "in the West, among the intellectuals, the old passions are spent"—that, for the radical intellectual who articulated the revolutionary impulses of the past century-and-a-half, the two decades between 1930 and 1950, with their tragedies and horrors, "meant the end to chiliastic hopes, to milleniarism, to apocalyptic thinking—and to ideology". This was true of the majority of the intellectuals formed politically during these decades. With the emergence on the scene of new generations for whom the lessons of these decades were not based on experience, but were at best an intellectual exercise and at worst an unknown or irrelevant past, the chiliastic impulse began to revive. A belief that it was dead-for-good, that after "the tragic self-immolation of a revolutionary generation that had proclaimed the finer ideals of man [after a] destructive war of a breadth and scale hitherto unknown, [after] the bureaucratized murder of millions in concentration camps and death chambers", the West would become immunized to the ideological bacilli, was a rationalist fallacy. Daniel Bell pointed out that "for the radical intelligentsia, the old ideologies have lost their 'truth' and their power to persuade": but he disregarded his own dictum that "what gives ideology its force is passion". Like 18th-century rationalists he overestimated the temporary effectiveness of reason and overlooked the future force of passion. The chiliastic urge has proved so enduring in the history of humanity that it was unlikely that it would disappear definitively. In his time, Max Weber thought that there inevitably would be "rationalization" of society because of "routinization of charisma" and functional bureaucratic necessities. In a similar spirit it was assumed that memories of Hitler and Stalin would have made a more lasting impact, and rationally would permanently extinguish chiliastic attitudes in the West.

There is, to be sure, a new factor. The nuclear facts of life may ultimately confront humanity with the stark alternative of an end of ideology or an end of history. "The End-of-Ideology" school was quite right in being critical of ideological passions, of the fanaticism which was ready to sacrifice the present for the alleged happiness of future generations. Daniel Bell was right in stressing with Jefferson that "the present belongs to the living", and with Herzen that "each age, each generation, each life has its own fullness". Raymond Aron was right in saying that "ideological dogmatism must disappear for ideas to become alive again".

But if "the End-of-Ideology" was and is a good prescription, it is not a good description. Ideological passions have begun to flourish in the West again; and it is the students, the one category of the population which is supposed to learn critical thought, who display the old ideological dogmatism and are moved by new mental stereotypes. In an age of television and mass communications *idées reçues* are received instantly.

I T WOULD, of course, be quite wrong to overlook the legitimacy of many of the students' grievances. Many of them are not only justified but are of general importance. Complaints about authoritarianism, bureaucratization of institutions, helplessness of the individual in the face of big organizations, commercialization of values in the West—in short, all that is drawing attention to the negative aspects of "the quality of life" in industrial societies—is intrinsically valuable and commands sympathy. If noble libertarian professions of faith on the part of the students against the stifling of the human spirit by "the bureaucratic and technocratic structures in the advanced industrial society" were sufficient to bring us, through ideological generalities and violent militance, one inch nearer to the overcoming of the problems and dilemmas inherent in modern technical-scientific civilization, there would indeed be greater sympathy with student protest.

It is, to be sure, arguable that such protests are an early alarm bell against the social sclerosis which prevents the adaptation of human institutions to the consequences of technological change. There may be something in this; but, intellectually, "the Movement" has not produced a single idea of how to cope with the present problems of social change—and what kind of institutions are to replace the existing ones. When faced directly with this question student leaders fall back upon the age-old ideological clichés. There is always that old Utopian escape-hatch that they do not want to produce a "blueprint for the new society", but that it will emerge in "the fire of the struggle". [14]

This was the psychological mechanism which permitted Marx to preserve some of the Utopian ideas in the 19th century (such as the anarchist idea of "the withering away of the state"); but his was, after all, a serious analysis of the society of his time. Reading the publications of "the Movement" today and listening to student leaders makes one realize that they are not the reformers of the coming "technetronic" society. They look more like its Luddites. [15]

---

[14] As Tariq Ali said on the BBC television programme:
"It would be incorrect of us to lay down dogmatic rules or lay down even a dogmatic blueprint of the society which is going to emerge. We feel that such a society will evolve through the process of struggle itself. We know we are opposed to this society, we know roughly that we are in favour of socialization, we are in favour of workers' control, we are—most of us are in fact libertarian Marxists, we believe in 'all power to the Soviets'. We believe that that slogan is not dated at all, that it has not been properly applied. We believe in the abolition of money, we believe in the appropriation of all private property."
(*Newsweek*, 24 June 1968.)
[15] George Lukacs wrote in his recent book, *Conversazioni* (De Donato, Bari, 1967):
"If we say that manipulation [of the people] is a consequence of technological development, then we have to become (in the manner of Marcuse, Adorno, and Horkheimer) a breed of Luddites, struggling against technological development. . . ."
Lukacs touched here on what for a Marxist is the crux of the matter. Marx started as a romantic, but after his "Young Hegelian" phase, he made the problem of "production" the cornerstone of his theory.
Professor Adam Ulam argued, in his *Unfinished Revolution*, that when it was adopted in Russia, Marxism was transformed into Leninism, because the natural reaction to

It would also be a doubtful idea to look at the Student Revolt as an example of the Hegelian "cunning of reason", a mystical concept which resulted from the grafting of 19th-century optimistic and teleological views of history onto 18th-century rationalism. The student revolt is not going to cure whatever malaise may exist in some contemporary Western societies. Its elderly ideologists are, in Herzen's phrase, "not the doctors, they are the disease". They express the present-day crisis of rationality, and represent the return to the Messianic hopes of earlier ages.

NOR IS IT POSSIBLE to apply Sorel's idea about great myths

> "which enclose with them all the strongest inclinations of a people, of a party, or of a class, inclinations which recur to the mind with the insistence of instincts in all the circumstances of life; and which give an aspect of complete reality to the hopes of immediate action by which, more easily than by any other method, men can reform their desires, passions, and mental activity. . . ."

In *Reflections sur la Violence* (1908) Sorel referred to early Christianity, the Reformation, and the French Revolution as examples of such myths which brought about a profound transformation (although the Utopian aspirations contained in them did not, of course, come to pass).

> "The myth must be judged as a means of acting on the present; any attempt to discuss how far it can be taken literally as future history is devoid of sense".

Is the idea of "Student Power" such a myth, a substitute for Sorel's own myth of a "general strike"? It is enough to ask this question (or listen to Mr Tariq Ali or M. Cohn-Bendit) to have no doubts about the answer.

But is not the French "Student Revolution" of May 1968 a *prima facie* case that "student power" can indeed move mountains and that as such it falls

---

industrialization in underdeveloped countries is radical populism or anarchism. (The earliest and the most extreme reaction to industrialization was, of course, Luddism.) The populist attitude of the intelligentsia has often been explained in terms of the discrepancy between their cultural and national aspirations and the economic backwardness of their countries.

Now, for the first time, a radical populism has emerged in the industrial countries, claiming Marx as its patron, but hankering after the romantic attitudes which are pre-Marxian and anti-industrial. History has made a full circle. The scientific-technological revolution of late industrialism has produced its own Luddites who, unlike the earlier ones, do not smash machines, but some of whom want to withdraw from society (and presumably live eventually on the surplus produced by the computerized economy). They will then be like the Roman proletariat which (according to Sismondi) was parasitic on the state. Marxist theoreticians have reached a point where they either have to give up the romantic-Utopian ingredients of Marx's early thought, or his later "productivist" approach to social analysis and history. Paleo-Hegelian neo-Marxists, like Marcuse and his followers, should logically give up Marx altogether and go back to Arcadia.

within the Sorelian analysis? After all, the very thing which Sorel had envisaged has in fact happened, namely, the general strike. Yet the lessons of May 1968 in France may be diametrically opposite to the hopes of the students. What has been demonstrated is not only that the French Communist Party refused to take the plunge in a revolutionary situation and to make a bid for power,[16] but that in this situation the aspirations of the French working class remained within the established social (though not political) order. It would have been very surprising indeed if the Marcusian "anti-consumerist ideology" had much appeal to the workers, just as the revolt against the affluent society has little appeal in the economically underdeveloped countries. A temporary fusion of the resentment of the *Raznochintsy* of the scientific age, the mass of the new students who still look on the universities as stepping-stones to the *élite*, with the old frustrations of the French working class, can easily conceal the basic differences between the two categories. In all the industrial countries, technological development led to university expansion, creating a mass of new students who retained however the old, *élite* aspirations. Education became the most important avenue of social mobility, hence not only the new character of the universities, but also their new role in the battle for status.

Inevitably, the changing function of the university in industrial society generated new problems and tensions. These were seized upon by the New Left, which groping for good causes stumbled upon the question of university reform. It proved to be a "winner" with the students and some professions, but it had no immediate appeal outside the universities. In France, the working class has for a long time now faced the painful problem of its integration into the French "bourgeois" society. Hence the strength of the revolutionary anarcho-syndicalist tradition in France. This accounts for the temporary fusion between the students and the workers, but their different aspirations are quite obvious.

Paradoxically, the outcome of the crisis may undermine this revolutionary anarcho-syndicalist tradition and diminish the chances of the Student-Worker alliance in future. In Germany, Great Britain, and the USA it is not likely in any case. In France it was also easily predictable that whoever emerged as the ultimate political victor, de Gaulle, the politicians, or the French Communist Party, the students were bound to be the political losers who, sooner or later, would cry "Treason!"[17] Ironically, by focusing attention on university reform and on the problems of the social gap between the workers and the "bourgeoisie", they may have contributed to the eventual modernization of the "structures" which they despise, and to the undermining of the possibilities of a future revolutionary action.

---

[16] And if it did, what would have happened to the Trotskyite, Maoist, and anarchist students?

[17] Cf. Alfred Kastler, "Comment les étudiants ont été trahis . . . ." (*Le Nouvel Observateur*, 19 June 1968.)

P OLITICAL behaviour cannot be explained simply in social terms (status envy) or as being due to economic factors only (lack of occupational prospects or the "over-production of the intelligentisia"). History and local cultural and political traditions also play an important role.

In France the myth of the Revolution is still strong, and its rhetoric so pervasive that the population as a whole begins to act their parts when the occasion arises. The extent of this historical Pavlovian conditioning is quite extraordinary. In May 1968, France was not only undergoing a revolutionary conflict, it was re-living previous ones. The past was almost as much a referential point as the present: 1789, 1830, 1848, 1851, 1871, 1936. The roles were distributed and it was somewhat difficult to distinguish between the real actions for real motives and the play-acting.

The language used put the problems of a technological age on the Procrustean bed of French revolutionary rhetoric.[18] Edgar Morin wrote about the students occupying the Sorbonne as the storming of "the university Bastille" (*Le Monde*, 5 June 1968); it seems, however, that no students were ever broken on the rack there. Nevertheless, this was the first occasion on which today's "rebels in search of a cause" have found themselves engaged in a real battle. They were clearly determined to make the most of it, imitating their ancestors, magnifying their own grievances, and demonizing their opponents.

What does one do if one wants to play a historic role and history does not oblige? One brings the prestige of the great revolutionary days to the humdrum contemporary problems of civil society, such as, for instance, university administration. If one does not face the real horror of the *Gestapo* one wins the crown of martyrdom by grappling with the *CRS*. The brutalities of the police produce the cry: "*De Gaulle: Assassin!*" and the students' paper (*Action*, 11 June 1968) splashes it on the front page together with the photograph of a maltreated student. In short, where "the grievances are not of the essence", and yet there is a revolutionary tradition, one can have an *ersatz* revolution.

---

[18] "Events here during the past two or three weeks have emphasized the extent to which the minds of educated Frenchmen, whatever their political views, are imbued with the atmosphere and concepts of Paris nearly two centuries ago. They look backwards to Danton, rather than forward to an age of computers and automation."

(*Daily Telegraph*, 3 June 1968.)

"This military epic [of the Revolution] gave an epic colour to all the events of internal politics; party struggles were thus raised to the level of the *Iliad*; politicians became giants, and the revolution, which Joseph de Maistre had denounced as satanical, was made divine. The bloody scenes of the Terror were episodes without great significance by the side of the enormous hecatombs of war, and means were found to envelop them in a dramatic mythology; riots were elevated to the same rank as illustrious battles; and calmer historians vainly endeavoured to bring the Revolution and the Empire down to the plane of common history."   (Georges Sorel, *Reflections sur la Violence*.)

Sorel refers to the French attitude to the Revolution as being comparable to the way Christians believe in Christianity.

Faced with this "Herostrates complex", Golo Mann asked the Berlin students "to stop playing at Lenin" (*Encounter*, July 1968). A sympathizer of "the Movement" described this psychological urge rather well, rooted as he is in the tradition of *The Playboy of the Western World:*

> "What is new, for this period of history, is that the Left has recovered for the moment something which once belonged to it, but which it had largely lost: a zest for play-acting. The glum rectitudes of scientistic socialism had tended to repel the dramatic from politics; the appeal to the imagination through play-acting was regarded as a Fascist speciality: this is among the reasons why some of the Old Left think they discern traces of Fascism in the New Left. . . ."
>
> (Conor Cruise O'Brien, *New York Review of Books*, 20 June 1968.)

A French sociologist was somewhat more ironical:

> "After all, our revolutionaries of 1792 adopted Roman hair-styles and borrowed their phraseology from the ancients, swearing only by Brutus, Cato, and Caius Gracchus. Our 'Marxists' are relatively less anachronistic. . . ."   (Jules Monnerot, *Le Monde*, 8 June 1968.)

THE ANSWER TO THE QUESTION whether May 1968 was the last revolution of the 19th century or the first revolution of the 21st century is that it was neither. It was a confrontation of the 17th-century national fantasies of *le roi soleil* de Gaulle with the 18th-century social fantasies of the present-day student Camille Desmoulins. (There was play-acting also in the 1956 Hungarian revolution, but there the grievances *were* of the essence, and they united the whole country around the symbols of its historic traditions.) For the students, wrote a sympathetic journalist, the Revolution "is not just a far-away goal and an ideal, at the same time a means to an end, the Revolution is life itself" (*Magazine Litteraire*, May 1968). In the same magazine Daniel Cohn-Bendit referred in an interview not only to the influence on him of the contemporary revolutionaries, but also to the influence of Rousseau. Some two hundred years ago the following was written (by Linguet to Rousseau, 1764): "Your ideas are the magic fables of politics; with a stroke of a wand suddenly emerges a society with all people equally endowed, equally rich, and equally happy. . . ."

Such a high pitch of "idealism" is not just a function of adolescence, it is the material from which "True Believers" are made. It is usually accompanied by some sort of Utopian beliefs. Professor W. H. G. Armytage has shown in his book, *Yesterday's Tomorrows* (1968), that such beliefs always included a dose of nostalgia about the past, and the present ones are no exception. In his analysis of the French Student Revolt, Edgar Morin referred to the double fear of the students: the fear of the "one-dimensional" character of life in a technical-bureaucratic society, and the contrary anxiety about not getting an assured career in it. This underlies the ambiguity of the revolt which is "modernist" and "archaic" at the same time. Others have called it "the Utopia of the epigones".[19] But whatever the label, there is little doubt about the naiveté of the visions of the future offered.[20]

IN VIEW OF the historical correlation between the quest for Utopia and the totalitarian tendency in politics, it is important to know whether the present quest is to be attributed mainly to the passing phase of adolescence or to the rising, and more permanent, chiliastic wave.

No doubt, both elements play a role in the Student Revolt. It can be looked upon as a contemporary youth movement and compared, as Walter Laqueur has done (*Washington Post*, 7 January 1968), to such movements in the past. It can also be seen as a phenomenon similar in its tendency to previous ideological revivals, sometimes related to, but in the longer perspective independent of any particular social category, and therefore more enduring.

Because students are a transitional group, with a rapid turnover, they are peculiarly subject to ideological fashions. From this point of view their present beliefs may not last long: fashions change rapidly in our time. But the students argue that "the present generation gap is not merely fashion: every generation rebels, but few have had such good reason" (Steven V. Roberts, *New Leader*, 9 October 1967). This is certainly not due to the deterioration of the relative position of the young in relation to other age groups; it must have something to do with the more general reasons affecting this generation of youth. But how can one estimate the relative importance of such reasons?

The problems of affluence and of organizational pressures may be felt as keenly by this generation as the problems of poverty and of political dictatorship were felt by an earlier one. Objectively, the hunger marches and bloody totalitarianism in the 1930s are in a somewhat different class of phenomena than such questions in the 1960s as "public squalor and private affluence" or the helplessness of the individual "in an era of big universities, big businesses, big governments, and even big foundations". But subjectively, they may produce the perception of "relative deprivation", and this is what matters. In a situation of acute generational egocentrism, even nursery mishaps may be put on the same plane as Auschwitz; and the adolescent sufferings of contemporary young Werthers made into a subject comparable to the martyrdom of the concentration-camp victims. If there is searching for a "cause", sooner or later one is found; if Vietnam did not exist,

---

[19] Wolfgang Rieger, "Die Utopie der Epigonen", *Die Zeit* (17 May 1968).
[20] One example:
    "The critical problem is this: how can we now take the first steps to what will be, finally, a qualitative change in man? . . . Our only assumptions are that human nature has virtually unbounded potentialities."
(John and Barbara Ehrenreich, "From Resistance to Revolution", *Monthly Review*, April 1968.)

something else would have been embraced, even a poor substitute. It is, however, not very sensible to reproach the present generation with being concerned with their own contemporary events. It is also normal that they display in their current excitement a certain lack of a sense of proportion. What is disturbing is the fixation with the future which is very similar to the senile fixation with the past on the part of some of their mentors.

IT IS AMUSING TO HEAR students saying that "it's useless to talk to anybody over 30". Is it only a failure of communication between generations? Such adolescent egocentrism can be exploited. Mussolini had his *"Giovinezza"*; Karel Capek described in his allegorical play on fascism, *The White Illness*, a demagogic leader whose programme is based on the removal of everybody over 30 (which would have included not only Dr Edmund Leach but also some of the present leaders of "the Movement"). What is behind this tendency towards infantile regression, or adolescent solipsism?

It is certainly not any feeling of intellectual superiority on the part of those who display so much "know-nothing-ism". Some of them look at their elders as if they were all a band of retired army colonels discussing the Second Zulu War. Many observers have noticed the element of anti-rationalism in the current wave.[21] It was discernible early enough, as can be seen from the comment of two American authors on a book sympathetic to "the Movement",[22] who wrote in their introduction: "They think that the ivory-towered men of ideas have cheated them, lied to them, and that action and spontaneous experience will show them truth. . . ."

The followers of a movement which exalts romanticism, anti-rationalism, *Gemeinschaft* (community feeling), makes action a self-justificatory criterion. Those who are fascinated by violence, can—and do—evoke memories of a movement which extolled all these elements not so long ago, before its leaders met their fate in the Berlin bunker and the Milan *piazza*. However, *comparaison n'est pas raison*. There are many important differences between the present-day "happenings" and those instigated by fascism.

UNLIKE FASCISM, the present movement has a libertarian component. It is anti-authoritarian, does not believe in hierarchy, and

---

[21] Cf. the perceptive articles by the President of the Students' Union at the London School of Economics, Colin Crouch, in *The Guardian* (12 & 13 June 1968).

[22] Paul Jacobs and Saul Landau, *The New Radicals*, p. 7. Among recent writings on students' revolt cf. the special issues devoted to it by *Problemi del Socialismo* (March–April 1968), *Der Spiegel* (FU 64, May 1968), *Encounter* (July & August 1968), *Neues Forum* (June–July 1968), *Il Mulino* (June 1968), *Kursbuch* (*13*, 1968). Interesting articles on the subject appeared also in *Le Monde Diplomatique* (June 1968), *New Society* (30 May & 20 June 1968) and in *Interplay* (June/July 1968).

In his letter to *The Times* (12 June 1968), Professor G. R. Elton wrote about the student movements' "firm opposition to reason and its reliance on explosive emotions. It exalts the fervent assertion and denies all virtue to reflection. . . ."

so far has little respect for organizations or leaders (much less *the* leader). It is not nationalist. One cannot take just some of its characteristics—the tendencies displayed in it are so contradictory— and define "the Movement" on this basis. It has traits of Fascism and Maoism, Trotskyism and Anarchism, as well as some inchoate and unprecedented characteristics. To take only some of them as the basis of definition would be a clear case of *pars pro toto*.[23] Perhaps the nearest label applicable would be "radical populism".[24] It obviously appeals to the youth, with its longing for romance, "Causes", and Utopia. What are its prospects?

If one assumes that humanity, for demographic reasons alone, is not likely to give up a scientific-technological civilization, a movement which, however vaguely, resents it, has of course no future, at least in the sense of achieving its ostensible goals based on resentments against this kind of civilization. As a youth movement it is likely to be relatively short-lived, as were other youth movements. History, to use Pareto's remark, is a cemetery of such ephemeral phenomena. It is the chiliastic tendency which it represents that is most pertinent to the question of its future. Sorel rightly understood that such movements cannot be analysed simply in terms of their ostensible goals.

The current revival of Utopianism in the midst of a scientific-technological "Second Industrial Revolution" was generally unexpected. But it is paradoxical only to those who either think in terms of economic determinism or assume a necessary relationship between technology and rationality— despite the experience with Marxism, which appeared in the early phase of industrialism and whose success was due to its chiliastic character. If at present a motley crowd of student ideologists and their elders refer to themselves as "Marxists", it is to preserve their chiliastic faith in Utopia. The fact that "empirical history" has amply disconfirmed Marx's predictions is of no greater relevance to them than a disconfirmation of a prophecy on which the faith of other millennial and messianic movements in the past was based, (believers in the Second Advent, Sabbatarians, etc.).

In a study of the subject,[25] Leon Festinger has demonstrated that "when prophecy fails", the sectarian "True Believers" usually not only do not

---

[23] Cf. Tibor Szamuely, "Fascism Then and Now", *Spectator* (21 June 1968). Cf. also Günther Zehm's article in *Survey* (July 1968, "Is There a Left-Wing Fascism?").

[24] In an article drawing attention to the parallels between the Russian *Narodniki* and the American New Left (in *Western Politica*, No. 1, Spring 1966), Milorad M. Drachkovitch quoted George Orwell: "Much of left-wing thought is a kind of playing with fire by people who don't even know that fire is hot." He also quoted the remark of Alasdair MacIntyre that "there are unhappy signs of a new populism of the left in which the old *Narodnik* illusions are being applied to students and the poor".

Two years later, Paul Goodman writing "In Praise of Populism" (*Commentary*, June 1968), diagnosed a "world populist revival" which led him to abandon his earlier gloomy idea that we are doomed. At least for him, if not for Marcuse, the future now "looks brighter".

[25] Leon Festinger, *When Prophecy Fails* (1956).

abandon their faith, but try to strengthen it by intensified proselytizing. Needless to say, the mass of students does not consist of "True Believers". Festinger's thesis applies only to the activists in the political *groupuscules* and their spiritual mentors from the alienated intelligentsia, many of whom have shown a kind of adolescent fixation.[26]

What are the prospects that the true believers, old and new, will continue "to define the issues", will be able to transmit their messianic fervour to the new generation of student-activists, and—the most central question of all—will be able to reach other groups in the Western populations? The French experience may not generally apply, but it raises certain points.

THE FIRST IS THAT the *groupuscules* somehow managed to achieve a *tregua Dei* in their sectarian bickering. Cohn-Bendit and other student leaders understood that the movement could advance only on the wave of vague sentiments articulated in general slogans rather than on the basis of a specific programmatic platform, each point of which would create dissent among the contending factions. The student masses could be mobilized only in this way.

But there is always a price to be paid for such a consensus. The cohesion of an amalgam which includes pacifism and guerrilla violence, libertarianism and authoritarianism, youthful enthusiasm and archaic ideas, is under severe strain; and the French defeat will inevitably lead to the end of "the truce", the reassessment of events by separate doctrinaire groups, and to a wiser political

---

[26] Two examples of the old "carriers of chiliasm" exhibiting in their doctrinal fundamentalism the "Festinger effect":

"It is necessary to make humanity rise to a point where it will be really fraternal, where any form of oppression, whatever it may be, will become impossible, where the mutual aid and the feeling of responsibility towards collectivity will be regarded as an elementary duty, and where labour will become a need for happiness which will last through life. . . . In the communist society, and only in such society, man, as it has been announced, will be liberated and will make freely his own history. This is the point, as Engels used to say. It is the incomparable merit of the Chinese communists to keep alive this great Marxist hope, while the modern revisionists, through ignorance and lack of courage, tend to bring us back to the past." (Jean Baby in *Le Monde*, 27 September 1966.)

"I even suppose that Socialist Man will offer the psychoanalyst far richer and more reliable material for research and conclusions, because in him a future Freud will be able to watch the working of the instinctual drives directly, not through a glass darkly, not through the distorting prisms of the analyst's and the patient's class psychology. . . . Yes, Socialist Man will still be pursued by sex and death; but we are convinced that he will be better equipped than we are to cope even with these. . . . The average member of socialist society may yet rise, as Trotsky anticipated, to the stature of Aristotle, Goethe, Marx, who, whatever their sexual instincts and aggressive drives, embody some of mankind's highest achievements so far. . . . We have to raise socialism back to its own height. We have to explain to our working classes and intelligentsia why the Soviet Union and China have not been able to produce and could not produce Socialist Man, despite their remarkable achievements which give them a right to our recognition and solidarity. We must restore the image of Socialist Man to all its spiritual splendour." (Isaac Deutscher at the second Socialist Scholars' Conference in New York, *National Guardian*, 24 September 1966.)

differentiation among students. In other words, the element of youthfulness will become less pronounced and the political side of the movement will become more prominent. In the next period many of the students will probably lose their penchant for Utopia and acquire more earthy political attitudes. Others—the activist "true believers"—will find it difficult to maintain a "non-denominational platform", which was the precondition of their initial success.

M. Cohn-Bendit, who claimed an affinity with Leszek Kolakowski, might find relevant some of the ideas expressed by the latter in his book on *Religious Consciousness and the Church Affiliation* (Warsaw, 1965). Kolakowski analyzes in detail the fate of the Dutch sects at the time of the 17th-century Counter-Reformation and comes to the following conclusion:

> "Historically, the attempts to create a non-denominational Christianity appear to us as purely negative phenomena. Their existence can only be perceived in relation to the organized religion against which they rose. As they cannot basically transform the collective and hierarchical forms of religious life in line with their own ideas, which would signify (and in some cases does in fact signify) the adoption of a realistic, rational structure denying the very premise of their protest, the non-denominational Christians are at best able to create inside (or parallel to) the church communities, pressure groups which force their opponents to assimilate some of their ideas in an emasculated form, leading to some modification of organized religion. Non-denominational Christianity, to the extent that it means anything in social life, was a negative force influencing the reintegration of the positive Christianity; but it had no real power to disintegrate the Churches. Favourable circumstances can shake it into an effective reform movement. But it can take social root only if it accepts the principle of organization, that is if it denies its own principles. . . ."

The anti-structuralist character of the students' protest and its anti-organizational ideology kept the movement inchoate, but afloat on a non-denominational basis. Yet, in the age of big organizations against which many of them protest, it is unlikely that the semi-anarchistic character of the movement can continue.

Some of its more tough-minded leaders are bound to discover—as did Lenin faced with his own *Narodnik* tradition—"the principle of organization". Some of them already operate the levers of manipulation in an organizational form. But after the French experience many more in "the Movement" asking themselves the eternal populist question, "What is to be done?" will come to deny the very principle of its protest. This would mean that the one attractive feature of "the Movement", its rejection of "the Apparatus", will disappear. If "total change" and not reform is the goal, the only form of struggle which would look to the activists as having an effective chance would be an *organized* struggle. They would, perhaps reluctantly, come to the conclusion that if you want to change "the System" in an age of organization, you have to have one yourself.[27] The tender-minded would of course, fall by the wayside and write about "the Movement Betrayed" and about another "God that Failed".

THE REAL QUESTION will be, however, whether it would not also mean undermining the one element which kept "the Movement" going, through a wider appeal—whether indeed it would not mean a return to ineffective sectarian bickering and political sterility. Even more acute for the activists in "the Movement" is the dilemma involved in the question of reaching broader "popular masses". The Utopian fundamentalists, coming as they do after the experience of Social Democracy's (and also the Western Communists') timid collaboration with "the System", may find that the role of a Leninist "detonator", activated by a dose of Maoist voluntarism, is not hopeful, if there is no material to detonate. This would still appear to be the case in the industrial countries of the West, where popular discontents are limited to partial claims, claims unlikely to lead to the overthrow of "the System", even of the Gaullist system.

Their one hopeful thought is connected with the strategic vulnerability of the complex modern mechanisms of state, society, and economy. Military strategists noted long ago that increase in power goes with a partial increase in vulnerability (e.g. in the last War the bombing of ball-bearing factories and petrol dumps). Strikes in a strategic sector of the economy are almost as effective in paralyzing much wider areas of the economy as more general strikes. (Marcuse emphasized this in one of his lectures, where he used the example of the liftmen's strike in New York.) However, as the French experience has shown to the activists, even a General Strike following an activated student body capable of occupying the universities is not sufficient to achieve a victory. If the goal is articulated in terms of political power, the prospects look even less hopeful. Apart from France and Italy, there is no credible "left-wing" alternative to "the Establishment".

EVER since Stirner said, "We are the first generation in history which realized that . . .", the sentiment has been repeated in subsequent generations with monotonous regularity. The feeling of historical uniqueness is common to every generation entering the political scene. This

---

[27] Here is the comment of Maurice Duverger in *Le Nouvel Observateur* (15 May 1968), the schizophrenic organ of the older followers of the New Left:

> "In modern societies, complex and compartmentalized, the 'masses' strictly speaking do not exist. They cannot really act, if not through the parties, trade unions, and groupings of this type, without the support of which nothing durable and profound can be achieved."

has been true ever since the "idea of history" became predominant in Europe. It is justified by definition, but surely it has become more than a little suspect. In the form of its current pathological exaggeration, it has outrun the individual solipsism of Stirner's *Der Einzige* towards a generational solipsism of youth ideology. There is a tendency to stress only the differences.[28] It is particularly neurotic at present, when "the acceleration of history" has not only rendered the adaptation to change more difficult, but has also made it even more necessary to learn from all the past failures of—to use the slogan of the Sorbonne students—imagination seizing power.

It would be, however, an optical error to look at the phenomenon of "the Movement" alone and make on this basis generational generalizations. It cannot be taken in isolation from the previous generation against whose "authority" the revolt is ostensibly directed. If so, then never in history has "authority" been so willing, indeed so eager, to give the impression that it is not authoritative. The revolt coincides with a general evolution towards permissiveness, from the family to the public level. It makes one suspect that the two phenomena may be related in the way, as Erich Fromm argued, "escape from freedom" and fascism were related. Perhaps after "escape from authority" the phase will come of a search *for* authority. As students' disturbances create, in any case, a "backlash", a reaction in favour of order and stronger authority, a new authoritarian dialectic may be released which will leave the present phase behind: leaderless as well as permissive. In any case, there is little doubt that the older generation indulged in the double error of both taking the revolt too seriously and not seriously enough.

Too seriously, because the question whether the tendencies existing in "the Movement" will develop depends largely on the older generation. The spectrum of reactions ranges from an exaggeration of the danger through the flattery of youth to the masochistic breast-beating of some elderly band-wagon-jumpers. The sensation-hungry mass media tend to magnify every event, but even serious press accounts of M. Cohn-Bendit as a "revolutionary genius" with student masses all over the world "seething in revolutionary discontent" bordered on the ridiculous.

In Great Britain in particular, the ideologists of the movement face a difficult task in the empirical, non-ideological, suspicious-of-general-concepts intellectual tradition of this country. Somehow, even revolution has

---

[28] John Sparrow quoted the following exchange: " 'Can't we discuss this as human beings?' asked a senior member in a 'provincial' university the other day, having reached an impasse in argument with a student leader: 'I am not interested in you as a human being' was the cold reply. . . ." (*The Listener*, 4 July 1968.)

Stephen Spender reported a not dissimilar conversation with a Sorbonne student:

"He told how he had been asked by someone why he had not explained things adequately to the authorities at his university, and how he had answered: 'because one does not enter into discussions with people who are non-existent'. . . ."

(*New York Review of Books*, 11 July 1968.)

a tendency here to dissolve in compromise, and the flames of revolutionary passion lead to such inspiring acts as the Hornsey Art School's students repainting their loos. This is hardly "the storming of heaven".

In the United States the problem is different, but also there the "student problem" is not to be put on the same level as "the Negro problem". Only an exaggerated sense of historical self-importance can lead to a "political scientist" to begin his article on the subject with the words (Dankwart A. Rustow in *New Leader*, 20 May 1968): "Since 23 April, Columbia University has been experiencing a major convulsion reminiscent of the Great Revolution of 1789".

I F THE NOTION of collective guilt was not so primitive, whether applied to nations or to generations, it would be arguable that it is not the young, but the older generation that is the problem.

There can be little doubt that in many cases *les parents terribles* are worse than *les enfants terribles*. Some of them have moved from revolt against "poverty amidst plenty" in the 1930s to a revolt against affluent society in the 1960s, at the time as they themselves moved from poverty to affluence, to practise alienation at $50,000 a year. The intellectual Establishment of New York and London, thrilled with revolutionary prospects, and displaying the characteristic *Salon-Maoismus*, contributes to the orgy of snobbery attendant upon the current Utopian wave. Long before the "Black Power" spokesman asked the students assembled at the London School of Economics to establish a "Revolutionary Socialist Student Federation", whether they know how to make a petrol bomb, the *New York Review of Books* published a diagram of and a recipe for a Molotov cocktail on its cover page. This has not prevented, of course, its political writers from deploring "American violence".

In France the self-abasement of the elderly "progressives" reached its peak during the May "revolution". At the meeting of Jean-Paul Sartre with the students at the Sorbonne, Max Pol-Fouchet exclaimed with pathos appropriate to the occasion: "Representing a generation which has failed, I ask you not to fail!"

The members of the Italian "progressive intelligentsia" are no less sentimental. Even the Communist poet and film director, Pier Paolo Pasolini, reproached them (*Expresso*, 16 June 1968) for trying "to regain virginity by making a show of adulation for the adolescents", lines which embarrassed the Party in its attempts to pass itself for the champion of students.[29]

It would not be surprising if the students, finding themselves between

[29] The electoral poster of the *PCI* addressed to the young voters presented a policeman threatening a young man with a stick. The caption ran: "Your first vote to say *no* to the authoritarianism in the University, in the factory, and in the state." (*Rinascita*, 17 May 1968.)

political abuse[30] and generational flattery, were somewhat bewildered. A generational gap is not an abnormal phenomenon, but this one is somewhat unusual.

It is from this viewpoint that the question of Student Revolt not being taken seriously enough should be approached. "Class '68" is not the last in history. Flattery tends to inflate students egos; but, at the same time, it tends to injure their intellectual potentialities, by applying to them double standards of assessment. Their chance of overcoming the adolescent *Sturm und Drang* will be diminished if their elders flatter them, and take their ideological pretensions with an uncritical sentimentality. The elderly "progressives" will not get the gratitude of the young for all their attempts at ingratiation. New *gurus* will replace old *gurus*, as new fads are already replacing old fads. Their prospects are as dim as those of the white "liberals" who tried to ingratiate themselves with the Negro racists. In both cases masochism led to the transgression of the line separating self-abasement from an authentic sense of equality.

Politically, the Student Revolt will have of course different effects in different countries. But generally it provokes a Hobbesian reaction among the middle- and (where it is integrated) the working-class. It strengthens the authoritarian tendencies it set out to oppose. It is directly responsible for the shift of the French electorate towards the "paternalism" of de Gaulle, which the students so deplored. If there is a "second round" resulting from the inflationary effects of the wage rises, neither the students nor any libertarian cause will benefit from it. In the USA the disturbances have created a backlash which increased Richard Nixon's electoral chances. In Italy the

---

[30] The Communists overtaken "from the left" in the West, and "from the right" in the East were particularly abusive.

L'Humanité poured scorn on the student leaders. Georges Marchais, a leading Party figure, referred to M. Cohn-Bendit as "a German anarchist", and to "the German philosopher, Herbert Marcuse, who lives in the United States" in order to play on chauvinistic sentiments. The East German press, after an enthusiastic initial reaction to the student riots, became much more critical, pointing to "the limits of the abstract democratism of 'anti-authoritarian' methods of organization" (*Forum*, May 1968).

The Soviet press, like the French Communists, castigated the "false revolutionaries" and "ultra-leftists". The Polish *Trybuna Ludu* (19 May 1968) wrote about "the half-baked pie peppered with sexualism and narcomania".

But the Chinese press has denounced "the traitorous activities of the French revisionist leading clique . . . supported and carried out in co-operation with the Soviet revisionist ruling clique" (*Renmin Ribao*, 6 June 1968). By "slandering the progressive students as 'anarchists'" they have been "again unmasked as dirty scabs" (*Peking Review*, 7 June 1968). For good measure the pro-Chinese Belgian communist paper, *La Voix du Peuple* (24 May 1968), reiterated that "in the case of Poland and Czechoslovakia, the students' 'movement' was closely linked with the 'ultra-revisionist' trend, aiming at the accelerated re-establishment of capitalism on the political, cultural, and economic level".

On the other hand, the Polish leader, Zenon Kliszko, Gomulka's close friend, said on the subject of the French student revolt that it had been inspired by "the imperialist diversion [which] deliberately passes off upon various youth groups a black flag to prevent a mass defection of the younger generation to the red flag" (*Zycie Warszawy*, 21 June 1968).

revolt strengthened the Christian Democratic stronghold. In Germany it has the same effect, not to mention the improved position of the neo-Nazis— whose paper, *National Zeitung* (21 May 1968), splashed its first page with the headline: *"Rettet Deutschland vor den roten 'Studenten'!"* In Britain it certainly does not improve the electoral chances of the Labour Party.

S OCIALLY, the Student Revolt may have a marginal effect on the problem of university reform. The argument that it is the "threat of revolution" (first used by the father of John Stuart Mill at the time of the 1832 Reform Bill) which is necessary to make the conservatives implement reforms has some validity in it, but only when there is strong opposition to reforms. Some countries, like France, need university reform very badly, others need less radical adjustments. But in each case the problem is that of a mass of universities producing an "educational proletariat" with *élite* aspirations. A trend towards "educational factories" is, of course, quite incompatible with the original idea of the university. Yet, although it may be true (as Kingsley Amis said) that "more means worse", to reverse the trend towards the expansion of higher education in advanced industrial societies is neither desirable, nor feasible. In the future there may come to be a greater status-differentiation between various establishments of higher education and a better adjustment to the occupational requirements of society.

It is difficult to guess what modifications in the social structure of modern societies will be necessitated by "technetronic" and demographic developments, not to mention the effect of the advances in biochemical sciences. But whatever they are, they cannot be introduced by "revolutionary means", although they may well involve radical decisions.

One thing is clear. To look at present-day social change through the spectacles of the myth of the French Revolution is an exercise in anachronism. At the time of Louis XVI the average life-expectation was about 30 years; now, in the industrial countries of the West, it is about 70. Thus, the confrontation of two trends—towards the increased role of youth and towards longevity—present a new situation. When our "generation in revolt" reaches the age of those they are revolting against it will form (barring catastrophes) a more sizable part of the population, both relatively and absolutely, than the corresponding age-group does at present. The real social problem will exist long after the present ideologies of Youth disappear.

The student unrest may or may not be a portent of things to come; however, the shape of the future will depend more on the rest of society than on students. The young, as so many in the West emphasize, have a right to engage in rebellion and to dream of Utopia. The real issue is whether this could become a millenarian movement embracing other social groups, and whether or not it could lead to a capitulation of the older generations possessing more historical experience.

H ERBERT MARCUSE'S *One-Dimensional Man* ends with a quotation
from Walter Benjamin:

"It is only for the sake of those without hope that hope is given."

This was a cry of despair at the beginning of the Nazi-fascist era. Is the present
situation really comparable? Have the students, whatever their grievances or
forebodings, nothing to lose but their hopes?

"We have become more conscious of the future", wrote Edward Shils,
"and at the same time the shape of the future is more opaque or
appalling. . . ."[31] To embrace Utopia may conceivably provide an easy
emotional way out. If one is too long on a bleak diet of the dead past and
mediocre present, one turns to a bright future for psychic sustenance. Yet the
paradox of Utopianism is that historically it has invariably led to results
grimly at variance with the original ideals of the true believers.

With the present "information explosion" and the "acceleration of
history", the future is becoming the present soon enough. Even science-
fiction finds it difficult to keep up. When the idea of "Imagination Seizing
Power" was entertained in the past, the interval between conception and
execution was not so hectically brief. Even so the bright Utopian hopes did
not survive for long the seizure of power in those 20th-century instances
when modern image-makers were strong enough to take control.

Alas, students of revolution realize this better than revolutionary students.
They know what happens to imagination when it is seized by power.

(1968)

---

[31] Edward Shils, "The Future and the Intellectuals" *Bulletin of the Atomic Scientists* (October
1967).

14. *Détente*: An Evaluation*

IN THE PRESENT Soviet terminology *Détente* or "Peaceful Coexistence" denotes a strategic alternative to overtly militant antagonism against the so-called "capitalist countries". It does not imply the abandonment by the Soviet Union and its allies of conflict with the liberal Western countries. It does not mean the cessation of the slogans about class warfare and about the "ideological" conflict between the "two systems" with the aim of replacing the capitalist (democratic) system by the communist system. The point is emphatically and repeatedly made in Soviet theoretical pronouncements intended for consumption within the Communist bloc. *Détente* means a change of methods. Head-on conflict is to yield to indirect methods of combat, using non-military means, described as "ideological": in Soviet practice this term covers subversion, propaganda, political blackmail and intelligence operations.

Historically the first period of *Détente* occurred in 1921 when, following the victory over the White Armies, Lenin decided that his country required a long period of consolidation of power and economic rehabilitation. At this time the Soviet Union entered into regular diplomatic relations with those "capitalist" powers which were willing to reciprocate, and engaged with them in extensive negotiations and collaboration aimed at propping-up the Soviet economy. This period came to an end around 1930 with the triumph of Stalin's one-man dictatorship and the drive for the militarization of the Soviet Union.

Immediately after Stalin's death, (and particularly after 1957 when Khrushchev established himself in full authority), the policy of "Peaceful Co-existence" was renewed. Its initial intention seems to have been twofold: to slow down the military effort of the United States, as well as to break out of the diplomatic isolation in which Stalin had placed the Soviet Union. Khrushchev's successors maintained this policy in full vigour. In addition to the original aims of *Détente*—the expansion of the Soviet system and the enfeeblement of the liberal democracies—they had a new aim, namely the securing of Western financial aid and the technical assistance for their lagging economy.

The Soviet Government expects the policy of *Détente* to accomplish the following:

---

* This text was slightly revised, and then issued (in 1974) as a formal statement by a group of students of Soviet and international affairs which included Robert Conquest, Brian Crozier, John Erickson, Joseph Godson, Gregory Grossman, Bernard Lewis, Richard Pipes, Leonard Schapiro, Edward Shils, P. J. Vatikiotis.

(1) To weaken the Western alliance by making it appear to be unnecessary, indeed, dangerous to peace.

(2) To reduce the pace of the American defence effort and to eliminate the United States presence in Europe.

(3) To secure from the West financial and technological assistance which would directly enhance Soviet military power by making easier the continuous build-up of the military sector of the economy.

(4) To isolate China and to counter the political consequences of the fact that the Soviet Union is involved in a hostile confrontation with both East and West.

(5) To legitimize its domination over Eastern Europe by making it appear historically irreversible.

As theoretical writings appearing in the Soviet Union make it quite clear, the ultimate result of a carefully pursued policy of *Détente* should be a decisive shift of the world balance of power in favour of the Soviet Union and its bloc. This shift, it is expected, will permit the Soviet Union to achieve further expansion without recourse to general war, largely by the use of methods of internal subversion and external intimidation.

It is only if this policy is frustrated and its aims are abandoned by the Soviet Union that conditions for a genuine *Détente* may arise. Until that time, the West, while not relinquishing hope for the relaxation of international tension, must distinguish between the real targets of Soviet policy and the smokescreen used to camouflage them. A genuine policy for peace, providing a convincing promise for the future, must rest on public opinion which is aware of the realities of the international situation (including the need to preserve the Western position in the balance of power) and not on illusory slogans about "Peace" and "Friendship", or stern condemnation of the "Cold War"—without any substantive changes in conduct by the Soviet leaders. Above all the West must not allow itself to be deluded into believing that the policy of *Détente* is directly related to the avoidance of nuclear conflict between the United States and the Soviet Union—as both countries, for different political reasons, tend to suggest. In fact the determination to avoid nuclear conflict has characterized the policy of both the United States and the Soviet Union for many years before talk of *Détente* became fashionable—the first striking instance was on the occasion of the Cuba confrontation of 1962, and the last one was on the occasion of the nuclear alert during the October 1973 Middle East War. There were other less striking examples.

Whilst *Détente* does not mean the abandonment of the Soviet posture of ideological struggle, it tends to foster in the West the idea that it has to accept tacitly Soviet political practices as a necessary condition for avoiding a nuclear war. This false alternative provided in the past the underlying premise for those advocating unilateral Western disarmament. Today it is

Western government spokesmen who often use this simplified dichotomy to justify an attitude of silent indifference towards victims of Soviet persecution. This can only confuse the Western public about wider political issues. Contrary to official suggestions, a defence of Solzhenitsyn or Sakharov does not in any way increase the risks of a nuclear war. The Soviet Union does not accept "ideological co-existence", and there is no reason why the West should compromise its own fundamental values and ideas. Avoiding ambiguity in this respect, also on the governmental level, can only decrease the risks of nuclear confrontation in the long run.

ONE OF THE MAJOR POINTS raised about *Détente* has been whether, and in what sense, it is connected with—and should be connected with—a "liberalization" in the internal affairs of the Soviet Union and of other countries in the Soviet bloc. The question has been dramatized in particular by the amendment, through which Senator Henry Jackson, supported by large majorities in the United States Senate and House of Representatives, has sought to deny to the Soviet Union "most-favoured-nation" treatment and similar trade advantages unless and until it permits the free emigration of its subjects. Although in practice, this has primarily until now revolved round the question of Jewish emigration, the amendment expresses a general principle and does not limit its application to Jews.

The Jackson Amendment and similar demands have been denounced by the Soviet Union as "intervention in its internal affairs". For it is a matter which would require altering Soviet law, or at any rate, Soviet treatment of their own citizenry. But this argument, even at its own level, is false. No change of law is required, only a change of practice. The United Nations Declaration on Human Rights, though not legally binding, is an expression of international principle which is held to be generally applicable; it specifically covers the free movement of people. The Soviet Union has accepted the Declaration of Human Rights. The observance, or non-observance, of these international standards should certainly be regarded as one touchstone of the reliability of Moscow's attitude to the formally accepted obligations which constitute a part of the general guarantees which the Soviet Union has undertaken to give as part of its contribution to *Détente*.

The Jackson Amendment, and the demands made by representatives of many Western countries at the Helsinki and Geneva talks for a free exchange of people and ideas between Russia and the West, puts the problem in its clearest form. Those who defend the policy of *Détente* in the way in which it is understood in the Soviet Union argue that international negotiations between powers are simply a matter of realistic policies to which ethical issues of this sort are irrelevant. A supplementary argument for the Soviet form of *Détente* is that whatever the current conduct of the Soviet leadership, international *Détente* will in the long run, more or less automatically, lead to an improvement in the Soviet treatment of its own citizens, if only through an increase in the standard of living.

This argument has no foundation in experience. For centuries Russia has sought (with some success) to import Western technology, but this has never had any effect on the internal nature of its regime, Tsarist or Soviet. The Soviet authorities are, of course, well aware of the fact that the United States and other Western countries believe that *Détente* will lead to a liberalization of the Soviet regime, and that is why there has been a progressive tightening-up of controls in the Soviet bloc during the period when *Détente* has been mooted. There are certainly signs of fear inside the USSR among the hard-liners, or those who fear for their own privileges (the hack-writers and venal intellectuals, for example), or the *KGB* officials, that the United States arguments for *Détente* may be right: This is why Brezhnev has repeatedly been reassuring them in his speeches that *Détente* provides the best platform for ideological warfare, and, following up words with deeds, he has been intensifying persecution of dissent.

The Soviet leadership makes no secret of the fact—and indeed states it in speech after speech and document after document—that its opposition to Western ideas and to any significant "liberalization" is total and irreconcilable. Such a persistent and unrelentingly hostile attitude is quite incompatible with any development of real progress towards genuine friendly relations between the two sides. Until genuine "liberalization" takes place, or at least until there are some signs of serious progress in that direction, we may unreservedly take all the other elements of *"Détente"* in current Soviet policy as temporary and tactical. They are not evidence that the Soviet Union is inclined to reduce its hostility towards the Western countries.

The Fate of Culture

W HEN FACED WITH the prospect of *Détente*, the internal Party line in the Soviet Union and Eastern Europe hardened to prevent any undesirable cultural developments which might undermine the Party's ideological domination. The increasing cultural rigidity was most pronounced in the Soviet Union itself where a determined effort was made to end the phenomenon of *samizdat* and to crush the dissidents. The KGB arrested many of them: some were sent to mental prisons, some to camps with harsher sentences than were usually given to dissidents sentenced earlier. The most important of the *samizdat* journals, *The Chronicle of Current Events*, was finally hunted out of existence. "Case 24" as it was called by the *KGB*, culminated in the Yakir-Krasin trial during which the accused, after a year of preliminary "investigation" in prison, cooperated with their prosecutors and—broken men—"confessed" in a manner reminiscent of the infamous Moscow Trials of the 1930s. There was, of course, no similarity in the gravity of the charges and the accused earned themselves a reduction of the already lenient sentence by "freely" denouncing their own "misdeeds" during the press conference at which they were presented to foreign correspondents. There was, however, another ominous sign recalling the technique of the 1930s: during the same press conference, the state prosecutor, Malyarov, declared that the two most prestigious Soviet dissidents, Sakharov and Solzhenitsyn, "are not immune" before Soviet law, a clear indication that they might also be arrested, which indeed is what happened to Solzhenitsyn later on.

At the same time the *KGB* succeeded (after a five-day interrogation) in breaking Solzhenitsyn's friend who had typed the manuscript of *The Gulag Archipelago*. Having disclosed the manuscript's whereabouts to the *KGB*, the woman was released (only to commit suicide). Solzhenitsyn and Sakharov, faced with an impending threat to themselves, appealed to Western public opinion. They denounced the increased oppression in the Soviet Union and reproached the West for its lack of moral stamina and courage in defending universal cultural values, as well as for the short-sightedness of its policy of sacrificing freedom for the chimera of pseudo-*Détente*. Already, during President Nixon's visit to Moscow in May 1972, Sakharov had warned that the Soviet leaders would take the new agreements as a green light for increasing internal repression, since they would assume that such repression would no longer affect Western policy towards the Soviet Union. In this they may have been mistaken—although the American administration has indeed been attempting to dissociate its foreign policy from the question of internal Soviet rigidity. Secretary of State Kissinger and Chancellor Brandt—both refugees from Hitler—declared that they would be pursuing the same policies even if Hitler and Stalin respectively were still in power. It is an ironical situation in which Sakharov and Solzhenitsyn stand for the cultural values of the West . . . while Western statesmen are ready to sacrifice them for the sake of an unrealistic *Realpolitik* which (as Sakharov noted in this message to the American Congress) would in the end also undermine Western security.

In contrast to the political leaders' non-committal reaction, Western cultural and scientific milieux, and Western public opinion in general, have been overwhelmingly sympathetic to Sakharov and Solzhenitsyn. As the latter stated, this was the only factor which had until then prevented his arrest. The publication in the West of *The Gulag Archipelago* prompted another campaign against Solzhenitsyn, the style and vocabulary of which was not very different from the assaults of Soviet propaganda in the Stalinist period. He was soon to be expelled from the country.

THE POINT so forcefully made by Sakharov and Solzhenitsyn, and only very rarely encountered in Western writings on *Détente*, is the extreme importance of internal Soviet policies as an indication of the Soviet Union's future external behaviour. A more liberal internal policy could be regarded as a test of the nature of Soviet political evolution. It would not be a sufficient guarantee that the Soviet Union had ceased to be expansionist, but it would constitute a necessary precondition for its evolution in this direction. Internal cultural control based on ideological mendacity (doublethink, doubletalk and double standards) suggests that similar attitudes and methods will also be used in foreign relations, and raises the problem of Soviet reliability *vis-à-vis Détente.* That is why the question of the "free flow of ideas, information and people" is of paramount importance in gauging the future of East–West relations. In the long run, the official attitude of the communist countries to cultural developments is the only indication which makes possible an assessment of Western security on the political, rather than on the military plane. The West can disregard this fact only at its peril. Yet the Soviet view of *Détente* includes both pressure to prohibit any Western criticism and the acceptance by the West of the principle that so far as the Soviet Union is concerned, the Soviet leaders are to be free to pursue the "ideological struggle". The most pungent comment on the double standards evident in the Soviet definition of *Détente* was given in the *New York Times* (3 February 1947): "The Soviet contention clearly is that Moscow is free to tell lies about the West but the West must not tell the truth about the Soviet Union."

The Soviet formula for this is that the "free flow of ideas" must not violate "the customs and sovereignty of each country" (which means, in effect, that ideas and information are free to flow within the bounds allowed by Soviet censorship). The official Soviet idea is that international cultural relations are to be limited to innocuous state-controlled "cultural exchanges"—as if culture were a commodity which could be manipulated and exchanged. But the fact remains that the works of Pasternak, Akhmatova, Sinyavsky, Nadezhda Mandelshtam and Solzhenitsyn which emerged in the post-Stalin literary revival remain largely inaccessible to Soviet readers. Yet, unofficial literature, unofficial art and unofficial history writing are the only manifestations of living culture in the Soviet Union. The official culture is dead, unable to produce anything of value.

It is not surprising that it is only the unofficial culture which attracts surreptitious attention in the Soviet Union and Eastern Europe, and that it is eagerly followed in the West which has become a temporary repository for unofficial Russian writings.

The reason why the official culture is dead was put succinctly by Lydia Chukovskaya, recently expelled from the Soviet Writers' Union, in an open letter in defence of Sakharov:

"There are written laws and unwritten ones, and in Russia there exists one unwritten law which has more force than the whole collection of our laws put together and which the authorities never fail to apply. In Russia there is only one crime for which the authorities never pardon anybody. This one law, the strictest of all, lays down that every person must be severely punished for the slightest attempt to think for himself. To think aloud, that is."

This attitude to free thought as a crime and a sin, also determines the official attitude to culture, whether it is a work of literature, art or history. Solzhenitsyn illustrated it in an interview with two Western journalists in Moscow:

"Vaganov, head of the regional archives in Tambov, refused to let me look even at newspapers which were 55 years old. In the central military historical archives, a rigorous search was recently carried out in order to discover who, in 1963, had turned over to me material about the First World War and how this had happened. . . ."

The access to historical materials remains a closely guarded privilege in the Soviet Union. It is granted only to ideologically reliable historians who can produce such works as, for instance, the new history of the Second World War, which accuses Britain, France and the United States of plotting to smash the Soviet Union. Thus, even in a time of *Détente*, Soviet leaders remain faithful to the Orwellian idea that "he who controls the past controls the future".

THIS ATTITUDE IS NOT CONFINED to cultural controls in the Soviet Union, but extends abroad where no such controls can be exercised. Soviet authorities try hard to dampen critical thought in the West, although not very successfully, under the cover of *Détente*. Examples of this are many: the campaign to silence Western broadcasts to the Soviet Union and Eastern Europe, the expressed intention to use the Universal Copyright Convention to prevent the publication in the West of unofficial Soviet writings, and the campaigns in the West identifying *Détente* with the Soviet state and Party interest (as once upon a time they identified it with "Peace"). More often than not, in this particular sphere, Soviet behaviour is so crude that it has the effect of turning the Western public against the Soviet Union. It is, incidentally, sobering to recall that it was the American administration which suggested that the Soviet Union should sign the UCC and that it seriously considered this a "triumph for international cultural relations", instead of realizing that the Soviet Union would try to use the Convention as an extended arm of Soviet censorship.

The fundamental naiveté of so many political perceptions in the West is ultimately due to lack of understanding, not just of the mechanisms of the Soviet political system, but of the mentality rooted in the political culture underlying it. It is the Western lack of political comprehension which makes possible Soviet attempts at cultural exploitation of *Détente*. The situation would indeed be laughable if it were not so tragic for the Soviet artists and writers, and if it were not for the threat which it poses for the West through the extension of Soviet political influence, the infiltration of Soviet *doublethink* and the possible debasement of Western cultural standards.

The fate of culture in the age of *Détente* depends, in no small measure, on the steadfast attachment of the West to its own cultural standards and the avoidance of confusion which pseudo-*Détente* could bring to them as a result of Soviet political pressure.

The Military Balance

I T IS generally assumed in the West that *Détente* by its very nature reduces the need for reliance on military strength. It is thought that relaxation in international tension is the obvious occasion to reduce military establishments and to run down weapons programmes. An inspection of military programmes in the Soviet Union and among its allies, however, shows that they do not share this Western view.

Even in simple numerical terms, *Détente* has brought no diminution, nor even a levelling, but rather a programme to expand both Soviet strategic offensive and defensive systems, as well as adding to the capacities of general purpose or "conventional" ground, sea and air forces. Behind these military armament programmes lies an extensive civil defence programme, a major military training programme for Soviet adolescents and a mass of well-trained reservists, continually swelled by the Soviet conscript system. In brief, there is *no* sector of Soviet military policy where expansion, diversification and modernization cannot be observed. The growth of the Soviet Navy serves as but one example of this relentless process.

In terms of strategic offensive weapons the SALT-1 agreements of 1972 served the Soviet Union handsomely, investing it with a 40 per cent advantage in ICBMs—1,618 for the Soviet Union to 1,054 for the United States—and missile-launching submarines—62 to 44, over 30 per cent more submarine-launched ballistic missiles—950 to 710—and a massive three-fold lead over the United States in total destructive power. It was argued, nonetheless, at the time that the United States could afford this numerical disadvantage by virtue of superiority in technology, namely the multiple independent targetable warhead (MIRV). Strategic bomber forces were not included in this initial agreement. In the 21 months that elapsed after the SALT-1 agreement, the Soviet command steadily increased the numbers of its ICBM force to well over 1,500 and increased its submarine missile strength to some 580: numbers, however, tell only part of the story, since four *new* ICBMs with large yield have been developed; an improved version of the DELTA-class missile-carrying submarine, capable of carrying 16 rather than twelve 4,000-mile range SLBMs is under development; and at least one of the new ICBMs is mobile. All the while ICBM plants have been modernized, facilities for testing missile engines expanded, and new "cold launch" techniques for ICBMs developed, utilizing varied diameter canisters enables the Soviet Union to circumvent the SALT-1 limitation on numbers of *missile-silos*, since they make it possible for one silo to house a range of missile types.

Thus, the "numbers game" has been exploited in favour of the Soviet Union; while the other factor which it was believed at the time of SALT-1 would prevent the balance of advantage from tipping in the Soviet favour, namely, United States superiority in technical innovation has crumbled. The Soviet Union has itself developed MIRVs for its massive new ICBMs, thereby compounding the Soviet lead both in numbers and in missile throw-weight (meaning more MIRVs on bigger missiles). Meanwhile, a new strategic bomber, the *Backfire*, is entering the Soviet arsenal and adds to the strategic offensive potential (while the USAF B-1 strategic bomber is not yet in full production).

THE MOMENTUM of this Soviet build-up shows no signs of relaxation. Ominous though that is in an era of *Détente*, the Soviet conduct at the SALT-2 negotiations gives much cause for uneasiness: the Soviet Union's requirement for permanent numerical advantage, coupled with the energy with which it pursues its own technological progress, could only result in consigning the United States to permanent strategic inferiority. It follows, therefore, that Soviet objectives aim at overt strategic superiority as opposed to the mere "insurance" of limited numerical advantage. "Parity" no longer suffices. While the Soviet MIRV is disquieting, the most alarming element of the strategic weapons build-up is its scope and rate, with significant long-term implications. The pattern of *Détente* based on undisputed Soviet strategic superiority has not been fully explored in the West. Existing evidence is sufficient to suggest that military superiority is incompatible with the mode of political accommodation which is what the West thinks *Détente* ought to be. This kind of *Détente* could best be served if the Soviet Union accepted this conception. The crisis at the SALT-2 negotiations tends to confirm that it does not.

Meanwhile, the Soviet general-purpose forces have grown and continue to grow. The Soviet Navy, modern and powerfully armed with a wide range of missiles, displays its oceanic presence and presents an oceanic challenge. The Soviet Air Force modernizes and improves its tactical air power, with ultra-modern aircraft, such as the *Foxbat*, and significantly adds to its capacity for strategic and medium-range air-lift; this was shown in the recent Middle East War.

It is in the European theatre, however, that Soviet policies of military reinforcement expose the emptiness of the talk of political *Détente*. Over the past five or six years, the ground forces of the Soviet Union, which form the core of the power of the Warsaw Pact Countries, have undergone major improvements in combat capacity. In the past three years some 9,000 tanks have been added to the Soviet tank force, more than 4,000 armoured personnel carriers have been introduced into Eastern Europe, tactical air power has been improved both in quantity and quality, the number of nuclear weapons assigned to the ground forces has been increased, more than 1,000 additional guns have been provided for the Soviet divisions and stocks of conventional ammunition has been augmented. A marked improvement has also taken place in the Soviet logistical system, with emphasis on serving armoured and missile units. The net result is to give the Soviet command a preponderance in the European theatre of at least 3:1 in armour and of more than 2:1 in tactical aircraft. And once again, in line with the SALT-2 negotiations, Soviet conduct during the present (1974) talks on the reductions of forces shows no sign of yielding any element of this superiority.

Even on this brief inspection, the Soviet policy of preaching *Détente* while increasing military strength is demonstrably the reverse of our own. More than that, however, the *Détente* sought by the Soviet Union is viewed by that country not as the justification for accepting the prevailing military balance, but as an opportunity to spur forward towards unchallengeable superiority.

Economic Consequences

SOME OF THE MOST uncritical attitudes generated by *Détente* in the West are in the field of East–West trade. The understanding of its limitations and of the Soviet motives involved is quite inadequate not only among the general public but also among Western businessmen and governments. Yet such understanding is of crucial importance for a realistic view of the prospects for *Détente*.

Soviet purposes are related to the current difficulties confronting the Soviet economy. They include the decreasing rate of growth of the GNP, the exhaustion of employable reserves of manpower, the balance of payments deficit and the inefficiency which is particularly apparent in agriculture and in the Soviet inability to respond to demand and to generate technical progress.

Having rejected any far-reaching economic reform which might, or might not, have raised efficiency, but which would certainly have antagonized many powerful vested interests in Soviet society, especially the Party apparatus, Soviet leaders have opted for the other major course that bore some promise of countering the unfavourable trends in the economy: massive assistance from the West. This policy is all the more attractive because, while it is expected to bring large amounts of capital into the Soviet

Union, the repayment is to be mainly in the very commodities that the Western-financed projects would produce. At the same time, the flow of Western technology and know-how is expected by the Soviet leaders to narrow the growing technological gap with the West and to improve Soviet export capacity. The Americans, the Japanese, and the Europeans are to build up whole industries for the Soviet Union and develop vast regions there at very little cost to the Soviet Union itself, and with minimal risk to Soviet institutions.

Contrary to widespread Western belief, the "more liberal" Soviet economic strategy abroad is quite compatible with a conservative policy at home. Indeed, this double-pronged economic strategy is an alternative to domestic economic reform which the Soviet leaders feared might jeopardize the stability of existing Soviet institutions and generate political strife. The risks to domestic political control from increased Western contacts can be minimized by police methods designed to isolate the bulk of the population from contact with the West. Past experience has shown that such contacts in the economic sphere involve only a relatively small and select group of Soviet citizens. To the extent that some risks are nevertheless present, they are counterbalanced by the promise of additional economic benefits which might assuage the growing consumer demand. They are countered prophylactically by the tightening of control over dissidence that we have witnessed in recent years. Contrary to some Western expectations, past experience shows that a more reactionary policy at home can well be combined with economic advances to the West.

The paramount Soviet target in its economic *Détente* offensive is the gaining of large long-term credits at low interest rates (chiefly from the USA) in order to finance the purchase of equipment and technology for the development of oil, natural gas and other mineral resources. Such assistance from the West may not only increase Soviet overall economic strength, but it could also enable the Soviet government to engage in military spending on a scale which would otherwise be impossible, given the competing claims of investment and consumption.

The economic *Détente* strategy of seeking large Western credits may thus bring not only enormous economic advantage to the Soviet Union internally, but also to Soviet military and foreign policies, particularly as it will tend to create groups in the West with vested interests in Soviet-derived profits and in the protection of Western loans. These groups can be politically manipulated in the free societies, while the appetite for profits among businessmen is also easily exploitable.

But it is not necessarily true that what is good for Pepsi Cola, or for the Chase Manhattan Bank (and their European equivalents), in their dealings with the Soviet Union is also good for the United States or Western Europe. Yet very little homework has been done in the West on the problems involved in close relations with the Soviet economic state monopoly. Instead of soberly assessing the disadvantages of a free enterprise system in a situation in which the Soviet state monopoly can exploit economic competition among Western firms while it makes only deals it chooses to make, many Western business leaders have shown themselves to be remarkably eager to take Soviet economic propaganda at face value. Whether the enthusiasm will survive the diminishing prospects of governmental credit guarantees following the passage of the Jackson Amendment is another question.

Not only was the short-sightedness and the "band-wagon" psychology of the supposedly hard-headed Western businessmen amazing—so was the small amount of public discussion in the West on the questions whether assuming the role of the Soviet Union's banker was in the national interest of the Western countries; and whether it was wise to invest in the development of Soviet resources of energy (especially after the experience with the Arab oil embargo) rather than in Western sources. At a time of inflationary pressure, is a substantial outflow of capital from the West to communist countries desirable either politically or economically? And is it true, as advocates of *Détente*-at-any-price never cease to proclaim, that trade promotes peace?

A REALISTIC ANSWER to these questions is quite different from what the Western public was led to believe in the period between President Nixon's visit to Moscow in May 1972, and Secretary Brezhnev's visit to Washington in June 1973.

The private interest of business corporations and banks is not equivalent to the national interest, much less to the interest of the West as a whole. Competition for investment in the Soviet Union and the granting of large long-term credits to it would not only divide the West, and strengthen economically, politically and militarily its most dangerous and avowed adversary, but would also reduce political options for the West in the future by making it (particularly the United States) dependent on the USSR for a substantial amount of the energy supply and other essential goods. It would give the Soviet Union a lever on Western policy through the very fact of its indebtedness and its control over the new sources of energy on which the West would come to rely. Moreover, this Western policy may produce the opposite effect from the intended one of "*intermeshing*" Western and Soviet economic interests, of "*Gulliverization*" of the Soviet Union. Trade and investment generates friction and conflict even among friends, history provides enough examples to show that they do not ensure peace. Germany was the largest trading partner of Russia just before each of the two world wars, and the high point of Russian–Chinese trade was immediately before the break between Moscow and Peking.

Political as well as economic realism would thus dictate caution in granting credits for the export of Western technology and commodities to the communist countries, sober assessment of each deal (after the grain deal fiasco), and realization that Soviet purposes in expanding trade are as different from the Western ones as are the economic rules of the game adhered to by the two sides. So far, there is no evidence that the tough problems involved here have been generally comprehended either by businessmen, or by governments, or by the public of Western countries. Yet there is little doubt that the original euphoria over trade and credits as the miracle weapons for dealing with the Soviet Union—bringing both profits and peace—has subsided and a more realistic mood is slowly expanding in the West. The effects of the Soviet-American wheat deal and of the Arab oil embargo have not been lost on the Western (particularly the American) public. These have dampened the early enthusiasm. But the policy's premises which have generated unrealistic expectations and illusions are still operative.

One example should suffice. A US official very much responsible for the 1972 "Wheat Deal", faced with a Soviet proposal to re-sell to the United States some of the still-undelivered grain at a much higher price than Russia had paid for it, still justified the original deal on the grounds that it "constructively helped the process of *Détente*" and defended its "historic importance" in opening up agricultural trade with Russia. Vladimir S. Alkhimov—the Soviet trade official who offered to sell at a much higher price grain—originally sold to the Soviet Union at subsidized prices—which would replenish the US stock diminished by exports to the USSR—made a less euphoric comment:

> "Look at Alaska, which we sold you for $7 million back in 1867. That was cheap too, but you don't hear us complaining."

Clearly the Soviet attitude to *Détente* involves a rather long view of economic reciprocity. In the meantime, the Soviet Union is trying to narrow down the "technology gap" by acquiring advanced American technology. The American Control Data Corporation and other firms are helping to close this gap. According to spokesmen of this firm, by spending $3 million in three years, the Soviet Union gained 15 years in R & D. Lockheed and other aircraft firms compete for deals with the Soviet Union which will provide that country with access to the latest American jet-liner technology, design and know-how. But at the same time as the Soviet Union is negotiating the purchase of most advanced items, like the high-speed electronic computer "Cyber", Soviet technological achievements remain inaccessible to the West.

The economic and technological advantages of *Détente* are thus somewhat one-sided, and in the long run this asymmetry could be dangerous.

Soviet Aims in Western Europe

A S HAS BEEN SEEN, the policy of *Détente* was primarily envisaged by the Soviet Union in relation to the United States, as having two objects in view: *first*, to obtain American capital and technology as a means of reviving and expanding Soviet industry, and of developing essential resources, particularly oil; and *secondly*, to negotiate, in partnership with the only other serious nuclear power, settlements of conflicts all over the world, with the need to avoid nuclear confrontation with the United States always in mind. *Détente, vis-à-vis* the United States, from the Soviet point of view, is a continuation of the *old* "spheres of influence" and "hot line" policy in improved form; and a *new* exploitation of American willingness, consequent upon the end of United States involvement in Vietnam, to trade with the Soviet Union.

The relationship with Western Europe is regarded quite differently by the Soviet Union. Before the dramatic change in United States policy in 1971, the aim of the Soviet Union was to obtain its capital and technological requirements from Western Europe, while Soviet propaganda was mainly directed towards encouraging economic disunity between Europe and the United States. The United States is, however, a much more attractive supplier of capital and technology than Europe—because of the EEC, of which the Soviet Union disapproves as an entity, and because expanded business relations with the EEC might act as a new temptation to certain "bloc" countries, especially Poland and Rumania, to develop their own economic ties with the EEC and to escape thereby from the Soviet stranglehold. Moreover, as far as Europe is concerned, the Soviet Union can reasonably hope to exploit to the maximum its already overwhelming preponderance and its military proximity, in order to increase its political influence—and especially so if isolationist and economic pressures inside the United States may lead to US withdrawal from Europe. The Soviet Union may also hope to gain political advantage from exploiting the divisions which exist between the individual countries of the EEC and any economic and political discord between the United States and Europe.

Soviet policy regarding the European Security Conference shows that the Soviet Union hopes (vainly so far) to replace an effective defence system (NATO) by meaningless declarations and treaties which would leave Europe virtually disarmed against the Soviet Union. It also seeks to consolidate social and cultural relations in the only form acceptable to the Soviet Union: namely, state-to-state relations, in which all contacts are organized and therefore controlled by the state. If this policy were to succeed, which at present seems unlikely in view of the position taken by several European powers, this would give the Soviet Union a powerful argument for claiming to stifle all criticism of the Soviet Union in Europe—which in practice covers all objective discussion of Soviet reality, and in particular to bring about the closing down of certain wireless stations, especially Radio Liberty. This has been one of the main aims of the Soviet Union for years.

Whatever the outcome of the present MFR and "Security" talks, the policy of the Soviet Union towards Europe is likely to remain for a time radically different from its policy towards the United States. In the case of the United States the Soviet Union may well offer for some time the concession which Polyphemus offered to Outis, that of "being devoured last". In Europe, where the Soviet Union hopes for an ever-increasing military preponderance, its policy aiming to increase Soviet political influence as that of the United States declines, is likely to employ the following tactics:

(1) Clandestine subversion. This has the particular advantage which the Soviet Union has enjoyed for half-a-century of conducting subversion and "Peaceful Coexistence" side-by-side—such as entertaining the British Foreign Secretary while arms are being supplied to the Provisional IRA for the purpose of killing British soldiers.

(2) A vigorous policy of misinformation, e.g. through feeding false stories to press correspondents and through the recruitment of conscious or unwitting agents of influence.

(3) The exercise of pressure on scientists and university teachers by withholding of visas from those who have not been sufficiently congenial to the Soviet Union, as a warning to others.

(4) The exercise of pressure on businessmen, who are interested in trade with the Soviet Union, to use their influence to prevent unwelcome criticism.

(5) If the opportunity arises, direct political action (reinforced by military pressure). This is not difficult to imagine if one thinks of the situation already obtaining in Scandinavia, which has to live under the shadow of the vast Soviet Baltic Fleet. This danger of political pressure under cover of military preponderance would clearly increase if isolationism grows in the United States and if the present discord between the United States and Europe is not repaired.

The Middle East

THE MIDDLE EAST CONFLICT is not a local dispute. If it were, it would have been resolved some time ago. As it is, however, neither side in the conflict is able to impose its will on the other.

Nor are the great powers simply "sucked into" the conflict. On the contrary, the Soviet Union has exploited the conflict for a variety of purposes. These include:

(1) The neutralization and detachment of Turkey and Iran from the Western alliance.

(2) The outflanking of NATO, assisted by a prolonged energy crisis, and the disruption of the EEC.

(3) The acquisition of a bridge to Asia and Africa.

(4) The isolation of its own Muslim subject peoples against influences from the region.

(5) The control of the route to India, which is particularly important in view of the rivalry and conflict with China.

In short, the Soviet Union is in the Middle East because of its vital interest in the confrontation with the West, i.e. the United States and Western Europe; the conflict with China; and the vast oil resources.

The arms deal concluded in September 1955 with Egypt inaugurated a period of massive Soviet military, technical, and economic assistance, which was soon extended to Syria and Iraq. During the Suez War in 1956, the Soviet Union exploited to its advantage the instant and unequivocal American opposition to the Anglo-French military action. It was thus only after President Eisenhower had publicly warned his Allies of this position that the Soviets issued their threats against Britain and France. Yet the myth grew among the Arabs that the Soviet Union was responsible for "the frustration of the Anglo-French venture". In the decade from 1957 to 1967, the Soviet Union used its greater military, technical, and economic assistance programmes in the region (e.g. arms supplies, the Aswan High Dam, increased aid to Syria and Iraq) to impose the nearly total dependence of these states in their domestic, regional, and international policies. At the same time, it sought to isolate the United States from the region, and to divide the policies of Western European states.

Although the Six Day War in 1967 ended in the defeat of Soviet clients in the Middle East, and was a blow to its military assistance policy in the region, it nonetheless produced a still greater dependence of Egypt, Syria, and Iraq on the Soviet Union for arms and economic aid. Even while the relations between these states and the Soviet Union deteriorated, the programme of massive rearmament was accelerated on a greater scale.

D ESPITE THE ACCEPTANCE of Secretary of State Rogers' plan, and the ending of the war of attrition on the Canal in August 1970, the Soviet Union immediately took advantage of the standstill to introduce more missiles on the ceasefire line. Despite the publicized expulsion of the Soviet military advisers and technicians from Egypt in the summer of 1972, the treaties of friendship and cooperation, which were signed with Egypt and Iraq in the early seventies, provided for the continued massive infusion of

Soviet arms, consultation and collaboration in regional and international policies. Military assistance to Syria was increased and accelerated.

In part, it was the Nixon-Brezhnev *Détente* agreement in May 1972 which prompted some of the Arab clients of the Soviet Union to reconsider their relations with Moscow. By 1973, however, it was clear that *Détente* was having no effect in reducing—on the contrary, it increased—the Soviet military activity in Iraq and Syria. Simultaneously, the Soviet Mediterranean fleet, and particularly its amphibious and air operational strengths, was greatly increased. It continued to use shore facilities in Egypt and Syria, and was complemented by a stronger presence in the Indian Ocean, where the West had been weakened by the British withdrawal from the Persian Gulf.

I N THE WAR OF October 1973 it became clear that the Soviet Union had prior knowledge of the coordinated attack on Israel by Egypt and Syria. *Détente*, however, was not understood by the Soviet Union to mean sharing this information with its American partner, in spite of its formal obligation undertaken in the US-Soviet agreement of 24 June 1973. Nor did it exert any effort in seeking a cease-fire. On the contrary, it urged, in a series of notes, the non-belligerent Arab states to join in the fight. And for some time before that it had been encouraging them to apply the "Oil Weapon" against the West. (Later it urged them to continue the oil embargo against the United States until the moment it had been lifted.)

On the third day of the war the Israelis halted the Syrian advance in the North. On the fourth day, the Soviet Union began a massive airlift of arms to Egypt and Syria. Its allies, North Korea and North Vietnam, supplied pilots for the Syrian air force. Even when the imminent collapse of the Egyptian Third Army at the end of the second week of hostilities forced the Soviet Union to seek an immediate cease-fire, it did so by threatening disruption of the *Détente*. No sooner was the cease-fire agreement worked out in Moscow with the United States Secretary of State, Dr Kissinger, than the Soviet Union ventured a repetition of its August 1970 performance by seeking to introduce further, more sophisticated weapons into Egypt.

THE IMPORTANCE of the Middle East, in contrast to Vietnam, in the confrontation between the United States and the Soviet Union derives from the proximity of the region to Europe and Russia. It is the meeting place of three continents, Africa, Asia and Europe. It is a vast reservoir of oil, upon the availability of which depends the life of all the industrial countries in the West.

The Soviet Union has shown a keen appreciation of this importance. At the end of the Suez War, it made the transition from a far-away, silent spectator, to a strident agitator in the area. Its violation of the August 1970 standstill agreement on the Canal revealed the complaisance of the United States, which, in turn, encouraged the steady Soviet build-up and expansion of its military presence in Egypt, Syria, and Iraq. Seen as a signal of the West's weakness, the Rogers Plan led to a hardening of the Soviet-Arab line.

More recently, the Soviet Union has developed links with the Palestine Liberation Organization, which could be used as a "destruct mechanism" of a possible peace settlement.

WHILE THE SOVIET UNION USES *Détente* as an instrument for the advancement of its own policies in the Middle East, the dilemman of the United States is clear: in order to detach the Arabs from the Soviet Union, it must restrain the Israelis and press them into accepting an accommodation which can seriously weaken their security.

This also means saving the Soviet Union from defeat. It will continue its policy of expansion in the region, notwithstanding *Détente*, in spite of the alleged "End of the Era of Confrontation" between the super-powers, and, whatever the consequences of the diplomatic efforts of Dr Kissinger to achieve peace in the Middle East. One cannot help remembering that in June 1973 Dr Kissinger declared that the United States and the Soviet Union "will make an effort not to become *inextricably* involved in the Arab-Israeli conflict" and the two countries signed a solemn agreement to "continue to exert their efforts to promote the quickest possible settlement in the Middle East". The ink was not yet dry on this declaration when the Soviet Union began to speed up its arms deliveries to the Middle East which made possible the October War.

Trade Unions

M OSCOW'S POLICY of *Détente* in the free trade union and labour field has been given succinct expression in its unrelenting drive for exchanging "East–West delegations", close cooperation "to promote the interests of the working class", and the ultimate re-unification of unions in the communist-controlled World Federation of Trade Unions (WFTU) with those affiliated to the International Confederation of Free Trade Unions (ICFTU). The Kremlin's purpose in promoting these exchanges was described by the ICFTU in 1955 as:

(1) winning moral respectability and legitimacy for their state company unions.

(2) misleading the workers of the West by making them accept these organizations run by the Communist Party, as *bona fide* trade unions.

(3) facilitating communist infiltration and subversion in Western countries.

(4) promoting the expansionist interests of Soviet imperialism.

Repeatedly, the Western non-Communist trade unions have asserted that for the sake of "labour solidarity and human freedom", free trade union organizations should avoid exchanging delegations with any country which denies its people fundamental human rights specified in the United Nations Charter, denies its workers the right of freedom of association, prohibits genuine collective bargaining and the right to strike, and penalizes those who advocate free trade unionism and democracy.

However, in recent years, in part as a result of the eagerness for *Détente*, the principles of Communist trade union policy have been less clearly perceived. Thus the German trade union leaders (*DGB*) have officially defended their changed view by citing Chancellor Brandt's *Ostpolitik* and their moral obligation to support it through "*Ostkontakte*".

The British Trade Union Congress, after meeting with the former head of the Soviet secret police, Alexander Shelepin (now chairman of the Russian "equivalent" of the TUC) called for a new trade union relationship between East and West. Its general secretary, Mr Len Murray, recently told a *Trud* correspondent in London that

> "what the Soviet trade unions are doing for the working man and their activity in concluding and implementing collective agreements is really impressive. At the same time, it will be interesting for Soviet colleagues to acquaint themselves with the experience of the British TUC's work in various spheres, in particular with our experience of relations with state power."

In Italy, there has been constant talk of a trade union merger and while trade union unity has not yet been realized there is a sort of *de facto* unity in existence. In January 1974, representatives of Eastern and Western trade union centres met, for the first time in 25 years, in Geneva to discuss a joint programme of action. The very convening of such a conference constitutes a significant advance for the Soviet Union. At this meeting, it was agreed to convene late this year an ostensibly "non-ideological" conference "on humanizing the industrial environment". Indeed, *Détente* already seems to have contributed to a lowering of all previous barriers against Communist penetration into almost all Western trade union and labour movements. An outstanding exception has been the relatively small *Force Ouvrière* in France and, of course, the AFL-CLO in the United States.

More significantly, many trade union leaders in Western Europe have begun to indulge in wishful thinking about the nature of the Soviet trade unions. Some have, on the basis of their brief visits, concluded that they should no longer view East European trade unions as "mere transmission belts of their State Communist parties".

Détente in the trade union movement has to date been completely one-sided, benefiting only the Soviet Union and the Communist parties in the West. Contacts and exchanges have not brought more rights, freedoms, and social justice for the workers in Communist countries—if anything such contacts, exchanges, and dialogues have in fact strengthened the Communist union officials in their efforts to hold down the workers in the interest of the Communist Party and the government which it monopolizes. Nor have they brought about a *rapprochement* between East and West European workers. Only trustworthy and dogmatic East European *"apparatchiki"* are selected for such exchanges. There is already substantial evidence that these so-called new relations have considerably accelerated the process of infiltration of the free trade unions, to the economic and political detriment of the West.

Détente, in Soviet eyes, is not incompatible with subversion. What the Russians understand by it is consistent with what the West means by "subversion".

In the Soviet view *Détente* entails the *de jure* as well as the *de facto* recognition by the members of NATO and other Western countries of the permanent division of Europe on ideological lines, and the validity of the Brezhnev doctrine which "justified" Soviet military intervention in any communist country which departs from "socialist" principles, as defined in Moscow.

In the Soviet view "subversion" is what Western countries would be doing to the Soviet Union (and other Communist countries) if Moscow conceded that principle of free movement of persons and ideas which is required for a genuine *Détente*. Similarly, as understood by the Soviet Union, the "Cold War" includes all Western activities considered by Moscow to be hostile, including any Western criticisms of the Soviet treatment of political dissidents. "Peaceful Coexistence", on the other hand, is regarded in Moscow as essentially a transitory—although possibly prolonged—phase in relations between the Soviet Union and non-Communist states pending the "final triumph of communism". During this phase, the Soviet Union reserves the right to subvert other countries, while sealing itself off from, and in other ways resisting, any exposure to non-communist ideas and influences.

In the Age of Subversion

THERE ARE THUS two sets of rules: on the Soviet side, a right to operate anywhere and to subvert any other country; and on the Western side, the obligation to avoid criticisms of the Soviet Union and of all countries under Soviet protection, and to abstain from communicating to those countries any ideas which their rulers think might make their citizens critical of them.

Soviet spokesmen have said repeatedly that "Peaceful Coexistence" implies the intensification of the struggle between the world systems. The intensification of the struggle implies, above all, more subversion in all its forms.

The forms of subversion include: agitation and propaganda (*agitprop*), misinformation, espionage, and the clandestine training, financing and arming of terrorists, saboteurs, and guerrillas. There is naturally overlapping between these main categories. In all of them, the *KGB* plays a major role; in some, the relatively smaller military espionage organization, *GRU*, is also involved. *Agitprop* and misinformation are intimately linked.

The "agitation" of selected social groups, such as industrial workers is carried out by Communist parties through the penetration of trade unions. They may, and often do, proclaim their independence of Soviet control but in fact, to a smaller or greater degree, conform with the policies of the Soviet Union. The Leninist end view is the weakening of Western economics and their currencies, with the aim of discrediting their governments and their economic systems and alienating the citizens from their institutions.

Another important technique has been propaganda and agitation among conscripts or enlisted men in the armed forces of the NATO countries. Misinformation about the nature of the states which these armed forces are required to defend plays an important part in this activity. In other walks of life misinformation is disseminated by pro-communist sympathizers and by the various left-wing groups which are not sympathetic to Moscow but in some cases are penetrated, and often quite unwittingly by non-Marxists who repeat fashionable arguments which such left-wing groups have seized upon and promoted. Nor should the special rôle of the various international "front" organizations—such as the World Peace Council and the World Federation of Trade Unions—in propagating views which aid Soviet policy be overlooked.

The expulsion of the 105 Soviet agents from the United Kingdom (in September 1971) drew attention to the scale of Soviet espionage in Western countries. Broadly speaking, with the one exception of Belgium, other NATO countries have preferred to expel "their" *KGB* and *GRU* men discreetly and in small numbers. In neutral as well as NATO countries in Western Europe about 70 per cent of all accredited Soviet diplomats are, in fact, spies. Nowadays, such personnel are as likely to be in quest of industrial and technological secrets as of military information.

Although the Soviet media frequently denounce terrorism and other political violence, clandestine aid to terrorist groups is highly organized. In Mexico, Guatemala, Colombia, Chile, Ulster, the Middle East, and Africa, there are well-authenticated instances of Soviet involvement. The Lenin Institute in Moscow provides regular "guerrilla" courses for selected groups of Communists from Western and other countries; non-communists are more likely to be given facilities in Tashkent or Odessa. This should not be surprising as Soviet leaders themselves regard subversion as compatible with "*Détente*" and "Peaceful Coexistence" with increasing subversive activities.

Détente and China

THE CHINESE ATTITUDE towards *Détente* is basically determined by the Sino-Soviet conflict.

When after the "Cultural Revolution" China emerged from self-imposed isolation and entered the mainstream of international political life on the level of state relations, it was the result of its perception of the growing Soviet menace. It was this factor which necessitated a shift in Chinese foreign policy. This brought about restoration of diplomatic relations with those countries which had recognized China before the Cultural Revolution, efforts to win recognition from other countries, entry to the United Nations, and *rapprochement* with the United States. The Soviet invasion of Czechoslovakia and the "Brezhnev Doctrine" made China even more acutely sensitive about the danger of Soviet expansionism.

The shift in Chinese foreign policy has as its primary motive the reduction of this danger. This led not only to a new policy towards the United States and Japan, but also to the support of the idea of a strong, united Western Europe which would continue to tie down Soviet military forces and provide a political counterbalance to the Soviet Union on its Western flank. Hence the Chinese criticism of the Soviet *Détente* moves in Europe (*Peking Review*, 8 February 1974):

> "The Soviet Union . . . while making further military deployments in Eastern Europe, took pains to press for the heads of the European governments to meet before the end of last year in the third stage of the conference on European security and cooperation, so as to lay what it called a 'solid foundation' for European security and cooperation. It hoped in this way not only to consolidate its overlordship in Eastern Europe, but also to lull the vigilance of the West European countries, divide them and edge the United States out so it could not put the whole of Europe under its sole domination . . . The Soviet leading clique has tried its best to advertise 'relaxation' of the international situation. However, the reality of the stepped-up Soviet arms expansion and war preparations in Europe and its intensified contention with the United States in the Middle East have relentlessly exploded the *Détente* myth. . . ."

While the Chinese assert that for all their talks about *Détente* the two super-powers are engaged in a struggle to achieve world hegemony, the Soviet press maintains that the Chinese "modified at the 10th Party Congress [held in 1973] their foreign policy in such a way as to be able to use various forces, including the imperialist circles, for their struggle with the Soviet Union, the paramount obstacle on the way to Peking's hegemony" (*Mezhdunarodnaya Zhizn*, January 1974). In their interpretation of the "Cultural Revolution" the Soviet analysts point out that this shift has occurred at the plenary meeting of the Central Committee of the CCP (in Lushan in Summer 1970):

> "During this meeting the substance of the secret talks between Peking and Washington, which were already conducted for some time on the instructions of Mao Tse-tung and Chou En-lai, were first disclosed. Everything points to the fact that other Chinese leaders, including Lin Piao, were unaware of this . . . The new line of Mao contradicted the resolutions of the 9th Party Congress. In his speech at this Congress Lin Piao . . . referred to the 'latest Mao directive' about the 'new historical period—the period of simultaneous struggle with the USA and the Soviet Union.' Now Mao proclaimed a completely 'new stage,' a stage of collaboration with the American imperialism to conduct a struggle with the Soviet Union. This new turn proved to be too sharp even for such an old hand as Lin Piao." (*Voprosy Istorii*, December 1973.)

There can be little doubt that during the Cultural Revolution there were important differences of attitude among the Chinese leaders about the problems of foreign policy, and that some of these differences persisted after it was over. But it is extremely doubtful that any Chinese leader could afford (or was inclined to take) a pro-Soviet line; the differences were about strategy and tactics.

There is also little doubt that the American-Soviet *Détente* efforts were seen with growing distaste, if not alarm, by Peking and that the new internal struggle (which erupted after the 10th Congress, although it is basically concerned with the internal affairs) may well get entangled with the issues of foreign policy. It is not just a question of struggle for succession, but also of basic future orientation of China which is involved in the esoteric formulations of the attacks on Confucius and Lin Piao, Beethoven and Antonioni. Whatever the symbolic status of the "sick horse" sold by the Chinling Production Brigade to the Taoyuan Production Brigade in the opera "*Three Ascents of Peach Mountain*", one can be quite certain that Mao's successors will have to face the same dilemmas as he does, and that their margin of manoeuvre in foreign policy will also be limited. Given its geo-political context and the nature of the Sino-Soviet conflict, China can either have a policy of equidistance *vis-à-vis* the Soviet Union and the USA, or a policy of *rapprochement* with the USA (with the Soviet Union being "Enemy Number One"). The Sino-Soviet *rapprochement*, the regular bugbear of Western analysts, is unlikely in the present state of Sino-Soviet relations, and even in the post-Maoist period, although factional struggle can be seen as offering an opportunity eventually to be exploited by the Soviet Union.

In this situation the American advances to the Soviet Union cause irritation among Chinese leaders. They look with growing concern at the Soviet-American summit meetings (as Chou En-lai made clear in his speech at a banquet for President Nyerere in March 1974). They have shown their disappointment on several occasions. When Dr Kissinger visited Peking in October 1973, not even a common communiqué was produced. Shortly afterwards the heads of the respective diplomatic missions were withdrawn from Peking and Washington. The visit of Dr Kissinger to Moscow in March 1974 caused another painful reaction on the part of the Chinese leaders.

They perceive the American *Détente* policy *vis-à-vis* the Soviet Union as jeopardizing both European and Chinese security interests.

US-Europe Relations

IT IS NOT just the *Détente* policy itself that has caused the present state of disarray in the Atlantic Alliance, but it has certainly contributed to this disarray. The fact that the post-Gaullist regime in France is straining the Alliance to breaking point is not sufficient explanation for it. It was the Nixon Doctrine which helped to release the forces detrimental to the Atlantic Alliance, and made possible their narrow-minded nationalistic ascendancy.

At the moment, however, the problem is not how to apportion the blame—this can be left to future historians—but how the special relationship between the United States and Europe, which was and is the only realistic basis for the survival of Western civilization, can be preserved.

For that purpose it is not sufficient to concentrate on the details of day-to-day politics of the Alliance, on the mechanisms of decision-making, on the accommodation of national interests, on the "atmospherics" favouring or undermining such adjustments, in short, on the pragmatic side of American and European diplomacy. No less important is a wider historical context of such analysis which is concerned with the fundamental purposes of the Alliance.

It is only within this context that success and failures of diplomacy can be judged. Diplomacy, however brilliant, is no substitute for policy; and policy (particularly one which stresses its "realistic" character) has to be assessed by its results. Looked upon in this way the policy of *Détente* has very little to show in terms of either promoting Western interests or Western cohesion. Shuttle-diplomacy by Dr Kissinger may be dazzling; but just as it is difficult to see what were the actual results of the peripatetic efforts of General de Gaulle, so it is difficult to see the positive historical consequences of Dr Kissinger's travels to implement his "Grand Design" for the "Structure of

Peace". The epigones of the General try to imitate his foreign policy performance, but *où sont les neiges d'antan?* What happened to the "Grand Design" on "Europe from the Atlantic to the Urals"? What remained as a result of all those diplomatic tours to Russia, Latin America, Canada ("*Vive Quebec libre!*")? Similarly, a comparison of the aims of American policy—as formulated by President Nixon and Secretary Kissinger—shows a striking contrast between promise and fulfilment, between hopes raised and the results obtained.

During the period of the implementation of this policy the balance of power has shifted against the West. Instead of a new "pentagonal balance" we have witnessed the disenchantment, to a smaller or greater degree, of Europe, China and Japan, the three pillars on which the new "structure of peace" was supposed to rest. The American-European relations in particular are worse than ever before in the last half century. What is more, such dangerous symptoms do not elicit sufficient anxiety on either side of the Atlantic to foster initiative to improve the situation. They are smothered by the soothing perspective of *Détente*.

The dangers involved in the present drift in the Atlantic Alliance would suggest that the fundamentals of this policy should be soberly assessed and brought home to the general public. Otherwise no realistic cure for the present ills of the American-European relations can be achieved. Diplomatic or administrative palliatives would not be sufficient to have this particular world restored.

Past and Future

D ÉTENTE is not a modern Soviet invention. Its tactical beginnings are to be found in Lenin's views on Bolshevik strategy and tactics in 1921. Western enthusiasts proclaimed its existence already in Khrushchev's time. But the present policy of *Détente* emerged as a result of a United States initiative, a concomitant to America's reduction of its global commitments. It was conceived as a means which was expected to facilitate American disengagement from its confrontation with the Soviet Union; to permit a policy of balancing between Moscow and Peking (made possible by the resumption of American-Chinese relations); and to promote an increased international rôle for Europe and Japan.

As has been noted, the results of the *Détente* policy in its present form do not conform to its political premises, to its proclaimed purposes, and to the expectations raised with the public at large.

The Soviet Union has deftly turned the tables and used *Détente* to promote its own interests against the interests of the United States and of the Western countries in general, rather than accept *Détente* as a *modus vivendi* leading to a "structure of peace". Western policies were immediately handicapped because of the illusions generated by the Western perception of *Détente* as based on genuine relaxation and reciprocity, while the Soviet Union saw it as an opportunity to lull Western public opinion into a lack of vigilance towards the perils it was facing, to divide the West by exploiting the differences between America and Europe, in short to promote one-sidedly and vigorously its own political and strategic interests.

The experience of *Détente* in action during the period since it was proclaimed is a string of Western disappointments, of political developments which were directly contrary to the hopes of the architects of this policy. There has been since then a general weakening of the Western position strategically, economically and politically.

FIRST OF ALL, *Détente* was presented as promising increased security for the West, i.e. for both America and Europe. The SALT-1 agreement was hailed as a turning point in the arms race. It was seen as a genuinely reciprocal arrangement stabilizing the strategic balance, thereby dispelling American and European anxieties about security. The acceptance of nuclear parity with the Soviet Union was interpreted as a step towards further reciprocal measures of arms control (through supplementary arrangements in SALT-2) rather than a step which put on agenda the possibility of the Soviet Union reaching for military superiority, the American debate about the proper response to it and the highest military budgets in the peacetime history of the two countries. It is not surprising that the Western public fed for years on the optimistic fare of *Détente*, is puzzled and bewildered, and that the West is at a disadvantage in matters of security-spending (Soviet leaders do not have to "sell" it to their public politically). The repeated visits of Kissinger and Nixon to Moscow are not likely to affect this picture in favour of the West, as is now quite clear.

As far as Europe is concerned, the Soviet-supported Middle Eastern war resulting in the Arab oil embargo has struck a heavy blow to the NATO alliance. A combination of the *Détente*-induced complacency and of the most short-sighted economic nationalism has seriously undermined its cohesion. For the first time the prospect of European neutralism as a first step towards the "Finlandization" of Europe has acquired reality. Politically, the Western world has reached such a point of disarray that *Time* Magazine has even referred to "*the West*" as an obsolete concept.

I T IS NOT DIFFICULT to see that the present kind of *Détente* policy has contributed to this outcome. The exaggerated American preoccupation with Soviet exigencies resulted in a neglect of European susceptibilities and the universal hopes generated by *Détente* lowered the Europeans' concern about their security so much that Dr Kissinger's "*Year of Europe*" turned out to be a resounding flop. Later, there was a chain reaction to the treating of

Allies as a nuisance and of enemies as friends. One cannot absolve the Europeans for their vacillations and the short-sightedness of their conduct. During and after the Middle East War the European "Allies" indeed behaved in a most reprehensible and un-allied fashion. The fact remains that American policy instead of strengthening the Atlantic community has only deepened the already existing European malaise and contributed to the weakening of the Alliance.

While the Soviet Union is registering slow and intermittent, but cumulative, political gains and becoming more menacing, the West is bickering. At a time when the internal situation in many Western countries is at its most dismal since the War, when *Détente* has clearly not brought any *quid pro quo* for all the Western concessions made for its sake, when the newly recognized East Germans are already occasionally resuming the tactics of traffic obstruction to Berlin (a problem which *Détente* was supposed to have solved) the picture of political disunity, both within Europe and between Europe and America can only gladden the heart of the Soviet leaders.

The political illusions of *Détente* have certainly contributed to this picture. The Soviet press is gloating with satisfaction over the mess on both sides of the Atlantic, and the Soviet leaders are only too keen to profit by the French-American quarrels. The politics of blackmail, so successfully practised by the Arab countries, may not remain the monopoly of those countries. *Détente* will not preclude its application by the Soviet Union as well, once it feels that it can be used without undue risks. The Watergate paralysis in the United States and the economic beggar-my-neighbour policies of the European states may offer new opportunities to the Soviet Union. Its imperial aggrandizement is predicated on the weakening of the political will of its opponents.

A genuine *Détente* is, of course, most desirable, but in its present form *Détente* proved to be an effective instrument in the process of weakening the West, as it has hidden from it the political and military realities of the situation and lowered the threshold of risks for the Soviet Union. It made possible the presentation in the West of political failures as successes for peace, of businessmen's fantasies about profits as rational enterprises in the interests of the state, of Western military decline as an achievement leading towards strategic stability. It is time for the West to recover its sense of reality if Western civilization is to survive. The Soviet attitude to *Détente*, even in its present form, is not irreversible, it may well one day be followed by a more militant posture as happened before when the Soviet Union decided that the circumstances were ripe for a change of strategy.

I T IS ONLY AS the end product of a well-thought-out and firmly executed policy, supported by public opinion aware of the issues, that a genuine *Détente* may come. It can only be a result of the Soviet recognition of its necessity, and it would certainly be welcome. No one wishes a recurrence of military confrontations which carry with them unforeseen consequences.

However, *Détente* cannot be based on illusions. It must be a two-way street. The Soviet Union must contribute to it by giving some indications that it does not intend cynically to exploit it as an opportunity to improve its ability to subvert and destroy the West. *Détente* will not be genuine as long as "Peaceful Coexistence" is for the Soviet leaders only a euphemism for a conflict by all means short of war.

An evolution of Soviet policy towards a meaningful *Détente* would require its moving away from this position. Among the measures that can be taken as indications of such an evolution in the Soviet Union would be the following points:

(1) Abandoning the "ideological war" against the West.

(2) Decelerating the arms build-up.

(3) Giving up the idea of military superiority in the SALT-2 negotiations.

(4) Providing a proof of a serious approach to *Détente* at the talks on European security by liberalizing the movement of peoples and the flow of ideas.

(5) Stopping the sabotage of the peace efforts in the Middle East.

(6) Discontinuing the supply of arms to the so-called guerrilla movements and desisting from other forms of subversion.

IF NONE OF THESE STEPS is taken, Soviet assurances about *Détente* will remain empty. If, however, some of them are taken, even gradually, it would be an indication of an evolution in the right direction. When all of them begin to be implemented it would be a sign that the Soviet Union is genuinely interested in *Détente* and is prepared to take its place as a responsible member of the community of nations.

(1974)

15. The Question of European Unity

EVER SINCE the First World War, Great Britain has shown symptoms of a marked reluctance to face changes in the international situation. Decisions to meet new challenges affecting her position were made after long delays in the recognition of their true nature. This was the case with the abandonment of the Gold Standard and with the slow acceptance of the need to resist Hitler.

Historically, the change in the international situation amounted to the ending of the Era of European expansion and domination which began in the 16th century. The First World War radically undermined European imperial positions; the Second World War destroyed them completely. European empires everywhere began to crumble. The fact that Britain was one of the victors of the last War did not make much difference to the outcome: the "end of Empire" was part and parcel of the general European contraction. The fate of Great Britain was substantially linked here with that of Europe as a whole—the real question was how she would adjust herself to the post-imperial era.

Since the Second World War the British position in the world balance of power has become immeasurably weaker. Yet the demise of Empire did not make the national inhibition about facing international reality any less pronounced. This was partly due to the luck of the British in avoiding the fate of other European countries during the last War—German occupation—and also to British political wisdom in carrying out the Imperial withdrawal in an orderly fashion. There were thus no traumatic experiences to bring home the full realization of the salient features of the new situation. On the other hand, the British reluctance to join the European community had deep historical roots, reinforcing the attachment to the *status quo* of yesterday and resulting in the politics of nostalgia.

The pattern was not unfamiliar. At first there was the refusal to admit the necessity of choice and then there were delays in making it, so that when the decision about the application to join the Common Market was finally made its implementation became difficult and the price of entry and of adjustment higher than it might have been if the decision about it had been arrived at more promptly.

Britain emerged from the War weakened but because of her stand during her "finest hour" her prestige was higher than ever. Yet when she could have had the leadership of Europe on a plate she was against European involvement. Her post-War foreign policy was based on a cosy rationalization in the form of the "theory of the three concentric circles": the special relationship with America; the hub of the emergent Commonwealth; and cross-Channel connections. When the Common Market was formed Britain did not believe in its success; if she had joined it at the time much of the present discussion about the price of entry would have been irrelevant.

Those who are not in principle against "joining Europe" must surely realize that there were political and economic costs involved in the delays which were due first to the British and then to the French unwillingness to promote the European idea. It would be a pity if now that the governments of the two countries are ready for it, Britain should fail to use this historic opportunity. If it is missed it would involve paying a far higher price than those who concentrate on economic issues are willing to contemplate. They no longer invoke now "the theory of the three concentric circles" but simply engage in *Greuelpropaganda* about the economic price of joining the Common Market and the loss of cultural identity and political sovereignty which it allegedly involves. But they do not put forward any coherent argument about the future over-all orientation of British foreign policy and the premises on which it is to be based.

When Dean Acheson remarked that Britain had lost her empire but had not yet found a new role in the world, he came in for a good deal of criticism in this country. Those who were most upset about it are now opposing the European orientation. But they use only negative terms in the discussion of Britain's position and her prospects. They are not able to provide any positive alternative to joining the Common Market more adequate than "the theory of the three concentric circles". And what has happened to these circles?

THE SPECIAL RELATIONSHIP with America has undergone a steady erosion, not in the sense that the language ties are less important, or that British security (like that of other West European countries) is no longer dependent on the American umbrella, but in the sense that British influence in Washington is now hardly of a special nature, scarcely different from French or German. One does not have to read Harold Wilson's memoirs to know that; for years now it has been little more than a nostalgic myth rooted in the reminiscences of the Churchill–Roosevelt era.

Likewise the evolution of the Commonwealth hardly advanced British influence in the world. Britain faced here a developing situation in which she had political obligations without the corresponding ability to "ride in the whirlwind and direct the storm". Cases like the Central African Federation, South Africa, Rhodesia, Biafra, the Indo-Pakistan war, and the recent internal aggression-cum-genocide in Bengal illustrate the incapacity of the "mother-country" to deal with a number of her Commonwealth children. Even cricket matches, those symbols of the "invisible ties" between the Commonwealth countries, became targets for violent demonstrations. The meetings of Commonwealth Prime Ministers showed increasingly the weakening of political cohesion.

The "third circle"—the European Community—has in the meantime become an economic success. But its political development was sabotaged by de Gaulle's *folie de grandeur*, a policy of empty gestures allegedly promoting *la gloire* but in fact only satisfying de Gaulle's nationalistic ego; it was a compensation for the psychological complexes inherited by France during the War, at the time of *le chagrin et la pitié*.

Now that Pompidou is quietly shedding the Gaullist legacy, the past experience with "the three circles" would strongly indicate that a refusal to join the Common Market might signify for Great Britain a rather unpleasant situation in which she would find herself falling between three stools, two of which are by now two-legged; the stability of the third may depend very much on the British decision to become a member of the Community. If she does, it will contribute not only to the momentum of European unification, but will help to maintain the internal stability and balance of power in the Community.

EVEN MORE IMPORTANT is the growth of Europe as a political factor in the international balance of power. This is imperative if East–West equilibrium is not to be upset by the simultaneous process of growth of American neo-isolationism and increase in Soviet strength. In the last decade the position of the United States as the protector of the West has been seriously undermined by the internal effects of the Viet Nam war and other manifestations of home-front unrest.

The combined psychological effect was the rise of neo-isolationist tendencies on the American political scene. The American "withdrawal symptoms" may not prevail; Senator Mansfield may be less dangerous to European security than alarmist observers fear; but the tendency he represents is bound to have some effect on the American posture in foreign policy and thus on the world balance of power. The American commitments in Europe may be maintained but, as Secretary Connally indicated, the US expects Europe to carry a bigger share of its own defence burden. If the American role in the maintenance of the balance of power is not increasingly supplemented by *the expansion of the role played by Europe*, it is not difficult to imagine the end result of this process: a dangerous vacuum of power in Europe which would, sooner or later, be exploited by the Soviet Union. If Britain joins the Community she may or may not become richer, but she will be in a politically stronger position and would have a better chance of remaining independent. The alternative course may eventually result in the break-up of the European Community. And the Balkanization of Western Europe could be a stage in the subsequent Finlandization of individual West European countries.

Thus, the interests of the West in general, of Europe, and of Great Britain coincide at this point: there is a clear and obvious need to prevent the appearance of a power vacuum in Western Europe which will be, if the present equilibrium in Europe is upset, a step towards a scramble among European nations to make their own separate arrangements with the Soviet Union and open the way to an eventual Soviet hegemony over the whole of Europe and not just one half of it. If the present shift in the balance of power against the West is not halted by the European effort to make up for what Raymond Aron has called "the end of the American era", such catastrophic consequences cannot in the end be excluded.

But even if the European Community does not break up, despite its inability to maintain a momentum by expanding from Six to Ten, what would be the consequences of non-entry for Great Britain herself?

THIS IS A SUBJECT on which the anti-Marketeers prefer not to dwell; but one can imagine the *dénouement* which such a development could entail.

Externally, Britain's prestige would fall; all "three concentric circles" would take her less not more seriously if she did not join. International faith in the future of Britain would slump. Her margin of manoeuvre in foreign policy would shrink still further. Internally her morale would fall: *pauvre Angleterre* would become the continental epithet. Britain might indeed become "the sick man outside Europe".

In such a situation a likely course for British foreign policy would be to seek at any price a close *rapprochement* with the Soviet Union to counteract the effect of past foreign-policy failures. This is a course which would commend itself to a small number of anti-Marketeers, but it is doubtful how many among those for whom Mr Kosygin is not (to use Mr Wilson's expression) "part of the British way of life", will share his euphoria, so artificially generated in his 1971 speech of 17 July, about Mr Brezhnev's Tiflis speech. The great majority of the British people still takes its democratic ideals and institutions sufficiently seriously to be less enthusiastic than Harold Wilson about the London–Tiflis axis. Mr Wilson's reference in the same speech to President Nixon's visit to Peking as opening up "new hopes, immeasurable horizons" (in contrast to the "aridities and infertilities of the Cold War" language of Mr Heath's pro-European policy) was clearly designed to please the "progressive" Left at the Labour Party conference. What Mr Wilson did not mention on the occasion was that while Soviet propaganda decried the White Paper as the continuation of "Cold War" (as it always denounced anything leading to the growth of West European unity), Chinese propaganda has shown a positive interest in the process of European integration. According to the official Hsinhua Agency, British entry would constitute an embarrassment to the "dual hegemony" of the USA and the USSR. That the Soviet Union would try to prevent facing the Chinese colossus in the East and a unified Western Europe in the West is only too natural. Is there any reason, however, for Britain to help such Soviet policy? And to be on the side of the Soviet Union against Western Europe?[1]

Yet in the long run this is a likely outcome of the attitude of "splendid isolation" in 1971. As past experience has shown, this attitude was not a wise one when Britain was still a great power. It is even less realistic in a world where, having lost that status, she can easily move from the position of an intermediate to that of a small power. The Beaverbrook press provided a shining example of such an attitude. The *Daily Express*, in its anti-European crusade, did not even realize the ironic incongruity between its imperial nostalgia and its reporting of current political events. For instance on one and the same editorial page of its issue of 17 June it announced that Mr Heath should "forget about Europe" and complained in a big headline "Now MALTA PLANS TO GIVE BRITAIN THE BOOT."

THE ANTI-MARKETEERS avoid facing post-War realities and especially the political limitations inherent in the diminishing stature of Britain, Europe and the West in the international balance of power. They prefer instead to concentrate on the narrow economic issues of today, frightening the British housewife with the prospect of rising food prices (and at a time when they have already been rising steadily here without British participation in the Common Market).

Perhaps the most astonishing feature of the Common Market debate is its concentration on economics. It is of course an important factor; but historic decisions of this kind must ultimately be made on political grounds. Nor must one forget that economic forecasting is something less than an exact science.

The arguments of the most formidable spokesman of the anti-Market case, Professor Nicholas Kaldor, suffer from that most common deficiency among professional economists, the lack of political perspective; they may also be economically unsound. In his contribution to a 1963 *Encounter* Symposium, Professor Kaldor predicted that the decision to join would make Britain a "depressed area", a fate to be avoided by "a comprehensive policy of

---

[1] The Left-wing *Le Nouvel Observateur* (19 July) wrote that China:

"was furiously hostile to the 'European' policy dreamt of by General de Gaulle, 'from Atlantic to the Urals', which could result in the increase of Soviet power. The same motive accounts for the surprised French, Canadian, and Italian diplomats hearing their Chinese counterparts approve the entry of Great Britain into the Common Market. . . ."

Similarly, the correspondent of *France-Soir* in Peking, Maurice Delarue, wrote that:

"the Chinese now even support European unity, because they consider it a counter-balance to the hegemony of the super-powers, and approve the expected British entry into the European Community."

vigorous economic planning" in association with the Commonwealth (which he thought was "gaining strength"). Subsequently, Professor Kaldor had a chance to advise the British government on how to implement "a comprehensive policy of vigorous economic planning" (just as previously he had had a chance to advise many underdeveloped countries on their economic policies).

But somehow the "white heat" of Mr Wilson's "technological revolution" failed to achieve economic growth comparable to that of the Common Market, and British economic decline followed the previous (and subsequent) pattern. It is, of course, perfectly possible that it will continue even if Britain joins the Common Market. The pro-Marketeers advertise the rise in Common Market real wages in contrast to what has happened in Britain. Yet it is clear that even if the immediate effect of joining and the price of adjustment are not very drastic, they would obviously involve a transitional period of economic dislocation before the more positive economic effect of the Common Market *Grossraumwirtschaft* can accrue to British industry. Whether the latter will actually rise to the challenge or not obviously does not depend on economic factors alone. Opinions, hopes, and fears here go beyond the strictly economic field.

It is embarrassing that one has to repeat such elementary truths because economists tend to forget that real social psychology is more complicated than is implied in the simplified assumptions of economic analysts. But Professor Kaldor, whose advice to the under-developed countries was so often followed by riotous outburst when his policies were implemented, should be aware of the pitfalls of economic analysis divorced from a sound political perspective. Keynes wrote "The Economic Consequences of Mr Churchill" when the latter failed to realize the implications of clinging to the old Gold Standard in a new situation. Someone will surely write with equal sharpness on "The Political Consequences of Professor Kaldor" if Britain fails to join the Common Market.

How politically naive Professor Kaldor is can be seen from his reply in the *New Statesman* (16 July) to the argument used in the White Paper on the Common Market that it is not really possible to make valid numerical estimates of some economic factors on which the anti-Marketeers dwell:

> "If the government persists in saying that no such estimation is possible, how can they say, in the same breath (para 56) that 'the government are confident that membership of the enlarged Community will lead to much improved efficiency and productivity in British industry, with a higher rate of investment and a faster growth of real wages'? If nothing can be estimated or 'quantified', where does this confidence come from?"

How touchingly simple-minded is the political perception of a distinguished economist! It assumes that political confidence can only come from quantifying the unquantifiable rather than from a wider understanding of politics and history. It is baffled by an approach which, while taking into account the best economic estimates wherever they are possible, refuses to fall into a semantic trap—namely, the naive behaviouristic reductionism of the "dismal science" and the "quantification lunacy" of some of its practitioners.

IN MY VIEW of the general debate, it is the underlying political attitudes of both pro- and anti-Market experts which determine their opinions and not their expertise.

The element of rationalization and/or of tactical hypocrisy was extremely obvious in this debate, where many Parliamentarians pretended that they were "waiting for the final terms" from Luxembourg and Brussels before they could make up their minds, although it is perfectly clear that in fact they have made up their minds on other grounds. And *rightly so*—because the issues transcend the marginalia of the final agreement. As the young participant in the *Guardian*'s "Young Eyes on Europe" wrote: "Maybe in 50 years' time my children will say that being a European is more natural than being a Briton. At any rate they will have completely forgotten if our butter in the 1980s was expensive. . . ."

The Common Market debate has been particularly striking not because the two major parties were divided, but because it united the extremes. Not since the Stalin–Hitler pact have we seen such strange bed-fellows uniting in a common cause. For both John Gollan and Enoch Powell "going into Europe" is a "sell-out". The League of Empire Loyalists and the Communist Party joined hands to denounce the iniquities of the Europeans. For the *Spectator* and the *New Statesman* neither Wogs nor Capitalists begin at Calais; but the arguments used in these two journals to oppose entry were often not too far from this level. For example, Mr Peter Shore, in what he believes to be the best form of his socialist conscience, remarked in the *New Statesman* that the benefits from the Community's agricultural budget which will accrue to Britain are small, because they "*will be focussed on the miserably poor peasant farmers of Southern Italy and France. . . .*" But his socialist heart weeps for the plight of the New Zealand farmers! It was also in the *New Statesman* that its ex-editor, Paul Johnson, tried to trace the anti-European genealogy in Britain as far back as the first anti-marketeer, Ethelred the Unready.

Was the *Spectator* any better? In its Conservative post-imperial pique it put forward a common platform with the new jingoism of "Little Englanders" from the Labour Left. Like Enoch Powell himself, it was now *against* all "the three circles", combining colour prejudice with anti-Americanism and anti-Europeanism. It thundered editorially (5 June) against "the European-Europe fanatics" and said in hysterical exaggeration that if they "get their way . . . we will then have no need of policies of our own or any means with which they might be implemented". It has even discovered (eight years after the French veto) that it is the French who are luring the English into Europe!

IT IS AMUSING to recall that the present attitude of *The Spectator* was expressed 14 years ago in similar form by the Gaullist deputy in the French parliament, Leo Hamon: "The [Rome] Treaty strips France of her personality, deprives her of a way of life which, as the country will see when it returns to its senses, is being sacrificed for a mirage." Today M. Hamon, as the official spokesman of the present French government, has changed his tune, in line with that of M. Pompidou. *The Spectator*, however, has gone on repeating his old arguments about the "loss of sovereignty" and the "diminution of national identity" which will be sacrificed for a mirage. What unreliable tunesmiths!

In the Common Market countries the polemics of yesterday are forgotten. The experience of the progress of the European Community has rendered the arguments of its opponents quite obsolete. But it is worth recalling that the same pattern of an unholy alliance of the reactionary Left and the nostalgic Right was very much present in the political struggles about the formation of the Common Market in the countries of its six would-be members. As Richard Mayne reminded us in *The Listener* (24 June 1971):

> "its fiercest opponents—like the fiercest anti-Marketeers now—came from the outer fringes of Left and Right. The extreme Right, in Italy Monarchist and Neo-Fascist, attacked the proposed merger of national sovereignty; the communists opposed what they called German rearmament, meaning German contingents in a European army."

In France, the Gaullists voted against the ratification of the Rome Treaty, as did the Right-wing Refugee Party in Germany, the Flemish nationalists in Belgium, and the Right-wing Protestants in Holland. Not to mention the Communists in all these countries.

It is also pertinent to recall that socialists in Western Europe favoured British entry all along, and that at their meeting in Brussels (28 June) they greeted with enthusiasm the prospect that it might now be accomplished. Yet the socialist *Tribune* disregarded such expressions of socialist solidarity and castigated the pro-European attitude of the Labour pro-Marketeers as "phoney internationalism".

The pro-Marketeer Labour leaders (some of whom signed the *Times* pro-European manifesto, but who changed statesmanship for New Statesmanship) were no less dazzling in looking for intellectual excuses for their political contortionism. Few could take their sophistries seriously, and it is likely that they only succeeded in discrediting themselves. Of all the arguments used in the Great Debate theirs were the most pitiful, with their Janus-like duality of declared pro-Europeanism in theory and anti-

Europeanism in practice. In comparison with their belated turn-coating, the celebrated "double-crossmanship" of the editor of the *New Statesman*, however incompatible with the stand of the Labour government in power (in which he was a Minister), seemed a shining example of political forthrightness. Intellectually, their search for an alibi, after they had overcome the inhibitions on their European commitment ("To rat or not to rat, that is the question"), could not be taken seriously. It was too obviously another example of a blatant (and short-sighted) political opportunism. It reminded Harold Macmillan of the attitude of their predecessors in the 1930s: "They were in favour of rearmament—*but not under Chamberlain.*"

No less amusing was the campaign in *Tribune* on "the Common Market pedigree" in which its editor and several left-wing Labour MPs denounced it as a capitalist "baited trap", a big-business enterprise "born out of the Cold War", only to appear on one advertisement page of *The Times* as the signatories of an anti-Market manifesto together with several right-wing Tory MPs whom they considered as their most reactionary opponents.

But perhaps the most strange combination produced by the political opposition to British entry into the Common Market was that of the Soviet Party Secretary and some Sovietological experts. While Mr Brezhnev opposed the move and the Communist parties mobilized their forces to denounce what the *Morning Star* called "HEATH'S 'NOBLE IDEAL'—A SIX SELL-OUT", Tibor Szamuely wrote in the *Spectator* (2 January) that "today, with Brandt's *Ostpolitik* in full swing, the EEC might actually be quite useful to Russia" and that "there is always a strong chance that the British Government will drag the country into an increasingly neutralist, even pro-Soviet Europe".

Yet the trophy for originality must surely go to A. J. P. Taylor, who with a fine historical sense wrote in the *Encounter* symposium that "entry into Europe is the greatest non-question of all time". The historical imagination shown here about an issue which for so many seems (in George Ball's words) one of "the most important decisions of the century" truly equals that demonstrated in Mr Taylor's evaluation of Hitler and the non-question of his primary contribution to the causes of the Second World War.[2]

---

[2] Mr Kenneth Tynan must also be given a dunce's cap. He defined the European Common Market (in a letter to *The Times*, 27 July) as "the most blatant historical vulgarity since Hitler's Thousand Year Reich".

The creator of *O Calcutta!* was afraid that "going into Europe" would preclude socialism in Britain. It is surprising that he is not interested in international intercourse and wants only to promote "socialism in one country". Is it only in Britain that there should be no exploitation of man by man (or *vice versa*)? In any case, surely, he is not exactly the person who can be taken as an arbiter of taste and a scourge of vulgarity.

Nor can Tynan who supported Rolf Hochhuth's slanderous fantasy that Winston Churchill had ordered General Sikorski's death (he argued that, in his eyes, this only increased Churchill's stature!) be considered a particularly well-qualified public figure to give lessons in political morality.

IF THE CURRENT SYMPOSIUM in *Encounter* (and that of 1963) shows anything, it is that intellectuals tend to reflect the mood of the country in general. Judging by some contributions, the main difference between the pro-Marketeers and anti-Marketeers is the degree of their indifference towards Europe. But political sophistication is not to be confused with political wisdom. Between 1963 and the present, British public opinion shifted against the Common Market; if it reacts in favour, the attitude of some wavering British intellectuals will probably also change accordingly. George Ball wrote (*Newsweek*, 14 June) that:

> "with chagrin at prior rejection combined with the loss of momentum, many in Britain have now grown hesitant, not out of delusions of power but fear of weakness—the sense that they may be swallowed up by an alien entity larger than themselves—a fear that seems strangely out of character for a people who have struggled so bravely and overcome so much."

The Spectator (5 June) illustrated this attitude perfectly:

> "The alternative is the continued existence of the nation with its own identity, its own institutions, its own sovereign Parliament, and the ability independently to pursue to the best of its abilities the policies which best fit its own interests as from time to time its own electorate determines."

But such "ability independently to pursue" is rooted in illusions which the electorate will share only as long as the anti-Marketeers succeed in playing on its most obscurantist prejudices and its nostalgia for the past, as well as in identifying the cause of European unification with the idea of "rising food prices", ignoring the causes of the present inflation in Britain. British entry into the Common Market is not, of course, a sufficient condition for the unification of Europe. Few serious pro-Europeans are utopian or euphoric about it. Given the complacency of the public about the problems of European defence and other difficulties, one can easily predict that British entry will be followed by a series of internal tensions within the enlarged Community. But it will still be a step in the right direction. What is at stake is the future not only of Britain but of the European civilization of which she forms an important part.

SINCE THE FIRST WORLD WAR, we have known (in the celebrated phrase of Paul Valéry) that civilizations are mortal. But there is nothing automatic about it, just as there is nothing inevitable about "post-imperial decline". Historical alternatives do exist. Professor Hugh Trevor-Roper has drawn our attention to previous cases of the "recovery of Europe" in history, and there is no reason why it should not happen again.

In the 17th century it was only Spain which failed to adjust itself to the new situation. While other West European countries overcame the severe economic and political crisis and successfully developed new intellectual and scientific ideas, economic techniques, and administrative arrangements, the Spanish Depression of the 17th century resulted not only in the decline of the Spanish empire and the renewed isolation of Spain from Europe, but in a long epoch of intellectual inertia and political and economic stagnation. As an historian of the period put it, the reason for this failure was the

> "unredeemed mediocrity of the Castilian ruling class at a moment when the highest gifts of statesmanship were required. [It] lacked the breadth of vision and the strength of character to break with a past that could no longer serve as a reliable guide to the future . . . At a time when the face of Europe was altering more rapidly than ever before, the country that had once been its leading power proved to be lacking the essential ingredient for survival—the willingness to change."[3]

The failure to adjust itself to the new reality and to create a modern centralized state which was then needed was partly due to the unwillingness of the Spaniards to draw on experience abroad. This had its roots in the hostility to values and ideas in the heretical part of Europe (to which there is no parallel in the present circumstances). It would be doubly ironic if the situation faced by present-day Britain should make it necessary for some future historian to write similar words about 20th-century Britain's failure to adjust through unwillingness to change.

THE QUESTION OF "readjustment" is of course different for 20th-century Britain than for 17th-century Spain; but still it is a problem of change. Productivity and scientific-technological progress are now such dynamic problems in comparison with the relatively static agricultural economies in the past that it is unlikely that, even if Britain were not to enter the Common Market, the detrimental effects would be as long-lasting as those which followed the Spanish failure in the 17th century. Yet as *The Economist* (10 July) stressed, the economic consequences of non-entry may be serious for a country so dependent on international trade as Great Britain:

> "At the time of France's first veto in 1963, Britain's leading technological firm was Rolls-Royce. The failure to enter Europe in 1963 doomed it to trying to live on penny packets of orders throughout the next decade. When the opportunity for a big order came at last, it felt

---

[3] J. H. Elliot, *Imperial Spain*, 1469–1716 (1963).

that it had to seize it, even for a risky product on the most disadvantageous terms. If we do not enter Europe, it can be prophesied with sickening assurance that Rolls-Royce's fate is only too liable in the 1970s to overtake our remaining major computer manufacturer, our remaining stake in major aircraft and aerospace manufacture, and that other British technological leaders will slowly relapse towards the lower range of their capabilities (so that ICI will become more of a paint firm, and less of a trail-blazer of chemical revolution). In America, Japan, and Western Europe the growth industries of the next two decades are going to be, first, the knowledge-based industries, springing up through this computer age; and, secondly, the producers of urban systems and pioneers of urban development. . . . A Britain that stays outside Europe's potential market of 290 million people will miss this tide, just as it missed the last one. . . . These are the probable realities of the economic threats before us, or at any rate before our children. They are at least more likely than it would have seemed in 1958 to say that we would have fallen by now to an urban Italian's standard of life. Any anti-European politician . . . who talks instead of the danger of ½ per cent on the annual cost of living index, or about New Zealand cheese, or about Caribbean sugar, will be seen, in history, as the most inconsequential ass. . . ."

The loss of the Mediterranean and American trade contributed significantly to the decline of 17th-century Spain. This time it is not a question of the ethnocentric, narrow-minded Spanish grandees despising manual labour and mercantile motives, but the stick-in-the-mud insularity of so many British trade-unionists which is a threat to foreign trade prospects and which lessens the nation's capacity to adapt itself to new circumstances and situations. Their real objection to going into Europe has nothing to do with the actual terms of entry, but like that of their Tory anti-Marketeer counterparts, is rooted in their conservatism, ignorance, and xenophobia. It is rationalized in "socialist" and "progressive" language, but it provides the ground on which the two meet, an auspicious ground for the fossilized mentalities of a Douglas Jay and of a Gerald Nabarro.

THE POST-WAR CHANGE in the international situation in which European countries were no longer able to play an important or even independent role in world politics led to the emergence of the "European idea". The initial step in its implementation was the formation of the Europe of Six. It provided a prospect that European countries might eventually reach a position from which they could influence historical developments and not merely be the objects of the antagonisms and agreements of the Super-Powers.

Now that the waning of American influence increases the uncertainty about American protection—now that the bi-polar world of the two Super-Powers is slowly giving way to a multilateral balance of power in the world—now that it is clear (even without President Nixon's visit to Peking) that China and Japan will sooner or later play a major role in it, it is no less obvious that individual European countries will not be able to play any such role.

If they want to have any say in the decisions which will in future influence their interests and their destinies—and ultimately the fate of European civilization itself—they have to pool their resources economically and politically by voluntarily sharing their sovereignties in a world where the sovereignty of a small country often equals its impotence. It was after all, as George Thomson, the unfortunate Labour spokesman for Europe, wrote in *The World Today* (July 1971), the bitter practical experience of the limitations of British power in the modern world, suffered by successive British governments, which led both the Tory and Labour governments to apply for membership of the Common Market. Or, as *The Times* (8 July) put it:

> "Ever since the War—and one could certainly trace the process back further than that—the situation of Britain has been one of narrowing opportunity. In the words of the White Paper the decision against entry would signify that 'in a single generation we should have renounced an imperial past and rejected a European future'. This, as *The Times* rightly said, 'would be a sort of suicide, a turning away from the challenge of life and a withdrawal into the supposed security of *rigor mortis*. . . .'"

Even if this remark has to be taken only metaphorically, there seems little doubt that such a course would contribute to a further decline of Great Britain. The role it would at long last have found would be to become the "backwater of Europe".

Are there pains in readjustment? They are likely to be far less severe than the pains of non-adjustment. The former will be temporary, the latter permanent. And, in the long run, the chances of the recovery of Europe (and not only of its Western part) depend on the successful accomplishment of the process of renaissance where, and when, it appears possible.

(1971)

16. On Literature & Revolution

The Destiny of Writers in
Revolutionary Movements

"THE Great October Socialist Revolution had a decisive influence on
world literature . . ."—thus begins an authoritative book on the
subject published by the Soviet Academy of Sciences.[1] The claim echoes
Trotsky's prophecy in his *Literature and Revolution*: "The art of this epoch will
be entirely under the influence of revolution." The year was 1924. Trotsky
characterized revolutionary art as having "a limitless faith in the future" and
ended his book predicting that

> "man will become immeasurably stronger, wiser, and subtler. . . . The
> average human type will rise to the height of an Aristotle, a Goethe, or a
> Marx. And above this ridge, new peaks will rise."

Since this was written there have been rather ample opportunities to
observe the influence of revolution on art and literature. We are still some
way to Trotsky's ridge. "The average human type" in post-revolutionary
society has not yet reached the height of an Aristotle or a Goethe, not even the
average member of Brezhnev's Politbureau. But it is already possible to see
the pattern in the encounter of literature and revolution. It emerges from the
comparison of their confrontation in different countries and provides an
insight into the nature of our epoch; or perhaps even into the question of the
human condition itself.

What is the basis of the revolutionary appeal to writers? what is their fate
after the revolution? what happens to their hopes and fears? how does the
revolutionary experience affect their attitudes? what happens to literature as a
result? And finally, how does the revolutionary idea itself change? These are
the questions to be studied in the comparative context of various revolutions
if the cultural implications of contemporary revolutionary longings are to be
seen in historical perspective and their probable outcome on future occasions
assessed.

THE INVOLVEMENT OF WRITERS in revolutionary movements is
parts of a wider problem of the intellectual in politics. Until modern
times an intellectual could have a direct effect on it only as an adviser to the
prince, and how frustrating that was, Aristotle and Ibn Khaldun, Machiavelli
and Sir Thomas More can testify. Indeed, it inspired the latter to write his

---

[1] A. I. Puzikov, V. P. Shcherbina, Ya. E. Elsberg, *Velikii Oktyabr i Mirovaya Literatura*
(Moscow, 1967).

Utopia. As he confessed in his letter to Erasmus, in his dreams of an ideal society he imagined himself "in the part of a sovereign of Utopia".[2]

Thus at the very beginning of modern times, when, emerging from the religious ages, the ancient dream of paradise is brought to earth,[3] one sees the intellectual inspiration of the utopian tradition in the twin sources of schematic idealism and political frustration. (John Milton, who was involved in a revolution, wrote in *Paradise Lost* that it is "better to reign in Hell than serve in Heaven".) It was, however, only the emergence of the phenomenon of the intelligentsia which brought utopian thought and the revolutionary idea together. The old mythological and religious ideas—the myth of redemption, millenarianism and chiliasm—were now transformed into a secular gnosis: the idea of a perfect society through violent change. When the gate to the now secularized Heavenly City is forced, history will begin anew through the total reconstruction of social relations on just and rational lines. The persistence of the notions of an ideal enclave and of salvation in all their historical metamorphoses is so striking that it clearly corresponds to enduring human psychological traits and not just to changing social needs. They also, of course, depend on historical conditions and on the existence of social categories to which they have a special appeal and which act as vehicles for their dissemination.

Intelligentsia is such a category. Its character and evolution were different in different countries and therefore it means different things in different contexts. But despite the difficulties with its definition, it is one of the concepts[4]—like populism or romanticism—which one cannot do without.

The internal differentiation of the intelligentsia at various times and places had a marked influence on the attitude of writers towards the revolutionary idea. The classical case is, of course, that of the Russian intelligentsia, which evolved from the stage when it was dominated by the populist (or even nihilist) toughmindedness of the *raznochintsy* to the post-*Vekhi* period of professionalization and the shift from social and political to cultural and aesthetic interests of the literary Silver Age before the First World War. The writers who were still committed to the revolutionary idea—and they were a minority—reflected a split among the intelligentsia. But even among them, the author of the symbolic *Burevestnik*, the "stormy petrel of the revolution", Maxim Gorky, was responding to the shift in the mood of the intelligentsia. When the long-awaited revolution finally came, this life-long friend of Lenin

---

[2] Quoted by Melvin J. Lasky in his book on *Utopia and Revolution*.

[3] The world "paradise" derives from the Old Persian *pairidaera*, denoting an enclosed park or orchard. Cf. John Armstrong, *The Paradise Myth* (London, 1969); also Frank E. and Fritzie P. Manuel, "Sketch for a Natural History of Paradise", in *Daedalus* (Winter 1972), pp. 83–128.

[4] It was first used in Russia in the 1860s and for a long time was considered a *sui generis* Russian phenomenon. Later it was applied to other undeveloped countries; nowadays it is applied also to industrial and "post-industrial" countries.

wrote his *Untimely Thoughts* (1917–18), which were so critical of Bolshevik revolutionary practice of terror and censorship.

THE SOCIAL PRECURSORS of the literary and professional intelligentsia had already appeared in politics before the French Revolution as the *philosophes* and the Physiocrats. They were reformists, not revolutionaries.

It was Rousseau with his abstract idea of absolute popular sovereignty (including the right to regicide) who was the literary precursor of revolution. He is the archetype of what has today become the stereotype of the "alienated intellectual". His revolutionary fantasies strongly resemble the ideological rationalizations of later revolutionary longings, rationalizations which were formulated by and which appealed to subsequent generations of political *literati* (who were, naturally, using the idiom appropriate to their age and its *Zeitgeist*). There is already in Rousseau the idea of alienation malevolently imposed by contemporary society. Lost happiness and lost virtue result from *l'homme naturel* becoming *l'homme civil*.

Both Stirner and Marcuse are of course direct descendants of Rousseau. There is the elitist concept of the enlightened revolutionary vanguard which presaged all the populist and Marxist dreams of the 19th and 20th centuries:

> "How can a blind multitude, which often does not know what it wills, because it rarely knows what is good for it, carry out for itself as great and difficult an enterprise as a system of legislature?"

This can be done only by a Legislator, "the engineer who makes the machine". One can already see here Robespierre waiting in the wings to enthrone the Goddess of Reason as a Supreme Being in Notre Dame, and to rule by terror to force people to be free. Even the geographical projection of Utopia already exists in Rousseau (not yet in Sir Thomas More). *Le noble sauvage* really exists; and, although the Encyclopaedists were sceptical about utopian writings, the contemporary "intelligentsia" was looking for him in Bougainville and other exotic places with the same positivistic curiosity as our contemporary true believers making pilgrimages to their own Utopian locations: Moscow, Peking, or Havana.

The *philosophes* of the Enlightenment with their liberal ideas of education and their moderate, if naive, notions of reason in politics were not yet true devotees of Revolution. They were all dead by the time it came (with the exception of Condorcet); but like Condorcet, they would probably have fallen victims of the Terror if they had still been alive. They had been too influenced by Locke, by the example of British constitutionalism, and by Voltairean scepticism to accept Rousseau in practice, when they had not accepted him in theory. And yet (as Coleridge had noticed) there was "a natural affinity" between their philosophy and despotism "notwithstanding their proud pretensions as the emancipators of the human race". By the time the Revolution came (and the Goncourts wrote that it began in the *salons* attended by the *philosophes*), it was a different part of the intelligentsia which played the predominant role in it: the provincial lawyers (like Robespierre), the self-educated adventurers (like Marat), the clerks, the *roturiers*. . . .

And the stage was set for the first enactment of this tragi-comedy of errors which is periodically provided by the confrontation between the theories of political *littérateurs* and revolutionary practice. The writers (though not always literature) are its frequent victims. Those among them who embraced the revolutionary myth of salvation often suffered the pangs of disillusion—which does not preclude subsequent generations of literary intelligentsia from being again attracted by the revolutionary idea, as moths are attracted by flame. It is true that more recently many such writers have preferred to worship this idea at a safe distance. But it is a fact attested by history that, like the rest of humanity, writers are not necessarily discouraged by unrequited love; and, like the rest of humanity, they are moved by passion and myth rather than by reason and historical experience.

WHEN CONDORCET WAS in hiding during the Terror, he wrote his celebrated *Sketch of the Progress of the Human Spirit* in which he asserted (like Trotsky) that "the perfectibility of man is absolutely infinite", it has no limits, and "the present state of knowledge assures us that the new era will be happy". Condorcet wrote these words in March 1794. Exactly three weeks later he was arrested and took poison to avoid the guillotine. Trotsky had 15 years to live before the ice-pick of Stalin's assassin reached his brain, confirming his 1924 prediction in *Literature and Revolution* that "life in the future will not be monotonous", rather than his prophecy there about the perfectibility of man.

For *belles-lettres* the period of the French Revolution and the Napoleonic era were barren. Trotsky explained this in *Literature and Revolution* as being due to the fact that Frenchmen were busy making the revolution, a somewhat lame explanation. What happened was that many writers went into exile, and not a few of those who remained feared for their lives. Not all of them could say like Sièyes, "*J'ai vécu*", when it was over. During the Terror, the poet Camille Desmoulins, Robespierre's friend, was executed;[5] and so was another poet, the most notable of his generation, André Chénier. The literary historian, P. E. Charvet, remarks that "emigration as an inevitable concomitant of the revolution was to have important and valuable consequences for French literature".[6]

During the Napoleonic era *l'esprit Voltairien* and the liberal spirit of Montesquieu vegetated in the *Institut*—subject to the despotic police controls exercised by Fouché on behalf of the Emperor who introduced stringent

---

[5] Robespierre, who as a young lawyer denounced capital punishment, refused a plea for mercy from Camille Desmoulins' friends. He was then approaching the time of his own execution.

[6] *A Literary History of France* (London, 1967), Vol. IV, p. 32.

censorship and who contemptuously called the liberal intellectuals, *metaphysiciens nebuleux* or *idéologues*. Madame de Staël was banned from Paris; her *De l'Allemagne* was prevented by the censor from appearing; she was placed under police supervision, and eventually escaped abroad. Benjamin Constant was in constant opposition to Napoleon and moved to Germany during the last phase of his reign. He published his masterpiece, *Adolphe*, only in 1819 (although he had written it in 1806). It was only after the fall of Napoleon that French literature flourished again, with Chateaubriand and Hugo, Lamartine and Vigny, Stendhal and Mérimée.

THE FRENCH REVOLUTION HAD a powerful effect on writers abroad. It aroused at first a considerable sympathy among them, but later their enthusiasm waned and in many cases turned into positive disillusion. The Revolution was seen as the champion of the suffering and the weak, of the poor and the oppressed, providing new hope for the downtrodden and for the whole of humanity. It was to introduce the rule of reason and equality.

> *Bliss was it in that dawn to be alive,*
> *But to be young was very Heaven!*

Wordsworth explained what made him so enthusiastic:

> *The attraction of a country in romance!*
> *Where Reason seemed the most to assert her rights . . .*

But soon came the "disappointment sore" when Wordsworth discovered that revolutionaries became "oppressors in their turn", a familiar reflection which will echo down the ages with every subsequent "God-that-failed". Coleridge, who also originally embraced the revolutionary idea, wrote in bitter disillusion:

> *Slaves by their own compulsion! In mad game*
> *They burst their manacles and wear the name*
> *of Freedom graven on a heavier chain!*

Goethe, Kant, Beethoven, all were disappointed. Goya summed it up: "The dream of Reason produces monsters," and the observation became a *leitmotif* with disillusioned writers. Hölderlin wrote that "What has always made the state a hell on earth has been precisely that man has tried to make it his heaven." Later on Dostoyevsky, having abandoned his youthful revolutionary beliefs, in his reaction against the revolutionary nihilism of *Nechaevshchina*, echoed the theme: "The policy which starts with unlimited liberty ends with unlimited despotism." The sentiment has been expressed again and again by many writers down to our own days.

In France after the Restoration literature reflected a disappointment with the world, a disenchantment with the revolutionary idea. The early phase of

French romanticism was a delayed reaction against the Enlightenment's belief in Reason and in the infinite perfectibility of man. With the passage of time, the memory of the September Massacres, and the Terror—the transformation of pure Reason into the fanaticism of revolutionary practical reason, and the aggressive militarism of the Napoleonic era—all faded; and they no longer inhibited the imagination of writers as they had done earlier.

In the 1830s romanticism acquires a revolutionary connotation in France and elsewhere. In France the revolutionary myth thrives on the identification of patriotism with revolution. It is the fiery rhetoric of Saint-Just and Danton, the pathos of the revolution as a theatre, Valmy and the glories of French arms under the Emperor, that appeal to the defeated nation and its writers. The son of a Napoleonic general, Victor Hugo, reflects this evolution.

The scepticism of de Tocqueville was to be appreciated only in the future. He was the first thinker who understood that a revolutionary movement transforms religious belief into a political belief but retains the basic characteristics of the former; that it shares with religious movements a dogmatic fanaticism although its faith is not transcendent. But in the 1840s the hope and the despair again became absolute and took an exclusively political form. Revolutionary secret societies deriving from Babeuf's and Buonarotti's *Conspiracy of the Equals* develop in a society which has a large reservoir of marginal men, of the ambitious but frustrated would-be intellectuals, of Julien Sorels and Rastignacs who have little chance "to take possession of Paris". The revolutionary idea is being embraced again—Marx and Engels study "the French revolutionary tradition".

AFTER THE FAILURE of *Les Trois Glorieuses* the pendulum swings again. Baudelaire regrets his revolutionary "intoxication" and so does Flaubert (whose *Éducation Sentimentale* was read with special pleasure by the middle-aged during the *événements* of May 1968). After the heady "June Days" of 1848 and the *coup d'état* of 1851 French writers moved away from the revolutionary "intoxication". For Baudelaire the vision of a rational Utopia is an inverted reflection of the terrestrial paradise. The Utopians, "the entrepreneurs of public happiness", are frauds who engage in the manipulation of man in the name of fiction. In his *Le Poème du Haschisch* Baudelaire ironically remarks that "Jean-Jacques [Rousseau] had drugged himself without hashish. . . ."

In the historical vicissitudes of the romance between Literature and Revolution in France the most illustrious among its contemporary *amoureux*, Jean-Paul Sartre, strikes at both Baudelaire and Flaubert with particular passion. In his books on them he dismisses Baudelaire as a mere rebel, who unlike the real revolutionary does not want to change the world, and Flaubert as a bourgeois intellectual who "despite his efforts to view the world as an

aristocrat" retains "a bourgeois view of the bourgeoisie". In Sartre
revolutionary optimism is now slightly dimmed, but it still shines forth:

> "Will the human condition be cleansed of exploitation, alienation, and
> all that is disgusting in this society? I'm not so sure. . . . Historians
> claim revolutionaries never know where or when to stop. But it is the
> contrary. They always do stop, so that the next generation of
> revolutionaries has felt obliged to go after the previous generation. . . .
> Perhaps it would be better if for once a revolutionary movement was
> ready and willing to go all the way." (*N.Y. Times Magazine*, 17 October
> 1971.)

Nothing can express more neatly the revolutionary commitment to Utopia
after so many disappointments: he, Sartre, is not certain that it can be
achieved in the future. But he blames previous revolutionaries for having
failed to achieve it in the past by not going "all the way" (whatever that can
mean in the context of Sartre's expressed preference for "a revolution
without terror").

With the French Revolution it was still possible to use the argument of its
Scottish fellow-traveller (who later became disillusioned), Sir James
Mackintosh, who was impressed in 1791 by "its unexampled mildness and
the small number of individuals crushed in the fall of so vast a pile". With the
Russian Revolution it is not possible to use such arguments (the number of
victims of the French Terror was 20 thousand, of the Soviet Great Terror—20
million). So the rationalization moved to the more callous: "You can't make
an omelette without breaking eggs." But the end, Utopia—and the means,
Revolution—remained the guiding stars of the intellectuals and writers
looking for historical shortcuts and total solutions.

The Pilgrims to Moscow

OUR OWN revolutionary epoch provides striking illustrations of the
relationship between Literature and Revolution and of the destinies of
writers caught in between.

On the most general plane there is an ironical contrast between the
mortality rates of pro-revolutionary artists and writers under revolutionary
and non-revolutionary régimes. Paradoxically, one can almost say that for
them a natural death is natural only in the non-revolutionary régimes. If this
appears somewhat exaggerated it is certainly wholly true that as a rule they,
and other writers, enjoy far greater creative freedom in pre-revolutionary
than in post-revolutionary societies. The point is rather obvious; the cases of
the last two Nobel Prize winners for literature, Solzhenitsyn and Neruda, are
symbolic in this respect; or one can mention Brecht; or Picasso, who joined
the French Communist Party in 1945, but whose "formalist" paintings still

cannot be seen in the Soviet Union.[7] And there is of course a legion of other examples.

It is, therefore, not surprising that many writers who fervently believed that on their Moscow pilgrimages they "saw the future and it works" were not inclined to settle in their dreamland when they were faced with the choice.

When Lion Feuchtwanger visited Moscow in 1937, he discovered there "genuine freedom" (and wrote a book justifying the Moscow Trials);[8] but he preferred to live his refugee life under "formal" bourgeois freedom, first in France, then in America. So did Heinrich Mann who lived in the USA and who died at the very moment when, after years of hesitation, he had decided to go to the DDR. Brecht did go, but he retained his Austrian passport and his Swiss bank account.

IT IS FAR EASIER for writers to preserve their revolutionary attachment and faith in Utopia if they are not compelled to live in it. Not surprisingly, the revolutionary experience of our epoch elicited contrasting reactions from inside and from outside. The number and the quality of the writers who either temporarily or permanently embraced the revolutionary idea and identified it with the Soviet cause is astonishing.

It includes Anatole France, George Bernard Shaw, Romain Rolland, Henri Barbusse, Theodore Dreiser, Upton Sinclair, André Malraux, Julien Benda, Jean Guehenno, Paul Nizan, André Gide, Paul Eluard, Louis Aragon, Jean-Paul Sartre, Simone de Beauvoir, Sean O'Casey, Panait Istrati, Martin Andersen Nexö, Ludwig Renn, Johannes Becher, Theodor Plievier, Halldor Laxness, Ignazio Silone, Cesare Pavese, Elio Vittorini, Vasco Pratolini, Carlo Levi, John Dos Passos, Edmund Wilson, E. E. Cummings, Richard Wright, W. H. Auden, and many, many others.

Many of them have given up their faith, others have undergone considerable evolutions. Each of them, to be sure, presents an individual case; but all of them, at one time or another, embraced the revolutionary myth, whatever the differences in their background and personality. Like their predecessors at the time of the French Revolution, they hailed the Russian Revolution as a lodestar of freedom and justice.

From the beginning they displayed not just political naïveté in their pilgrimages to the revolutionary Mecca, but also a readiness to condone political violence. The venerable sceptic, Anatole France, declared that "if

[7] When Brezhnev visited the Louvre, where Picasso's paintings were displayed to honour his 90th anniversary, he was asked to comment on them. His comment on Picasso should be recorded for posterity: "He had a good idea to use a dove as a symbol of peace." (*Daily Telegraph*, 1 November 1971.)

[8] Feuchtwanger wrote the following about "confessions": "If that was lying or prearranged, then I don't know what truth is." Quoted in David Caute's study of *The Fellow Travellers*, from which some of the subsequent quotations are taken.

one wishes to see an era of justice established, one must be resigned to what may come to pass in its accomplishment—to injustice, cruelties, blood. . . ." He had no idea of what the scale of such phenomena might be in the 20th century. (Despite Party disapproval, he defended the Russian Social Revolutionaries who were tried in Moscow in 1922.)

Later on, a pattern gradually emerged which combined a selective moral indignation with the acceptance of terror and despotism. Its premises were expressed by Brecht's *Die Massnahme*, in which he put the Party above morality;[9] by Auden in his poem *Spain*, where he proclaimed "the conscious acceptance of guilt in the necessary murder": and by Merleau-Ponty providing in *Humanisme et Terreur*, a perverse "dialectical" justification for Stalin's *univers concentrationnaire*.

THE OBTUSENESS OF some contemporary comments on the Stalin era defies comprehension. And they were being made not only by such asinine fellow-travellers as Hewlett Johnson, Anna Louise Strong, or the Webbs, but by literary figures of great standing. Romain Rolland felt that Stalin provided the best guarantee that *les droits de l'esprit* would be defended; George Bernard Shaw commended him as a "good listener"; Heinrich Mann argued that Stalin would rather renounce the title of Marshal than that of intellectual; Feuchtwanger wrote that "it is irksome to Stalin to be idolized as he is. . . ."

At the time of the Great Purge, when Akhmatova wrote her lines in *Requiem*:

Eta zhenshchina bolna	*(This woman is sick to her marrow-bone,*
Eta zhenshchina odna	*This woman is utterly alone,*
Muzh v mogile, syn v tyurmiye.	*With husband dead, with son away*
Pomolites obo mnye	*In jail. Pray for me. Pray.)*

(tr. Stanley Kunitz.)

Aragon wrote about the accused in the Moscow Trials that "to claim innocence for these men is to adopt the Hitlerian thesis on all points".[10] When David Rousset wanted to reveal the facts about Stalin's slave camps, Sartre objected and wrote that the "workers of Billancourt must not be deprived of their hopes".

---

[9] Brecht wrote there that the fighter for communism must be able "to speak the truth and not to speak the truth". The scene of confession of the comrade about to be liquidated by the Party anticipated the Moscow Trials and provided their rationale in advance.

A far less casuistic discussion on the subject was conducted by the Berlin Academy of Sciences and Literature in 1780. Cf. *Est-il utile de tromper le peuple?* (ed. Werner Kraus, Akademie Verlag, Berlin, 1966).

[10] Nadezhda Mandelshtam wrote in her memoirs, *Hope against Hope*: "When I see books by the Aragons of this world, who are so keen to induce their fellow countrymen to live as we do, I feel I have a duty to tell about my own experience. . . ."

The Case of Russia

WHAT HAPPENED TO the hopes of the Russian writers? In his revolutionary "classic", *Mother*, Gorky predicted that after the revolution "Russia will be the most brilliant democracy in the world". When the revolution did come, he was not so sure. Among the writers who emigrated were: Bunin, Berdyaev, Andreev, Merezhkovsky, Zinaida Hippius, Remizov, Balmont, Khodasevich. Also Alexei Tolstoy, Tsvetaeva, Ehrenburg, and Prince Mirsky—all of whom later returned.

But retrospectively the 1920s look like a golden age of Soviet literature. The yoke of "socialist realism" had not yet been imposed: there was a spiritual breathing-space for writers under the *NEP*; the struggle among various literary tendencies was to some extent permitted. Artists and writers of the *avant-garde* could still cherish some illusions about its alliance with the political "vanguard". But the Party was growing increasingly monolithic and it was only a question of time before literature was to be *gleichgeschaltet* too. Zamyatin, who anticipated Stalin in the figure of "the Benefactor" in his novel, *We*, also anticipated the effects of such *Gleichschaltung* when he said that unless Russian writers were permitted to write without the shackles of a dogma, "our literature will have only one future: its past". And that is indeed what happened. Mandelshtam sensed it early enough when he wrote in 1923 the poem "My age, the beast . . . ."

In 1930 Roman Jakobson wrote an article: "The Generation That Squandered its Poets" in which he described the fate of four Russian poets who accepted the Revolution and one who rejected it. He referred to the "execution of Gumilyov, prolonged spiritual agony, unbearable physical treatment, the demise of Blok, cruel privations and the death of Khlebnikov, the premeditated suicides of Esenin and Mayakovsky. . . ." What was to follow, however, made it quite clear that it was not a "generation" which squandered its poets and writers.

At the First Soviet Writers' Congress, attended by a galaxy of Western literary fellow-travelling stars such as Gide and Malraux, Zhdanov boasted about the optimism of Soviet literature: "Our literature is permeated with enthusiasm and heroism". The re-converted Gorky, by then the official Grand Old Man of Soviet literature, proclaimed the obligatory character of "socialist realism". He described Dostoyevsky as "a renegade who never understood the workings of the human mind", and declared that "the real literature, the real truth lay among the folk heroes, those ancient and ever-present heroes of the labouring classes—Prometheus, Svyatagor, Ivan the Simple, Petrushka, and finally Lenin. . . ."

Malraux hailed the construction of the White Sea Canal (built with slave labour) and accepted "socialist realism" as a "valuable" method, only to proclaim his particular brand of heroic myth: "I feel that, just as Nietzsche took what was then known as the brute attitude and elevated it into a Zarathustra, so we should set up once again, in a realm beyond all ridiculous sentimentality, those values that bring men together and restore a meaning to the idea of manly brotherhood. . . ." It was a fittingly incongruous note on an occasion which opened the surrealist era in Soviet life and literature.

In two years' time Gorky was dead, allegedly as a result of the combined efforts of his doctors who, in order to wreck Soviet literature and revolution, sabotaged his health. A year later, Gide, who in 1932 wrote that his "conversion has a religious character" and expressed his conviction that "the Soviet Union points the way to redemption", declared that "one must see things as they are, not as one pictures them to oneself in a wishful dream", and concluded that "the Soviet Union has disappointed our fondest hopes".[11]

This was to be the *leitmotif* of the whole generation of Western writers who had enthusiastically adopted the revolutionary idea and became disillusioned with the Russian Revolution, as their ancestors had become disenchanted with the French Revolution. Except in this respect, there was little parallelism between the two revolutions; but the parallel between them became an obsession with the Russian revolutionary movement and, however illusory, played a part in shaping the attitudes and actions of those involved in it.

THE SQUANDERING OF POETS AND WRITERS continued, only in a greatly intensified form, under *Yezhovshchina* and *Beriovshchina*. Solzhenitsyn summed it up in his *Open Letter* to the Fourth Soviet Writers' Congress:

> "Many writers have been subjected during their lifetime to abuse and slander in the press and from rostrums without being afforded the physical possibility of replying. More than that, they have been exposed to violence and personal persecution (Bulgakov, Akhmatova, Tsvetaeva, Pasternak, Zoshchenko, Platonov, Alexander Grin, Vassily Grossman). . . . The leadership of the [Writers'] Union cravenly abandoned to their distress those for whom persecution ended in exile, labour camps, and death (Pavel Vasiliev, Mandelshtam, Artem Vesely, Pilnyak, Babel, Tabidze, Zabolotsky, and others). The list must be cut off at 'and others'. We learned after the 20th Party Congress that there were more than 600 writers whom the Union had obediently handed over to their fate in prisons and camps. However, the roll is even longer. . . ."

And the list continues to this day, although since Stalin's death the treatment

---

[11] In 1934 Samuel Putnam wrote in the then Communist *Partisan Review* (Vol. 1, No. 5, p. 36) that "in finding communism André Gide has found that youth which all his life he has sought". On Gide's death in 1951, the Communist *l'Humanité* commented that "a corpse has died".

of artists and writers is less harsh: Brodsky, Sinyavsky and Daniel, Bukovsky, "and others". Solzhenitsyn himself is, needless to say, the most famous example.

WHAT WERE THE CONCLUSIONS about the confrontation of literature and revolution in the Soviet Union drawn by those writers who wanted to bear witness to the epoch?

Pasternak, Sinyavsky, Solzhenitsyn, and Nadezhda Mandelshtam are quite explicit about it. They represent a contemporary religious revival in Russia; but their ethical philosophy and historical reflections probably provide a common denominator for many others who do not necessarily share their personal faith.

In *Doctor Zhivago* Pasternak is ambiguous about the Revolution itself, but quite unambiguous about its later manifestations:

> "Reshaping life! People who can say that may have lived through a lot, but have never understood a thing about life . . . they look on it as a lump of coarse raw material that needs to be processed by them. . . . But life is never a material, a substance . . . life is the principle of self-renewal . . . it is infinitely beyond your or my obtuse theories. . . ."

> "Marxism is too uncertain of its ground to be a science. Sciences are more balanced, more objective. I don't know a movement more self-centred and further removed from the facts than Marxism. Everyone is only worried about proving himself in practical matters, and as for the men in power, they are so anxious to establish the myth of their infallibility that they do their utmost to ignore the truth."

On another occasion Pasternak added the ironic remark:

> "They really ask for very little, really for only one thing: to hate what one loves and love what one detests. And that is the most difficult thing of all."

In his essay on socialist realism, Sinyavsky made explicit the connection between such compulsion (of which Socialist Realism was made an instrument in literature) and the utopian teleology of the Revolution, what he calls "the Purpose":

> "So that prisons should vanish forever, we build new prisons. So that all frontiers should fall, we surround ourselves with a Chinese Wall. So that work should become a rest and a pleasure, we introduced forced labour. So that not one drop of blood be shed any more, we killed and killed and killed."

In his novel, *August 1914*, Solzhenitsyn expressed some critical thoughts about the Russian radical intelligentsia. Its representative, a young populist, Sonya, is criticized by her father for adopting revolutionary shibboleths. Quoting Gorky's *Burevestnik*, he characterizes the call to revolution there as "irresponsible". He advocates political moderation and solid fundamental work by technical specialists to overcome Russia's industrial backwardness:

> "A reasonable man cannot be for revolution, because revolution signifies a prolonged and mindless destruction. First of all, revolution, any revolution, does not renew the country, but tears it up for a very long time. And the more bloody, the more protracted it is, the more the country has to pay for it, the more likely it is to be called GREAT."

In her *Hope against Hope*, Nadezhda Mandelshtam explains the lack of resistance to the prolonged post-Revolutionary horrors by the hold which the Revolutionary myth had on the radical intelligentsia:

> "The decisive part in the subjugation of the intelligentsia was played not by terror and bribery (though, God knows, there was enough of both), but by the word 'Revolution' which none of them could bear to give up. It is a word to which whole nations have succumbed, and its force was such that one wonders why our rulers still needed prisons and capital punishment."

THIS IS THE CRUX OF THE MATTER, as the legitimacy of the régime is based on the acceptance, even if only tacit, of Revolution as the road to the Communist Utopia. Its erosion would undermine the legitimacy of the Soviet régime.

The Party is, therefore, extremely sensitive on this point (and always has been). It is, of course, based upon Marxist *Gesetzmässigkeit*, a *zakonomernost* of history which positively guarantees the consummation of the belief, the attainment of "the Purpose". This is the inner core of legitimacy underlying the ideological control-mechanisms, including the doctrine of Socialist Realism in literature. Anything that puts into question the validity of Marxist "laws of history" challenges the dogma of not only Socialist Realism, but also of the Revolutionary myth (with its concomitant Utopian perspective). It *ipso facto* contributes to the erosion of the régime's legitimacy which requires at least a lip-service to the historical certainties of Soviet ideology.

Since Khrushchev's "secret speech" a slow drift away from such prescribed certainties can be detected. It was reflected in literature where the hard core of Communist ideology has been directly and explicitly challenged by the four writers quoted above. Pasternak and Solzhenitsyn in particular have made a frontal attack on the Marxist view of history. Pasternak dismisses it in *Doctor Zhivago* as "a comical survival of the past" not to be taken seriously, and Solzhenitsyn in *August 1914* makes one of its heroes say that "history is not ruled by reason", but is "irrational".

The Case of China

ONE OF THE PERSISTENT THEMES which constantly appears in the encounter between Literature and Revolution is the clash between literary sensibility and political controls, between the writers and the revolutionary rulers. It has been illustrated again and again, but the case of China is in some ways the most striking.

In China both modern literature and the revolutionary idea were Western imports. The Chinese intelligentsia was also in a sense a product of Western cultural influence. It began to emerge after the fall of the Manchu dynasty in 1911 and the resulting disappearance of the Chinese scholar-official. Nowhere else was the relation between modern literature and revolution so intimate at the beginning, and nowhere else has the divorce between them been more drastic.

Modern Chinese literature begins with the advocacy by Dr Hu Shih of the use of the vernacular in place of classical Chinese as the medium of literary expression. His article proposing this, written when he was a post-graduate student at Columbia University and published in the literary journal of Peking University, *New Youth*, was a signal for the original Chinese Cultural Revolution (usually called "Literary Renaissance") in 1917. The same Peking University where students enthusiastically welcomed the idea was soon to become the hotbed of the May Fourth Movement and a recruiting ground for the emerging Communist movement. The same kind of motives had originally moved them to break with the past.

First, the felt need to abandon a moribund but sacrosanct literary tradition which had become esoteric and *précieuse*, and had degenerated into a system of obscure allusions and pedantic stereotypes. The learned but barren language of outworn clichés was to be replaced by the living language of the vernacular in which Chinese novels had been written in the past.

And secondly, the decaying Chinese society which had not been able to produce a *Meiji*-type of reform had to undergo a renewal through revolution in order to be able to stand up to the foreign powers which humiliated China in the 19th and 20th centuries.

Thus, Marxism in China appealed to motives which in Europe were present in the Reformation with its Vulgate and its Peasant Wars; in the French Revolution with its patriotic calls to arms in defence of the Republic; and in the Russian Revolution, before which the populist intelligentsia keenly felt the discrepancy between its own political and cultural aspirations and the economic and social backwardness of the country. Obviously, more was involved here than just an alliance between a literary *avant-garde* of the European type and a Leninist political vanguard. But the misconceptions underlying the intimate relationship between literature and revolution in China were no less profound than elsewhere.

THERE WAS A VARIETY of ideological positions among the new Chinese writers in the 1920s. All of them aspired to progress through modernization. Some embraced liberalism, some communism, some anarchism—all imported creeds. In the 1930s the Chinese intelligentsia became more radical and the majority of writers joined the Party-sponsored "League of Left-Wing Writers" which was established in March 1930 with the help of the most famous modern Chinese writer, Lu Hsün. After the outbreak of the war with Japan many of them went to Yenan.

Yet the conflict between the Party and revolutionary writers had already started before.[12] Lu Hsün, Feng Hsüeh-feng, Hu Feng, Hu Ch'iu-yüan, and Su Wen constantly came into conflict with the League's Party supervisors (Ch'ü Ch'iu-pai and Chou Yang who became a Chinese Zhdanov). Lu Hsün died in 1936; and, like Gorky in Russia, he was canonized in China as the patron saint of Communist literature.

In Yenan, where the writers began to misbehave by producing some critical writings, a "Forum on Literature and Art" was organized in May 1942. It played the same role in subsequent literary development in China as the First Soviet Writers' Congress played in the Soviet Union. In China, stringent Party control of literature had already been introduced before it had taken power in the country, at a time when Mao felt it no longer necessary to woo the writers (who were previously mainly concentrated in Shanghai). Mao Tse-tung himself laid down the canon. In his two speeches to the Forum he called the writers sternly to task and told them that they must be "oxen for the proletariat and the masses". He declared: "Our aim is to ensure that revolutionary literature and art follow the correct path of development". He defined it as being called "to perform faithfully functions of a component part of the revolutionary machine as a whole". He added:

> "Will not Marxism-Leninism then destroy the creative spirit? Yes. It will destroy any brand of creative spirit which is not of the masses and of the proletariat. . . . The intellectuals must identify themselves with the masses and must serve the masses. This process may, in fact it definitely will produce much suffering and friction. . . ."[13]

It did. Ever since, the Party has tried to coax the recalcitrant writers by periodic campaigns designed to "remould" them. The first of these was immediately after the Yenan Forum and was directed against Wang Shih-wei, the author of the popular book, *The Wild Lily*, who had the temerity to criticize in his writings the high-handedness of the Party cadres. Wang Shih-wei disappeared soon after the Yenan Forum and was never seen again. Another writer, Hsia Chun, the pupil of Lu Hsün, who defended Wang Shih-wei at Yenan, disappeared in 1948.

---

[12] Cf. Merle Goldman, *Literary Dissent in Communist China* (Harvard, 1967).
[13] Mao Tse-tung, *On Art and Literature* (Peking, 1960).

AFTER THE ESTABLISHMENT OF the People's Republic in 1949 many other writers got into trouble for not conforming to the Chinese version of "socialist realism" or simply to serve a didactic purpose as negative examples in various "campaigns". Earlier, Hsiao Chün, the most prominent Manchurian writer, was made the target of a rectification campaign, after the Red Army took over Manchuria (where he fought with the guerrillas). He was purged in 1948. Feng Hsüeh-feng, the friend of Lu Hsün, and a participant in the Long March, was repeatedly attacked in 1954 and 1957. His fellow-member of the League of Left-Wing Writers, Hu Feng, was being denounced all through 1955 in a nationwide drive against him. No less vicious was the campaign in 1957 against the famous woman writer, Ting Ling (a Stalin Prize-winner), who was made to sweep the office of a Party bureaucrat as her punishment. In the same year of the anti-Rightist movement, the epic poet Ai Ch'ing was purged, as were other less well-known writers who had been unwise enough to betray some of their inner feelings during the preceding period, the short liberal interval of "the Hundred Flowers".

Subsequently, there were other clashes between the Party and the writers, such as those with the lyrical poet, Ho Ch'i-fang, in 1959 and 1960. But gradually the spirit of defiance had less and less chance to assert itself until it was decisively crushed in the Cultural Revolution. This was directed not only against the Party opponents of Mao, but also against historic Chinese cultural traditions. The intellectuals and the museums were attacked by the Red Guards and the campaign against the Confucian tradition continued after the end of the Cultural Revolution.

But it was not just the antics and excesses of the Red Guards after 1966 which crushed the Chinese literary intelligentsia who emerged from the Chinese Renaissance after 1917 and so enthusiastically adopted the cause of revolution in China. They were eliminated "as a class"—not like *kulaks* under Stalin at one blow, but through the continuous harassment of various campaigns which were conducted to teach them Mao's Yenan directives, on how "to serve the masses" (and their Helmsman).

Before the Cultural Revolution some writers were made to rewrite their works published in pre-Communist China and—like Sholokhov, Gladkov, and Fadeyev in the Soviet Union—they did not flinch from the task. The most famous case is that of Pai Chin, the popular Chinese anarchist writer (whose adopted name derives from Bakunin and Kropotkin). Since Mao's victory he has renounced his views, accepted communism, and has taken out of his books all the numerous (and enthusiastic) references to anarchism.[14]

---

[14] Olga Lang, *Pai Chin and His Writings* (Harvard, 1967). He Ying-tzi, the author of the "classic" Maoist play written in Yenan, *A Girl with White Hair*, re-wrote it during the Cultural Revolution and eliminated the rape of the girl "to avoid wounding the feelings of peasant audiences". (*Le Monde*, 18 February 1972.)

DURING THE CULTURAL REVOLUTION literature in China simply ceased to exist. Nothing was published but the utter trash of devotional writings extolling the genius of Mao and attacking his enemies. It was symbolic that the cradle of the modern Chinese literary and revolutionary movements, Peking University, was closed during the Cultural Revolution. The relation between Literature and Revolution cannot be illustrated by a more extreme example. The burning of the books under the Chinese Emperor in the first century BC was not done in the name of revolutionary ideology, but on the advice of a court official who recommended it in his memorandum to the ruler. He added that "people wishing to pursue learning should take the officials as their teachers".

After the Cultural Revolution some books began to appear, but they seem to be designed, like literature in Stalin's Russia, for the edification of the Chinese *vydvizhentsy*, of the peasants and workers promoted from "the masses" (for whom Peking University has been reopened). But it is not only the literary tastes of the Chinese intelligentsia which were sacrificed in Mao's permanent revolution, but also their social role. In the process of their re-education, they were urged to be both "red and expert"; during the Cultural Revolution they suffered a further social decline.

Before the Chinese Revolution the literary intelligentsia was a small, but important, group; after the Cultural Revolution it practically disappeared. It is unlikely that it can play anything resembling its previous role. The new cultural policy which led to some relaxation of the shackles imposed by the Cultural Revolution and the erratic releases of non-Marxist books banned by it—such as Montesquieu's *The Spirit of the Laws*, Rousseau's *Social Contract*, and Thucydides' *History of the Peloponnesian War*—cannot revive the social formation which has been crushed. Nor will the new foreign policy orientation make Western cultural influence play a role even remotely comparable to what it was in the pre-War period. The "rehabilitation" of Chinese literary classics, previously prohibited, may restore some cultural continuity, but will certainly not revive the scholar-official or the Western-influenced intelligentsia.

The Case of Cuba

A LESS EXTREME EXAMPLE of the conflict between literature and revolution, though in its international aspect a most interesting one, is Fidel Castro's Cuba. It illustrates the same pattern arising out of the logic of confrontation between the victorious revolutionaries and the *literati*. Here, again, there are basic differences from the other cases; and yet the outcome, as far as this relationship is concerned, is similar.

When Castro came to power, he had the support of the middle class intellectuals who detested the Batista régime. There was not much intellectual content in his ideology. Castro was no intellectual; he described himself as "a revolutionary man of action". He quickly divested himself of those supporters from the 26 July Movement who were more liberal and less revolutionary than himself. But he was no communist; for various reasons the Communist influence in Cuba was insignificant. When Castro proclaimed himself a "Marxist-Leninist" he confessed that he had read *Das Kapital* only up to page 270. The Cuban revolution did not have behind it the theoretical–ideological framework which existed before the seizure of power in other revolutions. It was elaborated only afterwards, in a confused form, to provide an ideological fig-leaf for a revolutionary drive. As Che Guevara put it in his *Notes for the Study of the Ideology of the Cuban Revolution*:

> "This is a unique revolution which some people maintain contradicts one of the most orthodox premises of the revolutionary movement, expressed by Lenin: 'Without a revolutionary theory there is no revolutionary movement'. . . . The principal actors of this revolution had no coherent theoretical criteria. . . . The Cuban Revolution takes up Marx at the point where he himself left science to shoulder his revolutionary rifle. . . . The laws of Marxism are present in the events of the Cuban Revolution, independently of what its leaders profess or fully know of those laws from a theoretical point of view. . . ." (*Verde Olivo*, 8 October 1960.)

Castro, fired by similar revolutionary ardour and indifference towards theory, also stressed that "it is anti-Marxist to try to enclose Marxism in a sort of catechism",[15] thus at first making a virtue out of the lack of necessity.

IT IS BECAUSE of this refusal to develop a systematic ideology and a doctrinal bondage, because of the apparent spontaneity of the Cuban Revolution, of its perpetual militancy and of the relative insignificance of the Party functionaries, that Fidel and Che had such an appeal to the bohemian intelligentsia of the 1960s who were again being fired by the revolutionary idea.

Castro's *barbudos* lowered the profits of razor manufacturers in all the universities of the world. The romantic appeal of *Guantanamera* was not quite comparable to that of *La Marseillaise* or *Die Internationale*, but Castro, while maintaining his ultra-radical populist posture, allowed *avant-garde* films and literature. Both the Left Bank and Greenwich Village were enchanted. Rossana Rossanda, then still in the PCI, wrote enthusiastic reports in *l'Unita* about Castro's cultural tolerance; and so did Jean-Paul Sartre in *France Soir*—Castro's Cuba became his next Utopia after the Soviet Union. And he did not even have to write on returning from a visit to Cuba (as he did in 1954

---

[15] Fidel Castro, *Major Speeches* (London, 1968).

on returning from the USSR) that writers expelled from their Union can rehabilitate themselves "by writing better books". Left-wing intellectuals flocked to Havana from all over the world as they did 40 or 50 years earlier to Moscow. Cuban films merged nostalgically with *Potemkin*, and *Casa de las Americas* with the Left Book Club. Progressive *bien-pensants* were invited to sit on various literary and artistic juries in Havana.

Yet in Havana the prospects of the literary *avant-garde* were gradually looking less and less rosy. At first there were small clouds on the horizon, such as the establishment of the "National Council of Culture" which could interfere with artistic work. But in his speech in June 1961, Castro, in striking contrast to Stalin and Mao, assured the intellectuals and writers that there was no need to fear:

> "The revolution cannot by its very nature be an enemy of freedom. If some are worried about whether the revolution is going to stifle their creative spirit, that worry is not necessary, that worry has no reason to exist. . . . The existence of an authority in the cultural order does not mean that there is reason to be worried about that authority being abused."

Yet clouds were getting bigger, and as they did so more intellectuals began "voting with their feet". Many, including even such Castro supporters as the former editor of *Revolucion*, Carlos Franqui, or its former literary editor, Guillermo Cabiera Infante, went into exile. Those who remained faced increased pressures for conformity. The case of Herberto Padilla, the well-known Cuban poet, was the culmination of these developments.

When Padilla received the annual literary prize in 1968 for his book of poems, *Fuera del Juego*, the Army journal, *Verde Olivo*, furiously attacked the jury for this decision and called Padilla all sorts of names for his sins, which included, of course, lack of revolutionary enthusiasm. Had not Fidel himself said that "the revolutionary cannot be anything else but an optimist"? According to *Verde Olivo*, Padilla was one of those "whose spinelessness is matched only by their pornography and counter-revolution". This was no longer the kind of chiding which was applied at the time when Che Guevara wrote in the same *Verde Olivo* (in his *Notes on Man and Socialism in Cuba*): "Why should we try to find the only valid prescription for art in the frozen forms of socialist realism?. . . ." The increasing pressure on Cuban writers was reflected in further attacks on Padilla. The Young Communists' periodical, *El Caiman Barbudo* (*The Bearded Alligator*) published in 1968 several articles denouncing him viciously. One of these articles, written by the cultural official, Lisandro Otero, was particularly Zhdanovite in tone and style.

This did not prevent Susan Sontag from writing an article in *Ramparts* (April 1969), "Some Thoughts on the Right Way (for us) to Love the Cuban

Revolution", in which she proclaimed that "the Cuban revolution is astonishingly free of repression" and asserted that "no Cuban writer has been or is in jail, or is failing to get his work published".

Padilla was arrested in March 1971 and after slightly more than a month in jail, he confessed, in the best Stalinist style, to all the charges which were brought against him. Yes, he was a counter-revolutionary, a bad poet, and an insidious and malignant person. He had provided information to the two CIA agents, K. S. Karol and René Dumont (two left-wing friends of Castro living in Paris, who had become too critical in their recent books on Cuba). Evidently, more than one didactic target was involved.

When *Le Monde* published a whole page about the affair, the Left Bank intellectuals could not stand it any longer. Sartre, Simone de Beauvoir, and other "progressives" addressed a strongly-worded open letter to Castro protesting about the Padilla affair (*Le Monde*, 9 April 1971). On 22 May 1971 *Le Monde* carried a second letter whose 61 signatories included Susan Sontag, Alberto Moravia, Jorge Semprun, and Carlos Fuentes.

> "The lamentable text of the confession signed by Herberto Padilla can only have been obtained by means which are the negation of revolutionary legality and justice. The contents of this confession, with its absurd accusations and delirious statements, as well as the painful parody of self-criticism imposed on Herberto Padilla . . . recall the most sordid moments of the Stalinist period, with its prefabricated judgments and its witch-hunts."

Padilla, according to *Prensa Latina* (the Cuban news agency), denounced the signatories' "treachery" (*Le Monde*, 30–31 May 1971):

> "You will say again that I have not written this letter, that it is not my style, you who have never been interested in my style, bourgeois liberals who have always considered me an underdeveloped writer and only pay attention to me now to attack the revolution . . . very well, continue to serve the CIA, imperialism, international reaction. Cuba does not need you."

Castro himself made the position clear in a speech addressed to the "First National Congress of Education and Culture" (held in Havana on 30 April 1971). The Maximum Leader contemptuously dismissed the protest and its authors:

> "In these years we have become better and better acquainted with the world and the people who live in it. Some of these people were described here in clear and precise terms. Like those who even tried to present themselves as supporters of the Cuban Revolution, among whom there were some real tricksters and sharpies." (*Casa de las Americas*, No. 65–66, March–June 1971, p. 25.)

Castro denounced the "bourgeois liberals" and "pseudo-Leftists", the "snobbery" of "Western fashions", declared that his approach to art was political, stressed the need to combat "cultural colonialism", and denied the right of a few "lost sheep" to their dissident ideas. His retort to the literary fellow-travellers of the Cuban revolution was loud and clear: no criticism is allowed and no "false friends" who indulge in it will be tolerated. Internally, the implications of the "Padilla affair" for Cuban writers and intellectuals were no less clear. They were spelled out in a *Declaration* adopted by the Congress:[16]

> "All trends which are based on apparent ideas of freedom (*libertinaje*) as a disguise for the counter-revolutionary poison of works that conspire against the revolutionary ideology on which the construction of socialism and communism is based are inadmissible and to be condemned."

The Congress' *Declaration* listed a number of measures aimed at a uniform line in education and culture, including firm ideological indoctrination and stricter control of all media of communication. The not-sufficiently-vigilant editor of the weekly *Bohemia* (Enrique de la Osa) was dismissed, while the former editor of the hard-line *Verde Olivo* and one of Padilla's harshest critics (Luis Pavon) was nominated the head of the National Council of Culture. Padilla's wife, Belkis Cuza, rejected the protest by the left-wing Western writers against the treatment of her husband as "a shameless provocation".[17] The Director of *Casa de las Americas* (Haydee Santamaria) found it necessary to dissociate herself from their expression of solidarity with its defence of intellectual freedom, stressing in an open letter to the Peruvian writer Mario Vargas Llosa that *Casa de las Americas* loyally supported the official line.

The protesting Western left-wing writers were banished to the enemy camp. One more love affair between "progressive" literature and revolution came to an end.

Fate of the Literati

THE POINT which emerges from a scrutiny of millenarian revolutions is only too clear: whatever their other effects, whether they are considered beneficial or harmful, they invariably have a disappointing, and often tragic, outcome for the writers caught in the mechanics of revolutionary and post-revolutionary régimes. Others may or may not benefit from the revolution, the writers—*qua* writers—most certainly do not.

---

[16] *Casa de las Americas* (March–June 1971), p. 16.

[17] *Le Monde* (23 April 1971) reported that she had praised "the friendship of the comrades of State security, whose tenderness towards me in my situation brought tears to my eyes. . . ." Juan Accocha, a close friend of Padilla, wrote in *Le Monde* (29 April 1971) that his "confession must have been signed under torture", an allegation Padilla subsequently denied.

The conflict between writers and rulers in Eastern Europe confirms this. The conflict was aggravated by the fact that the revolutionary regimes in Eastern Europe, with the exception of Yugoslavia, were imposed from outside. There were no indigenous revolutions. But there, too, writers have suffered a similar fate and reacted in a similar manner to that of their fellow writers in more authentically native revolutionary régimes. The story of the plight of writers in Poland, Hungary, Czechoslovakia, and other East European countries need not be recounted here, nor their struggle for intellectual freedom. The East German *Aufstand der Intellektuellen*, the Polish October 1956, the Hungarian 1956 Revolution, the Prague Spring of 1968—in all these the writers played a paramount part. Everywhere in Eastern Europe they became disillusioned with the "revolutionary" régimes imposed on them. And that applies also to the revolutionary writers.

In Poland there was little revolutionary literature before the last War. The work of the three representative Communist poets extolling revolution was published in the 1920s under the title *Three Salvoes*. Ironically, the title was almost prophetic, though not in the intended sense. Of the three authors, two were killed by Stalin (Wandurski in 1932, Stande in 1938). The third, Broniewski, was imprisoned in 1940 when he too found himself in the Soviet Union. He was sent to a concentration camp, but later managed to leave the Soviet Union with General Anders' Army. After the War he returned to Poland and later wrote a sycophantic *Ode to Stalin* which was included in school readers. He became a chronic alcoholic and died a broken man. He has since been canonized as a revolutionary bard—but his poems about Soviet prisons were, of course, carefully suppressed (as was, later, the *Ode to Stalin*).

Another prominent Polish communist writer, Bruno Jasienski, was one of the orginators of futurism in Polish literature. In France he wrote a novel *Je Brûle Paris* (a *pendant* to Paul Morand's *Je brûle Moscou*), which was serialized in *l'Humanité*. He emigrated to the Soviet Union where he became editor of *Literatura Mirovoi Revolyutsii*, the organ of the World Association of Proletarian Writers (WAPP), and later of the Polish-language paper in the USSR, *Kultura Mas*; he wrote a novel, *Man Changes His Skin*, containing lyrical passages about the re-educative role of the *NKVD*. But he was denounced in 1937 by Pavel Yudin and arrested. He died in a concentration camp in 1941.

Another Polish revolutionary poet—who, although not a Party member, was editor of the Polish communist *Literary Monthly*—Alexander Wat, was imprisoned in Lvov in 1940. He returned to Poland after the War a physical wreck as a result of his tribulations in the Soviet camps. He died in exile in Paris.

Three other Communist writers survived the War and became prominent in People's Poland: Andrzej Stawar, Stanslaw Wygodzki, and Igor Newerly. The first died in Paris, where he had written for the emigré monthly *Kultura* a book critical of the Communist régime. The second went to Israel, having been purged as a "Zionist" in 1968. The third has become one of the leaders of the liberal intellectual opposition, first under Gomulka and then under Gierek.

Similar cases occurred in other East European countries. In Hungary, the great poet, Atilla Jozef, who later committed suicide, had broken with the Communist Party before the War. In Czechoslovakia, the Communist poet and writer, Zavis Kalandra, was arrested in 1948 as a Trotskyite and later executed. After experiencing life under Communist régimes more and more writers became disenchanted. The lists of contributors to *Irodalmi Ujsag* and to *Literarni Noviny* (later *Listy*) tell their own story.

The pattern of disillusionment in the East European countries after the War is not confined to older writers who "embraced the Revolution", like the Polish writers mentioned above, or (say) Tibor Dery in Hungary. It extends to the younger writers who were educated in these regimes: Hlasko and Mrozek in Poland, Bierman in East Germany, Kundera and Havel in Czechoslovakia, and many others. In the period after de-Stalinization disillusionment often led to cynicism. It has become the prevalent trait among those writers who are on the "revolutionary" bandwagon but can no longer make themselves believe in the Newthink.

From Prague to Stanford

THE attitudes of the intelligentsia in East and West are sometimes equated; but it is the contrast which is more striking than any similarities. There is no substitute for experience. The writers caught between the Revolution and Utopia know that in practice they face a choice between intellectual prostitution and martyrdom. They know how difficult it is to avoid this choice. For a majority of them all sorts of compromises and rationalizations, from self-deception to Newspeak, are inevitable. The few heroic ones who choose martyrdom—like Solzhenitsyn—are the exceptions. It is extraordinary that this heroism of *chestnye pisateli* ("honest writers") is necessary to do what would after all appear to be the most ordinary thing: to write as they really feel. This elementary prerequisite of the literary vocation requires almost superhuman courage, involving as it does a challenge to the state which imposes on the writer an ideological straitjacket and an obligatory perception.

When a Mary McCarthy or a Graham Greene points out, perhaps with a touch of jealousy, that in the Communist countries, unlike in the West, writers "are at least taken seriously", they fail to notice that this is because writers there constitute potential channels for articulating attitudes based not on the official, but on an authentic individual perception—something which a Western writer takes for granted as a natural right.

The contrast between the intelligentsia East and West is striking indeed. What divides them more than anything else is life-experience: first hand knowledge in the one case, theoretical knowledge in the other. While Susan Sontag evokes with lusty enthusiasm what she calls "a promiscuous idea of revolution", the attitude of those writers who have been compelled to live with it is somewhat less enthusiastic about this revolutionary promiscuity. Many examples could be given, but intellectually there has been nothing more comic (or pathetic) than the encounter between the representatives of the "New Left" and those of the "Prague Spring", the first concerned with the idea of revolution, the second with its lack of a "human face" in practice.

IT IS CERTAINLY NO ACCIDENT that at present the revolutionary idea is sincerely cherished among writers or intellectuals only where it has not triumphed, in places where post-revolutionary *praxis* can be safely disregarded. It is much easier to believe the revolutionary myth of our time on the Stanford campus than—say—in Czechoslovakia or Poland; and therefore the number of "true believers" is greater in Stanford than in those two countries taken together.

Revolution, East and West

Y ET—more seriously—the question of the persistence of the revolutionary idea remains. Its vicissitudes and metamorphoses cannot be understood in terms of any "laws of history", of postulated historical regularities or consciousness, whether Hegelian or Marxian, Leninist or Stalinist, Maoist or Marcusian. As with other religious or mythological ideas, its destinies cannot be explained in terms of "historical materialism".

The concept of social revolution made its first appearance in the 16th century. It was based on the metaphorical application of the notion of the cyclical movement of heavenly bodies (*De Revolutionibus Orbium Caelestium* was the title of the Copernicus treatise) to social unrest.[18] It was already used in this sense by Montaigne, but acquired its modern connotation only after the Glorious Revolution in which ideological longings were still expressed in religious terms. (Cromwell's soldiers marched with the Bible in their hands; the radical Fifth Monarchy men engaged in theological debate.) Between the Glorious Revolution and the French Revolution the revolutionary and utopian urges became secularized. The search for the City of God, for the New Jerusalem, gave way to the search for the City of Man; or, as Melvin J. Lasky put it,

> "the idea of revolution moved from astronomy to sociology, the idea of utopia from theology to politics".

---

[18] Melvin J. Lasky has traced it in detail in his book *Utopia and Revolution*; also cf. "The Birth of a Metaphor", *Encounter* (February and March 1970).

In the 19th century the revolutionary idea underwent further transformations. It was now linked with the idea of history (which replaced the idea of God). In Vico history was still governed by "Providence"; in Hegel "the problem of history is the problem of consciousness"; in Marx it becomes a natural process governed by scientific laws. In Vico history is still cyclical; in Hegel it is already progressive (through the dialectical development of the world spirit); in Marx it also unfolds dialectically, but in Marxist historical materialism Hegel is put on his head.

Engels claimed at Marx's funeral that he did for history what Darwin had done for biology; but whatever the status of Darwinism today, there can be little doubt that the original intellectual baggage of Marxism had to be abandoned. It had undergone such theoretical mutations that its historical expansion and continuous attraction as a revolutionary creed can be understood only in terms of its mythopoeic appeal, not of its heuristic merits.

AT FIRST IT WAS A THEORY of social change through the development of the forces of production. But, rather than removing the fetters on production in countries where it was supposed to develop only if "the capitalist integument" were to "burst asunder" through a proletarian revolution, Marxism, contrary to its own premises, moved into a growing number of *undeveloped* countries. The history of Western industrial countries did not confirm the social and political expectations of many generations of Marxists, beginning with Marx himself. In Russia, Marxism underwent a populist voluntaristic inversion by Lenin, who made the first revolutionary step away from Marxist orthodoxy by deciding to jump over the Marxian stages of economic development. Since 1917 revolutionary "Marxists" have been enlarging the extent of such historical "jumps". There are no more agonizing doctrinal discussions about whether a country is or is not "ripe" for "socialism". It can now be delivered from all kinds of social "wombs", from the nomadic People's Republic of Mongolia to be the tribal "People's Republic of Congo (Brazzaville)". Under Stalin, Marxism became in effect a doctrine about forcible industrialization of a backward economy, hardly a Marxian perspective.

While the new Marxist gospel was spreading, it was steadily losing its original intellectual character through adaption to local backgrounds— resulting in the Russification, Sinicization, Latinization of Marxism, and through the concomitant erosion of its general theoretical premises. Ideological unity came to an end. As with other schisms, each major polycentric splinter claimed universal validity for its own orthodoxy.

The twisting of Marx's own intellectual perspective through selective quotations of the canon reached the point of absurdity. In China Liu Shao-chi was attacked for the anti-Marxist heresy which the official Maoist press called "the reactionary theory of productive forces . . . [which] describes social development as a natural outcome of the development of productive forces only, especially the development of the tools of production". (*Peking Review*, 10 September 1971.)

MOVING FROM THE Far East to the Wild West, one is struck by a Marxist revival in industrialized countries, but intellectually it is a phenomenon which has very little to do with Marx's own theories. Western Marxism is being kept alive as a "critical theory" by increased injections of Hegelianism. Marcuse went back not only to Hegel, but beyond that to Rousseau. As he put it in his *Eros and Civilization*: "From Plato to Rousseau, the idea of a pedagogic dictatorship exercised by those who are generally thought to have acquired a knowledge of the true good is the only answer. This answer has been forgotten." They always know better: the secular elect of predestinarian history, the Hegelian *illuminati* and the Marxist *cognoscenti* of the historical process, the Lukacses, the Brechts, the Marcuses. But it is the Lenins, Stalins, and Maos who decide what is the "true good".

Marcuse (as Lucien Goldmann enthusiastically observed)[19] "brought 'critical theory' back to Utopia". But how Marxian—and how critical—is this new version of "critical theory"?

Marx would scarcely recognize it as his child or grandchild. Goldmann assures us—somewhat defensively—that "for Marcuse, the concrete form of the reality principle in contemporary society is the principle of productivity". Contrary to Goldmann's assertion, which is complimentary and formulated in Freudian language, Marcuse himself is not at all inclined towards such a reactionary Marxian deviation *à la* Liu Shao-chi. In fact, he removed Marx's "forces of production" from their pedestal in the centre of the theory. The reason for this is, of course, precisely the opposite of Mao's. For Marcuse it is not a question of the weak development of the "forces of production", as it is in China, but of their super-abundance in America. For him, the central preoccupation is not the question of liberating the forces of production in a capitalist society (as it was for Marx) but of liberating man from the "surplus repression" in the hated affluent society created by capitalism. Like Max Stirner—"Saint Max" so harshly criticized by Marx in *The German Ideology*—Marcuse dreams of the complete release of instinctual drives and envisages "the state of unrepressed gratification", of "non-repressive sublimation".

---

[19] Lucien Goldmann, "Understanding Marcuse", *Partisan Review* (No. 3, 1971). In a recent interview (*Politique Hebdo*, 2 December 1971), Marcuse said:

"The coming revolution, the revolution of the twentieth and twenty-first centuries, requires as an introduction a radical transformation of the needs, of the consciousness, and of the sensibility. . . . The emergence of the new sensibility will probably have as a first consequence the reduction of productivity. . . ."

Surplus Value & Surplus Repression

T HE REVOLUTIONARY IDEA has thus taken another turn: this time
from economics to psychoanalysis, from Marx to Freud (and beyond),
from sociological to psychological Utopia.[20] Marcuse is sceptical about what
he calls "the materialist concept of reason in history" and, having abandoned
"productive forces" as the analytical linch-pin of the theory, he also dismisses
Marx's chosen class, the industrial proletariat, as the historical instrument of
revolutionary liberation. Indeed he rejects Marx's class analysis altogether.

> "Today, the force of negation is concentrated in no one class. Politically
> and morally, rationally and instinctively, it is a chaotic anarchistic
> opposition; the refusal to join and play a part, the disgust of all
> prosperity, the compulsion to protest."[21]

He does not indicate, however, how the liberation of the Id is to be combined
with the ecological balance, or the permissive society with the pedagogic
dictatorship. Once "repressive tolerance" is abolished, a "revolution without
terror" will no doubt solve these simple problems quite easily. Today
hypocrisy is the tribute which revolution pays to liberalism.

BUT IT IS ONLY intellectually that Marxist theoretical tergiversations are
contradictory. Consistency and continuity are provided by the revolutionary
and utopian elements underlying the Marxist appeal. It is only thus that one
can understand its persistence and expansion, and indeed its emergence. In
this perspective, the Utopian urge (and the cosmic hubris) of Marcuse is
similar to that of his Promethean predecessor. Here is what Marx wrote
about communism in *The Economic and Philosophical Manuscripts*:

> "It is the definitive resolution of the antagonism between man and
> nature, and between man and man. It is the true solution of the conflict
> between existence and essence, between objectification and self-
> affirmation, between freedom and necessity, between individual and
> species. It is the solution of the riddle of history and knows itself to be
> this solution."

---

[20] But "psychological radicals"—Norman O. Brown, Herbert Marcuse, R. D. Laing—
cannot provide a solid basis for a Utopian ideology which would serve as an inspiration for social
movement. It is too esoteric, and therefore is likely to be ephemeral. *Das Kapital* may not have
been read by the masses, but the economic category of *"surplus value"* could be easily translated
into demotic language: "exploitation". How can it be done with the psychological category of
"surplus repression"? Even the new revolutionary categories of Marcuse, the Students and the
Blacks, the *lumpenproletariat* and the *lumpenintelligentsia*, cannot easily identify with or act upon
his ideas. No wonder that the "new revolutionaries" are no longer very interested in Marcuse.
Like him they believe in the dictatorship of the minority, but they are not concerned with such
intangibles as "surplus repression".
[21] Herbert Marcuse, "The Concept of Negation in the Dialectic", *Telos* (No. 8, Summer
1971), p. 132.

What Marx called "empirical history" or "the real movement of history" has hardly brought these lofty goals nearer in any post-revolutionary society. Yet intellectual rationalizations of secular Utopias are indeed related to "the real movement of history". They are constructed on the basis of contemporary reality, and like all fantasies they both embody certain of its elements and are somewhat limited by it. In the pre-Industrial age Rousseau idealized primitive man; emerging industrialism was the basis of Marx's "scientific" vision of the future; and "post-industrial society" provides the context for Marcuse's projected Psytopia (or Eupsychia). As with all Utopians, it is not only a vision of the future but also a return to the past—to the "noble savage" in Rousseau; to "primitive communism" (elevated to "full communism" at a higher technological stage) in Marx; to the child-like instincts of man corrupted by capitalist affluence in Marcuse. There is, thus, a convergence here of the blessed future and of the innocent past, of Utopia and Arcadia.[22]

Fig-leaves of Theory

THE 19th and 20th centuries also witnessed a further convergence of Utopian and Revolutionary ideas. As Peter Struve shrewdly observed, revolution itself becomes Utopia. The instrument merges with the goal: the emotions invested in the vision of the ideal society are transposed onto the mechanism which is supposed to bring it about. For those "dreaming revolution" the future indefinite becomes the future definite. In this way they can retain their quasi-religious intensity of feeling about the coming redemption, concentrate on the struggle for power, and postpone thinking about the real problems a government in any society has to face until the post-revolutionary advent of Utopia.

For "true believers" *in partibus infidelium* the disappointing nature of the post-revolutionary experience reinforces rather than weakens this shift in their mythopoetic focus. Faith is preserved by ignoring experience and concentrating emotionally on revolutionary means rather than on Utopian ends. But if the persistence of the revolutionary idea is due to those

---

[22] However, with all their illusions, Rousseau and Marx were thinkers of genius who were not simply escaping from reality. Marcuse, on the other hand, raised "infantile regression" to the status of ideology.

It is difficult to imagine how such an ideology can begin to be implemented. Presumably after the Revolution people will still be acting "at first" on the basis of their "corrupted" instincts, which will not disappear overnight with the disappearance of "capitalist society". It was discovered in the Communist countries that a New Man cannot yet be created because of the alleged "survivals of capitalism in human consciousness". How would our new liberators handle such "survivals" in human subconsciousness after the victory of the People in 1984, when it will be necessary to exercise a "pedagogic dictatorship" on their behalf?

Would not "surplus repression" have to be dealt with by Red Mental Guards on People's Psychoanalytical Couches?

psychological factors which facilitate the "Festinger effect", its expansion also depends on the appeal of this idea to categories other than "true believers". This appeal varies. Social conditions are not the only factors which enhance it. Political and cultural traditions, as well as the credibility of the revolutionary idea itself, play an important role in specific historical instances of revolutionary failures and successes.

In our own time the New Left itself has severed the umbilical cord which linked economic and class conditions with the emergence of a revolutionary situation in the traditional Marxist approach. Régis Debray moved Leninist "voluntarism" from the exploitation to the creation of a revolutionary situation. New revolutionary techniques are to bring about, if not the millennium, at least the dictatorship of the minority which is necessary to establish it.

Historically, the quest for secular salvation leads to a progressive narrowing down of the gap between the hope and the implementation. If revolution is a short cut to Utopia, revolutionary impatience first telescopes the "bourgeois" and the "socialist" revolutions; then the "bourgeois revolution" disappears as a necessary precondition for a "socialist revolution"; and, finally, there is not even any need to wait for a revolutionary situation to bring revolution about: terror becomes a short cut to revolution, for which rural or urban guerrillas have to establish *foci*.

All the old "theoretical" discussions, in which generations of Marxist revolutionaries spent their lives chopping logic and splitting hairs over this-or-that formulation, in which an ocean of ink was spilt over the proper location of a comma in myriads of documents analyzing revolutionary prospects, turned out to be irrelevant after all. Historically, the only reality behind these exercises was the revolutionary will embracing the revolutionary myth. In this respect there is really little difference between Lenin and the contemporary "new revolutionaries", except that in their case the "theoretical" fig-leaf is even more transparent.

Appeal's End

REVOLUTIONARY revivalism came to the West when the revolutionary myth ceased to be associated with the Soviet Union. The word "revolution" re-acquired a mythical undertone among the Western intelligentsia, particularly among those who, according to Sartre (and Hegel), are defined as intellectuals through their *conscience malheureuse*. But most of the prominent writers were not so easily taken in. And it was not just a matter of "once bitten twice shy" (although this played a role), or of the once-young writers on the Left moving to the Right at a more mature age (although this also played a part). It was the whole experience of the revolutionary epoch they had gone through.

Reflections on it began with the literature of disillusion by Koestler, Orwell, Silone, Sperber. This had a powerful effect; but it was the actual impact of contemporary events that made most of today's outstanding writers less than enthusiastic about revolutionary developments and the role of writers in them. "Poets aren't the unacknowledged legislators of the world", Auden said, "it is the secret police who are." No less characteristic is the reflection of Saul Bellow in *Mr Sammler's Planet*: "There were no revolutions that he could remember which had not been made for justice, freedom and pure goodness. Their last state was always more nihilistic than the first. . . ."

Even the old Communist writers in the West reflect the same disenchantment, although they remain loyal to the Party. Aragon declared in an interview (*L'Express*, 20–26 September 1971) that he "always rebelled against socialist realism" and that he would never have joined the Communist Party if only he had read Gladkov's *Cement* at the time. It is the same Aragon who had written *Pour un réalisme socialiste* and who now proclaimed:

> "Stalinism created conditions of credulity for people like me, it is true. But one cannot say that I was a Stalinist in the sense that this word has acquired for me today. . . ."

There is nothing like the semantic power of retrospective reinterpretation! But it is surely indicative that such declarations are made by a writer who in the 1930s wrote a eulogistic poem about the GPU, and attacked Picasso for drawing a not sufficiently reverential portrait of Stalin after the death of the beloved leader.

Aragon is not alone. A similar statement was made by Pablo Neruda, author of an *Ode to Stalin*, who complained that the Stalinists had done him "the greatest wrong". (*Le Nouvel Observateur*, 25 October 1971.)

If two such old Stalinist literary war-horses feel compelled to make such declarations, it is clear that as far as the Soviet Union is concerned its revolutionary appeal is dead and buried. Indeed, of all the prominent Western Communist or (once) fellow-travelling writers mentioned in this article only seven are given as representing the "socialist realist position" in the Soviet book on literature and revolution I quoted earlier. Six of them—Romain Rolland, Theodore Dreiser, Heinrich Mann, Arnold Zweig, Paul Eluard, Bertold Brecht—are safely dead. The seventh is Louis Aragon.

Aesthetics & Society

AS FAR AS Marxist literary aesthetics is concerned, nothing can better illustrate its utter bankruptcy than Lukacs' *boutade* that Solzhenitsyn's *One Day in the Life of Ivan Denisovich* is the only Soviet "socialist-realist" book. There is more to it than a paradox by an erstwhile Stalinist theoretician of art with bourgeois literary tastes. He argued, quite seriously, that Solzhenitsyn is a "socialist-realist" writer and that Lukacs' favourite concept of a concrete universal can be applied to *Ivan Denisovich*. But even if it is true (though Lukacs did not quite say so) that a concentration camp represents a "concrete universal" of Stalinist Russia, this still does not help us to realize what constitutes the artistic superiority of Solzhenitsyn over—say— Dudintsev, who deals in his *Not by Bread Alone* with a problem which also constitutes a "concrete universal" in the Soviet Union.

We are some way from the period when Marxist aesthetics was explaining *Don Quixote* by referring to Cervantes as representing the interests of the impoverished *hidalguia*[23]—or the *Crimean Sonnets* by Mickiewicz as reflecting the movement of grain prices on the Odessa stock exchange. But despite the valiant efforts of Lucien Goldmann and Roland Barthes, the central problem of how to avoid reducing aesthetics to the sociology of art still baffles Marxists. One can learn many interesting things in *Le Dieu Caché*, but not what constitutes the continued appeal of Racine. Marx frankly acknowledged his own difficulties *vis-à-vis* this problem in respect to Greek art. He believed that "material transformations can be determined with the precision of natural science", but in the same *Outline of the Critique of Political Economy* he wrote:

> "The difficulty does not lie in the fact . . . that Greek art and epic are bound to certain forms of social development. The difficulty is that they still provide us with artistic pleasure and in a certain sense represent for us a norm and an unattainable standard."

Yet Marx never faced the contradiction between his view of art as, simply, reflecting various social formations, and his belief in the timeless value of Greek art. He tried to cope with this difficulty by saying that Greek art represents "the childhood of mankind" which "exercizes its charm as a never recurring stage", but this is a lame explanation. Not only Greek, but all great art, has this timeless value which points to the ultimate autonomy of the intellect *vis-à-vis* the Marxist economic base.

Ultimately, Marx was as helpless in his analysis of revolution as he was in his analysis of art and literature. He wrote several drafts of an answer to Vera Zasulich, who had asked him whether Russia could attain socialism without going through the stage of capitalism but, perhaps for Freudian reasons, he never sent them. Vera Zasulich is still waiting for a reply.

The building of "socialism" in so many undeveloped countries still poses the same unanswerable question to those who start their analysis from Marxian premises. No matter what additional qualifications are introduced

---

[23] Cf. L. B. Turkevich, *Cervantes in Russia* (Princeton University Press, 1950).

into the theory, they cannot answer this question, just as they cannot explain the spread of Marxism itself (or Christianity, or Buddhism, or Islam) in terms of the relation between the economic base and ideological superstructure.

Literature and the continuing attraction of great art cannot be explained by any kind of historicism. Pasternak said that "poetry and history are separate universes, one exists in eternity, the other in time"—the poet is "eternity's hostage to time (*Vechnosti zalozhnik u vremeni v plenu*)". Malraux wrote that "eternity is contained within the work of art", Blake that "eternal principles of characters in human life appear to poets in all ages". Clearly, there is sufficient universality in human problems and sufficient consonance, despite all the changes in style and form, between great writers and artists and their audience throughout time, to make a mockery of any aesthetic theory which tries to reduce the analysis of art to historical or sociological relativities. The relativity of tastes is an important but not a crucial question in aesthetics.

Among contemporary Marxists Arnold Hauser is still trying to rescue Marxist aesthetics by insisting on the iedological nature of thought, on the relativity of knowledge, and on their correspondence to class and social background. But Lucien Goldmann, while adopting the same approach, admits in his introduction to *Le Dieu Caché* that Marx's question about Greek art is still puzzling. His own answer to it contradicts the basic premise of Marxist aesthetics and hardly amounts to an attempt to face the problem squarely:

> "A philosophy or work of art can keep its value outside the time and place where it first appeared only if, by expressing a particular human situation, it transposes this onto the plane of the great human problems created by man's relationship with his fellows and with the universe."

This is as lame as Marx's own "childhood of humanity" explanation, and anyway it practically concedes the case by treating it as a question of hermeneutics rather than of history. Marx and the Marxists always denied the existence of "eternal values" and insisted on historical relativity. But literature is concerned not just with *la condition sociale* but with *la condition humaine*, and that means that it cannot abandon some of the most important human preoccupations for the sake of an *ersatz* religion which disregards the mystery of man's existence, bans metaphysics, and, having raised the revolutionary phenomenon to a totemic position, fails to explain it. Marcuse refers to the "aesthetic anthropology" of Marx, but it is better to call it (with Rufus Mathewson) "a 19th-century anthropomorphic positivism". In its narrow perspective it cannot deal satisfactorily either with aesthetic questions concerning literature or with anthropological questions concerning religion, because it turns away from what is to human beings, literally, a question of life and death. An attempt to impose this arid positivistic perspective on society inevitably leads to the trivialization of literature. When rigidly enforced it can only result in shallowness of thought and feeling. It can produce neither the *Divine Comedy* nor the *Human Comedy*, but only the *Optimistic Tragedy*.

The cheap juxtaposition in this title of Vishnevsky's play could be matched only if Hollywood were to produce a film of *Oedipus Rex* or *Antigone* with a happy ending. Such juxtapositions make the rationale of human suffering and sacrifice incomprehensible and tragedy meaningless. Optimistic tragedy makes as much sense as metaphysical positivism or hedonistic transcendentalism. In Vishnevsky's play there is not even a happy ending, only a promise of one in the inevitably bright future. It is, of course, an expression of the secular progressive belief in a "scientific" unfolding of history as an escalator to higher and better things; but it is hardly compatible with the concept of tragedy.

Kafka & Dostoyevsky

FOR writers who have a less superficial view of the human predicament the trivialization of human problems and of their literary perception is much more crucial than the question of external censorship of their writings.

It is a situation in which the the sensibility of the writer has to be sacrificed to the ruling ideology. When writers try to perceive things along the expected lines, they have to deny their own authenticity. Censorship interferes only with freedom of expression; obligatory perception and self-censorship—with creativity itself. Poets are worse hit as they rely to a greater degree than others on involuntary or subconscious thought in the "act of creation". If they manage to censor themselves they cease to be creative; if they do not, they are politically vulnerable. That is why there have been so many victims among them.

It was no accident that the call for "sincerity in literature" (by Pomerantsev) was the first demand for cultural change made in the Soviet Union after Stalin's death. Then came the insistence on the restoration of genuine meanings to words. *Samizdat* emerged because neither was made possible. Freedom of thought is inseparable from freedom of expression, but in Soviet conditions the former is particularly important.

One example can make this point clear: the character of the official "rehabilitation" of previously taboo authors. This is often misunderstood in the West. There it is taken as straight proof of liberalization and of the extension of freedom of thought for the Soviet intellectual public. In some sense this may be so, if the writings were not previously available. But public rehabilitation is done in such a way that the essential message of the authors in question is twisted and emasculated.

Two sensitive cases, Kafka and Dostoyevsky, illustrate the point. Both were "rehabilitated" despite the dangerous implications of their thought. But how were they presented? Kafka was the subject of a critical reappraisal in which the die-hards continued to attack him, while even those who were appreciative spoke and wrote in such a way that the very essence of Kafka's concern with the human condition vanished altogether.[24] What is one to make of the following appraisal?

> "In the creative works of Kafka there is a criticism of great force. However, Kafka projected the characteristic traits of bourgeois society onto human society in general. He absolutized and almost deified the evil strength of capitalist bureaucracy."[25]

Could any reader think that *The Castle* might have some relevance to Soviet bureaucracy or *The Trial* to Stalinist purges? Perish the thought! They are relevant only to "bourgeois society" and "capitalist bureaucracy". There are no "eternal truths", literature only "reflects" its own time and society. Therefore Kafka can only "reflect" the horrible experience of Austro-Hungarian administrative practices, but cannot be taken as a guide to Soviet society. QED. It may be that despite all this, the "rehabilitation" of Kafka and other non-*kosher* writers means (as Max Hayward said) "a gradual extension of Soviet consciousness". But one should also take into account the official efforts to determine its depth and quality.

As FOR Dostoyevsky: after years of being reviled, the author of *The Possessed* was eulogized on the occasion of the 150th anniversary of his birth. The former standard view of his "arch-reactionary thought" has been forgotten and *Pravda* (11 November 1971) announced on the day of the anniversary:

> "There is no reason why we should abandon this great writer to the reactionaries. We cannot reconcile ourselves to reactionaries and idealists who claim Dostoyevsky as their own."

In order to appropriate Dostoyevsky and make him into one of the progressive predecessors of Soviet literature, a "delicate" reinterpretation was necessary. Lenin's comment that Dostoyevsky was "arch-bad" is no longer quoted. *The Possessed* is no longer described as "a furious libel on the Russian liberation movement" (*Bolshaya Sovetskaya Entsiklopediya*, Vol. 15, 1952), but as "an anatomy and critique of ultra-Left extremism" (B. L. Suchkov in *Literaturnaya Gazeta*, 17 November 1971). Even Gorky has been recruited to the ranks of the followers of Dostoyevsky! The two writers have been presented as akin to each other in an article by N. Zhegalov, "Dostoyevsky and Gorky", in *Literaturnaya Rossiya* (12 November 1971).

---

[24] Cf. Guy de Mallac, "Kafka in Russia", *The Russian Review* (January 1972), pp. 64–73.

[25] L. G. Andreyev and R. M. Samarin, *Istoriya Zarubezhnoi Literatury Posle Oktyabrskoi Revolyutsii*, Vol. I (Moscow, 1969).

The article concludes that only in socialist realism can there be "a deep, creative assimilation of the traditions and the legacy of the classics". Indeed. Roger Garaudy has done this in a more sophisticated way in his *Réalisme sans rivages*. But he has been excommunicated, so one cannot even say that when there is no Stalin, then everything is permitted—not even within the narrow framework of "socialist realism". But whatever is permitted to the Soviet literary critics bears no relation to the essence of Dostoyevsky's genius. He saw the implications of the marriage between revolutionary mythology and utilitarian ethics in Russia more clearly than anybody else. Today brings this judgment on his insights:

> "Dostoevsky was a genius at foreseeing, but what he could never foresee was that his novels would participate in the construction of socialism."[26]

Ivan Karamazov was right: if there is no God, then everything is permitted. However, he could hardly have imagined that it would lead to the transformation of Dostoyevsky into a "progressive writer"! Could anyone visualize the author of *The Possessed* "participating in the construction of socialism" under Brezhnev?! Even Stalin would have been surprised to see that while Trotsky is still branded in the Soviet Union as a counter-revolutionary, Dostoyevsky is no longer regarded as one. Fifty-five years have passed since the revolutionary upheaval; the average human being is not appreciably nearer the level of Aristotle or Goethe, but Smerdyakov is still in charge of *Agitprop*.

I N THE WEST, it is Trotsky rather than Dostoyevsky who has been undergoing a revival. He has been romanticized by Isaac Deutscher, Peter Weiss, and Richard Burton. His "permanent revolution" has been preached by the "new revolutionaries", many of them of impeccable bourgeois origin (like Tariq Ali or Teresa Hayter, enacting *The Possessed* without having read it).

The wave of revolutionary romanticism in the 1960s affected, of course, Western "progressive writers". But apart from them, the general response of writers has been different from what it was in the 1930s. Far fewer have been ready to fall for the same kind of myth. Others displayed sympathy for the "new revolutionaries"—on them the lessons of the '30s were lost. But they were no longer pro-Soviet, and their "revolutionary" commitment was no longer unambiguous. It was somewhat constrained, reflecting the fashions of the day rather than a deeper involvement. As usual, whether in New York or Paris, they were influenced by the moods of Greenwich Village or the Left Bank, although many of them were now living in far more fashionable quarters. But, there were fewer writers among the militant "progressives"

[26] V. Dneprov "Dostoyevsky kak Pisatel Dvadtsatogo Veka", *Inostrannaya Literatura*, No. 11 (1971), p. 200.

than in the '30s; they were far more vague in their ideas; still, they were ready to jump on the revolutionary bandwagon, even though they were not quite clear in which direction it was rolling in the polycentric world, or indeed whether it was rolling at all. The appetite for revolutionary myth and progressive equivocation has been fully displayed during the past decade in the representative journal of "Radical Chic", the *New York Review Books*.

The Use & Abuse of Myth

T O ANALYSE various revolutions it is, to be sure, necessary to study the social and economic conditions at the time, the state of political institutions; the needs and hopes of the population; the existence and characteristics of the counter-élite; the effectiveness of military controls, and many other factors on which the success of the revolutionary idea depends.

But the idea itself rests on a myth, and in order to understand it one has to analyse the nature of myths. This would go beyond the scope of this essay. It is sufficient to say that there is a fundamental ambivalence in the concept of myth which goes back to the Greek philosopher Euhemerus, who first tried to "decipher" myths as allegorical history. Hegel and Marx regarded myths in the same light. Both were strongly influenced by the rationalistic perspective of the Englightenment. Marx's concept of ideology as a mask has a strong affinity with the view of myth as nothing but a form of embellished "false consciousness".

Freud, Jung, Frazer, and Malinowski went beyond this perspective and considered the psychological and social character of myths. Sorel was preoccupied by their political function. Cassirer examined (in terms of neo-Kantian epistemology) their relation to language and the state. Mircea Eliade and Joseph Campbell analysed their functions on a comparative basis, starting with the Jungian premise that myths are public dreams.

Lévi-Strauss explicitly rejected the idea that their significance can be seen in terms of "truth" and substituted the criterion of "coherence" in his Structuralist approach. In this approach myths are seen in the light of their social function, not historically, and their "meaning" is no longer related to the question of "reality". It can be argued, of course, that any epistemological quest must in the end stumble on the problem of the 'hermeneutic circle". But that does not mean that one can avoid philosophical premises even in the most sophisticated anthropological analysis of the concept of myth. The ambivalence may be implicit or explicit; but it is there. Coherent or not, myth may be regarded as mystification or as deeper truth, whatever its function and whether it is considered necessary or not.

THE QUESTION becomes clearer and less esoteric when one considers the relation between myth and literature, which is more relevant to the question of the relation between the revolutionary myth and literature. The ambivalence inherent in the concept of myth—seen *either* as a falsehood *or* as the profoundest symbolic expression of moral, aesthetic, and existential choices, justifying life and "making sense" of it—is particularly pertinent in literature. This is so because literature is peculiarly involved both with the ends and the means served by myths. As John Armstrong put it (in his study of *The Paradise Myth*):

> "Myths are the most accurate means that the human mind has devised, representing its own immeasurably complex structure and content. They are essentially poetic formations. . . . Men create myths because the intricacies of our mental life require a more subtle and sophisticated medium of expression than abstract discourse can provide. Besides being inadequate and unenlightening in this field, abstractions tend to leave us cold."

The literary Western Marxist revisionists like Roger Garaudy and Ernst Fischer tend to accept this view, despite the fact that they subscribe to the positivistic legacy of Marxism. Garaudy wrote that the creation of myths

> "is the essential function of art from Homer to Cervantes, from Goethe's *Faust* to Gorky's *Mother*, which questions the world and at the same time challenges the order of the world in the name of that heroic image which man at all times has made of his destiny and his future".

Quoting this in his *Art Against Ideology*, Ernst Fischer "essentially agrees" with it, only adding that the creation of myths is not the only essential function of art: "Art can carry out one of its functions—that of criticizing the *status quo*—by the use of myth, but equally well by the use of anti-myth. (*The Marriage of Figaro, Madame Bovary*, and *Anna Karenina* are all, it seems to me, devoid entirely of any mythic character.) . . ."

In contrast to Fischer, Roland Barthes, combining semiology and Marxism, concentrates on the legitimizing function of myth, which permeates "bourgeois" culture, obscures bourgeois reality, and tries to conceal it in order to perpetuate the *status quo*. A revolutionary society does not need any myth which would create a mystifying picture of itself. Deciphering mythology is for this Parisian "anti-Stalinist" *gauchiste* simply a question of destroying the false pretences of "bourgeois" society. "Left-wing myth is inessential."

Here Marcuse is joined by Barthes: the first is ready to apply the concept of tolerance only to the Left, the second applies the concept of myth (in the pejorative sense) only to the Right. Both push aside not only Kantian universals, but also some of Marx's own views of man and history in their obstinate political Manicheism. How anybody seriously concerned with the problem of contemporary myths can disregard the revolutionary myth is beyond comprehension.

With "anti-Stalinists" like Barthes, who dismiss the Stalinist myth as "inessential", one really does not need the old Stalinist *apparatchiki* from *Agitprop* to perpetuate it. The sophisticated blindness of the *gauchiste* intellectual is sufficient in itself to make us understand another element in the persistence of myths. It is the need to rationalize the *credo* "when the prophecy fails" (which I called earlier "the Festinger effect" with reference to Professor Festinger's book on the subject). Both Barthes and Garaudy, despite their contrary views of the concept of myth, share an ideological approach to it. For the first it is negative because it preserves the "bourgeois" *status quo*. For the second it is positive because it brings about change in the *status quo*. Which only goes to show that both are still prisoners of the revolutionary myth: they are ready to idealize change *per se*, rather than view it on its merits.

Consequences

VIEWED IN THIS WAY, revolution loses its mythical character and becomes a problem of political and social change which is to be assessed in terms of its costs and consequences. It can also be seen as not just a mechanism of political and social change—which is how it is usually viewed—but as a complex process in which some institutions and patterns of behaviour change, while change in others is prevented or delayed.

It is arguable, for instance, that without the Revolution industrialization would have developed more quickly in France; that without it the Reform Bill would almost certainly have been enacted in Britain much earlier; that without the October Revolution the institution of autocracy would have been weakened, not strengthened in Russia (with all the attendant derivative instances of arrested development from agriculture to technological innovation, from the freedom of the press to the rule of law).

When Clio is raped she takes her revenge. In all the countries where major revolutions have taken place and/or major revolutionary changes have been introduced, continuity reasserted itself with a vengeance after a time. Perhaps to reassert their identity, the societies in question cling even more closely to their traditions whatever they are, when their evolution has been interrupted by a revolutionary "jump". This precludes rather than accelerates change in those traditions which are not, or no longer, desirable. It also reinforces the nationalism of these societies, making a mockery of revolutionary professions of friendship towards other peoples.

PERHAPS THE MOST pertinent new factor introduced by millenarian revolutions arises from the merger itself of the ideas of Revolution and Utopia. It means that the new authority established by the revolution owes its legitimacy to the implementation of Utopia and that implies a permanent revolution unless the idea of Utopia is abandoned or rendered innocuous by semantic-ideological reinterpretations. But to get off the tiger is awfully difficult; it undermines revolutionary legitimacy and raises the cry of "revolution betrayed".

The price of normalization is usually very high. In France the "rule of Reason" ended with *Thermidor* and *Brumaire*; it was only the Napoleonic wars and the Restoration which restored the evolutionary equilibrium. The building of the classless society—the Communist Utopia—makes the task of terminating revolutionary change in society even more difficult, particularly as the idea gives legitimacy not just to one authority but to authorities in various countries and is also the basis of an international movement. The forcible collectivization and terror under Stalin, the Great Leap Forward and the Cultural Revolution under Mao, are just examples of the measures taken to implement Utopia through a permanent revolution. The dialectic of continuity and change has a different character in evolutionary and revolutionary perspectives.

Principles of Hope & Reason

THE COSTS and the consequences of millenarian revolutions stand in striking contrast to the hopes of the revolutionary intelligentsia. It discovers in practice that it is invariably the victim of the revolution and a target for liquidation as a social group. Revolution devours not only its children but also its fathers, and grandchildren as well, if the latter show independence of mind. Writers, who form part of this Utopia-fed intelligentsia, catch a glimpse of reality and begin writing anti-Utopias. Dreams turn into nightmares. Exploitation does not disappear, oppression becomes worse than before. As to internationalism, one only has to note the vocabulary of Sino-Soviet polemics; to listen to Radio Tirana; or to meditate on the fact that the editor of the Soviet magazine, *Druzhba Narodov* (*The Friendship of Peoples*), is a militant anti-semite.[27]

When the fate of writers in revolutionary movements and the course of post-revolutionary régimes is contemplated, and the scrutiny shows that revolution has too often been an instrument of their destruction, a melancholy conclusion is forced even on those who want to remain loyal to Utopia.

> "We [Irving Howe writes] have learned that the effort to force men into Utopia leads to barbarism, but we also know that to live without the

---

[27] Cf. the speech by Grigorii Svirsky at the meeting of the Moscow writers in 1965 (reproduced in *Le Monde*, 28–29 April 1968) and his *Letter to the Friends*, distributed by *samizdat* in November 1971.

image of Utopia is to risk the death of imagination. Is there a path for us, a crooked path for men of disciplined hope? . . . ."[28]

Others still believe in *la fécondité de l'Utopie*: "L'Utopie ce n'est pas le malheur, mais ce n'est pas plus le mensonge ou l'illusion."[29]

Obviously, for a certain type of political imagination, to attack Utopias is (as Thomas Molnar remarked) about as meaningful as to denounce dreams. This is particularly true for the revoutionary fundamentalists who hate reality so much that, like some Italian "new revolutionaries", they now contemplate an "apocalyptic strategy" in order to bring about their Utopian dream. We have, thus, a mini-Utopia for the moderates and a maxi-Utopia for the radicals.

But the problem is not to rescue Utopia but to rescue humanity from the consequences of the Utopian approach to politics. This does not imply the death of imagination; the imagination can be exercised in many different ways. "The Principle of Hope" does not have to be identified with revolution, as it has been by Ernst Bloch. Indeed, it requires an effort of imagination to see how to dissociate the two in a period of renewed revolutionary romanticism and of the adolescent inanities of the "new revolutionaries".

The Ecclesiast says that "without vision, the people perish". This is true, but we also know that with too much vision people perish too. A contemporary seer should be chastened by past experience of the political implementation of the myth of salvation, whether in its religious or secular form, and by the thought that it can now be combined with modern technology and modern methods of control.

If it is true that, as Max Weber said, "all historical evidence confirms the truth that man would not have attained the possible, unless time and again he had reached out for the impossible", it is also true that "the impossible" must now be defined in less Utopian terms, or, what amounts to the same thing, that the concept of Utopia must be radically redefined in line with our experience of its implementation.

Does it mean banning the ideal for the sake of the real? Not necessarily. Humanity still consists and will always consist of both Don Quixotes and Sancho Panchas. A political philosophy or literary vision which excludes one or the other would itself be utopian. But at different times different types of vision possessed a different inspirational quality and credibility. In our own time, unlike the time of Thomas More, Utopia is no longer credible for the politically mature; it inspires only the politically immature.

Campanella wrote in *City of the Sun* that "the whole world has gone mad",

---

[28] Irving Howe, "What's the Trouble?" (*Dissent*, October 1971), p. 471.
[29] Jean Daniel, "L'Avènement de l'Utopie", *Le Nouvel Observateur* (3 January 1972). The statement about *la fécondité de l'Utopie* echoes Malraux' remark, made in 1935, that "*le communisme rend à l'individu sa fertilité*".

and Herbert Marcuse echoes him by writing about the contemporary "explosion of insanity". But Campanella also proposed to build seven walls around his City (in Berlin they have only one) to protect the virtue of its subjects—while Marcuse writes about "liberation" and the end of "repression". Clearly, as a minimum condition, the definition of sanity for the redefined Utopia must be different from the one offered by Campanella, Marcuse, or R. D. Laing.

IT IS SOMETIMES ARGUED that in order to preserve Utopia it is necessary to preserve illusions, that, as Sorel said, "the future belongs to those who have not yet lost their illusions". But synthetic illusions, like synthetic myths, are not credible, as Sorel discovered with his own brand of synthetic myth.

If it is to inspire, a hope must be authentic and not rest on an artificially induced optimism conditioned by the suppression of historical experience. But the future has indeed belonged, in a certain sense and for a certain time, to those who had not lost their illusions—and whom Sorel admired as inspired by myths: communists and fascists. This is precisely the kind of future which those who want to retain hope not based on illusion have every reason to fear. Writers who—as past experience of their involvement in revolutionary movements testifies, often combine a mythopoetic predisposition with political naïveté—should be on guard against this type of seductive reasoning. The fate of their colleagues who adopted the revolutionary myth should be a warning against any attempt to rationalize it again and to perpetuate it by a self-willed illusionism.

This may not affect the fate of literature itself, which is a sturdy plant. But it may affect the fate of the writers themselves and, no mean consideration, of humanity itself. Great literature can come out of great suffering—but Solzhenitsyn is not an argument for the existence of concentration camps. Writers who avoid unnecessary illusions and casuistic self-deception help to make a non-apocalyptic future.

(1972)